Dear Mom

A FAMILY FINDS ITS PAST
IN WORLD WAR II LETTERS HOME

Michelle Cahill

Michelle Cahill

2015

Credits: Cover design by Ken Harris Graphic Design. Front cover pastel painting *43 Concord Street* by Mary Wardner Cahill. Author photo by Terry Lee. Black and white photos from the Cahill Family Archive.

ISBN: 978-0-9906425-0-3
Pleasant Street Publishers, Laguna Hills, CA
Website: www.PleasantStreetPublishers.com
Facebook.com/DearMomTheBook
Email the author: PleasantStreet75@gmail.com

Dedication

To my uncles, Tom and Jack, and their Dear Mom.

Preface

I never thought of time-traveling so, in 2012, I was shocked to be in 1940s Los Angeles, watching my family before I was born.

During World War II, the lives of my widowed grandmother and her children were plunged into chaos when five sons left for military service. For the close-knit Cahills, there was one constant: The boys wrote their mother often, and she saved every letter—hundreds of pages in a collection she called "Dear Mom."

Three sons returned home; two did not. Army fliers Tom and Jack died on bombing missions in Europe near the end of the war. My grandmother, her daughter and the remaining sons struggled through their loss. Eventually the "Dear Mom" anthology was stored, and our uncles' voices quieted.

My generation never knew Tom and Jack, but we always had their pictures. As was common in many families after the war, painful details of such losses didn't filter down, and our history became fragmented. Decades later, my cousins and I were curious about our uncles, but there was no one left to tell us their story.

In 2012 we were happy to stumble upon the "Dear Mom" letters that we never knew about, crammed among old photos. I was the first to read them and quickly saw it was time for Tom and Jack's voices to be heard. I had a notion of how the letters could unfold in a book, and this final version varies little from that early vision.

As I wrote this book, I had two lines of focus. The boys' war experiences were parallel—they both flew on bombers in Europe. But all the details were different: training, ranks, ratings, planes, combat assignments, theaters of operation, reference books, bomb group associations, websites, friends, documents and photos. Every organizational method I learned in forty years of working at Disneyland came into play to keep Tom and Jack "sorted" properly.

I hated studying history when I was in school, all those locations and dates to memorize. But through my family's letters, I became absorbed in the war. I found my uncles' names, planes and squadron buddies listed in books, on websites and in documents once *Secret*, now *Declassified*. Tom and Jack are part of world history, and I feel privileged to know who they were. Their letters and the photos found with them explained an elusive emptiness I always sensed, and they also helped me weave our family back together in my mind.

Through their letters, my uncles introduced themselves to my generation and detailed World War II behind the scenes. Their soldier stories are descriptive, touching and hilarious. I learned not only about Tom and Jack but also about flight training, the war they fought, Cahill family life and American culture of the 1940s. Transported back to a time that was not yet technology-obsessed, I began questioning today's more hurried lifestyle choices.

Though this book is about my family, our story is analogous to thousands of other families who made the same sacrifices during World War II. Maybe your family has a similar history you've known about only vaguely. Are there letters, documents or photos in your attic that can connect you to voices from the past?

Acknowledgments

I am most grateful to my uncles, Tom Cahill and Jack Cahill, who in 2012 introduced themselves to me in their entertaining World War II letters. Though I have the book's author title, they wrote about ninety percent of it, and I added the remainder for context, clarity and continuity.

My grandmother, Mary Wardner Cahill, is the core of our family's story. To me she was the sweet Nana who taught me how to knit and made me fresh fruit salad. I had no idea of the life she led before I entered it. Now I do.

My aunt, Patricia Cahill, was vital, preserving for decades her younger brothers' letters and hundreds of family photos. No better gift could she leave my generation. Patricia was our family historian, and more than once we've wished we could have her back with us, if only for one day. So many questions...

I also thank my brother and my cousins who supported me from the onset, agreeing it was time for Tom and Jack to tell their story. We are the nieces and nephews the boys envisaged in their letters.

My primary military connections were through the Mediterranean Theater's 57th Bomb Wing Association for Tom and the European Theater's 446th Bomb Group Association for Jack. Together they launched me on an exciting adventure. As I sought to learn more about my uncles, these groups were the touchstones to which I kept returning, relishing their resources. Through them, I connected with veterans and their family members who helped me understand seventy-year-old history.

Innumerable are the men and women featured in my uncles' letters, mostly soldiers, but not all. Whether they knew Tom, Jack, or both, or were family members or family friends, through them I learned about my family, the war and life in the 1940s.

In addition to people recognized by name in the body of this book, there are many behind-the-scenes supporters. In addition to good friends, these include a circle of local writers, various stages ahead of me, who shared their experiences in meetings, workshops and conversation. I would have been lost without their guidance.

As I look back, I see how life prepared me to meet this challenge. My interest in writing emerged a decade or so into my forty-year Disneyland career. I always knew I could write a decent sentence, but knew little about weaving them together at length. The first to grant me that chance was Anne Okey who managed the *Disneyland Line* employee newsletter in the 1980s. After seeing her request for "reporters" throughout the Park to contribute to the publication, I offered to write a feature on the Entertainment Division's All American College Band. She agreed and printed my submission with only a few edits. That first byline hooked me.

Later I worked in Disneyland Publicity where Lorraine Santoli taught me about press releases and gave me writing tips with a marketing edge. Now retired and an author, when asked, Lorraine was happy to read a draft of my introductory chapter. I was unsure of the book's potential, and she encouraged me to finish it. She said she is always honest with writers seeking feedback and would tell me if she thought my project had no merit or was a waste of my time.

The first person outside my family to read a full draft of the manuscript was another former Disneyland co-worker, Roxanne Brandt. She is of such high character that I knew she would not delude me if she had concerns about this project's appeal to readers. She called it a "page-turner." Continuing to be encouraged, I became more confident that it was not just my emotional connection to Tom and Jack or author-wannabe folly propelling me.

During the time I worked on this book, I took a nonfiction writing class taught by Patricia McFall at Saddleback College. I learned more about the craft, and it only took three sessions of this same course for her mantra—Details! Details! Details!—to stick in my brain. My editor, Deborah Heimann, helped me wade through the over five hundred pages of letters and new-to-me military lingo that has a bewilderment all its own.

Finally, I thank God and the Universe for waiting until I retired to unveil to me this family treasure. I would not have had time to explore the letters when I was working, and instead enjoyed three years of leisure bringing Tom and Jack into my life.

Concord, New Hampshire, 1926

Patrick and Mary Wardner Cahill with children: Mark on Mary's lap, Jack on chair arm with book. From lower left, clockwise, Bob, Tom, Maurice, Patricia, Frank and Jerry.

The Cahill Family

PATRICK CAHILL (b. 1879) m. **MARY WARDNER** (b. 1885)
June 2, 1910

Maurice (b. 1911)
Patricia (b. 1912)
Frank (b. 1914) m. Peggy
    Liz
    Katy
    Tom
    Ann
Jerry (b. 1916) m. Pinky
    Jack
    Steve
Bob (b. 1917) m. Jackie
    Patrick
    Michelle
Billy (b. 1919)
Tom (b. 1921)
Jack (b. 1923)
Mark (b. 1925) m. Germaine
    Elizabeth
    Maureen
    Mark, Jr.
    Jennifer
    Bill

Contents

Letters of Introduction

In 1945 my father lost two brothers. In 2012 I found them.

Most of my life, Tom and Jack were silent portraits on my grandmother's wall. They were my father's younger brothers, "the boys," Army fliers who died in World War II. We never forgot them but my generation grew up knowing little about them.

My mother, Jackie, told me how handsome they were. She met the Cahills in 1937 when she started dating my dad Bob. She later lived with the family for two years before they were married, after her family returned to their home state of Washington. Tom and Jack were jokesters and teased her mercilessly. They were "brothers" to her, and she loved them very much.

I thought that was all I'd ever know, but decades later I had a startling surprise.

THE FAMILY

A child arrived every year or two after Patrick Cahill married Mary Wardner in 1910, in Concord, New Hampshire: eight boys and a girl. My father was the middle child, and the only girl, Patricia, was my favorite aunt. The family was quite affluent until the stock market crash of 1929 prompted the failure of their half-century-old cigar-making business, S. Wardner & Co.

After my grandfather died in 1933 from complications of diabetes, my grandmother saw greater opportunity for her brood in California, where her mother and sister had relocated earlier. In 1937, my grandmother and the children—two school-aged, the others young adults—moved to Los Angeles, into the home of my great-grandmother, Nellie Wardner, "Gram."

Still struggling financially, the family happily adapted to the area's warm weather, sunny beaches and abundant live entertainment. Everyone was musical—Patricia was a gifted pianist. The Cahills often hosted parties in their large home. Bands also rehearsed there, sometimes to the displeasure of neighbors who called the police to quiet the revelry.

Later that decade, war began in Europe, and by 1943, five sons—Frank, Jerry, Tom, Jack and Mark—were in military service. The close family was torn apart with sons in different states, then different countries. Brothers away from home wrote to their mother often, and she saved every letter.

Three sons survived, but Army airmen Tom and Jack were killed on bombing missions in Europe near the end of the war. Our family received notification of their deaths two days apart in February 1945. Their sister and brothers stuck close by their mother, and over the next fifteen years, created my generation: thirteen grandchildren for "Nana."

WORDS I'LL NEVER FORGET

A few weeks before our 2012 family reunion, I realized that this decade and the next was the time when my father, his sister and his brothers would have celebrated their 100th birthdays. I suggested we could honor their century marks at our reunion. Cousins Katy, Elizabeth and Ann agreed, and we met at Elizabeth's to dig through a mystery stash of Cahill keepsakes. We hoped to unearth more photos so our generation and future ones could better know our history.

Elizabeth, who inherited this loot from Aunt Patricia, brought to us two tubs of memorabilia and said, "There are also some old letters in here that the boys wrote home to Nana during the war." I was stunned, had to learn more, and took home the mishmash of crumbling precious paper.

THE FIRE

Our family almost lost these letters. In 1950, my grandmother and Aunt Patricia moved south along the Pacific Ocean to Corona del Mar, a village of Newport Beach. It was a happy home where our families met often. At every gathering, we sang for hours, accompanied by Patricia on her Steinway baby grand.

In 1964, a fire ravaged this home, including Patricia's piano and Nana's portraits of her sons lost in war. My grandmother and my aunt moved to a new home, and my uncles' voices moved with them but remained silent another fifty years. I continued to know nothing about the letters that held the secrets of who they were.

THE PAPER TRAIL

Seventy years after my uncles wrote home, I had their letters. They literally rose from the ashes, some of which remained at the bottom of the containers that still smelled smoky. Many items had scorch marks and water damage. Tom and Jack left our family far too soon, and it was finally time for their voices to be heard.

I sorted the letters, determining there to be over 600 pages. One hundred or so were written by Frank, Jerry and Mark, my uncles who returned from war, and the rest were Tom and Jack's. I felt privileged to have something they touched. I never could have imagined how easily their words would acquaint me with them or how welcome they would be in my life.

As I read the letters, I was captivated, like when reading a novel, immersed in the story. But wait. This *is* my story, or at least my history. These were my dad's little brothers, and I was surprised by the emotion I felt. I would tear up on one page and laugh on the next.

Both wrote humorously, Jack in documentary style and Tom as a storyteller. The letters started with classroom studies. As I read further, into their flying escapades, my uncles became increasingly alive and engaging. I thought: This is a book. Fatefully, in a later letter, Tom wrote his mother saying that after the war he planned to write a book about his Army experiences. He didn't publish his book, but he did write it through his letters.

WHO WROTE WHAT

Though I'm the author of this book, I did relatively little of the actual writing. The number of pages my uncles wrote dwarfs my literary contribution.

A copy editor who reviewed my early work on this project thought my uncles' letters were so well written that readers would not find them believable for boys writing to their family. Such letters, she said, would be less cultured, more careless. Readers would think, as she had, that I had rewritten the letters to improve them.

Because I was a bit past mid-life when I "met" Tom and Jack in their letters, and they wrote them in their twenties, it felt like they were my sons or nephews rather than uncles. I was perplexed that anyone would think I would (or *could*) improve their writing, and proud like a mama that "my" boys' writing was so highly regarded.

Tom and Jack were educated in New Hampshire Catholic schools and learned to write well. I didn't need to rewrite their letters. In fact, occasionally I referred to a dictionary for clarification. I'm a bit lowbrow, and their writing was more classic and highbrow. *Apace?* Why didn't Tom just say *quickly?*

I do see a resemblance between their writing and mine, the loose and casual styles. For me to write well, though, I generate multiple drafts on a state-of-the-art computer with thesaurus, grammar guide and spellcheck. Tom and Jack had remarkable vocabularies, only one shot at their news, but they always wrote well, with a pen, pencil, or 1940s-era typewriter.

In a handful of the letters in this book, I omitted parts that were uninteresting, repetitive or of a personal family nature. I also broke up long sentences and paragraphs and finessed phrases that were unclear. The letters carry the story, but I wrote occasional transitions in *italics* to add definition or background. Other than these exceptions, the letters are pure and retain the boys' styles. They often wrote hurriedly, with limited resources and without time or focus to edit for proper sentence structure.

THE TIME CAPSULE

Our family's letters cover twenty-seven months, November 1942 through January 1945. They capture World War II behind the scenes—what they did when they weren't studying or dropping bombs. Early letters from Tom and later letters from Jack are missing from our collection. But chronologically weaving together their letters presents a complete picture of airmen during ground school, flight training and combat.

As I read the letters, I time-traveled back to my birth decade. There are mentions of numerous relatives, family friends and Army buddies throughout the letters. "Bells" kept ringing as I read names I remembered hearing in my childhood, but others, mostly related in soldiers' antics, were unfamiliar. I retained names of "unknowns" if their content was entertaining or furthered the "plot."

An unexpected bonus was to find six newsy letters my grandmother wrote, which I've included for literary seasoning and dimension. I also sprinkled in a few from brothers Frank, Jerry and Mark. It's comforting to see how much my family loved Tom and Jack and that the boys knew it.

Nana's references to my brother, "Little Patrick," her first grandchild, a mischievous toddler at that time, are hysterical. My brother and I got a kick out of reading her documentation of his impish behavior that our mother so often described. Nana wrote to Jack, "As he has some cute tricks and is learning to talk fast, I don't need to say how enjoyable having him around is, but he can run you ragged. Everything has to be out of reach, and you have to be about three jumps ahead of him in everything."

Money, or the lack thereof, was an ongoing topic in the letters. It is touching for me to see that the financial focus was on the family as a whole. The brothers kept only enough of their pay to cover basic needs and sent the rest home to their mother and sister who managed the family's expenses. They mentioned enclosing $10 or $20, which at first seemed small to me. When adjusted to 2015 dollars at 13:1, I realized these amounts had buying power then equal to $130 and $260 today.

To quote Jack, finally being paid after several weeks, "Money gets top billing I guess. I am to get paid Saturday to the tune of about 80 simoleons. I intend to send home about $30 and you can pay the telephone bill, and Bob and Jackie. I don't know how much if any will be left but you can use it on *yourself*, and I do mean *you*!!"

The family bank wasn't only for deposits. Their mother was always ready to send money to her sons. Tom wrote, "Could you send me some money 'til payday? I am flat with a Capital F."

It was uplifting to see that, after he received his commission as an officer and was to receive substantially higher pay, Tom wrote he soon would be able to send home more money to lessen the burden of brothers at lower pay rates.

Because of war rationing, letters related recurring angst about the scarcity of chocolate chips, which sometimes halted Nana's cookie shipments. Tom and Jack were always on the hunt for chips and contraband—chocolate candy bars for her to chop up. From Jack, after arriving at a new base, "As for chocolate bits, no dice. I had a box to send but I put them to use on the train down here. Meals were few and far between on that trip." Occasionally there would be a big score, as he later wrote, "The PX has an abundance of Hershey bars, the big ones. I will send home some come payday."

Though my uncles "spoke" in their letters, I couldn't hear the sounds of their voices. I seemed to need this and, as time went on, voices like their brothers emerged.

Tom's voice became similar to my dad Bob, who like Tom was pensive, and Jack's was like my Uncle Mark, who always laughed as he talked. A personality matchup in my mind, I guess.

Interestingly, Tom and Jack's letters "lengthened" my life, as I eavesdropped on my family for three years before I was born, while 1940s music played endlessly in my head.

MEMORIES FOUND

It is clear to me that if there had been no war the boys would rather have been at home with their family. But both loved flying and chose it, despite the increased danger. They were committed to the war, satisfied with their ratings and looked forward to seeing the world beyond New Hampshire and California.

It was fun for me to read about their social lives...girls, parties, dances. Jack's favorite training location was the town of Emporia, Kansas, where he was based for a few months. Most of the town's young men had gone to war. Jack wrote his mother, "The girls are abundant and as friendly as can be. They go for us in a big way as the manpower shortage has lowered their resistance considerably."

As Tom was leaving New Mexico for South Carolina, his brother Frank sent to him the address of a "real dish." Frank met this "choice bit of fluff," the sister of a friend, when he went with the friend to their home in New Jersey. Frank was married, but scouted for his brothers and hoped Tom could meet her if he was ever in that area. After receiving the information, Tom wrote to his mother, "You know with Jack, Jerry and Frank traveling all over the country, I should be able to build up a pretty good address book with the proper cooperation. I in turn will turn over my meager findings. Meager, except for one deal here in Albuquerque." I think the name of the "deal" was Kay.

Tom was a singer and shared a love of the arts with his mother, who was a landscape painter. After returning to Corsica from a leave to Rome, he wrote her about the superb performance he saw there of the Puccini opera *Madame Butterfly*. He also eloquently described the grandiose artwork at St. Peter's Basilica and an inspirational audience with Pope Pius XII.

Tom's squadron on Corsica had a pet dog, Jocko, who had a recurring role in his letters. He wrote, "I think once before I mentioned Jocko, the dog next door. Since his master went home on leave, he has been rather down in the mouth but is gradually getting over it. The other day we decided to bring Jocko along on a mission. He has about eight or nine missions already they say." Tom had arrived on Corsica only two weeks earlier, and at this point Jocko had more missions than he did.

In addition to introducing my uncles to me, the letters formed a military textbook. I learned the fundamentals of gunnery, radio, meteorology, flying, navigation and bombing...topics I never thought to explore.

Tom's vivid descriptions during pilot training had me swooping through the sky with him. He wrote about his first solo flight, "I eased back on the old stick and there I was, flying. At 500 feet, I leveled off and my first impulse was to holler—which I did. Boy, I was really having fun."

I was alternatingly fascinated and terrified following the boys through training and war. My grandmother must have felt the same…but more. I could easily imagine her laughing through many letters, but cringing at some as I did. I was surprised at the things they told her: frightening mentions of flying, guns, flak, bombs and bailing out of an airplane.

From France, Tom sent her a photo of a B-25 bomber with half of one wing shot away. His caption on the back: "Smitty and Hill brought this one back. My airplane but I wasn't flying in it that day." Is that something a mother really wants to know?

Despite the serious business of war, Tom and Jack were a hoot! It was remarkable to see that not even war stopped them from being funny. I shouldn't be surprised—they were just like their sister and brothers who I knew. A silly sense of humor thrives in our DNA.

FULL CIRCLE

When my uncles wrote to their mother, they didn't know this would be the only way my brother, my cousins and I would ever know who they were. For each uncle, we had only his name and one photo. Beyond that, to us, they were unknown soldiers.

As they recorded the last years of their lives, Tom and Jack painted pictures that interwove their war experiences and their love for our family. They also tossed in snippets from their childhood that enlightened us further.

I never could have imagined the power of a pile of paper. It transformed Tom and Jack from silent portraits into cherished family members, and changed me for the better in the process as well. I found an answer I needed but never knew to look for.

Winter 1942

TOM - PREFLIGHT CHECK-IN

Tom joined the Army on May 18, 1942. He qualified for aviation ground school, then preflight training as a cadet. Our collection from him begins with the form letter below.

Santa Ana Army Air Base
Santa Ana, California
November 10, 1942

Dear Mother:

I'm sending this from the Classification Center here at the Santa Ana Army Air Base, where I arrived today. I was met at the train and am now here with the rest of the future Army Air Crews.

I've been registered and assigned to Squadron 9, where I shall remain for about two weeks. During that time I will have my physical examinations and tests which will determine whether I become a pilot, bombardier or navigator. After being classified I will be assigned to another squadron here on this post, and then my actual preflight training begins. That preflight training will last for about nine weeks and then I will be sent to one of the flying schools to start my flying training.

You will, no doubt, think it is strange receiving this type of letter from me instead of a personal note, but here is why: Our commanding officer knows that during the excitement and process of getting settled during the next few days, some of us will be apt to forget to write to the folks at home. This is his way of letting you know where I am and that I shall be well taken care of in the Army Air Forces.

Another is my protection by National Service Life Insurance which is granted me free of charge all through my training period.

I know I'll have more nice things to tell you when I write a real letter. In the meantime, please let me hear from you. My address is: Squadron 9, Army Air Base, Santa Ana, California.

Your loving son, Tommy

We don't have the original of this letter in our collection. Luckily for legacy purposes, my grandmother typed multiple carbon copies of each of her sons' letters to forward to other brothers away from home. It was her way of keeping all the boys aware of the others' locations and activities, though the boys wrote to each other directly also. It seems like she also kept file copies for herself, as well as originals, because, for some letters, I found both the original and a copy, or the copy only. I think the copies are what she kept centrally available for family and friends in Los Angeles.

TOM - SETTLING IN
Santa Ana, California, November 12, 1942

Dear Mom,

I'm finally able to write. The last couple days have been pretty unsettled but now things have been more or less decided.

Last night the doc peeked down our throats with a flashlight and ordered me to report for sick call this morning. I'd already been assigned to fireguard duty so that meant going to breakfast ahead of the squadron with the officer of the day (OD) and adjutant. Then my duties began— namely inspecting "C" flight barracks for fire hazards.

After my other guard came back from chow I reported to the orderly room. Another sick call was with me and we waited in the line.

That's about all we've done. Wait in line and march. If you're not doing one you're doing the other. Anyway, we waited and waited. When we finally got inside and reported, the adjutant told us the sick calls had left long ago out the backdoor. He pointed to a column about a mile away and said, "On the double!"

We caught up with them just as they turned into the flight surgeon's building. We waited in line *again*! Finally they took my temperature, sprayed up my nose, gave me aspirin and cough medicine.

Well, this is about all now. The food is swell and plentiful and the fellows are OK.

Your loving son, Tommy
P.S. Favorite calls from upperclassmen to rookies: "You'll be sorreeeeee!" and "You *would* read those recruiting posters."

TOM - THE PSYCHO CHECK
Santa Ana, California, November 16, 1942

In birth order, Tom and Jack were #7 and #8 of the nine children, twenty-one and nineteen years old respectively when they went into the Army. In the letter below, you'll meet a few siblings: #2 Pat (Patricia) the only girl, #3 Frank and #9 Mark the "baby." Pat and Frank were in their late twenties at this point, Mark was sixteen.

Dear Mom,

Today we spent nearly eight hours in the psychology department undergoing examinations for classification. They are quite a strain and so this will be a short one.

Tonight we are all shining shoes and getting things in shape as we have a new commanding officer coming tomorrow and some major is going to inspect the barracks. Everybody here is in good spirits as our fates should be decided in the next few days. They are being pretty stiff as there is quite a bit of material here.

I went down to the phone booth yesterday to give you a buzz but there was a line a mile long and the boys were calling any place from LA to Boston. I'll try again sometime but I wouldn't wait at home for it. After we are out of quarantine, I think we can have visitors on weekends and perhaps Jack will take you down. He'd like to see the place.

We are up at five or five-thirty every morning, and I'm catching up on the stars and sunrises and sunsets I've been missing all these years. We don't have much to do but take exams and eat so I'm just getting fatter. They'll get even with me soon.

Next Friday could you send me a copy of *Time* magazine? I can't buy it here. I think it comes out Fridays and if you mail it right away I'll get it Sunday or Monday. Could you do that weekly? Lastly, could I have two or three sweatshirts—plain colors? If someone will charge them at Neeland's on their bill I'll pay for them when I get my check.

Everything else I need I can get here but they sell them faster than they can reorder. I'd appreciate the sweatshirts quam celerrime or sumpin'.

I'm glad to hear Mark is getting good marks in school. Tell him to keep it up. What has Frank heard from the draft?

Did I tell you I met the chaplain here, Father Clasby? He's quite a boy. There are not many Catholics here but among them are the cadet officer, our squadron leader, the adjutant and one flight lieutenant. That's the top of the list too.

Tell Grandma everything is fine and I'll write soon. Also I owe Pat a letter. Well, I guess that's all.

Your loving son, Tommy

P.S. I've just made you beneficiary and Pat alternate in ten grand gov't insurance.

TOM - WRITING GRAM

Santa Ana, California, November 23, 1942

After moving from New Hampshire to California, the family lived in the home of the children's maternal grandmother, "Gram." It was a large house, two-stories, located in downtown Los Angeles. Built in 1916, it had eight bedrooms and four bathrooms. Gram had access to the collection of letters the boys' mother compiled, but the boys wrote to her separately also. At this time, Gram was 85 years old and had health issues.

Dear Gram,

I've started to write before but always got interrupted. I can't plan much here as they are liable to call me out anytime. I'd hoped to write you first with the news of my classification but I won't know for three or four days, so I thought I'd better write now as when I do hear about my classification, I'll be busy moving to a new squadron.

That moving will really be a job. Uncle Sam has given me more and better clothing than I've ever had in my life. I got an overcoat that weighs a ton, raincoat, blouse (tunic), 2 olive drab wool shirts, 4 suntan suits, 2 pair dress pants, 3 flight caps, 1 garrison cap, 12 pairs socks, 6 handkerchiefs, 6 shorts, 6 jerseys, leather gloves, 2 neckties, razor, shaving brush, 4 towels and a pair of swell shoes. Oh, yes, a belt too. So don't worry about me on these cold mornings.

I also have another pair of shoes coming, a sweat suit, sneakers and shorts. I am being fed like a pig. I've had chicken three times and drink at least a quart of milk a day.

I had KP duty Saturday and saw them prepare the food. That place is cleaner than yours, Gram, and that is saying a lot. We served about five thousand meals that day. The floors are washed three times a day in the mess hall and more than that in the kitchen. For KP duty we get up at four in the morning, report at four-forty and if we are lucky we get off at eight-thirty in the evening.

We have a lot of Irishmen here but just between you and me they are not so hot—at least, not at shooting crap. One lost about forty dollars last night but I was smart enough to stay out of that game. I sort of teamed up with the guy next to me and we've agreed to kick the devil out of each other if we get in one of those games. I'll fix him if he plays and he'll do the same to me if I do.

I won't be home for Thanksgiving and I don't know about Christmas. I'll be able to have visitors next week if I can get any down here.

Well, I've gotta quit now. Get better quick as I'm sure you'll like jitterbugging once you get up and around.

Love, Tommy

TOM - PILOT TRAINING BEGINS
Santa Ana, California, November 30, 1942

In this letter, Tom refers to his successful classification for his preference, pilot training. He probably phoned his mother with this information; it doesn't seem to be "news" below. Jerry (or Gerald) was the #4 child (26 years old); my dad Bob was #5 (25 years old).

Dear Mom,

As I write this letter I am wearing a gasmask. Outside white clouds are billowing, but they are on the north side of the camp. There goes the "All Clear" for this area. We were warned this morning to carry our gasmasks at all times.

We got up at 4:30 this morning and went over to the mess hall to go on KP duty. However, it seems Squadron 19 was already there to do the job, so we left in no little hurry. It is quite a task of about sixteen straight hours without letup.

I don't know how much longer I'll be in quarantine. The real dope is scarlet fever. It is not serious as yet, and it is limited to this quarantine area. One squadron is completely isolated though. I don't know of any cases in our group yet, though one fellow went to the hospital Saturday night and hasn't come back yet. If he's got scarlet fever we'll be here forever.

We are all satisfied with our classifications and are waiting to get started. Last nite some of the fellows in the squadron put on a show under the direction of Bill Hart. I don't know as he is Wm. S. Hart's son or not, but he has been in pictures, and was just getting started when he came here. He was in *Somewhere I'll Find You* with Clark Gable and Lana Turner. He is very clever and a nice fellow.

They did a parody on "Der Fuhrer's Face," like this: "When the Captain says, 'Get on this work detail,' we say, 'Pile! Pile, Just Pile it up your - - -.'" They gave the adjutant an awful going over, and the takeoff Hart did on the captain was perfect. The CO was there and he got quite a kidding. I hope they do more of them.

Saturday night Pvt. Lou Alter and Margaret Whiting played and sang. Alter wrote "Manhattan Serenade," "Dolores" and other hits. Margaret Whiting is the daughter of another songwriter who turned out some good ones. They played the piano and sang, and led community singing. The temptation on my part was great.

I have been thinking of buying a better blouse, but I have just heard they are going to issue them when we get to or through primary. If this is true, I won't buy one because then I'll know I earned it.

Besides, if I don't get through primary, it won't do me any good anyway.

Lt. Naughton prepared a swell Thanksgiving dinner for us. He did it in such a thoughtful manner, and treated us like human beings who are more or less members of his family, that when we get to work under him, we'll really do a swell job.

Our own squadron leader, 2nd Lt. Macke, is a real nice fellow and only twenty-one. He is the only second lieutenant in charge of a squadron on the post. Most of the COs are captains or at least first lieutenants. Consequently, all the officers, well most of them, are jealous and are just waiting for him to make a slip. It's up to us to see that he doesn't and so we try extra hard. He shelled out for Cokes at the show last night for 180 of us, plays football with us, and it's going to be hard to find a better CO.

The food you sent is gone and everybody had some, but it looked like a lot of expense. I don't want you to use house money. Homemade cookies are always welcome, and I can buy candy bars for three cents each. When and if you come down I'll give you a whole carton to take home. Just tell me what kind. I'd feel a lot better if you take some money and go to a show once in a while.

It looks like I'll spend Christmas here unless I am very lucky. I'm going to send you some money around then to get yourself some pastels and all that goes with it.

We have some beautiful sunrises and sunsets here, and I think of what you could do if you saw them. There are colors here which I never suspected at those occasions, particularly orchid.

I may be moved by Saturday but I don't know for sure yet. Tell Jack to go easy on the gas so that he can get down here. Well, I guess that's about all for now.

Your loving son, Tommy

Tom's mother, who became my grandmother, "Nana," was a landscape painter. Three of her pastels were passed down through the family. My cousin Elizabeth and I each have one from our fathers, Mark and Bob. Steve received his from Jerry and subsequently gave it to me. It is of a beautiful California sunset, and includes, as was suggested by Tom in this letter, the color orchid.

JERRY - DON'T TELL BOBBY
San Diego, California, December 1, 1942

This is the first letter from Jerry. He introduces my mother Jackie and brother Patrick, born two days after the Pearl Harbor attacks. To differentiate him from the boys' sister Patricia, my brother usually has "young" or "little" before Pat or Patrick. To differentiate between the two Jacks—my uncle and my mother—my uncle is usually Jack, and my mother is Jackie, though both were called both.

Dear Mom,

Received your letter yesterday and Pat's today. Have been working for the past three nights and don't feel like writing a long letter so will just dash off a few thoughts.

Tell Pat I appreciated her letter. I'll try to write soon. The shoes you can keep until I come up again or ask you to send them. As for Christmas presents, just forget about them. You have enough worries as it is, and I can think of nothing I need or want.

Don't tell Bobby, but Jackie wrote me about him wanting to get in this war. Try and tell him that his job is where he is now, until he's called. None of us were doing any war work and he is.

Another thing, too, besides you and the rest of the family, he has Jackie and young Pat. He owes it to them and everyone else to stay where he is until he's called.

I know Tom, Frank and all the rest of us would feel better to know that someone was around you in case anything happened. You might also remind him that I stuck around for quite some time when he and Frank got married. Don't worry, if they want him they'll get him. Just tell him not to get hasty.

I have started my diary and will try and keep it, so it can be read sometime.

Don't forget to send Tom's address, and if any of his pictures that he took Sunday come out alright, send them along.

Well, I guess this is about all for now.

Your loving son, Gerald

My dad Bob worked all his life in aeronautical engineering. At this point he was working at Douglas Aircraft Co., thus Jerry's reference to his doing war work. He had a hernia that marked him "1B," temporarily deferred from military service. Both medical insurance and money were in short supply, so his surgery was delayed.

TOM - A SOLDIER'S WORK IS NEVER DONE
Santa Ana, California, December 3, 1942

Dear Mom,

So many times I have started to write Pat or Jack or other member of the family, but I always end up writing you. As all of you read all of the letters anyway, I guess they won't mind.

Yes, I got my shots Thanksgiving and before the big meal too. I just got another one today. We had three shots Thanksgiving, one smallpox, one typhoid and one tetanus. Today we got another typhoid and it was a double dose over the first one.

Two guys passed out at mess today and I felt like I'd like to for a while. After getting some food in me I felt better, though right now I have a headache and had chills this morning. That is about the average reaction.

The needle penetrating the muscle (which is getting a little tougher by the way) makes the arm and shoulder sore while the serum entering the system might raise hell in a number of other ways.

Next Thursday we get a triple dose of typhoid and the next two Thursdays after that I'll get more tetanus. What a life!

Your schedule looks pretty tough to me. Perhaps if Jack and Mark knew what I have to do, which is just what they'll have to do when they get here, they might start in now to help you more.

They will find that one of the worst feelings they will get here will be when they do things and think of all the work they could have saved you. I kick my pants every day because once you get used to it, it is not too bad.

I get up and dress at 5:30. At five-forty-five we have to be on the line outside for roll call. Between that time and 7:20 I have to make up my bunk, and brother, I mean make it up!

You get gigged for a wrinkle! Everything in my footlocker must be in the place where it belongs. My clothes must be free from dust, all buttons buttoned and hanging so that they face the door. My shoes must be shined and placed in proper order under the bed.

After this is done, the floor in my area must be swept and mopped, everything dusted, the windows wiped and washed about every week. I also have to wash and shave.

Some days I have added duty as today I had to do everything above but sweep and mop, and then get mops and brooms, brushes and rags enough to clean the entire barracks.

Then I had charge of cleaning the latrine. I had four guys working with me and we had to wash the shower room walls, floor and duckboards, the latter also have to be set outside to dry. Then wash a half dozen sinks and mirrors, nine toilets, windows, woodwork and floor.

The toilets have to be spotless and *dry* above the water for inspection. The inspecting officer will run his finger up underneath the rim and if he finds anything there!!! All brass and metal must shine.

After all these things are done, we go to mess. When we come back we can't use the latrines 'til noon and we have to clean up outside the barracks, washing the steps, etc. While nobody would probably be that fussy at home (Grandma never was) it will give you an idea of how little has to be done at home to be satisfactory. So, I hope they'll take the suggestion.

The CO told us we would be moving out next Tuesday so I should be able to have visitors a week from Sunday. This also means Saturday evenings from 5 to 9. When we transfer we will be split into two groups, the whole squadron to be divided halfway down the alphabet.

So I shall keep with my best friends here, DeMent, Halferty and Burtner.

I doubt if I'll get home Christmas unless I'm very lucky. C'est la guerre. I don't believe I'll phone this week unless I should move sooner than the CO said.

I'm going to lay down now until the next mail call. I hope everybody is cooperating at home. Meantime, I'll be waiting to see you all again.

Your loving son, Tommy

TOM - BARRACKS GOOFINESS
Santa Ana, California, December 4, 1942

Dear Pat,

We had quite a time in the barracks yesterday. There is a fellow named Cobery here from Massachusetts and he gets letters from a girl studying art in Boston. She writes very clever letters and illustrates them. The fellow who bunks next to Cobery is Halferty, the guy who phoned me after I got my orders. Well, this Halferty plays the piano and used to have a band of his own and is very funny to boot.

Cobery let Halferty read a letter aloud, censoring them where he thought it wise by reading silently. She wrote how she looked forward to "the day when her darling angel would come zooming out of heaven to take her in his arms!" It seems he told her he was a "Knight of the Air" now. (A Knight of the Air is a bunch of us who agree to say a decade of the rosary every night.)

Evidently he didn't explain thoroughly because she wrote back calling him her "Knight in Armor" and also said she was glad he was a Knight because a King is a King forever until he dies, but "once a Knight is plenty."

She mentioned too that she was going out with other fellows once in a while but nobody in particular just to prove she was still faithful to him. Whenever she mentioned a fellow, Halferty would stop reading and, you know that thing they play when the villain comes in, well, Halferty does that and goes through all sorts of contortions. He sighs and faints when she gets mushy and makes those letters the funniest things you ever saw.

Halferty looks just like that Bugs Bunny in the movie cartoons and is twice as funny. He doesn't seem to get much mail, so maybe sometime you could send some cookies to him instead of me. The name is Guy Halferty and he'll be in my squadron when we move.

After we got our shot the other day about ten guys in the barracks went to bed. They didn't want to go to the hospital because they might get kept there and miss moving out with the squadron. So, it was necessary to get food for them out of the mess hall.

I gave them my milk and another guy made a couple of pork sandwiches, we got a couple extra pieces of cake and all this we smuggled out in our zoot suits. DeMent was pretty sick and all he took was some milk. He heaved three times that day.

About Christmas, it looks pretty doubtful about getting home. As for shopping, I have not yet made a decision. So far, I think I'll send Mother some money for pastels, as I told her, and as it is so difficult to wrap and ship stuff here I may call it even with everybody else, asking nothing and giving nothing, but buying a new blouse for myself and calling it square.

I guess this is about all; glad to hear you are doing OK with the piano and say "Hello" to Mr. Tramblay for me. Tell Mom I'll try to call next week.

Love, Tommy

"Send some cookies to him instead of me." This is where Tom went from being a soldier in a picture to a member of my family.

TOM - BOOGIE-WOOGIE BUGLE BOY
Santa Ana, California, December 8, 1942

Dear Mom,

According to the upper classmen chances are pretty good that I may get Christmas off, but don't bank on it too much. We are on Alert and sleep with our clothes right at the foot of the bed, ready to evacuate at a moment's notice.

Visiting hours are Saturday from 5 to 9 p.m. If you do get down, go to the Cadet Reception Hall or Visitors' Room, whatever they call it. I'll try to be there or within call.

Incidentally, tell Jack we actually have a "boogie-woogie bugle boy" and he's in flight B! When he calls classes he plays "School Days, School Days, Dear Old Golden Rule Days."

This outfit is wackier than the nutty ninth but the pace is much faster and they mean business.

Love to all, Tommy

TOM - I'LL BE HOME FOR CHRISTMAS
Santa Ana, California, December 20, 1942

Dear Mom,

Four days and I'll be home! Here are plans so far. I won't have anybody staying at the house for the weekend except Saturday night. Boothe and Burtner have been given a special pass over the 100-mile limit to be with their folks. They told me to thank you anyway and of course, I don't blame them for going home if they have the chance.

I'm not sure yet but I think Mifflin, one of the fellows here who is from Phoenix and is meeting his wife in town, will come to Christmas dinner. DeMent will stay over Saturday night as he is going to be in Glendale and it will give us an early start Sunday.

On the ride to town from here there will be Duncan, DeMent, Booth and myself. I hope Frank won't mind. I figured as long as he was coming for me he wouldn't mind helping the fellows get to their homes. He knows what Christmas means and I'm sure will understand. It will be the best present he could give to me or the fellows.

Could you have Frank bring five dollars with him? I borrowed five from DeMent to send to Gerald and I want to pay him back. I'll pay you back as soon as I get my bonus.

The schedule will be to meet us at the gate at 7 a.m., December 24th. DeMent and I will go downtown and have pictures taken. Then, he'll go to Glendale and I'll come home. About getting back. Does Jack have the gasoline? He had better or I'm really up the creek unless Frank has an unlimited supply. This is going to be the best Christmas I've had in a long time. A day which had been getting almost monotonous has suddenly taken on a new tremendous meaning. Helping to decorate the mess hall has been great for me, and I'm glad to have been able to help make Christmas a little brighter here.

I'll try to call Wednesday during the day to make sure of all the above arrangements and tell of any changes. Haven't had time to write Grandma again but tell her I'm looking forward to seeing her. So, we'll see you.

Love, Tommy
P.S. If anybody is getting me a suntan shirt the size is 15 neck, 32 sleeve, 33 is too long.

TOM - THE LOST WEEKEND
Santa Ana, California, January 25, 1943

Dear Mom,

Sorry I didn't get in last weekend but my bus ticket was no good. By the time the five o'clock bus came I wasn't feeling well enough to make the trip anyway.

Friday morning we were scheduled for machine gun practice on the range. It was pouring at the time and we knew we would not go, but as we had no other orders we had to march almost a mile to the point where we were supposed to meet the convoy. Of course, the trucks weren't there and we had to wait for orders to go back. All this consumed about an hour and a half during which time all we did was absorb more water.

Our raincoats and shoes were good protection but below the raincoat I got pretty wet. I kept my feet more or less dry until about twenty-five yards from the barracks. I stepped in over my ankles and that took care of that.

I took off my clothes, put on my sweat suit and climbed into bed, which is about what everybody else did. From Friday noon to Saturday noon I was fireguard, and with classes Saturday afternoon, that left no time for phoning.

With seven others from our barracks I went into Santa Ana where we indulged (or in these times, is it called overindulged?) in thick steaks, went to the USO dance which wasn't bad and got back to camp and bed by 12:30.

The parade was called off on account of a flooded parade ground so there was not much doing except in blackjack. I might add that I generally have been making enough at this extracurricular activity to take care of what I spend during the week. While this is not an enormous amount, it runs from three to five dollars which is alright with me.

I went to sick call today and got my throat swabbed and a six-day light duty slip which means no drill, calisthenics or details for that period of time. Everybody here has a cold or sore throat and the main reason seems to be that somebody gypped our Uncle Sammy when they put the oil burners in, so that we have no heat or hot water unless we want to take a chance on things blowing up.

It seems that everybody is nicking this place. Laundry is 63 cents a week whether we use it or not and they shrink everything. So much a month for buses, use them or not, and Saturday night when we came in we had to pay a fare from Santa Ana. I hope all these chiselers get it in the neck when it will hurt them the most. Amen.

So far I haven't given any good news but I'll tell you my average in class is still 97.4. I missed two tests due to being fireguard and on sick call today but they just don't count that, and when they figure your tests they add your scores and divide by the number of tests taken. It seems too good a deal to be true and there must be a catch in it somewhere but so far nobody has found it. See you Saturday.

Love to all, Tommy

JERRY - GOOD LUCK, JACK
San Diego, California, February 3, 1943

Dear Jack,

Got your letter today and was quite surprised to think that you are going so far away, however it may be a good thing.

You know I'm not one to do any preaching but maybe I can tip you off to a couple things. Unlike my job, you know you have to keep in the very best condition at all times. For that reason it might be a good idea to cut down on your smoking and lay off the beer. I think you want to make the grade enough to give it all you can, and I know you won't regret it.

I know too that you will get along with all the boys and be able to take anything the Army dishes out. I'll be pretty disappointed if you don't come out on top and really make a name for yourself.

Good luck, Jack, and don't forget to write and let me know how you're getting along.

Your brother, Jerry

P.S. If I'm going to see Tommy and Frank in Berlin, how the hell can I see you in Tokyo? J.

JACK - THE TROOP TRAIN
En Route from Los Angeles to San Antonio, Texas, February 7, 1943

Jack's letter-writing career began on a train from LA to Texas. In his first twelve days, he wrote sixteen pages of letters to his mother and sister Patricia. He was only nineteen years old and very close to his family.

Dear Mom,

I'm on the train so the writing won't be so hot. We are in Arizona now but I don't know where. I didn't get much sleep last night, no one did. Stopped at Needles, Cal. this morn for breakfast, bacon, eggs, spuds, toast and coffee. Real good but had to sit outside the restaurant for an hour.

Just now in Kingman, Ariz. Pretty cold. Nothing but servicemen on the train. No liquor of any kind anywhere. That's OK.

Didn't see Tommy. Am riding first class Pullman. Next meal at 2 p.m. This is pretty country if you like desert. Those recruiting posters sure work wonders. There are about 600 of us, 36 per car, about 20 cars, all troops.

Can't write much on a train, will write in detail later.

Lots of love, Jack

P.S. Say hello to all and tell them I will write when I can.

JACK - YOU'RE IN THE ARMY NOW
San Antonio, Texas, February 10, 1943

Dear Mom,

Just a few lines to let you know I am OK. We arrived here early Tues. morning. Yesterday we kept pretty busy so I didn't have time to write. This is a large camp of some 50,000 men. It is an Air Corps ground school and the second toughest camp in the country.

Yesterday it was pleasant but later in the day it was windy and we had a regular sandstorm.

Last night five of us missed mess so we ate in the PX. I went to bed about nine. I just got to sleep when a guy came over and dragged me out of bed and we went to the MD and got two shots in the arm and a blood test. There was a shortage of blankets, but we were upstairs, the heat was turned up and it was quite comfortable.

We just came back from chow. The food is pretty good and plentiful but I miss home cooking. It is cold outside. I could sure use a knitted cap and a bunch of coat hangers. At least six or eight. We eat cafeteria style here. Will write in detail when I can, but we are about to be called out. Don't forget the hangers.

Your loving son, Jack

P.S. If I don't write don't worry. I'll be pretty busy for the next four or five days.

P.P.S. Send Frank's and Gerald's addresses and Tom's when he gets a new one.

JACK - THIS CAMP IS TOUGH
San Antonio, Texas, February 11, 1943

Dear Mom,

I have a few minutes before chow so I'll start this letter. Army life is OK but this camp is tough. Our CO Lt. Murray is a jerk. He is one of those 90-day wonders and is not liked any too well by anyone on the post. Things are unsettled as yet, tho we have our uniforms.

Gad! I have 3 OD shirts, 3 OD pants, 3 suntan shirts, 3 suntan pants, 1 suntan cap, 1 OD cap, 3 zoot suits, 3 long-johns, 3 service underwear, 2 ties, 2 pairs of shoes, 2 pairs of leggin's, 1 jeep hat (new edition), 1 GI toilet set, socks, handkerchiefs, 1 flight jacket, 1 blouse, 1 overcoat, woolen gloves (knitted), 2 barracks bags, and if I forgot anything, I don't know what it is.

The "407" is about the best squadron in this camp of some 50,000 men. They are mostly from Texas and Ohio. We cadets are known as the "Walking Air Force" and "The Flying Infantry." The camp has a happy spirit and when we arrived we were overly greeted with a friendly "You'll be sorreee!!!"

We got two shots the other nite but they didn't bother me much. The boys all sing a lot. On the way to and from chow usually. They sing the Air Force Song and the most popular, "Texas is a hell of a state, parlez vous!" (2 times), then "The worst of all the 48," etc. Of course they don't say "worst," but you are a lady. The food here is OK when you get used to it. I have learned to make a bunk one way. We were to have inspection today but didn't.

After lunch, 1:45 p.m. Just came in from chow. Potatoes, salmon loaf, string beans, soup, coffee, cake and ice cream. It gets a little better each time. In a few weeks we will go on a hike to the rifle range. It is 14 miles out. We go out one day, stay the next and come in the third. If our barracks chief goes with us, it will be easy as he is rather plump and does not look like the hard-going type. However, if the Lt. goes, it may be rough as a GI haircut. I will take anything he is going to dish out. This epistle will be interrupted at any time so if it doesn't make sense try and forgive me.

I went to the show last nite and saw *In Which We Serve*, 15 cents. Picture pretty good.

By the way, how are things at home? Is everything OK? I suggest that you turn in my insurance policy, as it will help out. I have $11,000 worth here. The regular GI and another $1,000 20-year endowment policy. I think I will write Frank next. He is farthest away. Tell the other folks I haven't forgotten them and will write when I can. Is Mark doing better, now that he has but one boss? He should. How's Pat's bowling coming?

I think we have an exam tonight but I am not sure. I am in an overflow area, i.e., away from the regular 407 area. It is quite crowded but not too bad. Our barracks should hold 63 men. We have 100. We are supposed to be here 30 days but I know the Army better than that. There is a football game outside, seven men in the backfield and about 14 in the line. Fooey!! I signed up for basketball on the squadron team. I don't know if I'll make it as there are ex-college players and everything here. But often you practice ball instead of marching!!

Not much more to say now but may add more before I mail this. Give my love to all.

Later 3:45 p.m. Dear Mamacita, Just came in from sports. Boxing, football, basketball, baseball, volleyball and foot-racing. I played football. I'm in no mood to get myself knocked out of this camp. I don't know what is next on the program. No one does. Every time you leave your barracks you have to straighten the bed, your spare clothes and all. It has been pretty cold lately. The wind is cold but the sun is hot. Every once in a while we get a dust storm. Our first day it was awful.

By the way, as far as I have seen, that stuff of pretty girls in Texas is so much baloney. I haven't seen any! I can get a pass in about two weeks but there is very little to do. Well, I guess this is it. Bye for now.

Your loving son, Jack

TOM - MR. BROWN'S PACKARD
Santa Ana, California, February 15, 1943

Dear Mom,

I had one of the best weekends in a long time. Saturday night, we went to a YWCA USO dance. Floyd reserved a room for us for the evening so that took care of the worry. The girls at the dance were all dressed in formals for Valentine's Day and it was really nice. In fact I took one home to Anaheim along with three other couples and didn't get back to the Y until 4 a.m. as we had to hitchhike back. At eight o'clock Sunday morning, Floyd woke us up and we ate breakfast and took a bus to Balboa Island in Newport Beach.

There Floyd knew some people who had a standing invitation open to him any time. What a shack they had! The host was a big-shot undertaker in Santa Ana and had plenty of what it takes, and what's more liked to spend it and share his good fortune with others. They even had a guest book there and it seemed that every cadet at the base must have stayed there. Anyway, they have a son about thirteen who took us all around the bay in their motor boat.

After that we walked across the peninsula and went swimming in the ocean. Swimming in February! It was kind of cold but plenty refreshing. Just being in trunks with no insignia or anything to remind me of my long invaded privacy was about the biggest kick I've gotten out of anything. After that, we changed our clothes at the house, ate, and Mr. Brown took us back to the base, in his Packard, no less. What a life!

School still keeps. I found out I got a 92 in Naval forces last week and I should have done better. Next time. A 90 in physics and a 100 in code. Code was sent at 10 words per minute and you have to take it for 5 continuous without missing a letter to get a hundred. This week it will be twelve words and that will complete the course.

Well, I should be in around 6:30 or 7 Saturday so I'll see you then.

Love to all, Tommy

JACK - WAITING FOR MAIL
San Antonio, Texas, February 16, 1943

Dear Mom,

I have been waiting for a letter but as yet none have come. I guess it takes about three days each way. The joint is getting organized now and the weather is coming around to be a little nicer.

We had drill today and this noon we had a smallpox vaccination and a typhoid shot. My arm will be stiff tomorrow so I had better do some writing.

Yesterday was Sunday so we did not do much. I went to Mass and to the show and we were issued gasmasks, mess kits and canteens.

In the afternoon we played blackjack. I usually confine myself to whatever small change is in my pocket. I played for three hours and won a dime.

We have done very little except play football and basketball, and sit in on lectures which is very tiring and not worth much. I have only saluted twice. It is still a sensation.

Today we had an inspection and what a mess. Almost everyone's roll was wrong including mine. The lieutenant lifted everyone's pillow up and took the cover. He left a clean one.

When mine came out he pulled 2 neckties, an OD hat and a magazine. I pulled the mag. out of the can and put it inside there in a hurry. One guy got his bed all torn up including the mattress corner so I ain't doing so bad.

I hope to be sent to Santa Ana. There are a few lamebrains here, but not so bad.

I miss you all terribly and hope to see you soon.

Your loving son, Jack

This is where I became attached to Jack. He was so young, away from home and his close family for the first time.

JACK - A LETTER FROM MOM
San Antonio, Texas, February 17, 1943

Dear Mom,

I got your *wonderful* letter today and you don't know how happy I was. It seems we just live for news from home. One fellow here, Joe Chaix (Checks), was sore as the devil because he hadn't heard from his girl. Tonight after chow he went to call her up and find out what is going on. Now there are five letters on his bed and he doesn't know it!

We stood retreat last nite and it is a thrilling event. We were interviewed last nite for our service record. It was a lot of bull but was a good sort of diversion. Today we had an exam. It was tough as they come. So far only 11 out of 1,100 have gotten a hundred on it. We had a physical this afternoon and it was a cinch.

Not much has happened since I last wrote but not much happens here anyway. The boys are in fine shape. Incidentally, we had hopes of going to Santa Ana but they have gone. We are here for a minimum of 21 days (too much), and when we leave 99% of us will go to some university or college for our preflight training for as long as today's test should indicate.

I wish I could get to USC but the Navy has that one. UCLA or LAJC would be fine but no such luck I fear.

We've marched a lot lately and I can see why Frank thought they might make him a whirling dervish. The weather here corresponds with that on the coast as far as winds and cold are concerned.

I guess I will close this off as I have a lot of work to do, and letters to write, and no more news anyway. Tell Pat I'll write her.

Your loving son, Jack

P.S. Tell Jackie and Bob to write if they can and I will find time to answer. Am busy as heck right now. In the Army you rush and wait. Lots of love, XXOO

P.P.S. Our barracks chief says he might go to LA. I might give him our address as he is a swell guy.

JACK - DOG-TIRED

San Antonio, Texas, February 18, 1943

This is Jack's first letter to his sister Patricia. My Uncle Frank told his daughter Ann that Jack and Patricia were quite close, though Jack was eleven years younger.

Dear Pat,

Well, this is one tired soldier you're hearing from. We have been on the go since 5 a.m. and it is 6:30 p.m. now. We rose at 5, fell out at 5:15 for roll call, came in and made our beds, swept out the barracks, and cleaned out in general. When I say made our beds I mean it; no wrinkles, the U.S. on the blanket facing fore and in the center. On the shelf I am allowed a gasmask, shaving set and a picture (if you can find room).

We got to chow at 6:35, at 7:30 (or before) we fell out and went to a lecture. It was on "military courtesy." Our barracks had seen it already...it was the same damn sergeant, same damn line, same damn gags and it concluded with me sustaining the same damn pain in the butt. It was a mess for a while as the machine (projector) broke down so a kid got on a piano and we all sang. We were told what to and what not to salute. One guy, when we were on salute to the colors said, "No, boys, you don't salute a barber pole!" It was funny at the time.

We came back from there and drilled for two more hours. Then noon chow, wieners, Phfftt!! We have potatoes every meal! Once in a while we have sweets for variety. After chow we went to the cow pasture. Three hours of phys. ed. and it is a good hike out and back. Everyone was dog-tired and when we returned a damn sergeant said, "Fall out in 20 min for retreat." I could have killed him. Well, retreat is the most inspiring ceremony in the business but it tires you to stand at attention for so long. As the Army does, we marched down there and back part way and stood retreat in our own back yard. We no sooner got in the barracks than we fell out again to sign the payroll (no pay yet). Well that brings us up to the present. Oh yes, we missed evening chow but they say it was no good so that is a help.

What is Johnny Routh's store address? I ordered some stars for Mom and owe him almost $15 on my watch. Let me know your circumstances, financially, as I may want to make a deal. I miss you folks a lot and wish I could get close to home. Write when you can and you may expect a prompt return letter. I have to write Bob and Jackie, Peg, Ben and May, and fifty others. Say hello to Babe especially and all the rest of the gang at the bowling alley.

There may be a lot of beautiful girls in Texas but I have yet to see *one*! Tell Mark I expect a letter, and if he knows what is good for him he had better lay off the cigarettes, and do all the calisthenics he can at school. I know from experience!! My throat is sore from this dust down here and smoking irritates it like the devil. Tony Martin of the cinema is at this camp and he is just a buck private, like *me*. Say hello to Mom and tell her I miss her lots!!

Write when you can get time.

Your loving brother, Jack

TOM - OLIVE DRAB
Santa Ana, California, February 23, 1943

Dear Mom,

Glad to be able to talk to you on the phone this morning. One thing I forgot. Could you send me some darning thread, olive drab or tan? I have a few socks to patch up and would be able to do it while I'm quarantined here.

Perhaps I can get out of quarantine on a Saturday night or Sunday afternoon. If I hear that I'll have only one more weekend I'll let you know. It's possible to get in and out of quarantine but if I got caught it would go rather rough. However, the chances of getting caught are small and it could be pulled off quite easily.

The main thing now is finding things to do. We are improvising ping-pong tables and playing cards mostly. I have lots of letter writing to do but I can't seem to find enough things to write about. There are loads of people I wanted to see in LA, some I haven't seen since I came down here and they'll all have to have letters.

The enclosed is some winnings I collected yesterday and hope you can use it for something not necessary. Take Pat to a show or just go downtown, get a fancy dinner. For heaven's sakes, don't spend it on the house. If I hadn't sent it, you never would have had it anyway.

Tell Mark to keep on the ball and whatever he does, to be sure to do a good job because later it might mean a buddy's life or even his own or his brother's. It is a rather hard alternative, but if he learns the lesson it will be worth it.

Love to all, Tommy

Spring 1943

JACK - JUST OUTSIDE OF HEAVEN
Emporia, Kansas, March 1, 1943

Dear Mom,

Needless to say I am sorry and ashamed for not writing to you sooner and more frequently. But as you know, we have been on shipping orders and my physical condition was none too pleasant. However I suppose you have my telegram by now, and both my mental state and physical condition have improved very much. By that I mean, Sheppard Field was a hellhole, and cadets were not any too popular with the commanding personnel.

Friday nite when I called, I was mostly rid of my sore throat. We left Sheppard Sat. morn at 10:15. We rode on a chair car (1903 model) and it was most uncomfortable after 17 hours of sitting.

The mail from Sheppard Field is lost I guess. It has not arrived for many of us. It snowed a lot today but the weather is nice and somewhat invigorating now. How are things on the home front? I wish they would pay me. I could help you out some, I think.

Well, Mom, we are just outside of Heaven. Emporia, Kansas is a town of about 12,000 hungry people. By hungry, I mean starving for excitement or a change in life. We are an answer to their prayers and vice versa.

The fact is some 850 boys have gone into the service from here. That is a lot for such a small place. Service flags are everywhere. That is where we come in. There has never been a contingent of troops stationed within 100 miles of here. Furloughs are few and far between, and they know little about how their boys look and act in uniform.

We are at Kansas State Teachers College. It has 500 students left, mostly girls. That is quite a drop from 1,800 to 2,000 regular students.

About our studies: Today we were segregated into 5 squadrons of about 100 men each. They were determined by the amount of education we have had, i.e., college grads and 3 years college went in "A" squadron. One and 2 years college or JC were in "B" squadron. The rest of us at the same level are in C, D and E. We will be here for about 20 weeks. In that time we will get preflight training and I think we receive 10 hours flight training. That is really swell.

We have a swell setup here and it is up to us to keep it such. The people are all for us. We have been ordered not to take advantage of them and to act as soldiers and gentlemen. It is only natural that it will be better for us and those cadets who follow if we do this. On the campus we are under the school as well as military rules. In town we are on our own.

The girls are abundant and as friendly as can be. They go for us in a big way as the manpower shortage has lowered their resistance considerably. We are free until 10 Wednesday nights and from noon Saturday to 10 p.m. Sunday. I missed Mass Sunday but it was no fault of mine. We were quite busy. The food here is wonderful and I have no complaint whatsoever except that it is a long ways from home.

Well now, I guess I had better close. I hope to write more frequently now that we are settled at a permanent station. It snowed a bit today but not enough to notice. The weather is a bit cold but clean and refreshing. Hope to hear from you soon. I haven't gotten your cookies yet or any mail either. It will be forwarded soon I guess. Tell Pat I have started several letters since my last one to her but have sent none. I will redeem myself soon.

Lots of love & kisses, your son, Jack
P.S. Here is a quaint remark. Army definition of a KISS: "Upper persuasion for lower invasion." (I guess that's risqué but thought you would get a kick out of it.) The ground is white with snow now! It reminds me of Concord, with the snow and all!

The KISS joke above…love it. This was one of many indications to me, in these letters, what it must have been like for my grandmother to have so many boys. I wish I had known her in those early years, but it is sure a treat for me to "eavesdrop" now.

JACK - QUARANTINED
Emporia, Kansas, March 3, 1943

Dear Pat,

I fear that I have neglected you considerably along the lines of letter writing. I feel like writing now, but my hands are still a bit numb with cold. It was 4 degrees above this a.m.

As I know you are a school lover, I will attempt a description of this place. The campus is about the size of Los Angeles City College but much prettier. In fact, I could say it has all the appearances of being beautiful though now the trees are bare of leaves and the grounds only partially covered with snow.

There is a small picturesque lake here that is only half-frozen over, and very thin ice forms on the surface. In some parts, ducks still swim but they are odd-looking fellows when it comes to skating. If it were the dead of winter, or the end of May, this campus would undoubtedly be among the most beautiful in the U.S.

The dormitories are nice and I have come upon a very good deal. I share a room with a certain young chap named Jerry Brame. He is a fine boy from Seattle. I think that this is the only room with two in it as the others have three, four and some have five and six. It overlooks the lake and we have in our room two Army cots, a desk, two chairs, a dresser, and in the large closet we have a bureau. It is really swell except for a loudmouth bunch of Texans next door.

8 hrs. later. Well Pat, I'm disgusted. For a few days we have been quarantined. That is the boys of the 407th and 408th have. It seems that some of the others in Texas had the measles and that put us on the spot. Well, 400 fellows from various squadrons at Sheppard traveled with us on the train. We go to chow with guys from Buckley Field, two of whom have since gotten measles. We mingle with the townspeople and congregate in the same auditorium, but when our afternoon off comes we are confined to quarters. I don't get it. Outside of that everything is fine although I missed chow tonite. I was asleep at the time. By morning my backbone should be well out in front.

I am reading Richard Halliburton's *Royal Road to Romance*. It is a very poetic type of book, but good reading.

The next day. 11:35 a.m. Dear Pat, I'm really disgusted. We will be quarantined for two weeks due to measles. It wouldn't be so bad but other guys who came down with measles in the last few days are on the loose. There have been about 150 invitations to fellows for parties and open houses, etc., and we stay in our rooms. Nuts!!

I guess you can judge that I am in no mood to write, so will close and hope you will remember only the cheerful part of this letter. There is nothing to write about here at present, but will keep you posted on whatever may result. I have rec'd no mail from Sheppard Field so far but hope to. I fear Mother's cookies will be lost by now. My tongue is hanging out for them at this time. If any come here they will be thoroughly enjoyed, as they go farther with two fellows than they would with 52.

Say hello to all, and give them my love. Be a good girl and keep 'em bowling. I would like to have you or Mom visit me here as it is permissible. Maybe it can be arranged in a few months but $50/mo. is not much to save with. I expect to be here at least three months. If Tom and Jerry could put up expense money, I could provide a ticket for Mom. It would be a rest for her. I miss you all.

Your loving brother, Jack

JACK - THE I.R.S.
Emporia, Kansas, March 3, 1943

Dear Mom,

Not much to report as everything of importance is in Pat's letter. My lips are chapped I might say though, and we march a good deal.

The main purpose of this letter is my income tax. As near as I can guess, I have to pay nothing. However, I am enclosing my form which I will ask Pat to attend to. It is not complete but as close to completion as I can come.

This is of importance: Either in my drawer in the small table in the front room, or in or under the top right hand drawer of the front room closet is a statement from Western Union. It gives my earnings for 1942 from them. I am not sure how much it is. It may be $200 or more but I am not sure. If you find it, OK. Then Pat can finish my blank. If not, put it down as $219.53 or something unless you can get a duplicate statement from WU. It is a big mess trying to fix an income blank to coincide with someone more than 1,200 miles off.

I had forgotten this tax business until I had mailed Pat's letter. If any payment is due, I will be able to cooperate with her except on the first payment. I have rec'd only $6 traveling money from the Army since I entered the service. I have $10 left so I may be able to coast through the month with ease, especially since we are quarantined for two weeks, and only get to town on Wed. & Sat. & Sun. anyway.

We have been eating in style lately but will start at our own chow hall on Monday. It is a new place and will have civilian cooks. Things should be OK but I will miss the 15 pretty waitresses that wait on us.

So far I have rec'd but a few letters from the coast. Tom owes me two, Gerald and Frank each one. They may have been lost at Sheppard. I guess I will start my correspondence all over again.

This is a terrible letter, but honest, Mom, there is nothing to report. Classes have not started yet, and all we do is march and get lectured. It is a dull life at present.

Say hello to all and Gram especially. I will write her when there is something to write about. Mark owes me a letter too. How about that! He would enjoy all these girls in town. Is he being a good boy? I would hate to have him let you down at a time like this! Have Pat write about my tax return. Hope you are feeling well. Will write again soon.

Your loving son, Jack

JACK - THE NEW CHOW HALL
Emporia, Kansas, March 9, 1943

Dear Mom,

Yesterday I made a killing by receiving seven letters. It is my first mail since I got here, and naturally I was very happy. I would have written last nite but there was nothing to write about that you didn't know. So I spent the time writing a girl at work as she was in the dark as to what I was doing.

Sunday, we poor unfortunates were about the only ones at chow. They planned on about 400 but only about 150 went. All that food couldn't go to waste tho so we just dug in.

For breakfast I had three loads of potatoes, three bacon, two eggs, four donuts, six hot biscuits and four cups of coffee. At noon, I slowed down a bit and had but three bottles of milk and two donuts extra. At nite, I duplicated the morning meal somewhat with an extra milk. It was delicious.

We eat in our chow hall now. It is beautiful. We eat cafeteria style and are served by eighteen nice young girls. It is run by civilians but of course sponsored by the Army.

It was formerly the student café. It was all worked over and is very, in fact scrupulously, clean.

In the main dining room, at one end is a modern soda fountain. On the other is a fine trophy display. On the other wall is a beautiful mural, painted by students, of campus life. It is very nice. Food is *really* good and plentiful. It is still unsettled as to whether we may have seconds or have more on first serve. We do both.

Classes started today and I'm afraid your son has his hands full. We get up at 5:45. We must wash and all and *clean* our rooms for inspection. And I mean clean and neat. We fall out for chow at 6:40 and if we have time, come back to our rooms and usually clean some more. Classes start at 8:00 sharp, and last exactly 50 minutes. We have in the a.m. geography (not elementary by a darn site), English, history and first aid. Then from 12:00 to 13:00 we have chow.

When we get done we start again. At 13:00 orientation lecture (military), 14:00 math, 15:00 physical training, 16:00 study, 17:00 retreat then drill for an hour. At 18:00 chow. Lights out at 22:00. That is mighty rough if you ask me.

We did very little in class today, just got used to the atmosphere. Nothing left to report except that I am tired. This quarantine is absurd and only kept as a matter of form.

I am overly pleased about Pat's job and will try and write her soon. A jump like that deserves a special letter at least. Tell Jackie I'll miss the cookies but know there was a good reason so she is by all means forgiven. You be sure and send me "tollhouse cookies" if you can. I am dying for some.

Glad to hear that Tommy is finally underway. Did he get my letters? I sent him two from Sheppard.

I got a letter from Gerald, you, Pat (2), Jackie, Mary Haworth (Douglas co-worker) and one from Betty Reilly.

George is deferred 'til June. He loves his girl more than his country by gosh! He's yellow or stupid, or both. Deferment for one study, one credit for trig! They'll probably take Bobby instead. Just our luck.

The Army has only paid me $6 expense money so far. My book is marked $20 part payment for February but I have not gotten it. If it can be arranged, I will send you the $20 if you *promise* to use it on yourself. I may need it for Pat's tax but I don't really know. Nothing to do but close now. Lots of love and kisses and tell Mark I am proud of him. I hope he doesn't age mentally too much, like I did with responsibilities, but I guess he will always be young.

Did you charge my telegram to the phone or didn't you receive it?

Lots of love and kisses, Jack
P.S. Got yours and Peg's tonite.

A new mention of a family member in the P.S. above: Peg was Jack's sister-in-law, married to his older brother Frank. Peg's family lived next door to Gram on Van Buren, and Frank met her when the Cahills moved in. Yes, Frank married the girl next door, who at the time of this letter was pregnant with their first child.

TOM - GOOD RIDDANCE, SANTA ANA
Hemet, California, March 11, 1943

Dear Mom,

It is with considerable pleasure I scratch out the Santa Ana address on this letterhead.

We arrived in Hemet this afternoon by train, the cars of which looked so old, I expected Jesse James' ghost to drop in any minute and hold us up!

Now I am housed in sort of a duplex bungalow. There are two separate rooms, each with a large closet, bath, two bureaus, two desks, four chairs and five bunks.

The bunks are wooden framed, sort of Monterey style, with 3/4-sized bed, *springs* and mattress. There are swell lamps for each desk and indirect lighting for the room.

The meals are served cafeteria style and so far are just as good, if not better, than at Santa Ana. Today we were issued sheepskin lined flying boots, gloves of the same material, helmet, goggles, leather jacket and a knitted woolen sweater!

Our schedule here will be much busier than our former one with the first bugle at five-fifteen and God only knows when the day ends. Tomorrow we will have Mass in one of the school buildings and I hope to go, and also perhaps take Communion.

The planes we eventually hope to fly are Ryans and they are pretty nice and seem to land like a bat out of hell. Some of the boys don't land quite soon enough and so they have to zoom up and try again. I don't believe we'll fly until Monday or Tuesday.

This is about all I have time for now. Don't worry a bit as there are only about four squadrons here. We get much better attention, with better quarters, heat and medical service, and as for flying, they haven't had a serious accident since they've been operating here. If you'll send me Jack's address I'll write immediately.

I don't believe I'll be able to phone for a couple weeks at least, due to quarantine. Say hello to Grandma.

Love to all, Tommy
P.S. As near as I can gather, I am about ninety miles from Los Angeles and forty miles from San Diego.

JACK - THE SOCIAL LIFE
Emporia, Kansas, March 13, 1943

Dear Pat,

I can't put this letter off any longer as it is one you thoroughly deserve. I am really proud of you for the fine job you have worked yourself into. I guess that makes you assistant manager of the plant doesn't it.

The quarantine was lifted yesterday. Last nite we shed the bonds that bound us and went to town. Being Friday, everything was closed except drugstores, etc. I visited one which was quite empty of customers. I had two hot chocolates, first since I left home. They were the equivalent of five full cups and needless to say were thoroughly enjoyed. A very charming redhead waited on me and we had a very pleasant talk. Meanwhile, Kate Smith was on the radio and she sang, "As Time Goes By." That is the song from the show *Casablanca* and it is really nice.

After a half hour here, I went up the street and met Jimmy Boswell and Murray Arthur. We talked a while, and they had six girls and were trying to get rid of four. Not me! Both are swell guys. Art Cowan from LA is here. I went to school with his brothers, Joe and Bill. He is a swell guy. Well, Mel Bushnell and Jim Bradford came by and so we all went to the College Grill. Brad is from Ventura, a swell kid, and Mel is from Visalia, Cal. One Gus Allman from LA went out with Cowan last night and met up with a bootlegger. Gus got drunk as hell. He is a character and has 513 hours in the air. Murray has over 800, and three years in the Marines. That is our little band as is left after Sheppard.

Things are beginning to move now. We have been set up in squadrons judging from an exam we had at Sheppard Field. I am in "C" which isn't bad considering most of the other guys in "C" have at least two years college or more.

So, I will be here for three months before I go to preflight. That's OK with me. The women are abundant here but beauty is kinda scarce. Last nite I went to the College Grill again. They have a "jukebox" and dancing space there. We had a lot of fun. They are having a dance in town tonite, I guess I'll cruise by.

I hope you got a substantial raise with your new job. You sure deserve it, and need it.

How is everything at home? I would sure like to be there. If my raise comes thru I would certainly enjoy having Mother here. I could hire a nurse for a week to care for Gram. It would do Mom a world of good.

Right now I could hardly hire a taxi. Write when you get a chance and keep up the good work.

Your loving brother, Jack
P.S. Take a drink for me as everywhere I land is a dry county or something.

Running into friends away from home...this letter began a trend of such happenings.

TOM - MY DOLLAR RIDE
Hemet, California, March 16, 1943

Dear Mom,

Things happen fast and furious around here. I got my "dollar ride," as they call it, yesterday. This consisted of 25 minutes of climbing, gliding, banks and turns. After we took off, the pilot started climbing and it seemed that we were just standing still. At first I didn't know what to think or feel. I looked over the side and got a funny feeling, but realizing that is what leads to getting sick, I said to myself, "Cahill, what the hell are you thinking? They've been doing this for years." So after that, all was fine but I certainly got some thrills.

We would be flying along when suddenly he'd bank and one wing would come up and practically hit me in the face while the other one looked like it might fall off any minute from the angle we were at. Of course, it wouldn't fall off, but that is how it looked. He let me take the stick for about five minutes and I was surprised at how little effort it takes to control the ship. That is, force, I mean. Actually there is rudder, ailerons, elevator, airspeed and a million other things to look out for. When we landed I never felt a bump, though the air speed indicator said 65 mph.

Today I had 40 minutes also adding to yesterday's maneuvers, stalls and spins. These are not at all dangerous, understand, but can be if you don't know how to get out of them. To stall, the pilot would point the nose up until it could no longer climb, that is, he had it too steep, then the motor would kick out and you could hear the breeze whistling through the wires when, whoosh, the thing just dropped the nose and down we went. Then you just let it go 'til it picks up flying speed, gun the motor and that was that.

The spin is worked into in something of the same manner only instead of dropping straight down, you seem to stand on the propeller while the rest of the plane goes around you. I still kept my breakfast in that one so I'm not thinking of airsickness anymore.

I handled the controls for about 15 minutes and had a bang-up time. If I progress as well as the average, I should solo in about two weeks or so.

The ships are very safe, checked every twenty-five or fifty hours and overhauled every one hundred so there is no danger of mechanical failure. These are considered just as hard to fly as a basic trainer though not as heavy, whereas if I went to a field where they had Stearman biplanes, then basic would be just like starting from scratch—if and when I get to basic.

Our schedule Monday was like this. Up at 5:15. Reveille formation at 5:25, then eat breakfast, clean up the cabin, etc. and meet the flight line formation at 6:40. On the flight line from 7 to 12. During this time we study maps, walk planes out to the line, start the motors and fly. At 12 we come back, get out of flying clothes, clean up and hit the school formation at 1 p.m.

Out of school at 4:10, march back to the cabin and out for calisthenics at 4:25. Back from calisthenics at 5:15, clean up, dress and hit retreat at 5:30. Eat at 6:00 and then a flight meeting from 7:15 to 8:15. After that we have the rest of the night to ourselves but the morning time is so short we clean up at night now.

We have flight meetings Monday nights only so tonight I have a little more time. So you see, I have to pay for my luxurious furnishings.

Oh, yes, at calisthenics we ran 1,300 yards. Today it was 900 and sprinted 50 yards eight times. One bunch were running down the road and got clean out of sight, couple miles I guess and we can expect that, no doubt.

Sunday I had free so took a few pictures and more or less caught up on my letter writing. I also did a few sketches which I'll bring home when the book is full.

I haven't gotten any mail here yet from anybody and don't know whether it is because they are slow forwarding from Santa Ana or there just isn't any. Incidentally, we are quarantined from the PX so if you could send some cookies, it would be swell.

DeMent ran into an old buddy of his here who is any Army check pilot, a lieutenant. He is one of the boys who give you the ride in the Maytag Messerschmitt which is what they give the would-be washouts their last chance to show their stuff in.

The food continues to be swell and I now eat all the salad they can dish out. The phone call I made sounded pretty ragged on my end. They don't have the Bell system here so the service is pretty lousy. I'll try to save the phone for special occasions.

Well, I've got to study my traffic regulations now and try to practice some of the stuff the instructor told me up there this morning. Traffic regulations are very important as there are sometimes one hundred and fifty planes in a ten-mile radius. Wrote to Jack but had to guess his address. See you later.

Love to all, Tommy

JACK - ST. PATRICK'S DAY
Emporia, Kansas, March 17, 1943

Dear Mom,

It is fitting and proper that I write you on this fine St. Patrick's Day. It grieves me not to be able to wear my green but Army regulations, you know!

The luck of the Irish is still with me I guess as I was afraid for a while that my dreams of flying were shattered. During our calisthenics, our instructor introduced a new exercise he calls the "Ripper." This should be enough explaining. Well, Mom, it ripped me all right. My stomach muscles were pulled around a bit in the lower center of my stomach. For a minute, the doc thought it might be a rupture but said no after a checkup. He should know, he is a good MD. He has two planes himself and is also, I think, a flight surgeon.

It hurts a bit when I walk so I am excused from drill, gym, etc. A rupture, you know, will wash you out. Heaven forbid.

Not much happens around here, we are off each nite from 8 to 9:30. We go about a block off the campus to the College Grill. We dance and fool around. I am not interested in women now. I seem to shun women and bootleggers. For the first time in my life, I realize the importance of education. As far as I know we have just six weeks of school before we start flying. I would like to hear from Tommy. Has he shipped out yet? Got a letter from Jerry last week, answered same.

I almost forgot—I won't need the hat now, maybe Frank can use it. And there is nothing I would enjoy more than the cookies, but with things as they are, wouldn't they be better there? I get plenty to eat here. The food is good and we may have seconds.

I am sorry things on the home front are so tough. I wish I could be there to help. When I can, I will send some money to you.

Well, May, my time's about up. Would like to hear from Mark but I guess he's a busy kid these days! Give my love to all and Gram, and I still owe her a letter. Lots of love and kisses.

Your loving, I miss home, son, Jack

"May" isn't a misspelling, it is a nickname for Mary—I remember hearing my dad call my grandmother that name sometimes.

FRANK - VISITING FAMILY IN RICHMOND
Lebanon, Pennsylvania, March 17, 1943

Dear Mother,

I started a letter to you up in the barracks, but did not get a chance to finish it and, since the typewriter was not busy down in the orderly room, I thought I would try again and see if I had any better luck.

I am considerably busier than I thought I would be on this cadre. We do a lot of drilling, mainly practicing in handling men, as each of us takes turns in directing the movements of the group. This is a good experience for me and I am learning quite a lot. Especially when you consider that I have had very little drilling myself to say nothing of drilling others.

In addition, we have classes in the various subjects which we will be expected to teach to the new recruits, when and if they arrive.

My own position here is somewhat peculiar. My transfer took me out of the jurisdiction of the 489th just when they were about to make me a staff sergeant, and when I pointed this fact out to my new company commander, he said at first that I would have to prove my ability to him in order to get my rating. Later, however, he called me in and told me that I was going to apply for OCS, and that he wanted me to take a course of training that would make things easy for me when I got there. Thus the drill and handling of men in the field.

In addition I am going to handle the initial setup of the supply room and will turn the job over to the new man after I have gotten it well underway. After that I am going to do personnel work. The lieutenant says that is all they teach you there anyway.

What I started to write about mainly was to thank you for the sweater. Like the stockings and cap, it arrived during a warm spell, but if I know anything about Pennsylvania, it won't be very long before I will find a good use for it. There is a little snap in the air tonight, in fact. It fits very nicely, for although I have lost a little weight, it has not gone from my waist.

Undoubtedly by this time Peg has told you about my little jaunt into the South. I had a marvelous time. The Lowrys were swell to me and took me all over Richmond and as far as Williamsburg, which is certainly something to see. I did not realize how tired I was of barracks and dogfaces until I got away from them. You know I hadn't been away from this post overnight until now, and you can't imagine just how much pleasure I got out of sleeping in a real bed, eating off of dishes and talking to civilians. They gave me a five-day pass which was why I was able to get to Richmond. It wouldn't be possible to do it on much less.

They had a very severe sleet storm in Richmond shortly before I went down there. Nearly every tree in the city in that area had limbs torn off or were completely broken down by the weight of the ice which formed on them. They had no electricity for nearly a week and all communications, including rail, were completely stopped.

Walter Lowry seems to be in good spirits and health, but is subject to occasional periods of depression, during which he talks mostly of his numbered days. Kate's passing away seems to have been a blow from which he never fully recovered. Having me to show around wasn't a bad thing for him as he loves to drive and of course has not been able to, on account of the restrictions on pleasure driving. He eased his conscience with the thought that showing a soldier the battlegrounds of the Civil War could not be classed as pleasure driving.

My pass expired Sunday, but I left Richmond on Saturday as at this stage of the game I am trying to keep my record fairly clean and wanted to make sure that I would arrive on time. Also I wished to avoid the necessity of standing up all the way from Richmond to Washington, as I had done on the trip down.

I got to Washington about seven that evening and discovered that there would be no train to Harrisburg until the next day unless I wished to arrive about three in the morning. All of the hotels were filled so I got a cot in a gymnasium through the USO. Katherine Crowley had sent me her phone number so I called her. She lives with one or two other girls and since the father of one of them was visiting there, and they had plenty of room, she suggested that I might be more comfortable at her place.

They came down and picked me up. We sat up until about four-thirty batting the breeze about the family and of course, Peg (mine) and Hector. Of course she doesn't know them but she didn't seem to mind if I talked about them. Particularly, she wanted to know how you were feeling. I told her that you had your hands just as full as ever in spite of the fact that your family was pretty well spread out over the continent. She wished especially to be remembered to you, and was indeed pleased to know about Patricia's good job.

I don't know when I will be able to get to Richmond again. There is a lot that I would like to see but doubt very much if I shall again be able to get a long pass until I finagle a furlough home.

Washington, though, I am going to visit again one of these weekends. Katherine showed me a lot of the public buildings, including the Mellon Art Gallery and the Smithsonian Institute, but of course only the outside of them. One of these weekends, though, I am going to get there on a Saturday morning and try to go through them. The Lord only knows when I shall be in this part of the country again, and I might as well see as much as I can while I am here.

Say hello to everyone for me. I intend to try to get caught up on my correspondence as soon as I can, but cannot say exactly how soon that will be. Take it as easy as you can. I hope that Grandma is improving. I am going to try to write her this week, probably over Sunday, if we don't start getting our strength in and I am not too busy.

Love, Frank

Some new names: The Lowrys are cousins of the Cahill children. Patricia was especially close to her cousin Lizbeth, one of Walter and Kate's daughters, who is mentioned in letters that follow. "Hector" was what the family called Frank and Peg's baby, scheduled for an August birth.

TOM - SPINS, STALLS AND SNAP ROLLS
Hemet, California, March 18, 1943

Dear Mom,

This will be rather short but I'll try at least to bring you up to date. I have now logged two hours and forty minutes in the air and I'm surprised at what I have learned already. But it makes me realize how much more I have to learn in sixty hours and that I can't afford to waste any time.

I'm getting my turns down pretty well, climbing and gliding ones. These are most important as they are the basic maneuvers for getting out of spins, stalls and any other spot, and also are the whole secret to the successful approach to landings. Yesterday I got pretty sick but did not throw up. I wasn't used to being up so long or doing so many turns. Today I stayed up longer and it didn't bother me a bit.

My instructor Mr. Kearns is a swell guy and today he said I had a tendency to be too easy in my banks. By doing everything with the ship then letting go of the controls, the ship will continue on its way a bit then just level off and continue a normal flight. Actually it will fly by itself but as the pilot generally has some place in particular he wants to go, he must learn to control it.

To show that you couldn't "hurt" the plane or be scared of it, he put me into a snap roll before I knew what was going to happen. A snap roll is level flight, around the longitudinal axis, upside down and around level again. More darn fun! It is difficult to tell, without any scenery, whether you are upside down or not. Spins and stalls are also fun. In fact this whole business is swell. Today he said I'd improved a great deal over yesterday.

I think I may get home next weekend. In any case, could you send me about five bucks? I have a lot of laundry and cleaning to get and there will also be my bus ticket. Everybody else here is in about the same fix I am so I'd rather not borrow. If you haven't got it, all right, as I can get it here. I gave Mifflin his pictures and sent a couple of my pictures to Marjorie so will have more prints made.

Love to all, Tommy

JACK - SICKBAY
Emporia Kansas, March 18, 1943

Dear Mom,

It will be a bit difficult to write this and possibly to read it. I am in sickbay. The med. decided on hot applications for my strain, and so it is OK by me. I don't know how long I'll be here but imagine only a few days.

I picked a good day to be here as it was terribly windy out and there was rain, snow and sleet off and on all day. I will not miss much school and what I miss is all review. I got 104 on an English test the other day. I have forgotten a lot but it will come back.

Rec'd yours and Tom's letters yesterday. One from Jerry today with $4 loan per request. I will be OK 'til payday. Tommy's letter was very nice. He gave me much good advice. I let the boys read it and they agree he really has something on the ball. He is lucky to be near home.

I wish Jerry could get a job like non-coms here. It is one of the best deals in the Army. Lots of spare time, liberty, authority, etc. He would make a good one! Should get a stripe if he does!

We had a woman here named Mrs. Laura Babcock. She was swell. She quit this noon but used to cook for kids in sickbay, usually 9 to 15 kids.

Her husband died last November. She is the kind of woman you like right away. Very kind and cheerful.

Her son has been in the Navy for six years. The kitchen is on the second floor across the hall from my room. She used to come in and visit all the time. Oftentimes she gave me cheese and crackers, pineapple juice, etc. She is swell and is going to visit me tomorrow! We call her Laura.

The doc was just in. I am to get a hot pack on my stomach every hour. The orderlies will be busy tonite.

Don't worry as I am perfectly OK and getting the best attention and food. Wish I were in Tommy's shoes, close to home!

Your loving son, Jack
P.S. I start flying in six weeks. They aren't going to let us solo, I fear! Damnnnn...

JACK - SICKBAY, PART TWO
Emporia, Kansas, March 20, 1943

Jack worked at Douglas Aircraft in Los Angeles before enlisting, and received updates from one of his work friends.

Dear Mom,

I never had a stamp so I didn't mail your letter. Rec'd letters from Mark and Lew O'Hearn yesterday and today I got one from Jackie and one from Ed Frige from work. I guess I will be here until Monday.

The food is swell and today we were visited by one of the cook's daughters. She was 25 today and is very pretty and she will soon start flying in Ferry Command. I'm in the wrong outfit!

The fellows all came to visit me, that is, those from our old barracks, and a few others. Some from the old group were sent to Wichita.

Not much to report. Frige said in his letter that we will get a straight $64.25 raise! Hell. Also said a new kid, now on a machine I ran, rolled it off track and ruined it. He says after Ray Bishop cooled down he finally decided on putting someone with brains on that machine. Remember the meal I used to get at work for 35 cents? It went to 46 cents before I left. Now it is 82 cents with a nickel cup of ice cream.

There is very little to do around here in sickbay. I draw pictures in my spare time when I can sit on my can. But it gets tired after a while, like right now for instance. Jimmie Boswell has been swell doing shopping for me and all.

They had a tough inspection today. Our room was one of a few that was perfect, no thanks to me. They had personal inspection on the parade grounds where they stood at attention and parade rest for 2-1/2 hours. Both positions are erect and tiresome. Parade rest is with your feet 12" apart and hands clasped behind your back. Very tiring. Am I lucky!

Well Mom, all for now. Will add more tomorrow. Am enclosing a picture I drew.

The next day: Nothing to write about. I eat plenty and sleep well, and will leave here tomorrow. Sickbay that is. Some of the boys are in town today so things are rather quiet except for a jerk practicing on his trumpet. Haven't rec'd cookies yet but should any time. Say hello to all. Tell "Blackmail Inc." (Mark) I will write him soon, without the name and address. Wise guy!

Love and kisses galore, your loving son, Jack
P.S. Income tax all taken care of for now.

TOM - UP, UP AND AWAY!
Hemet, California, March 23, 1943

Dear Pat,

Your most welcomed arrived today and many thanks. Now I can get my clothes off the cleaners hands and buy a bus ticket home. I'm pretty sure I'll be home this weekend as we are flying every day and the weather should continue fair. Thursday night, the Shell Oil Co. is putting on a show for us in San Jacinto. Friday night we have open post in Hemet until 9 p.m. because we won the white flag last week for first place in inspections. Then I'll be free Saturday from 12:30 to 9 p.m. Sunday which is pretty swell.

We are flying in the afternoon this week so we don't have to spend half the period waiting for the fog to lift. I now have four hours and forty minutes logged and today was not too bad. I handled the stick on the takeoff today which is a step in the right direction. I've now gotten used to the sensation of flying and can devote all my attention to the controls. My instructor had me put it into a spin today and bring it out myself. This I did except for one thing. The ship is spinning around like the devil and loses about two thousand feet in four or five seconds. Well, I got it out but in the spin I forgot to put on the throttle after we straightened out. I won't forget again.

The wind was blowing like the devil around five hundred feet where we were practicing some turns so I didn't accomplish much in that line today. Tomorrow we start on landings and that is the last thing we learn before soloing—and the hardest. After we landed today I was taxiing down the runway and he said, "I'll make a pilot out of you, or break your neck." If he thinks he can teach me, I can learn. Not a bit of airsickness and having a swell time.

Mother's letter also arrived today and I now feel up to date on everything in the family life. The cookies are at the post office and I'll pick them up tomorrow. Over the weekend I expect to stay home Saturday evening or Sunday afternoon. I'm not sure however just how my time will be worked out. Also got a letter from Bob and Jackie which I'll try to answer soon.

I've been thinking about buying a radio. We don't have any for sale here so could you look around for me? The one we have in the cabin is borrowed and lousy. I also don't always agree with my roommate's artistic tastes.

DeMent isn't in my cabin but the one next door. We were quartered alphabetically so we missed out. The fellows with me are all good Joes however and we get along fine. They are Calvin, Carstensen, Cassidy and Castrup. The first two are both married and divorced and you should hear them hash over how it all happened. Carstensen is going to remarry his former. He had in-law trouble. Calvin is mad as the devil because his ex has moved to Wilmington and he's afraid he'll run into her. Cassidy is married and expecting. He used to work as an extra in the movies. Castrup is from Chicago and only twenty.

Tomorrow I'm going to start practicing approaches and landings. The approach is the hardest part of it and determines usually the landing. Keep your fingers crossed. That is about the picture now. If anything comes up unexpectedly I'll phone but I hate to use this one, the service is so lousy. Thanks again for the five and I'll be paid in about ten days.

Love, Tommy

JACK - THE SHOESHINE PARLOR
Emporia, Kansas, March 23, 1943

Dear Pat,

There is really nothing to write about except amusements and idiosyncrasies. At night we go to town for a walk, Coke, hot chocolate or what have you. We usually go to the College Grill and dance, eat and so forth. We are free from 8 to 9:30 at night but we *damn sure* better be in by

9:30. On Friday we are off after our last class until 11:30, Saturday from around noon 'til 11:30 and Sunday all day 'til 9:30. Not too bad.

We have a few characters here that are amusing one might say, rather they are amusing via their idiosyncrasies. One Dr. Brown is the topmost card. In the last war he was a corporal in a liaison division and just carried messages around the camp. He stayed in the U.S. He bulls a lot (white lies). Anyway he runs around in riding breeches and boots as it is the closest he can get to a uniform. (Isn't that an idiosyncrasy?)

Yesterday he came into the library and we were all studying or something and he yelled, "Attention!" In the service, that means an officer is present so "snap to" soldier. Well we "snapped to" and saw not an officer but the old doc himself. Well, we started to sit down but he got mad as hell! He said he was "under orders" so evidently expected the courtesy due the captain, the colonel or "Der Fuhrer" even. It was funny as heck to see him fume and fuss.

Well, all for the present, but will "idiosyncrasize" more later.

Later.

Have a few minutes before math. There is a new lieutenant here fresh out of school, in fact there's two of them. One obviously likes to be saluted and meets us every morning on the way to class to satisfy his ideals.

They are getting rather strict here on certain things. Things that don't amount to a damn. For instance, in the closet hanging clothes from rear to front in this order: raincoat, overcoat, fatigues, flight jacket, blouse, suntan shirts, OD shirts, all pants on hanger covered by shirt. All buttons buttoned and facing the door. Phooey! But I suppose that is termed as discipline.

After I get out of here, the Army, I will spend one month on the beach and get tan, and then open up a shoeshine parlor. I am really getting good! Every day about three times. No hats on in any building, no smoking in chow hall, elbows off the tables in chow hall. Those boy-scout officers—more later.

Later again.

Just a few lines more before bed. Gus and Best and I went in to town tonight. Enjoyed a cheeseburger at the Snow White Café. Gus is a character, a bit fat and uses very good English. He is very nice mannered, intelligent and always ready with a gag.

He is indeed a swell boy.

Best has five years in the Marines and will be married four years tomorrow. Swell guy. Lights out! More later.

Later still.

Nothing to say. Slept like a bump on a log. Had to go on hall detail this a.m. That's the first detail I've had since I entered This Man's Army. Running out of space so will close now. Be good and don't work too hard.

Your loving brother, Jack

AUNT MARY - A LETTER FROM CONCORD
Concord, New Hampshire, March 23, 1943

Aunt Mary Cahill was my grandfather's sister. We found this letter, her reply to a letter from Jack. At this point the family had been gone from Concord for six years. She still called him "Jackie."

Dear Jackie,

You don't know how I enjoyed your letter, and how pleased I am that you are in such a nice place where it is comfortable. I hope they will keep you there for a long time. I know that you will try to do well in your studies as you are interested in them, and it is not the same as going to high school. It will do you lots of good to have a nice place to live in while studying, rather than old barracks without any beauty. You have a great opportunity to advance in education, and it will be worth a great deal to you in later life. After all, one can't have too much education to get the most out of life.

Your letter was so interesting that I have read it over and over again, and your writing has improved wonderfully. I don't see how you do so well being left-handed. I guess letter writing is a gift that runs in your family.

I still think you have a soft spot for Concord when you are reminded of it so often in places you see. I sure hope someday you will be able to come back again, when all the boys are here to greet you, but just now the place is practically deserted. The young men have gone off all over the world, and it is pretty lonesome for most of the girls, no dances, parties or anything, unless just the girls go.

Kate McDonald and Katie Donovan were very pleased that you wished to be remembered to them, as it is so long since you were here. I always tell them about my letters from my nephews and they think it is just grand for you all to write me so often, and I do too.

The same day I received your letter, I also had one from Patricia and she was so excited telling me about her new position. It must be very lonesome for her and the rest of the family with four boys gone from home. I bet Markie misses you all a lot, Bobbie too.

We have the Army Air Cadets here training in flying, and they are all so young in their green suits, and I always think of you and Tommy when they go by. Some of them go to 10:30 Mass Sundays. They always have loads of books and papers when they go back and forth to the hotel. One of the instructors staying at the house said that Concord had a wonderful airport, and after the war it would be one of the large training centers. They have taken on a great deal more land and the planes are going all day every day in the week.

How long did it take you to get from LA to Texas and how did you like the ride? And how long from there to Kansas? Gerald is the one who always said he was going to see the world before he was married, but it looks to me as though you are the one. At least you don't have to pay the expenses and I hope everything will be over soon, so families can be reunited and get back to normal. How I should like to be with your family again, and have Frank, Gerald, Tommy and you there. We wouldn't need any outsiders to make it interesting, as, by the time each one told his experiences, we would be pretty well entertained.

Elizabeth Lowry sent me a carbon copy of her long letter to your mother telling about Frank's visit to Richmond. I am so glad he went there, but only wish Elizabeth's mother could have been there, as she would have made his visit much more enjoyable, but nevertheless the hospitality was there just the same. Guess Frank is getting used to his Army life now, and I am sure it won't be so hard now that spring is here. It must have been hard for him to come during such terribly cold weather, and I did pity him. It has been the coldest winter on record here, and one day it was down to 37 below.

Last week we had the St. Patrick's concert for two nights, and it was very good, mostly patriotic and not all Irish as it used to be. There wasn't much humor to it, but it showed good training. Remember the time when you played something on the stage and the boy near you made a mistake and you gave him a nudge, and the people all laughed? Guess that was the time Markie jumped up out of a great big hat. He was a little kid then.

Be sure to write me again when you have time, as I certainly enjoy your letters and am anxious to know how you are getting along. I am so glad that you are physically able to train to be a flier, and do hope nothing will happen to keep you from finishing the course.

With lots of love, I am, as ever, your loving Aunt Mary

JACK - JOE THE BIGAMIST
Emporia, Kansas, March 24, 1943

Dearest Mom,

Your cookies arrived yesterday in fine condition and were most heartily welcomed. They did not get broken, but the oatmeal ones suffered slight casualties. They tasted very, very good and in spite of all your other duties, your ability as a cook has not decreased in the least. It took only three spurts for us to polish them off.

Everything is the same here except the weather and the ducks. It is misting outside but really not enough to notice. As for the ducks, we have about twenty of them here in the lake and we get a lot of fun from them. We smuggle bread from the chow hall and they fight like hell over it. They seem to carry on courtships among themselves and one Old Joe is a bigamist. He is loyal to all four tho and when any other quack tries to swipe his wives' bread he just beats the tar out of them. It is a very nice lake and some 20 feet deep. Some Sunday a.m. I am going in for a swim. Incidentally, could you send my swimming trunks or those tan ones I inherited from Tommy?

Also is it possible to buy tennis shoes there? We are supposed to have ration slips but can't get them. My "civvie" shoes are a bit tight but not uncomfortably so.

Guess this is all for now. Tell Peg and Mark that I will write soon but at present there's nothing to write about. You may tell Mark that I am acquainted with a more or less blond-redhead. She is quite cute and interesting, but the name, address, etc., is strictly a military secret. Also tell him that there are four nice fems at this table right now and they afford nice conversation. Jealous, is he?

Your loving, but wolfing, son, Jack
P.S. No mail. Best got some cookies from his wife. Oh boy!

JERRY - THE BOB HOPE SHOW
San Diego, California, March 24, 1943

Dear Mom,

Your letter arrived the other day right after I mailed one to you, but as yet the newspapers have not shown up.

Things are still pretty much the same down here although something is brewing that will probably blow up all at once. There has been quite a run on the dispensary the last couple of weeks by all the general servicemen. It seems that as soon as they are put on the list of men available for shipping, they suddenly develop what is commonly known as "overseas pains." It makes me sick to see the way that some of them buck for 1B, but it is probably just as well that they get it because they wouldn't be any good if they did get into action. Some guys just haven't got any guts.

I guess I forgot to tell you that I went to see Bob Hope when he was down here a couple of weeks ago. I didn't get to the broadcast but I did see the show he put on afterwards. It was much better anyway, as he was able to open up a little bit. Because we waited so long outside while the broadcast was going on, he said that he would give a little longer program, and he certainly kept his word. It lasted about an hour and a half and was really good. He certainly is clever and he does more of these extra jobs than anyone.

I haven't heard from Frank for two or three weeks so I imagine he is pretty busy. He never was one for writing anyway. Jack hasn't written either but there will probably be some mail this afternoon when I get through work. (If you call this work.) I also wrote Tommy this afternoon. I guess this will be all for now. Write and give me all the dope on anything, and I will try to write again soon.

Your loving son, Gerald

TOM - PRAYING LIKE NEVER BEFORE
Hemet, California, March 27, 1943

Dear Mom,

Our quarantine has been extended until the 1st so flunking the exam didn't make any difference there. However, next week we are getting off Friday night at about 5 until 9:30 p.m. Sunday. This will be swell if the quarantine is actually lifted. We have not had any new cases so it should be.

Thursday I had a terrible flying day and didn't think I could ever make a pilot. Friday, I discovered what I think was wrong and had a good day. My instructor said I should solo before I get home.

Today all I've done is sunbathe and write letters. The same program tomorrow. It seems that I've had letters from everybody and must answer. Had one today from Monette who is one of my best correspondents.

We had Mass Friday night in one of the schoolrooms and I went. The altar was a table with an airplane engine on one side and all kinds of gadgets on the other side. It was pretty much a Thanksgiving for me because I prayed as I never had before when I was getting ready to go up. If I had a day Friday like I had Thursday I'm afraid my flying hours would have been numbered. I know Who to thank and I'm not forgetting. I always have prayed but perhaps it was getting habitual. I'm not inclined to ask for much but when I do I need it badly.

The cookies and dates were swell and went just about as quickly. Cassidy's wife, about every week, sends him a box of Ritz crackers and a half-pound of cheese which he seems to be quite mute about. That's about it all for now. Have lots more letters to write and will let you know how things stand before I come home.

Love to all, Tommy
P.S. When I come home, I hope you can go out to dinner.

Monette was married to my grandmother's cousin Tom Herbert. She is mentioned in several letters and was close to the family.

TOM - THREE GOOD LANDINGS
Hemet, California, March 31, 1943

Dear Mom,

I've been far too busy to write anybody the last few days. The flying is very tough and I don't mind telling you I've been getting by only by the skin of my teeth. I've had to be flying mentally every minute on the ground and as a result cannot devote enough time to my ground school. My swell living conditions go practically unnoticed 'cause I just don't have the time to enjoy them.

Due to quarantine we were confined last weekend anyway. If I should fail any exams this weekend I'm going to go see the commandant and try to get off anyway because I need the change.

As I said the flying is tough. My coordination is not so hot and it makes other things difficult. My instructor said today that if I give him three good landings in a row tomorrow that I would get a cross check and if passed, then solo.

It has taken me longer than lots of other fellows here but once I get past the solo stage I hope to offer more competition.

If the quarantine is lifted and all other things conspire to let me out this weekend, I should arrive in LA Friday around 8 p.m. If early enough I may stop on the way home at St. Vincent's for the stations. Our bus back here leaves Wilshire and Figueroa at 5 p.m. Sunday so you see I shall have plenty of time for a change.

Don't go to any trouble and I'd like to take you out to dinner sometime during my stay. If you could get some doughnuts Friday at Welch's I'd love to have them for Saturday breakfast. I haven't had any for a heck of a while.

So, there is one more exam to go and that business of soloing to get by before I can get home in a decent frame of mind. I hope Jack prepares himself for a really rugged course. This and next week will decide how I come out. Say a prayer because I need them right now.

Love to all, Tommy

P.S. Will phone or wire if I can't get in. Will also send money for this month.

TOM - BRINGING HER BACK IN ONE PIECE
Hemet, California, April 1, 1943

Dear Mom,

Finally soloed today. It took thirteen hours and every one of them was tough. I landed her and took off twice, bringing her back in one piece. Our quarantine has been extended. I don't know for how long. Will write over the weekend with details.

We had a big check this month, so the enclosed. Take any amount for yourself and spend it as foolishly as you want. I expect Pat to see that you do this.

Love to all, Tommy

TOM - KNIGHT OF THE SKIES
Hemet, California, April 4, 1943

Dear Mom,

This week we even had bus tickets to go home on when they extended the quarantine. Our last case was Tuesday so if we don't have any this week I'll get home Friday night.

This morning nine of us went to San Jacinto to be color guard in a flag dedication at the church there. All the unquarantined cadets were in town so a bunch of our gang got to go. They had a breakfast in the school hall with us as guests but we all slipped a buck in the kitty. The priest was a guy as Irish as the Blarney Stone. He would whistle at the parish girls who were waiting on us, in much the manner of Hollywood and Vine, whenever he wanted anything.

We had an Army reconnaissance car which I don't mind telling you we put to good use. Our navigation instructor takes up the collection, and a couple of cute girls from the canteen go to that church and sing in the choir. If DeMent and I ever get a chance to go into town there, we will have something to start on.

I'm sorry I couldn't talk to you when I put in that call but I only had fifteen minutes excuse from the flight line. I don't know whether I'll get home this weekend or not and I won't know until Friday, so if you want to be on the safe side, don't look for me until I come in the door.

That solo was quite a ride. We did about fifteen landings Friday morning—my last day in which to solo. I couldn't seem to get the tail down. I'd land on two wheels then set it down while I should make my landings all three-point. Finally, my instructor told me to park it on the line. Usually when you solo you don't park to let your instructor out. He usually just gets out as you taxi up the strip. My heart sank because I knew that I hadn't made the grade. I was just in a position to park when he told me to go down to the end of the line. I got there and started to turn in when he stopped me.

He turned around and said, "Think you can do it?" "Hell, yes," I told him and wasn't a bit nervous. This is rather puzzling to me 'cause I know I'm not a hot pilot but I seem to have a screwy idea that I can always get down all in one piece. "Well," he said, "I'm getting out right here. You can kill yourself if you want, but I'd rather watch." Instructors are not supposed to solo a cadet until sure they are safe. Mine was not completely satisfied but I had to solo Friday or it would have been an Army check-ride for me.

So I zigzagged down to the end of the runway and turned around all set to go. The visibility was much better with the front cockpit empty so I shoved up the throttle and started down the mat. You have to be going at least 75 before the thing will get off the ground and so, when at that point, I eased back on the old stick, and there I was flying. At two hundred feet I made a sharp turn to the right to go around the field and land. At 500' I leveled off and my first impulse was to holler—which I did. Boy, I was really having fun.

Then I was almost ready to land. Our instructor only lets us go around once on our first trip so this landing had to be good. It wasn't. The tail still didn't go down properly and while I could have got it down and ended with a rather sloppy landing, I decided I'd go around again and see if I could improve. So I gave it the gun and bounced along a bit and off we went again. The next landing was better but not good and there I decided I'd better do my experimenting with Mr. Kearns in the front seat.

It seems that everybody in the squadron congratulated me because they know I've had a tough time catching on. It made me feel good that so many fellows were behind me and it gives me more confidence for the future.

I know you think I can do most anything, Mom, but frankly, flying is very difficult for me, and while I can do pretty well in stalls and spins, other things are much harder to catch on to.

Halferty gave me the best compliment of all. There have been days here when I've spent most of my time trying to figure out what I'd say to you and Jack and the rest of them if I didn't make it. I have no alibis whatever. Anyway, each day I managed to come back and give Kearns a little better ride. The improvement was hardly noticeable but there was some, and Mr. Kearns nursed my flying along when he should have put me up for elimination. Anyway, Halferty said I had more guts than anybody in the outfit to keep at it as I did, and he meant it too as he is very sincere.

I wasn't going to tell you this but Mark and Jack are both going to run into some tough sledding. Someday they may want to call it quits too, but if knowing that I finally did something which I had at times despaired of, they may try just once more and even again.

I'm not through here yet by any means and anything may happen but I've done one thing anyway. The rest of the course will be as tough or more so but I never intend to wash myself out. It is going to take somebody else to do that. We had two guys quit already and a couple more eliminated but I rather expected one of the two to quit. I'm really going to have an experience here.

I have not flunked any more exams and now that I've passed that solo I can devote more time to studying. I've "flown" here in our cabin by sliding a chair on the floor like rudder pedals, holding the top as a pivot and using one of those floor stand ash trays as a stick to improve coordination. That helped. But I think most of the credit goes to a prayer Fr. Clasby gave us at Santa Ana. Jack might like it, and you for the both of us.

"Dear Lady Mary, Queen of the Heavens, once again I dedicate myself to you. Protect your Knight of the Skies. Give strength to my wings and fidelity to my arms; help me ever to chart my course toward your Divine Son. I am sorry for ever having offended Him, because He is all Good and deserving of all my love. With your help I purpose nevermore to offend Him. Amen."

That's about all for now. Don't look for me this weekend until you see me.

Love to all, Tommy

JACK - CATCHING UP ON MAIL
Emporia, Kansas, April 5, 1943

Dear Mom,

I am on CQ tonite so I have access to a typewriter with which I intend to whack off a few letters. I hope that you will put up with whatever mistakes that I might make.

I am certainly glad to see that you went to Dr. Otto. It is senseless to worry about us, as you know by now that we are pretty well taken care of. I regret that situations prevent your coming here. The rest would do you a lot of good. All that is left is to take things as easy as possible and look for the very brightest side of things.

I agree wholeheartedly with your policy of Mark's five dollars, but if it's OK with you I would prefer that he have it for fun because he certainly deserves it. Understand, this is no way even a slight reprimand, but merely my assumption as to how I would feel were I in his place. However, the phrase "Mother knows best" is firmly impressed in my mind, and shall always be, as it has in the past, my unerring guide.

Tommy sure is getting his share of quarantines. I just sent you a money order. I firmly and emphatically suggest that you make good use of that ten when Tommy takes you out. That was my prime intention when I sent it. It will give me far more than ten dollars' worth of satisfaction to know that you are at last having fun.

As for me, I am enjoying myself thoroughly. Friday nite I went to the nurses home at Newman Hospital. They have a little dance session out there every Friday nite. There were about sixteen nurses to ten of us. We danced for about two hours and it was indeed a pleasure. I can modestly say that the pleasure was not all mine as they are confined considerably, and you know Mom the manpower situation has been critical here for some time. They all but dragged us in the door and we were a bit skeptical about going in. The idea didn't sound so hot to us at first, but it was a case of a name being deceiving I guess.

There was another instance like that on Saturday nite. The USO tossed three parties around town, at the junior high school, the YMCA and Sacred Heart School. We went to the one at Sacred Heart School. When we arrived, there were about 160 girls there, the most fellows we could muster up were only 25. It was much better than the one Friday nite and I spent a considerable part of the evening with a very nice young blond. She lives just across the street so I must get in contact. I guess I'm not much of a wolf as I have forgotten her last name.

That doesn't bother me too much tho as she will be at the dance on the 17th. There is a band coming up from Fort Riley, and they are plenty good. I think that they have three of Benny Goodman's men in there and the other eleven have been around. I am in pretty solid with the bigwigs of the USO local. I met one Mrs. Huffman and I am invited out to breakfast after Mass Sunday. She is a real nice lady. I am also well acquainted with a Mrs. Ramsdale and she is a very good talker. We had a nice gab session Sunday.

We finished up our course in medical aid on Friday and it was very simple. Also on Friday we had a brass hat here and we put on a parade for him. Needless to say, our "C" squadron was by far the best and he was very impressed with our band. We are the only detachment he has seen so far that had a band. He was strongly impressed by our action and our initiative. When a guy in his position makes a comment like that he really must figure we have something. The credit is due mostly to Capt. Shevlin who is the finest officer that I have ever met. He was in here tonite for a while and didn't crab a bit when two guys came in thirteen hours late on passes, tho they will be taken care of in the usual manner, i.e., fair and square.

We started a new set of classes today. It consists of two hours of physics, followed by a study period and then gym. We have a formation for mail call and then we go to chow. Then comes a lecture, which has lately been on aircraft recognition, so it is more or less up my alley.

As an attraction today, we had a series of pictures projected on the screen that were drawn by Milton Caniff, the author of *Terry and the Pirates*. The lieutenant erred a bit when he said that the author studied extensively in Asia. I recently read in *Coronet* magazine that he has never been near Asia. All that he knows about it he learned from books, magazines, pictures and talks with an old Chinese laundryman. Anyway, to get back to the point, after the lecture we have math, and then an hour lecture in physics. Of course we have our usual retreat and drill followed by another mail call.

We start flying in about a month, but I personally would rather have a month or so more of academics under my belt and start from scratch flying at primary. However, you know me better than to turn down such a chance.

Jimmie and I are well supplied with food at present. I made a visit to a local bakery and we have rolls, apples, popcorn, cigars, cigarettes and all. One would think that we were preparing for a siege.

We are on duty for fourteen hours tho so we will sure need it. We are excused from all classes and formation, but I think that I will go to physics as it is our most important study. I want to take advantage of a good teacher while I have one. He seems to know his oats. After that I can sleep as long as I want to.

Another roommate is on duty at Morse Hall. This kid likes to build planes too so we have each started a model, and it will take up our spare time and also keep us from spending money. We hope to convince Lt. Barnard on the idea of encouraging model building for recognition purposes. The model selection in town is rather lousy, and if we can get a decent demand then the Army will see that we get what we want, I'm sure.

Jimmie said that he wishes that I would receive some more of those cookies. I naturally more than second the motion but you must certainly wait 'til you are feeling real well and there is plenty of sugar around. He got a box of candy from his brother-in-law the other day. It was fudge that he made himself and he certainly is a good cook. Cooking is his hobby. We are about to compose a letter-petition to him demanding more of the same.

I sure would like a nice beer right now but all they have here is 3.2. When I get home would you mind very much if I almost drowned in a big Whiskey Sour?

That is one thing that I would like to taste. I know you don't like that talk, but a guy has to fall off once in a while and I have been pretty good since I left home.

Well, Mom, I have surely exhausted my source of information by now. I just remembered that there are a few pianos here and I might try and see if I have forgotten what little I knew before I came in This Man's Army.

Write when you get a chance and I know you will fill it with all the dope from there. Your letters are the most coveted of all. Tell Mark to drop me a line, and let your conscience be your guide about my suggestions for his fin.

Your loving son, Jack

TOM - FAILURE TO LAUNCH
Hemet, California, April 14, 1943

Dear Mom,

Today as I told you on the phone I was eliminated from further pilot training. Lt. Castro, who rode with me, was very fair and I must say that I was given every possible advantage. I gave it all I had but I just couldn't come through with the goods. The lieutenant said I could fly with four or five more hours of dual but due to the schedule which must be followed, such a course was impossible. In civilian life I should do well enough but the Army needs pilots with as little waste of time as possible. My instructor told me I was better off, as he would much rather have me be a good pilot than a dead one, and he knows what he is talking about.

After the initial disappointment which lasted for an hour or so, I took stock of things and realized that it was all for the best. My prayers certainly will not have been wasted and I still have as much faith in my ultimate outcome. Now I have the problem of deciding what to do. I think, though I'm not certain, that I have qualified for bombardier-navigator. The two jobs are now combined and I don't know how long it will take to get through. If I could be a gunner, it would take only five or six weeks, but if I'm qualified for the former, which has a longer training period, I think I should take it as personal gains should not be considered in this war. However, if they need gunners worse, I think I'll do that.

I joined because of a war and here it is almost 11 months since I enlisted and as yet I have contributed nothing but an added expense. I'll go before the Board Monday probably and then it will be decided. They are very fair and I'm sure I will get a fair deal. I have the privilege of removing any officer from the Board from the major on down, if I think he may be prejudiced in any way against me.

I told you DeMent also is up for elimination. I hope he beats them but our attitudes to begin with were about the same. We both preferred piloting but would take bombardier or navigator. Chastain, another good friend of ours was also eliminated and this list is getting longer.

I'm not ashamed but sorry that so many people thought I could do it. It may perhaps teach you all something...that I have not underestimated myself or been modest whenever anyone said I'd be a hot pilot. I knew what I was capable of but not what I was up against. Now I know both and you have the outcome. Will be in this weekend I think.

Love to all, Tommy

P.S. You may send this to the boys as I don't know just when I'll get to write them, and the less times I have to repeat this story the better. Meantime, don't worry, as mentally and physically I feel better than I have in months! May be sent to Santa Ana for a couple more months.

JACK - BLOOMERS UP THE FLAGPOLE
Emporia, Kansas, April 14, 1943

Dear Mom,

I have about 15 minutes to start this letter. We *have* to go to a show tonite. They are having a bond drive show and we are *invited* to it.

I do want to tell you how very much I enjoyed your cookies. I suppose "we" is a bit more appropriate. Some of the boys helped me out a little, but honest, Mom, I could have done OK alone. They all raved about them and said they were the best yet. Take it from them, Mom, because they have eaten all kinds since being in the Army. You might call us Experts on Cookie Judging.

I got a tooth filled today—on the Army. The dentist is a "Local Joe" and did a swell job. I hope to get the others fixed soon. It will take a little time I guess. Well, I'll try and finish this tonite after the show.

Cont. April 15. As you can see I had no time to add to this last nite. The show was pretty good and we never got home until after 11:00.

Things are popping around here and it happens to be our squadron commander who caused it, I think. A few days back he stole "B" squadron's flag. Well, "B" thought "A" did it so they ran a pair of bloomers up on the flagpole with "A" on them. Well last nite, the pay-off. "A" squadron lives in the Smith House. It is on Commercial St. which is the main drag. I imagine "B" was guilty of tearing up the house.

Sheets were hanging out of the windows, beds torn up and everything all over the place. The lights were on and so it was visible from the street. This is bad. You can see the impression it gives the public and you know how news spreads and increases in ferocity as it goes along, in a town of this size. We have heard nothing from it but I expect all hell to cut loose soon. By rights, our squadron commander should be washed out, but he has to be discovered first. Capt. Shevlin was so mad he almost cried, they say.

Everything else is as usual. Physics exam today. I did OK, I guess—will know later. I have been awfully busy lately, and it is hard to find anything to write about—much less the time to write it. This explains the shortage of letters.

I enjoyed the talk Sunday and I hope you are feeling better. If you still feel bad, see Dr. Otto again. I guess I will close. This is a lousy letter. It is hard to write about nothing. Tell them at home I will try and write as soon as possible. I have to go to class now. I just had a shot in the arm.

Your loving son, Jack

JERRY - DON'T KNOW IF I'M COMING OR GOING
San Diego, California, April 17, 1943

Dear Mom,

Am on CQ this afternoon so I will probably get a little caught up on my correspondence.

Received your letter yesterday with Tommy and Frank's enclosures. I was sorry to hear about Pat's accident and also about Tommy's disappointment. Pat, I hope, is alright by now. Tommy I know is OK. It is no fun to be sweating out something like he was for so long. It is too much of a strain. He shouldn't feel that he let us down though, because we all know that he did the best that he could. Maybe he was cut out to be a bombardier or navigator anyway. What he learned in his pilot training may help him out in his new job and certainly won't do him any harm.

As usual I am sweating out a few things down here. It seems that half of the time I am unable to tell whether I'm coming or going. Oh well, if I didn't have something to worry about I probably wouldn't have any fun.

There is some doubt as to whether or not I will get my furlough the first part of May as I had planned. Things are in pretty much of an uproar down here and we are losing most of our best men. If certain changes go through I will make sergeant, but my furlough will be canceled indefinitely. Incidentally, I have been recommended twice in the last week and there is a vacancy now. When I see it I'll believe it.

While I am writing I had better wish you a happy birthday. I wish that I could have sent you something but the bankroll, as usual, is very low. In fact I think I will have to borrow a couple of bucks from one of the boys to carry me over to payday. I don't know where all my money goes to, but I don't worry about it an awful lot as I usually have a pretty good time.

Kay Kyser is supposed to put on his show with his band down here next Wednesday, and if I can get tickets I will probably go. It will be for the second show and not the broadcast.

Well, I have to make out a final statement for one of the boys who is getting discharged next week, so I guess I'll have to close. I'll try and get home next week for Easter and hope Tommy can do the same. It will be nice if he is at Santa Ana for a couple more months. About Easter, I guess you know that it will be nothing new for me *not* to have a new suit. Will try and write again if anything turns up. Tell Pat to take it easy and sue the streetcar company for a million dollars.

Your loving son, Gerald

FRANK - DEAR PETUNIA
Lebanon, Pennsylvania, April 20, 1943

When I saw this letter, I had total recall of hearing Frank call Patricia "Petunia." Hadn't thought of this for decades. He opened this letter referring to her recent accident.

Dear Petunia,

The next time, duck! If you can't, let me know and I shall try to get you a steel helmet, excuse me, that should be HELMET, Steel, M-1.

That last is what is known in the Army as nomenclature. The only things which have names are the soldiers. I guess that they are not important enough to have any nomenclature. Before you are taught to use anything here, you must first learn its correct nomenclature. Nomenclature is made by taking the accepted name for anything and twisting it around so that it sounds like a foreigner's first effort, or like that "Basic English" which enjoyed a brief span of publicity a short time ago (about five years).

For instance, this letter is being knocked out on a TYPEWRITER, Portable, Elite type. I am sitting on a CHAIR, Barracks. Behind me is a SECTION FURNITURE, Four Drawer High, One Drawer Wide, Letter Size, Wood, Olive Green. That's nomenclature for a filing cabinet. It doesn't hold any more letters than an ordinary filing cabinet would though. Nearby is a STOVE, Heating, and this machine is on a TABLE, Camp, Folding.

I am dressed as follows: SHOES, Service, pr., 1; SOCKS, Lt. Wool, pr., 1; UNDERSHIRT, Cotton, ea., 1; DRAWERS, Cotton, pr., 1; TROUSERS, Herringbone Twill, Green, pr., 1; JACKET, Herringbone Twill, Green, ea., 1; CAP, Wool, Knit, M-1, ea., 1.

It's the damnedest thing; the Army describes them backward, but if you want to catch HELL, Plenty, just try to put them on that way.

Today I had to do a little scouting and patrolling in the quartermaster section of the camp, and when I got into the truck, what do you think met my eye? A sign that read "Nomenclature, TRUCK, 4x4."

There isn't much stirring here; otherwise, I should not be forced to pad my letters as outrageously as I did above. I hope that you don't mind though, and you may be sure that if anything happens, I will be sure to write and tell you about it. In the meantime, keep out of the way of flying glass, and if that is impossible get yourself a chainmail snood.

Speaking of coats of chainmail, I guess you probably heard the one about the knight who was a little eccentric, in that he preferred to perform his feats of knight errantry mounted on a Great Dane instead of a horse. One night he rode into an inn, and the innkeeper said: "Get the Hell out of here. I'm not putting anymore of King Arthur's bums up in my hotel." Then he saw how the knight was mounted and immediately relented. "You can stay," he said. "I wouldn't put out a knight on a dog like this."

Love, Frank

TOM - THE FIRST FATALITY
Santa Ana, California, April 25, 1943

Dear Mom,

Today Father Clasby suggested that you drop a line to the colonel in appreciation of his efforts, as Father says the colonel goes out of his way to help the chaplains here and we have better facilities than any post in the country. I know you're busy tho so I'm just passing it along to you.

We prayed for our old squadron mate who "spun in" yesterday. He was baptized just a couple months ago. That's the first fatality of anybody I knew personally but I guess it won't be the last by any means, so I'd better start getting used to it. It hardly seems that these guys know what they are in for but perhaps that is just as well.

Love to all, Tommy

MOM - THE PICTURE
Los Angeles, California, April 26, 1943, Letter to Jack in Emporia

I was thrilled to find several letters from my grandmother, "Nana." I saw her often, so it is easy to hear her "speaking" in her letters.

Dear Jack,

You darling! Nothing could be sweeter nor more pleasing to me than your picture. It is wonderful and I am so happy and so proud I could kick the ceiling if I didn't have stiffened old joints. It's grand, colossal, or whatever one says to express the nicest thing that could ever be given to a mother. That takes care of my birthday, Easter and Mother's Day. Haven't been able to do hardly a lick of work—just sit and admire.

Guess Pat will think I am nuts. As she is still recovering from her accident I have left it in her room but I find plenty of reasons to go in and just look at it. It is so good, it seems you are right there and are going to say something. Always keep that smile—no matter what happens. Your grandmother is delighted too, but she had just roused from a doze when I took it in to her, and she mistook you for Frank.

I had hoped to get some cookies off to you in time for Easter but didn't have the bits. Tommy brought me some chocolate bars from Santa Ana and I had just gotten some bits also, so made some last night. The box you are getting may seem small but there is a double layer of them and when I can I will send more. I guess they will probably taste as good now as for Easter.

Having Pat in bed makes it a little more difficult but she is as usual not much bother so far as extra waiting on her is concerned, but I have to keep her room looking good. It is a vast improvement on what it was. She has a new lamp in there and the bed is placed so that the head is between the closet door and the hall door. The room is much better looking. The dining room curtains are now in Gerald's room.

With part of my allotment I got some new glass curtains for the dining room—just plain but nice looking so that the room looks a bit less poverty-stricken than it did. I want to have things nice when you boys come home again, and if I can get a few things now and then that are going to improve it, I am going to do it. I can't go out much so I don't need much in the way of clothes, since thanks to you I have a good coat and dress.

Gerald got up for Easter. He is now a sergeant and Frank has again beaten him as he is a staff sergeant. Tommy came home too and went out with Monette. They went first to Morgan Thieme's house in Beverly Hills and then to Baldwin Hills to Ponzi's to dinner. The latter then took them all to Slapsie Maxie Rosenbloom's and they had a swell time.

Monette is going to be here another week and we are to go to Dan's to dinner Thursday night. I hope Pat is able to go. Gerald is getting no furlough. There seems to be quite a shifting around of personnel in the offices and his furlough is out. Morton Tuttle is in Miami with a radio unit. Peg is fine. Frank called her up yesterday but had to wait six and a half hours to get the call through.

Bob got his retroactive money from Douglas a week ago so maybe yours is being sent to you direct. I would suggest that you bank what you can, and then if by any chance you get a furlough you would have the money right on hand to be sent you for car fare, etc. I hope you will have a furlough at the end of six months and can come home.

Must close this now but am enclosing the start of another letter so you will know you were in my mind. Many thanks dear for the perfect gift—the card was wonderful.

Love and kisses, Mother
P.S. Sending cookies today.

Letter (unfinished) from Mom to Jack in Emporia, April 22:

Dear Jack,

Had hoped to get a nice long letter written to you for Easter but with my up and downstairs duties I don't have much energy left for letters. However, I know you will excuse any brevity so long as the letter appears.

Tommy called up and is going to bring home some chocolate bars which I can cut up and put into cookies so that is a help. He has qualified or rather classified as bombardier without any examination as they had his physical report, etc., there which he considers a miracle—to have it done so quickly at Santa Ana.

He understands that much of the pilot training is the same as bombardier and that he will only have to take what he didn't get which should take about three weeks and then he will move on to some other place. If he can qualify in the high twenty per cent after that training, then he can take navigation and get his wings and commission.

It sounds pretty good so here's hoping he makes it. He says some of the fellows back at Santa Ana have had as much as 200 hours of flying but for some little reason didn't make it, so he doesn't feel so badly about it after the comparatively few hours he had.

Here it is Saturday and I didn't get the letter off to you for Easter as I had first intended. It doesn't seem that there are hours enough left in a day for me to do all I have to do now.
End of unfinished letter.

TOM - THE RE-LAUNCH
Santa Ana, California, April 29, 1943

Dear Mom,

Just a quickie mainly for the purpose of enclosing the lettuce.

I just learned today that DeMent washed out and couldn't get bombardier training because he had shown signs of tenseness. I'm sure they are mistaken about that as I know him very well, but it is too late to do anything now. They are breaking up a good combination and it will be a long time before I'll meet another guy like him. He may get gunner training and I'll see him again but the Army is pretty hard on friendships. Of the two of us, I never doubted that he would get through. He's just a private now. This gamble that is cadet life turned him down.

I guess I got a break here but when I think of how long I've been signed up, I wish sometimes I'd gone in the Merchant Marine. However, I'll keep at this bombardiering with more of a vengeance than ever. There are more and more scores to settle every day.

Met a fellow today from Hemet who said the day that fellow crashed last week, his mother and fiancé were at the field waiting to join him for the weekend. It was probably just some careless mistake, but I hope Jack will be sufficiently impressed with the fact that you can't make them. Trouble is, when you get flying, you are up there, above, and all the troubles below are not given a thought. You are some place where you're not quite sure you are good enough to be, in awe of everything around you, and sometimes the very necessary but technical requirements of your situation are forgotten. The one place in the world where a fellow is really at peace—and you have to spend every second watching your plane, your instruments and other planes. I'm getting off the beam again so I'd better hit the hay. Had a swell letter from Frank. It took a while to catch up with my moving around.

Love to all, Tommy

TOM - STARVATION CORNER
Santa Ana, California, May 3, 1943

Dear Mom,

Sunday was just a waste of time but in the afternoon our outfit won first place in the parade for bombardier-navigator school. We had our first good meal in a week in the evening with steaks. Krushot, Hawthorne, Waddell and I are all in neighboring bunks and we generally share what we have. Last night we were sitting at the bottom of the table—Starvation Corner as well call it—and the steaks we got were about one-half the size of those the boys at the top had, so we retaliated by keeping the bowl of strawberries to ourselves for ice cream sundaes.

As the final touch to make all concerned feel good, I got our waiter to bring us another bowl. When it arrived at the top of the table, we hollered and reminded them of their steaks. They felt patronizing so only took enough strawberries to barely color their ice cream—and we had what was left in the bowl which was plenty. We were still eating our strawberries when they finished and stacked their bowls away with the garbage.

Lo and behold! Here comes our waiter with another bowl of strawberries and who are the only ones left at the table with bowls and spoons? Right! Krushot, Hawthorne, Waddell and I! We really pulled a fast one on them as they never did find out there was a first bowl.

Today we spent the morning at the range on the beach firing .30 cal air-cooled machine guns and Tommy guns, 22s and .45 automatics. I did best on the last named with a 6.4 for 9 shots. In the afternoon we went swimming, and all in all, it was the best day I've ever put in here.

At 8:30 tonight we are going to draw cadet blouses so I shall be quite improved in appearance when I come home this weekend, as I think I will. I'd like to take you to dinner. I may have a date later in the evening— dinner with you counts first.

Love to all, Tommy

MOM - MISSING EACH OTHER
Los Angeles, California, May 4, 1943, Letter to Jack in Emporia

Dear Jack,

This will probably have to serve as a Mother's Day greeting unless I can get out to get a card. Had hoped to get some cookies done and may yet but with the pressure of things to be done, don't dare bank on it.

While I think of it too, if you are going to Mrs. Babcock's to dinner on Sunday, be sure to take her some flowers or a corsage. She is being like a mother to you, and I presume it would please her, for it would be something that her own son would do were he here, or rather there, to do it.

It makes me feel pretty good to know that people are so nice to you but you are a sweet kid anyway (now don't say "Now, Mother" like the others do).

I really think you are, even if boys don't like to be called sweet. Anything that is thoughtful and kind comes under the heading of "sweet things" and you do lots of them.

Haven't heard from any of the boys this week but expect to before the day is out.

Sent Gerald cookies for his birthday but they wouldn't get there before Monday or Tuesday as I couldn't get them made. I hope you got your small box of them in good condition and that they brought a touch of home.

Jackie's mother is leaving Vancouver next Tuesday and will arrive sometime Wednesday. She has everything slicked up for her arrival. Incidentally, Little Pat does his walking all by himself now. He doesn't wait for an objective to go to—starts out on his own and is here, there and everywhere.

He certainly keeps Jackie on the run now. Says she walks about ten miles a day keeping up with him. He is so cute. He says "Nana" every time she goes to the phone.

Peg is fine. Jackie and I are going to have a shower for her soon. Some of her friends had said they were going to give her one but they have never gotten around to it so I guess it will be a pleasant surprise for her. I want to get a few things done upstairs first though before we have it. The place can stand some improvement and we need quite a few things.

I am going to start in and get the things we have needed so long and can hardly do without any longer—cups, saucers, glasses, sheets, etc. Am also going to try to make a few improvements in the house so that it will not look so shabby as it has in the past. We certainly had to let things more or less run down, but I should be able to make some changes without too much expenditure. I can get a few more ration stamps each week too and in that way increase my number of bonds.

Mark is going down to the Douglas Vernon plant today. Mr. Norris will send him to Santa Monica and thinks he can get him on the split shift working from four 'til eight in the evening in shipping or something like that, as four hours is not enough time to start him in training for other work. With Mark going in the Navy too, it would hardly be worthwhile. He had wanted to join the CBs in the Navy but you have to be twenty-one.

Frankie Collins and Kay were over Saturday night. Little Johnny is cute as ever.

By the way, Monette would like one of your pictures if you have one to spare. She says she wants a picture of each of you four so she can show them to her friends. We had a great time with her. She is peppy as ever—wish I could have a little of it.

As I am enclosing the last letters of the boys, they will tell you as much as I can about their doings so I will get this finished. Pat is back at work and feels like she has had a grand rest. She really felt back to normal yesterday.

I wish I could be with you all for Mother's Day but I can't of course. I will be with you in spirit though and you may be sure that I shall be thanking God for such a boy as you. Just keep on as you have been. Whatever you do, I am with you in it and don't do any worrying about anything. Just do your best and that is all anyone can do.

Keep me posted on what is going on and you know I'll be wishing you Happy Landings, perfect coordination and all that it will take to make you a pilot for I know that is what you want most to be.

I'm not going to put in anything that will make you homesick for none of us can have things as we would like them in war time. Missing each other has got to be part of the game for the duration, but we can all look with hope to a peaceful happy future when the world is rid of the rats.

My love, a big hug, and a kiss 'til I can deliver them in person.

Your own, Mamacita
P.S. Grandma is doing OK.

MOM - TOM'S ADVICE FOR JACK

Los Angeles, California, May 7, 1943, Letter to Jack in Emporia

The Tommy reference below is to his April 29 letter to his mother (The Re-Launch).

Dear Jack,

This will be a very short letter as I am fighting a cold and don't feel so hot, but will try to write you again in a few days, and also send you a new kind of cookies I have discovered to make.

Am enclosing a letter from Tommy, which will speak for itself. You will see what he has been up against and it may be of help to you in the future. You have no picnic ahead of you, and you can see that Tommy has what it takes else he wouldn't have gotten as far as he has. My heart goes out to him for being so gallant and brave and persevering under what to someone else would be most disheartening.

He wants you to profit by his experience, so do. Any advice he hands you comes from the heart as well as firsthand knowledge.

Everything is going on the same round here. Your grandmother is very well but as usual she has to complain that her leg stings so that she will get some sympathy. I don't know what she would do if she couldn't find something to fuss about. She is easy enough to take care of but I get so tired of hearing that old "my leg stings so."

If Tommy comes home this weekend, Gerald is coming up too because he hasn't seen him for so long.

This is all for now. I will write again in a few days, but think I am going to lie down for a while. I think I can nip this cold in the bud if I take it easy. Loads of love to you darling. Cut out the smoking if possible. Will write very soon when I feel a little more like it.

Yours, Mother

Gram was a diabetic, bedridden at this point. I believe she'd had a leg amputated and I think the "leg stings" were phantom pains, thus Nana's frustration.

MOM - A MOTHER'S DAY LETTER FROM MOM
Los Angeles, California, May 13, 1943, Letter to Jack in Emporia

Dear Jack,

Don't know how long this letter will be as the mailman is across the street and I want to get it in the mail as soon as possible. Yours received and contents noted and enjoyed immensely. Am glad you like flying and did so well on your first trip. Keep up the good work. You might possibly turn out to be a "natural."

I know it must seem something out of this world to be way up in the clouds. I know if I hadn't been on such an errand as I was when Maurice died, I could have enjoyed my plane ride but feeling as I did, it was a means to an end, getting there as quickly as possible.

Tommy was home for Mother's Day. Took me out to dinner and then we met Mrs. Miner and David at the Knickerbocker. We had a nice time. Tommy had his cadet blouse and was pretty proud of it. Aren't they something with their satin linings, etc. He looked wonderful as usual.

Said this week he is going to have a course in logarithms and trig or something complete in three hours. Also he was to have four hours in the pressure chamber at 38,000 feet—without getting the bends if possible. As I haven't heard from him this week don't know what he has been doing.

Am enclosing a copy of his last letter anyway and if I have time will put in one of Frank's and one of Gerald's.

I had a nice card from Gerald too. Enjoyed yours also. Both arrived in good season as well as your wire. Frank wrote me that he had intended to call me up but thought I might prefer the price of the call instead so sent me five dollars. I would have enjoyed talking with him, but I wouldn't want him to have to wait six and a half hours as he did the last time he called Peg to get the call through.

Pat paid for half of my new hat—a very simple black one. I had not had a new one for a couple years for spring so that I did need one. She also brought me a box of candy so I fared very well on Mother's Day.

Found the enclosed snapshot and wondered if you would like it. It is nearly three years old and is the only one I know of around as Peg's mother lost some of the films. As you are the youngest one gone, and farthest away of those with me, thought I should send it to you as the other two are able to get home.

Tommy doesn't know how long he'll be at Santa Ana, probably only this week, perhaps longer. They are rushing things along.

Mark likes his job at Douglas a lot and I like it because he is home early every night. Your grandmother is fine. Is hemming diapers for Peggy now, has nearly two dozen of them. The telephone bill is paid up to date. Between it and my insurance and Tommy's and Pat's, it took practically my whole check of $37.00. The telephone bill was $21.64—two months—some bill. Guess I told you your call from Emporia was $2.30. Tommy had tolls amounting to $6.60 on the last bill, and as he had his pay split when he moved, I couldn't get it this time as he was short, but it will come in handy when he does get it.

Well, this is all for this time. Will send you some cookies when I can, but think the next ones should go to Frank as I haven't sent him any yet.

We all enjoy your letters and they are going to be a lovely and interesting addition to "Dear Mom."

Loads of love—will write again whenever I can but have to write the other three also. Yours with hug and a kiss (thanks for the one on the card). By the way, the card was particularly beautiful.

Love, Mamacita

"The ones with me" that my grandmother mentioned refers to the three sons then away in the service, but who were living with her prior to that: Gerald, Tom and Jack. Frank and Bob both moved out earlier, when they married.

Mrs. Miner was a music teacher who gave Tom singing lessons. David is her son, a friend of all the Cahill brothers.

"Dear Mom" was my grandmother's reference to her collection of her sons' letters. She named this book before she knew it would be written, before she knew I would write it, and before she knew there would be a "me," her fourth grandchild.

MICHELLE - BILLY AND MAURICE

There are two Cahill sons I have not yet mentioned. In addition to Tom and Jack, other uncles my generation never met were Billy and Maurice.

Billy was #6 in birth order. My cousins and I don't know much about him; we only saw one portrait of him in our childhood, but were happy to find several more pictures stored with Tom and Jack's letters. They are darling snapshots of Billy playing or posing with his sister and brothers, showing his cute personality. In 1922, Billy died from whooping cough when he was two years old.

The previous letter from my grandmother to Jack, dated May 13, 1943, referenced Maurice (pronounced Morris), firstborn of the nine children. Maurice didn't move from New Hampshire to California with the rest of the family in 1937. He was 25 years old, with a life already established, and stayed in the family's hometown of Concord.

My mother told me the little bit I know about Maurice. She was sixteen years old in high school in 1938, dating my dad, when he suddenly stopped calling. She thought she had been "dumped" but later learned that he had gone to Concord suddenly because Maurice died. They resumed dating when he returned.

She said my father told her that Maurice, a bandleader, was going home late one night and had forgotten the key to the apartment where he was staying with a friend. He was climbing up to enter through a window in the building. Two police officers saw him, mistook him for a prowler and called to him to come down.

It is believed that Maurice didn't hear the policemen. He didn't respond or comply, so they fired and he died from a bullet that ricocheted off the brick building.

A newspaper account wrote that Maurice, also known as "Pat," was a "prominent youth." To compound this tragedy, the policemen were friends of Maurice's, and he had played poker with one of them the night before the shooting. Because of the darkness, the policemen did not recognize him.

The account also stated that my grandmother "urged that no action be taken against the two officers." I imagine if they were Maurice's friends, my grandmother may have known them since they were little boys.

This was tragic, of course, for our family, but also for his police officer friends who had to live with this for the rest of their lives.

As was the case with Billy, my generation had seen only one portrait of Maurice, as an adult. We found many more of him, mixed in with Tom and Jack's letters, including photos of him as a child with his sister and brothers.

TOM - FLAT WITH A CAPITAL F
Las Vegas, Nevada, May 20, 1943

Dear Mom,

Well, how do you like my new address? We arrived this morning, by Pullman no less, in which I had a lower all to myself. We live in barracks here, much better than at Santa Ana. There are two or three separate rooms and one long dormitory upstairs. Bill Hawthorne and I, by some very sharp maneuvering, managed to get the biggest room.

From the speech we just had, I expect to be here about seven weeks, five of ground gunnery and two in the air in AT-6s and Venturas! We won't have regular calisthenics but will have a couple hours of games.

Got to scram now; this is just to let you know where I am while I have a chance. The schedule will be pretty fast for the rest of the week, also the pressure chamber again. It is very hot here and as the ground is limestone reflecting the sun quite strongly we have all been issued swell sunglasses.

Love to all, Tommy
P.S. Could you send me some money 'til payday? I'm flat with a Capital F.

TOM - SWEETHEARTS ON THE RUNWAY
Las Vegas, Nevada, May 28, 1943

Dear Mom,

Yours arrived today and thanks. I hated to ask for the dough but everybody here is broke and I couldn't borrow from anybody. There is nothing to spend it on here but Cokes and milk shakes. I finish one, and before I leave the PX I'm as thirsty as when I went in. The solution seems to be just forgetting about it, and that I'm doing gradually and with some success.

We are the only cadets on the post—just one squadron. The management doesn't quite know what to do with us. We now eat in officers' mess—formerly used by the commissioned bombardiers and navigators. The CO keeps apologizing about the food which was good to begin with and keeps getting better. We have the table all set and waiting for us as we file in. GIs (in white jackets!) hover over the tables and refill everything as fast as it gets partly empty.

For instance, we had iced tea the other day. I was the first one to pour any out of the pitchers which are huge, and I spilled a couple drops on my plate. Just so I wouldn't have everything flavored with iced tea, I took a napkin and started to wipe it off. I hadn't taken two swabs at it when our boy dashed over, "You got a dirty plate? Let me get you a clean one." I told him that I had just spilled some tea on it, but he wouldn't believe it or he considered the plate unsuitable for use. He just took it out of my hands and off he went to get a clean one.

They don't quite know what to make of us. They know we are not officers and yet we are not GIs so they middle of the road it and treat us swell. On Saturday we make up for it as best we can with tips which might help them celebrate their passes better—the passes we can't have.

Yesterday morning everybody was up at 5:30. We should have been up anyway, but so far we have just ignored reveille. The reason we were up, one early bird hollered "WAACS!" We had been expecting their arrival and, at this daybreak, there they were. Only a dozen of them or so but they were practically the only women on the post. The biggest thing was they were eating in our mess hall! We have a whole mess hall to ourselves—and the WAACS. Of course they don't make any difference to me, but it does make the place seem more like ordinary camps.

Even without women, passes, and cool shade, this place is pretty swell due to the presence of some sweethearts—streamlined jobs running from four hundred to four thousand horsepower. All day long there is that whine and roar above that has become music to us whether we listen to it from the ground or sit right in the middle of it. Next week we'll add a rhythm section to that music when we actually start on gunnery.

Bill and I go over to the field every day hoping to hitch a ride to any place in anything with wings. We have basic trainers—which Bill has flown quite a bit and which he hopes to fly here—advance trainers, which we will fly in during some of our gunnery training, Venturas made by Lockheed which are actually combat ships and also Flying Fortresses! Bill and I went through a Ventura and a Fortress yesterday and boy are they terrific! With satisfaction we noted that the bombardier has practically a suite compared to the cramped quarters which the pilots and navigators live in.

I still can't get over the size of these Fortresses! From the navigator hatch, looking back, it looks a mile long. I think you could land a Ryan on the fin. We also investigated all the turrets. We get practice in those ball turrets which are under the belly but as the Fortress is the only one which has them, I doubt if we will get to try them in flight practice.

Due to the fact that our trips in the pressure chamber at Santa Ana were not recorded in our service records, we had to go up again. Today was the time for my section and about an hour in at 38,000 feet I got the "bends" and had to come down. I've been up twice before and never had a bit of trouble so I guess I just had a bad day. Bends are relieved by returning to an altitude just below that at which the symptoms first appeared, and then you would never know you had experienced them. I feel fine now.

Despite the heat, this place has a certain savage beauty to it. The mountains are just solid rock and limestone. Mt. Charleston is snow-capped. There seems to be hardly a living thing, birds or insects. There are patches of green grass by the nurses' quarters and the swimming pools—yes, I said pools—we use the officers' pool during regular athletic periods and the enlisted men's during free time. The sun's rising and setting is always beautiful and with night, the place cools just right.

Bill and I were evicted from the room we had because each barracks will have two instructors in it—for homework help I guess. The barracks are all painted ivory color which brightens things considerably and makes the chapel look like the one in anybody's small town.

We are away from that horribly childish treatment of Santa Ana. I don't mean the fancy mess here and all that. We can do without those things, but we are allowed to take care of ourselves as much as possible and trusted to behave in a manner of the cadets we are supposed to be—the manner they told us we should be at Santa Ana but never let us be. At least, after a month in that boy scout camp, we are again going to be part of the war effort—even if only a potential one. A machine gun instead of a rake or dish washing machine—more like it should be.

As I said before, a pass looks very distant, but if it is possible to get the time, and I get paid, I may fly in. As cadets we get along pretty well with the pilots here and there is a possibility of getting a ride to Burbank in a bomber or something. The airlines also use this field as a regular stop and a round trip costs about $25, an hour and a half each way and well worth it.

We were to have an hour of drill and one of calisthenics daily. This was cut down to fifteen minutes daily of close order drill. "I hope this is alright with you gentlemen," said the lieutenant. The drill will also be our calisthenics! I imagine we'll have an hour or two of physical training but that is just games and the swimming pool.

The payoff is listening to the radio announcers inviting us to the Las Vegas gambling joints, "Come to Hotel El Rancho Vegas for an evening's entertainment. Come and try your luck with some real sportsmen!" We have sportsmen here too, though on a smaller scale!

This is about all for now. I'm going to take a shower now—at least one a day and two or three if you have time is quite necessary. I think I'll get my hair cut too—but short!

Love to all, Tommy

TOM - CRYSTAL CLEAR
Las Vegas, California, May 30, 1943

Dear Mom,

The first week I actually have been training is now in the books. The veil of incomprehension which enveloped the .50 cal Browning machine gun last Monday has been lifted and it is now crystal clear—though I will admit the crystal is a little dirty in spots. However, this week should clear up everything. I got a 94 in my nomenclature and I think 100 on part functions though I haven't gotten my mark. The rest of the course is at times ridiculously simple as it was designed for GIs with 7th grade education but to keep us "Caydets" on the ball, we are required to get 80%, and officers 85%.

I am still eating like a pig and I'm starting tonight by not eating any supper, and in the future leaving the table slightly hungry in an effort to shed or at least hold down this fat I'm acquiring. At this moment I'm tipping the beam in the 170s and on me it doesn't look good.

Somebody found out that we have a few minutes free time and so now we go to code class every night which gives us nine hours of school per day and an hour of calisthenics. So chances are most of my letter writing will be done on Sundays unless I can write some time during classes.

There were a few passes issued to Las Vegas last night but I didn't try to get one as I was more in need of sleep and must also hoard my finances, but from reports Vegas is quite a spot. The only station we can get on the radio is station KENO, of all names, which also indicates Las Vegas pretty well.

This week we are scheduled to go out on the range and do some real shooting with 22s, shotguns (skeet and trap shooting) and maybe start on .30 cal machine guns. I also found out that when we start flying we will go to some place called Indian Springs, a few miles from here. I'll let you know if you should address my mail there.

Speaking of mail, I had an idea today. While you are typing copies of our letters why not make an extra one and send them to Aunt Mary? I'm sure she would enjoy them and it would keep her as well informed as I think she would like to be. I wrote to her today and realized how little she probably does hear from us. That does it I guess.

Love to all, Tommy
P.S. I'll try to finish up some sketches this week but I haven't had much time.

Summer 1943

TOM - THE AXE JUST FELL
Las Vegas, Nevada, June 6, 1943

Dear Mom,

Sorry I didn't get this written sooner but for one reason or another I couldn't get to it.

Right now I am in very good spirits. We have been out on the range all morning shooting skeet. Skeets are clay discs about 3-1/2" in diameter and are released on command from a sort of catapult mechanism. We have one from the left which starts high. Then we fire from seven different positions on a semicircle, each position calling for different leads on each shot.

The first time I didn't do so well and was rather discouraged as those things always do come hard to me, but today I did better and hit 32 out of 50. I had three sets of "doubles" when the birds were shot out one close after the other from both sides. My shoulder is rather bruised and after I learn to hold the gun properly all the time, I won't be bothered with that. We'll fire 50 more rounds tomorrow, and later we will shoot from the back end of a truck at skeets while moving at about 35 mph.

The skeets don't count much on our final grade, but now that I can do them pretty well, I don't expect much trouble on the machine guns. In school work I am also surprising myself because I thought I'd have quite a bit of trouble with all the mechanical subjects. I'm going to study more though even after we finish the course, as on these multiple choice questions, it is possible to eliminate obviously wrong answers then reason on the remaining couple. I think I had better know the stuff without too much time for reasoning.

I am in school now and this will be finished in snatches. We have just finished the final exam on .50 cal machine guns and there are a few minutes left in the period. I'm not in such good spirits as I was to begin with, as the axe just fell on our group. We have been getting away with murder and I could see it coming but to no avail. The lieutenant caught one of the boys talking while "at ease" and, as a consequence, our section will drill for an hour tomorrow at 4 a.m. We are lucky to get even seven hours sleep as it is, with classes until 9 p.m. every night, and he is hitting us just where it hurts the most.

The trouble with these guys is that here, while the schedule is long, the discipline is hardly noticed. Not being content with getting away with more than they ever could at Santa Ana, they try to do unreasonably wrong things, which will only make it really tough now, and God help the next bunch of cadets who come here.

I have not been swimming for a couple weeks as I just don't seem to have the time. I'll finally get paid Thursday and will send you some money. I don't know how much I will get but I'll forward as much as I can. I'd like to square up Gerald, but I don't know what it amounts to, so if you could let me know, I'd appreciate it. I'm going into Las Vegas this weekend but I shan't spend much.

There is a possibility of having a few days off after finishing this six weeks here but it is just a possibility. I'm going to try saving more dough for a quick getaway if it should happen.

Wrote to Jack and told him as much as I know about this racket. If he expects to continue as a mechanic of some kind after the war he shouldn't bother with gunnery. However, if he just wants to be in the air for this war, then I guess there will be no argument anyway.

It was swell to talk to you again and I was surprised that the connection was so good. I'll call again around graduation and let you know what I'm going to do. Best regards to everybody. I'll try to write Grandma this week, and Frank.

Love to all, Tommy

JACK - FOUR HUNDRED MILES CLOSER TO HOME
Emporia, Kansas, June 7, 1943

Dear Mom,

Tomorrow I leave Emporia for Sheppard Field. I don't expect I'll be there long. Of course anytime put in there is that much too long. Ironically enough I will land there June 9th. That is just four months to the day that I first hit that Godforsaken (and I'm not kidding) place.

You can appreciate my feelings in as much as I am still a buck private, although I have had four other ranks, namely, aviation student, aviation cadet candidate, student pilot, and aviation-cadet-student-pilot-candidate-private-first-class. It seems that most of the guys will have their wings and be flying before they are officially made kaydets. In spite of all the red tape you hear of, it can't hold a candle to the Air Corps. Not only can they make more tape, but it is three shades redder.

All I can say is I'll be 400 miles closer to home, and hope I am thru with student officers or as they are commonly called "self-appointed generals." Some are OK tho: One fellow I left LA with, Ed Best, is a swell one. He is cadet wing commander. That is top man over 6,400 guys. He has 5 yrs. in the Marines but doesn't look it. He will make good as he is every implication of the saying, "The truly great are modest."

I am going to miss the boys from Emporia but four are coming with me. One is Vic Walz. He hails from New Orleans (pronounced, he says, "oll-y-ins"). It is a little confusing as he talks thus: "The toikey is a poiple boid." It is the New Orleans guys, not Brooklyn. The New Yorkers put it on, with Vic it is natural.

I guess I've padded this letter enough. I rec'd your five and will get paid tomorrow. I'll send home $20. You can give Bob five, and you seven, and the other eight to the phone co. That leaves me two behind. I can't get along on 50 per, so I will try for a few stripes. This is a crummy excuse for a letter. I am not quite in the mood I guess.

Your loving son, Jack

TOM - THE BANK OF DEAR MOM
Las Vegas, Nevada, June 11, 1943

Dear Mom,
Just a quickie for the express purpose of the enclosed. I netted about $40 and am sending $25 to cover the phone bill, the five I borrowed, Gerald, and whatever is left is for the house. It is not much but as you can see it is about as much as I can spare, having borrowed from the boys here, I must repay it.

The third week and hardest part of this course is over now. I've been getting about 55 to 60% hits which is around average and is better than I expected. Will try to write over the weekend, and will write Mark also.

Love to all, Tommy
P.S. I don't believe I'll get paid now until the first week of July and may need to borrow again.

JACK - TEXAS. AGAIN.

San Antonio, Texas, June 12, 1943

I found no letter from Jack mentioning that he was eliminated from pilot training. He must have called his mother to tell her.

Dear Mom,

It is high time I was whipping out a communique to you. Like I said when I was here before, this is the hottest damn state going. My barracks are nice. Except for cockroaches, they are clean. My bunk is nice and comfortable except for an occasional bedbug or two. And the view is terrific. We get a beautiful view of the water tower and its cozy little checkered paint job.

We are conveniently located too. It is just a stone's throw to the chemical warfare practice area with all its nice smelling gasses. If the stone should happen to fall short, no harm done. It would land SMACKO! right in the sewerage. If the colonel thinks that having a PX and theater close by is compensation, he's nuts! With these nicely flavored and cleverly blended assets in mind, I took a sip of the most acrid tasting H_2O I ever laid lips on and departed for the service club.

Nine p.m. finds our lonely soldier, pen in hand, at the mercy of a terribly corny jam session and incomparably boisterous community sing, bitching his head off.

The place has changed some. It is a lot hotter and dustier.

I am a cinch for gunnery, but first I will have to take radio or armament. I think I will take armament. It deals with guns, bombs, bomb racks and pleasant manners of destruction like that there. My sole aim is to be a gunner and a good one. Armament will give me a good foundation for gunnery. Radio will beget me a good foundation for a job in peacetime. But everyone has to do their best now to insure peace in the future. So why in heck should I spend time on something I may not use? In a year's time I will be overseas, I hope. Needless to say, everything I learn here will help me there. Maybe save my life!

The Army is desperate for aircrew members. Every washed-out cadet is going in whether he likes it or not. I like it. I have a good chance when I finish gunnery to be assigned a ship. The crew will no doubt be brand new. We will fly around for three or more months touring the country. I will be a staff sergeant and get flying pay and expenses. Donaldson is a gunner. He washed out as a cadet. He has made up to 300 simoleons in one month!

We have a contingent of WAACS here. Some are very cute, others seemingly aggressive. They sure are snappy.

The guy who used to be CO of the post is now a major. He was busted twice from a brigadier general for being asleep at Pearl Harbor, and is up for a court-martial come the war's end.

Guess this is all the dirt for now. I will write more later. Tell all hello. I guess I won't be home for a while. Be good and say hello to Gram. I'm glad she's getting around.

Your loving son, Jack

TOM - DEAR JOHN
Las Vegas, Nevada, June 14, 1943

Dear Mom,

Before I go any further, let me say that I don't have the slightest objection to carbon copy letters from you. That any of us should feel slighted when it actually saves you a lot of effort would indeed be most selfish. The personal touch in your letter should not just be felt on an original copy, but understood and realized that it is there just the same, even if you did not write as often as you do.

I went to Las Vegas yesterday for the day so was not around to write. It is quite a town and all they say it is. Slot machines everywhere and games of chance all over the place. I only had about ten dollars left out of my pay so what I spent didn't make much difference. I guess I lost around five, winning at roulette but losing to the one-armed bandits. It was a lot of fun. Some of the boys lost all their dough and today are trying to raise money by selling everything from watches to Denver streetcar tokens. Pretty near everybody is asleep right now (noon break before school), as most of them came in pretty well crocked. I had a few myself, but was able to maintain a fairly steady course and not get sick even after eating hamburgers, onions, French fries and watermelon.

School continues and at last we are firing regular machine guns. Today I fired two hundred rounds from an upper turret mounted on a truck and one hundred from a lower ball turret. I got 95 hits in all, which is not exceptional but about average or slightly above. I thought that being in that little ball turret, which is less than four feet in diameter with a machine gun about six inches from each ear, would be plenty noisy, but I was surprised to find it was not nearly as bad as I had imagined. The guy firing in the next turret tho seemed to make a helluva racket and I'll have to put cotton in my ears next time.

We are all finished with shotguns and rifles for which I'm plenty glad. I never could fire the shotgun without getting the devil kicked out of me. The last time, we fired shotguns from the back end of a truck going about 25 mph at traps going in all directions. We fired about 50 rounds in three minutes or so, maybe a bit longer, so I just got off most of mine from the hip and managed to hit a few that way but, of course, didn't get a very hot score.

We have one more week here firing machine guns on the ground, then next week we will move to Indian Springs about fifty miles from here and start shooting from AT-6As. I guess they will just forward any mail from here.

Marjorie wrote to me just before you did so it was no surprise. It also was not much of a letdown but rather a relief. There was nothing unpleasant about it and it never kept me from going out with any other girls as you know. I guess you can dispose of the letters in my drawer. In these times I'd rather not be tied down any or have anybody else worrying.

That's about it for now. I don't know exactly when I'll get to write again but I'll try to make it sooner than this one.

Love to all, Tommy

JACK - THE EPISTLE
San Antonio, Texas, June 14, 1943

Dear Pat,

As I start this long-delayed epistle to you from the service club, I find myself in a very homey and memorable, or I should say reminding, atmosphere. With a jam session going on in the corner and the steady buzz of voices, it reminds me of the Fourth of July parties we've had, only this one is "king size," with no worry of cops, and everyone happy but sober. Except for lack of the two easily identified items mentioned, this is much like things the "House of Cahillshire" once knew. We used to fight neighbors and cops then. Now it is a fight against a common enemy, so that we may be free to be engaged in the throes of battle with the neighbors and cops again.

I may sound over-patriotic, if there is such a thing, but lately I've made what, to me, is an important decision. I had to choose a type of training that would enable me to take gunnery. That may not sound hard but under these circumstances it may mean plenty. It was radio or mechanics, and do my job here in the Corps and have a trade for the future, or take armament and give my all to gunnery and the brutal art of death and destruction to attain a common goal.

After due consideration I found that armament is my best bet. I don't remember if I said this to Mom, but I'll repeat, that every bomb I rack will, I feel, bring the end closer. If it does not destroy in whole or in part an objective essential to the enemy's success, its noise or action will sure help our foes get the "wind up." Panic can do more to win a war than actual destruction.

I am all for obliterating the poisonous influential roots behind the fanaticism and militarism of the Axis powers, if such be humanly possible, which I doubt. But I don't give a damn how we win this war, as long as we do it, and do it well and damn quick, so I can go home. Just what brought out such militaristic writing, I can't say. Let's accredit it to the fact that I have gotten nowhere in four months and can take it out on no one and let it go at that.

My sole aim now is to be a gunner and a good one and get home to take advantage of the liberties and freedoms our country has to offer. Lest I forget, I was interviewed today and I am going to take armament. Upon appointment to said school I will have attained the rank of PFC (so what?).

I feel very religious these days. Could I have "seen the light," "gotten religion"? I don't know. I went to evening Mass Sunday and had the honor and privilege of serving. It's funny to think that I once considered it a duty.

Tonight I went to Mass again in hopes of serving. Two boys were ahead of me but I found consolation in singing hymns that I sang in days gone by. It is strange but that, too, I considered more or less a duty and I never did really "sound off" in church. Tonight I sang, seemingly, with such devotion that I considered it an honor, and you couldn't tell me from St. John himself.

I sure wish I had followed thru on my chances to learn trumpet, trombone or piano. I'm dying to get in on this jam session, but find myself as helpless as a rookie in the field of combat.

You may personally administer your boot to the seat of my pants upon my return home. Remind me to take lessons on something when I get home.

Well, Pat, I guess this will hold you for a while. I am going outside to catch the tail end of Rubinoff and his fiddle who are making a personal appearance in the outdoor theater. Drop a line my way as I enjoy your letters a lot. This camp is still corny.

Be good, I'm glad you are OK now. Your accident gave me a scare for a while. Say hello to the gang at work and keep 'em bowling.

Your loving brother, Jack

TOM - HOME ON THE RANGE
Las Vegas, Nevada, June 16, 1943

Dear Mom,

Yours arrived just this minute. As you had already sent some of the enclosures, one being a copy of my letter, I am returning them, as one is initialed for Frank and you may not have another copy.

Things are going fine on the range. We are kept busy out there, and for the first thousand rounds of firing from turrets and flexible guns, I have an average of 31% hits. This is considered a little better than average, and with another thousand rounds to go on the ground range, I have a chance of building it up to a good score. Some difference in the characteristics of the turrets will make differences in the score but so far I have been shooting fairly consistently. On the .50 cal flexible range, however, I was both low and high man in our section for the day.

Firing the first fifty shots I was stopping the gun to pull the trigger instead of continuing a smooth track. The result was only four hits out of fifty! The second fifty rounds, though, I caught on and corrected it and got twenty-nine hits which was highest out of fifty for our group, but my total for the hundred was about average. Tomorrow I'm going to shorten my bursts just the merest fraction of a second and will be able to save a couple rounds each burst. The longer the burst the greater the bullet pattern and of course the last few shots will be entirely wasted.

We are also studying malfunctions out on the range. The instructor removes a part from the gun or uses a bent part, poor ammunition and things like that. We attempt to fire, or in some cases fire and then try to figure out what caused the stoppage. We take up twenty of the most common situations and must be able to recognize them without lifting the cover of the gun. I thought they would be quite difficult but so far I seem to be getting them.

Must go to school now so will mail this right away. Must answer Pat's letter but I just barely have time to write you alone and have been owing Carmen and Monette letters for weeks.

Love to all, Tommy
P.S. Will try to phone in a couple weeks.

A new family name, Carmen. She and Monette, mentioned earlier, are married to Dan and Tom Herbert, brothers who are Nana's cousins.

TOM - WHERE THE DEVIL GOES IN WINTER
Indian Springs, Nevada, June 21, 1943

Dear Grandma,

Today I flew again for the first time in a couple months now. This time the ship was much bigger, had about five times as much horsepower and was quite a bit faster than the one I used to fly in. I did not fire any guns today but took one along so the ride would be as much like the real thing as possible. There are about five planes in each group on a target which is towed by another plane. Each plane in turn moves in and fires at the target until ammunition is expended. To keep score, each gunner has his bullet painted a different color, and then it is quite simple to tally the hits.

Also different this time, I rode most of the way backwards. The rear seat has a swivel and I turn it around in order to get at my gun. Have two safety belts. One for while I'm sitting and another, much larger, for while I am standing. It is a little different standing but not much. Sometimes when the air currents drop the plane suddenly, a fellow's feet don't quite keep down on the floor but there is no danger. Actually in flying there is no motion noticed. A bump in the air is noticeable but unless you look at the ground, it seems exactly like standing still. I'll be flying every day now, sometimes twice a day.

This week we are at Indian Springs. There is actually a spring, a couple miles from here, and from the air it looks beautiful and so out of place that it might be a mirage. On the post here, there is exactly one tree. It is quite green and healthy. How it got here I don't know. How it lives I know even less, and it remains a constant source of wonder. The elevation is 3,100 feet and when we fire we go up to about 9,000 feet. It is quite cool there but not cold.

It is absolute wasteland out here and planes fan out for miles in all directions and never have to worry about shooting a living thing on the ground. The nights are cooler and the sun never seems to go down but it must sometime because we rise in moonlight.

The food is terrible. The flavor is governed by the tray you eat from. By tasting the grease on the trays, you can have anything from last Christmas' turkey to last night's potato salad. This is a slight exaggeration, of course, but conditions are not as good as they might be. Of course, we are miles from any place. I think this is where the devil goes to when it is

Winter in Hell. At Las Vegas, the food was wonderful, the kitchen and utensils spotless.

At Las Vegas we have Mass every night but Friday (Jewish services that night) and three Masses on Sunday. We have two hours of classes on Thursday night so I can't go then, but usually I manage to get to Mass and Communion most Monday, Tuesday and Wednesday evenings. You know the value of prayer, and since I have been in the service, I have recognized more than ever its necessity, and through it, I have been able to do things I never think I possibly could have done otherwise. The reverses now come about as easy as the successes.

I hope that things are easier for you now and that in turn should make it easier for Mother, as she has been through a great deal also and must be careful.

Well, I'm going to go to bed now. It is not time for "Lights Out" yet but I'm very tired and tomorrow I'll have about four hundred rounds to fire so I'll need all the sleep I can get.

I'll try to write more often in the future but I must rely on my letters to Mother to keep the family informed. Hope to get home in a couple weeks but so far it is just a hope.

Love, Tommy

TOM - CUTTING LOOSE IN THE REAR
Indian Springs, Nevada, June 23, 1943

Youngest brother Mark was the last son living at home, planning to go into the Navy in December.

Dear Mark,

Now that I'm flying again, it seems there is more to write about. I went up today for the third time this week and for the first time the air was fairly smooth. The other two flights seemed to be just up and down. I'd get my sight on the target and when I pulled the trigger we'd be fifty to two hundred feet above or below the target. Consequently I only got seventeen hits out of two hundred rounds yesterday.

Today, though, I flew in the morning and it was smoother, and I got fifty-seven out of two hundred which is pretty good shooting if I say so myself. If I can keep that up, I'll have a damn good average. Right now it stands at 18.5% and 12% is what the last class average was. It is really fun though to stand up in that rear cockpit and cut loose.

The actual target is about twenty feet long and I guess about six feet high. Shots in the tail don't count. Tomorrow we'll practice "cut unders," when the pilot slips into the target, slips away, in and out until the ammunition is gone. You get a little closer to the target at times this way but you also have to fire when moving away.

When he "peels off" after I finish firing, my feet are right out toward the horizon. I lose all sense of where the sky, the desert or horizon should be. To make it more fun I'm riding backwards or maybe sideways so can't prepare myself at all. So I have two more flights, one tomorrow and the last on Friday. Already I have enough hits to graduate so everything the next couple days is gravy and I hope to pile them up.

We fly in AT-6As made by North American. They are quite a change from Ryan PT-22s. My pilot is a 2nd lieutenant but a good scout. I have not saluted him in three days and if I do he'll probably get sore at me! He calls all his gunners "Skipper," flies any way you want him to and can really fly that crate.

How are you coming with the Navy? Don't worry about joining up too soon. I would do it before getting drafted for the simple reason that I think the Navy is a better deal than the Army. You have a defense job, I don't know how many hours you work but I know you should not be working at all. You've had a tough time of it already but that seems to be our lot. But even if you are working, maybe only part time, you are doing a good job, I know. That is important because I've seen lots of fellows who wear a uniform, people think how patriotic they are when in reality they are worse "slackers" than lots of civilians.

There are times when I wish I had joined the Navy, as long as I'm not going to be a pilot. I'd be at sea and on a good clean ship. There are lots of places like Las Vegas in the Army.

When you do join I imagine you will get a rating of some kind from your job. Pick something you want to do. Don't think it is selfish. As long as they need somebody for the job you might as well have it. You'll do better at a job you enjoy. However, the Navy is a big outfit and sometimes they can't always satisfy each boot they have. Then is your chance to really be a hero.

Gripe all you want—that's what guys are in the service for—to gripe. You'll feel better too, but don't believe all your griping or you'll be in a jam. I'm developing into one of the best gripers in the Air Corps. I can even gripe because the food was too good at Las Vegas and was only making me fatter! That's some pretty tall griping!

Well, old boy, take is easy. I hope you are not smoking too much. You know what Jack says about it, but you're big enough to take care of yourself now so I won't preach anymore.

Your loving bro, Tommy

JACK - GIRLS AND OTHER INTERESTING CHARACTERS
San Antonio, Texas, June 24, 1943

Dear Mom,

Rec'd yours today. I tried to answer it this afternoon but couldn't seem to concentrate. It is so ungodly hot here. I was surprised to think that you took me seriously about the women situation. I don't know how I got to talking of them, but in all sincerity, I aim to stay quite free from them for a while. Especially the ones in this town. They are fairly well spent.

I am, however, corresponding with a girl in Emporia in a friendly sort of way. I met her at the "rat-race" the night before I left. We went out after the dance and I got in about 3:30 Sunday. She's a good kid.

I have been transferred to the 32nd Training Squadron. The 1st sergeant is a big guy but not as good as T/Sgt. Higgenbottom in Emporia. Higgenbottom used to sing "Good morning to you," etc., and at the end someone would say in a falsetto, "Hi Sarge!" He used to wisecrack right back and it would go on for some time. I did KP for 3 hours the other nite. I was supposed to go on fireguard and didn't know it. It was easy tho. I had to see the 1st sergeant the next morning and I told him why I didn't go on FG, and when I termed my KP as "three hours on the swing shift," he laughed at my description and let it go at that. He is a good Joe.

There is an old master sergeant here. He was an aerial gunner in the last war and was at Pearl Harbor on December 7. He has been in for 26 years and he wears three rows of ribbons and gunner's wings on his chest. It weighs his shirt down on one side. He has no use for a 2nd lieutenant unless he wears wings. Those are the only shavetails he will salute. When he is dressed up, he looks every inch a soldier; when in fatigues, he is just an old "GI" without his teeth.

Once he was going into the PX and a 2nd looey walked out. He didn't salute him. The story goes that said officer asked, "Don't you salute officers?" He said, "Yeah, when I'm not too busy!" The looey replied, "How long have you been in the service?" Well, the sergeant brought forth his left arm and started counting his stripes. He counted eight and said, "Eight times three is twenty-four and two is twenty-six. How long have you been in 'John'?" The looey blushed and walked out. It will take an act of Congress to break him. That is actually, not literally.

There isn't much to write about, and I don't like to write a lot of crabbing, and that's all we do here. There are more ex-cadets here than they can handle. We may ship earlier but I doubt if we'll hit that much luck. I expect to go to the rifle range soon. I hope so. We will use the new M1 Garands. Guess this is all. Tell Gerald I wish him good luck in his new deal. All for now and love to all.

Your loving son, Jack

TOM - THE PLANE WITH THE CHECKERED NOSE
Indian Springs, Nevada, June 26, 1943

Dear Mom,

The week has gone by quickly, now we are finished with our firing and tomorrow I expect we will return to Las Vegas. I never thought I would be glad to get back to that place but I will be.

My final average in the firing was 13.7%. I'm satisfied with it because I made those hits at the required range or close to it. Some got over one hundred hits in a two hundred-round mission, but fellows flying with them say they were only about seventy-five yards from the target. I am not one to deny there are better shots than myself, but to pull in close to the target and whack up enormous scores is kidding nobody but yourself.

Yesterday was about the best mission of all. As I was setting my gun on the mount My Boy came out and said "How do you feel today Skipper?" I told him "fine" though I had been to the dispensary the night before and indulged in one of their "depth charges" which any GI will tell you is nothing short of dynamite. I think after the war I'll try to sell them as a substitute for "Drano." To continue, My Boy inquired about the condition of my chute and then said, "We've been flying pretty straight and level this week and I can only stand so much of that. Make sure one of your safety belts is fastened at all times. It's going to be a rough ride, Skipper." All of which suited me fine because it was getting rather boring just going up and coming down again.

The seat in my particular plane was facing the tail and would only turn about 90 degrees and in the direction away from my gun. One safety belt is attached to the seat and the other (like a window-washer's in an office building) is hooked to the cockpit. It is not quite long enough to allow me to sit down once I have it attached to the hook. Well, to a background of

"Under a Strawberry Moon," instead of the raspy voice of the man in the control tower, we took off in high spirits.

I soon found out what he meant by a "rough" ride and wished he could have carried out his intentions. When he rocked his wings I knew it was about my turn so I unfastened one belt, hooked the second one, loaded, charged my gun and moved it from "Safety" to "Fire." I just about had that done when he peeled off and I mean peeled off. At just about the same moment he leveled off, the target was in view about two hundred yards away so I started firing.

When my ammo belt was shot away, I waved my gun up and down and the next thing I knew we were almost upside down. With the seat just out of reach I was half-sitting, half-standing and helpless. When that gravity started working on me I couldn't have moved or fallen out if I were Superman. Then up he climbed again leaving my stomach somewhere around five thousand feet.

After the second hundred rounds the process was repeated, the radio all the while blaring out jive. Going home, I was expecting a slow roll or at least a snap roll. As I was looking out the tail I had no way of telling what would happen. Usually by knowing where the pilot is looking I can just about figure what he is going to do. We were flying a formation so tight that if it were not for the roar of the engines and slipstreams, I could talk to Brown in the next plane without raising my voice. They then started flying wingtip to wingtip which is the hardest formation of all to fly.

There was still plenty of time and distance to home and I was expecting anything.

Suddenly a plane with a checkered nose came from out of nowhere and the boys broke up that tight formation and moved into a comparatively loose echelon before you could say "Jack Robinson." It seems that the guy in the checkered ship was the flight commander and he frowned on all such horseplay.

The past students here had never flown before, that is, most of them, and to prevent unnecessary airsickness, only straight flying and gentle turns were allowed. It is not a question of safety, just making it easier for the students. As most of us had flying time, the pilots hoped for a break but they didn't get it. They have a tough job here flying eight hours a day with no fun at all.

Watching my pilot and the things he has to do, I began to realize that even with the extra time I had wanted in pilot training, I still might not have been able to do all that he did.

I have not heard any more about what happens after graduation. Chances are we'll go straight to bombardier school and when I do get home I'll be a lieutenant—I hope.

Love to all, Tommy

"My Boy" is Army lingo for "my pilot."

TOM - GOOD RIDDANCE, INDIAN SPRINGS
Indian Springs, Nevada, June 28, 1943

Dear Pat,

Sunday morning, our last day at Indian Springs (Thank God!), a bunch of us were going by the theater and we heard the piano playing. Feeling quite hep to the jive, we dropped in and there, of course, somebody was playing the piano. Obviously the piano would not play itself, but that anybody in such a Godforsaken hole could possess the talent and the courage to raise himself from the depths to which we had been lowered that week was remarkable and could not be believed just by hearing. We had to see.

Sure enough, he was sitting there beating it out, blond and as human as anybody can look in a zoot suit (GI style of course!). He had a style of improvising somewhat like yours but not quite the touch. Without turning around he complied with requests for anything popular.

Gradually his audience (and requests) were increasing, and being human, as I said before, he paused for a cigarette and discovered there were about thirty of us getting a free concert. He got rather bashful then but we talked him into playing some more. He played a blues medley that was really solid, drifting from one number to another so smoothly you couldn't tell where he left off. The session was finally interrupted for the chaplain (Protestant) who was going to have his morning service.

After it was over, the concert not the service, we drifted up to the PX and there gorged the jukebox with nickels to hear Bing, Ella Fitzgerald and Mr. James Dorsey. We got talking about the good ole civilian days, bands we'd heard, bands we played in, and I also told of how we used to have bands rehearsing all the time at the house.

There is really not a lot of music in Nevada, and talking this over I recalled the patient hours you have spent playing for me, and also recalled how long I have been owing you a letter—or a couple of them for that matter.

The radio station in these parts is "KENO of El Rancho Vegas," Las Vegas, Nevada. I get a bang out of the station letters and must admit that it suits no place better than Las Vegas.

Until a couple weeks ago it was purely a local station but now is a member of the Blue Network so once in a while we hear a decent program. Only once in a while though, because most of the radios can't reach Fred Allen, Kostelanetz or the New York Philharmonic. The last day flying at Indian Springs, My Boy in the front cockpit caressed these ears of mine with sweet music via the earphone. Much better than the control tower.

Saturday night, Sonja Henie's *Iceland* played up here. Though I had seen it once before, I went twice up here just to see those ice scenes. Being quite familiar with the action, I was able to watch each character just before he or she had some bit of business to perform and could see them preparing.

I enjoyed that as much as the rest of the show. *Coney Island* was here also and I took that in. I have not seen *Aerial Gunner* but outside of being a "corny picture" as the post paper calls it, it does have some shots of our training.

Speaking of training, in this week's *Life* magazine—the issue with the Trees in it—there were some "special devices" used by the Navy. We use most of the gunnery items. Also in that same issue is an advertisement by the Sperry Company showing a lower ball turret. It shows it better than I can without risking a court-martial.

Our schedule for this final week calls for 2,000 rounds of shooting. As we only fire 200 rounds per trip that means at least two missions a day and sometimes three. Today I was up three times in various Lockheed AT-18s for a total of about four hours. We were firing from Martin upper turrets, lots of fun. The first trip was a waste of time, the first gunner shot the target away. After we got a new target, the sight burned out and we had to come back. I didn't get to fire on that trip so it will mean that I have one more trip.

These are the fastest things I've been in, so far. They are what the Hudsons and Venturas were developed from. Coming home we were hitting 210 with speed to spare. It is exasperating to have to spend the rest of the week, every day flying as far as Los Angeles and back and never getting there.

Rumors continue to fill the air with weekend passes, furloughs, delays en route and a million other reasons for getting to Los Angeles but so far there has been nothing concrete. Had a letter from Monette today re-inviting me to Frisco. If I should get time enough I'll try to fly up there. Gotta scram now.

Love to all, Tommy

TOM - LEAVING LAS VEGAS
Las Vegas, Nevada, June 30, 1943

Dear Mom,

Two days more and our gunnery training will be over. There seems to be some argument as to whether our graduation will be Saturday or Monday. The secrecy would seem to indicate that we will move in a body to some new field and that action would rule out any possibility of a pass, furlough or anything resembling a vacation.

The latest rumor is Albuquerque. It seems to be the straightest dope of all, and as it is the best school in the country I would not mind.

I'm also sending you a booklet on Las Vegas Army Airfield—with post notes. It shows the brighter side—if there is one. Today I had two flights canceled but made the third one. Five more flights to go and I'll have my shooting finished.

The Eagle spread his wings today and I collected a full month's pay for the first time in ages. I'm holding on to most of it until I move. The amount enclosed is for you personally. If you have any immediate need let me know, but as soon as I know how I stand I'll send you some. May phone Sunday, but don't count on it as they are having quite a program here. Lights out now so I'll close.

Love to all, Tommy

JACK - KISSES ON THE BOTTOM
San Antonio, Texas, June 30, 1943

Dear Mom,

Rec'd yours today and tho I had wanted to write before this, I just couldn't quite make it. I have been very lax since leaving Emporia and Dear Old KSTC. I have left several things undone and also unexplained.

Money gets top billing I guess. I am to get paid Saturday to the tune of about 80 simoleons. I intend to send home about $30 and you can pay the telephone bill, and Bob and Jackie. I don't know how much if any will be left but you can use it on *yourself*, and I do mean *you*!!

As for chocolate bits, no dice. I had a box to send but I put them to use on the train from Emporia. Meals were few and far between on that trip. I will look around but I really can't promise anything.

There has been a lot of what to me is enjoyable confusion lately. It seems that a John E. Cahill has come to the 309th. The last three afternoons I have been called out for a physical, a general classification test and an interview. Each time I explained the error but only to have it happen again. It did, however, serve to keep me from the "cow-pasture," the scourge of the camp, where we have PT. It tears you down instead of building you up. I'm serious.

The mornings are interesting lately. Today we started preliminary marksmanship. We were lectured on the carbine M2 and the Thompson sub-machine gun. We learned to take them apart. You would be surprised at how simple it is. I was. The carbine is a honey. We will fire both guns soon. Tomorrow we take on the Garand rifle, or as the Army calls it, the U.S. Army, RIFLE, .30 cal, M2. Taking them apart is better known as fieldstripping them. Together, the parts are called the "nomenclature" and after the letter Frank wrote Pat a while back, I needn't say more about that.

I saw *Stage Door Canteen* last nite. It is a wonderful show. I wish you and Pat would take some of the money I am sending and see it. You would get a lot of laughs and the lovey-dovey part is the same, but still a little different, and to me in parts, the show was inspiring. Don't miss it. By the way, Ray Bolger gives you an idea on what Army drill instructors are like. Talking about voicing command!

I am very glad Mark is doing so nicely. He is, as they say in the service, "on the ball!" Outside of being a source of worry, I honestly believe the kid is entitled to his license. You know, Mom, he won't have much chance to drive, but if he is like I was, he will do some driving to the beach, etc., without a license, but of course with a competent person at his side. I don't think it will hurt anyone and he will be happy and know he has accomplished something. Strange to say, having a license adds greatly to confidence and relaxation, which is the essence to safe driving. Altho I know how you feel, only too well. But I think he should be rewarded for going thru such an ordeal as he is now. I understand the boy's feelings, maybe a little more than you do, Mom. How about it?

At present my appreciation for GI food is at a new low, but of course I don't expect home cookin'! No furlough 'til Thanksgiving at least, and no more news for now. Say hello to all.

Your loving son, Jack XXXOOO

JACK - GUNS AND STUFF
San Antonio, Texas, July 4, 1943

Dear Mom,

Well, I feel a lot better now. I am going to the rifle range tomorrow so I'll be leaving soon. However, several others classified as armorers are leaving for radio school. I don't want that and I expect I'll raise a bit of a stink if they try to give it to me. Compared to armament, radio leaves a very unpleasant taste in my mouth.

I got paid yesterday, as you notice by the enclosed MO. As you know, five is Bob's so will you see that he gets it. I rec'd Jackie's letter and Pat's and will answer them soon. I think that a $10 error was made on my pay so I will look into it tomorrow. I won $10 in a poker game today so that helps. I hope to get some shoes if I can get the CO's OK. I will send mine home as Mark can probably use them.

I've seen a few schoolmates but that's all. Between Tom, Frank, Jerry and I, the Army does a fairly good job at keeping us apart. C'est la guerre! I wish you could see *Mr. Big* with Donald O'Connor and Gloria Jean. It is a terrific musical along Mickey Rooney lines but better. I have nothing more to write about but will let Pat know about my experiences on the range. Say hello to Gram and all.

Your loving son, Jack

TOM - HEADING TO ALBUQUERQUE
Las Vegas, Nevada, July 5, 1943

Dear Mom,

Just a quick one for now. Graduation is at 12:30 and we leave here tomorrow for Albuquerque. There seems to be a rather long time between leaving here and arriving there, so it is just possible we might be going by way of LA. Though it seems unlikely, I'll be there some time Wednesday morning and may get time off to come home. There seems to be no way of finding out definitely so I'll just have to let it rest there.

I'm leaving this place without an ounce of any regret whatever. Someday I may come back here as an officer and oh, boy! Because we were cadets, we were disliked before we even arrived, but it is all over now and Albuquerque will be much better I'm sure. From fellows who have been there, it is supposed to be a very nice town, a good field and I'll be able to look up Mrs. Tuttle's sister. We may be there eighteen weeks in which case I should get off around Thanksgiving and that gives Frank a good stretch of time to beat me to a commission, but I wish all the boys could have one.

If I don't get to LA, I'll send you some money from Albuquerque. Don't write until I send my address.

Tell Mark not to worry if he can't be an aerial gunner in the Navy. A PT boat would be lots of fun, radio plenty hot and in fact almost any job in the Navy will be near action. Being at sea is quite a bit like flying.

Love to all, Tommy

Mrs. Tuttle mentioned above is a longtime family friend from Concord, New Hampshire.

JACK - THE VICTORY GARDEN
San Antonio, Texas, July 6, 1943

Dear Pat,

Rec'd yours the other day so I'll not delay any longer. Judging from your excursion of the airfield you seem to have caught onto the ways of the Army to a certain extent. Altho there are countless things that are a constant pain in the soldier's sitter, no layman will ever know the whole of it, and I doubt if the average soldier himself can call to mind most of them. You have seen things which, even tho I am in the Air Corps (the infantry branch it seems) I haven't seen myself. I have been *near* a B-25 and B-26 and have handled a Piper Cub. The biggest I've seen along the destructive lines is a .45 cal slug.

The weather here is, beyond a shadow of a doubt, much hotter than hell. The sun is merciless. The last two days have been tough. I've been to the rifle range and got a little experience, a little knowledge, a little soreness in the shoulder and a very little score. It was a lot of fun tho. Today I fired for record but did very badly. I fired the carbine and the Thompson sub MG. Both are mighty nice pieces and it is difficult to make a choice between the two.

The carbine is light, easy to handle, but doesn't have the power of the sub MG. It doesn't waste time knocking an enemy on his rectum tho. It is a semi-automatic, i.e., it will only fire one each time. The Thompson however is heavier but has a minimum kick and fires a bigger slug. The Garand is the best in the world I think and it will knock hell out of anything that cares to have hell knocked out of it. I fired it 60 times yesterday and 32 today. It is strictly infantry tho. The carbine is an Air

Corps design, with a similar operating mechanism. I understand that all planes are being equipped with racks to hold the carbine.

This is a corny letter, so I have just placed a call so that I can talk with you-all (Texan for "you" plural form). I talk funny now I think. I have been closely affiliated with Southerners, New Orleansers, Brooklyners and all the rest. I have reacquired part of my New England accent, with a smattering of "you-all" talk and "choips like a boid" lingo which comes from New Orleans, not NY.

I met a kid from Gorham, NH, yesterday and he knew you in school there. I forget his name but he described you as that "short little girl." He was glad to know you are in good health, etc.

You have yet to tell me of my record collection. Is it still in one piece and has it increased or decreased in size? I heard the "Elks Parade" tonight, which reminded me there are a lot of records I would like to buy.

Just now, a junior dust storm is in progress. It is really terrific. The dust and sand gets in your hair, even the small victory garden I have been raising the past week, just below my nose. This camp is getting worse.

The novelty of WAACS has worn off, but it is a kick to see them salute. They are so eager. They are doing a good job tho and have put more than one MP in his place. On Sat. nites everyone is frisked for liquor. The MP gets a lot of the spoils and some have gotten too much. They sometimes get over-eager when frisking said WAACS.

I had a letter from Gerald. He seems to be enjoying himself. He has about the same setup as I had in Kansas. Good deal.

A lot of guys have shipped out to radio including armorers. I hope I don't fall to the same fate. Guess that is all for now. Be careful and write again soon. When I send that package I will enclose a booklet that might acquaint you a bit with the Army.

Your loving brother, Jack

TOM - LT. DIXON'S SHINER
Albuquerque, New Mexico, July 9, 1943

Dear Mom,

Well, I have finally reached an *advanced* school! It was quite an adventure just getting here. Monday night we made final preparations to evacuate. Tuesday morning, our bags were all packed and labeled as per instructions and placed outside to be picked up, the barracks cleaned and floors oiled, and what happened? Our beloved CO came forth with this announcement, "Men, there has been a mistake in *reading* the orders. You will leave tomorrow (Wed) not today!" Can you imagine such a thing? The boys will tell you how many people handle shipping orders and yet nobody noticed it! When Wednesday arrived we were all delighted to finally leave, and to also see that our beloved Lt. Dixon had a beautiful shiner. We are not certain who did it, but if I ever find out, I'm going to deem it a special privilege to shake his hand!

After waiting three hours in train cars before finally leaving, our CO said, "I'm going to put you men on those cars and make damn sure you don't get off for a minute." Well, we didn't get out, but on the other side of the train which he couldn't watch, we were loading through the windows cases of beer, quarts of whiskey, and the porter fixed up one of the water coolers for storage and cooling of the beverages. We traveled in Pullmans and though they were not air-conditioned it was not a hard ride.

Thursday morning we were in Barstow, California, closest I got to LA. I couldn't call as I was in a troop movement but I knew you wouldn't be worrying. We stopped along the way for Fred Harvey meals. The food was delicious and the people we met along the way were very kind. We passed lots of desert camps, and it is no longer dull traveling across these wide open spaces as it was when we drove from Concord to LA. The railroads seemed very crowded and why we made such good time I'll never know. Along with my GI acquired talents of bed-making and shoe-shining, I observed the porter in his manipulations of upper and lower berths, and now may be a porter after the war! Though I can't quite compete with their talent for crap-shooting.

Thursday afternoon and evening we traveled through upper Arizona. I never knew Arizona was so nice. We could smell pine trees and the earth looked very rich in places. I don't mean to be discouraging, but I didn't see much cattle.

At about seven o'clock this morning we were roused to prepare to get off at Albuquerque. I didn't see much of the town but what I did get a look at was wonderful. It seems very clean, with well-kept lawns and plenty of shade trees.

Kirtland Field is about four or five thousand feet above the city, and we can look down on it and see just a long green valley. The town is a little bigger than Concord but of course much more up to date. From all reports it is a swell place for weekends.

This school is going to begin tearing us down Monday. It is going to be anything but a snap. Again we are "guinea pigs." This is the first squadron to go through the new eighteen-week course instead of the old twelve. We'll have six weeks of navigation, and our final missions will include navigating to some distant target, dropping the stuff and getting back again.

They told us to get all our sleep this weekend as we won't get any once the ball is rolling. We won't start flying for two or three weeks but when we do it will include missions any time from dawn until midnight. The night flights will be about every three days or so. Your little boy is going to have his hands full.

Eighteen weeks will end just before Thanksgiving, and as we have already been to gunnery school we might get a break at the end. It will be a year then and I think we should, but you know the Army.

I'm going to try to send you a package this week. We'll be quarantined tomorrow so I may not get a chance but I'll try. I'm sending you a pair of wings. They are exactly like the ones I wear and though I'm not an above average gunner, perhaps you'll like them anyway—sort of a down payment on those bombardier's wings which will take everything I've got to earn. They give me a rating to fall back on anyway.

I'm also sending film of photos I took at Hemet. Have two prints made of each shot. You keep one set of prints and send another to DeMent. He left his address with you I believe. You might put in a note that they are from me. Tell him if he sends me any money for them, I'll send his money back in the form of capsules of lice or something equally unpleasant.

They say it rained here yesterday, and as the altitude is over 5,000 feet, I guess I can expect some cooler weather. Because of the altitude we won't do much running faster than a dog trot. They have a horrible looking obstacle course here, and with my last two or three months of little or no calisthenics, it will be quite a strain. But with inspiration such as "Damn the Torpedoes, Full Speed Ahead!" and old stuff like that there, we will survive.

Our CO threatens short haircuts!

Hope I can get that package off. If I can't get an airmail stamp, this will have to go straight. I have a batch of them in my barracks bag but, with usual Army efficiency, mine and the squadron's belongings are now anyplace within the continental limits of the United States—or maybe farther.

Love to all, Tommy
P.S. I'll send a money order as soon as I can get one.

In my quest to learn more about my uncles' experiences, I searched related websites. My interest in Kirtland Air Force Base was sparked when I saw how Tom looked forward to training there, as well as being in Albuquerque. Through the Air Force Navigator Observer Association (AFNOA), which veteran navigators can join, I connected with retired Col. John C. McHaffie and his wife Barbara. For distribution to members attending the AFNOA 2005 Reunion in Albuquerque, Col. McHaffie compiled "The Short History of Kirtland Air Force Base." The McHaffies kindly sent this document to me. From this compilation I learned that, to fight a 1940s modern war, the Army saw the need to develop and produce more technologically up-to-date air weaponry. Projections were that tens of thousands of trained personnel would be required to win the war. Based on geographic climates, these schools were to be located in the Southwest, primarily New Mexico and Texas. Both states had ideal flying weather, as well as available acreage. Once established, Kirtland had a contingent of 150 AT-11 training planes. In 1942, the base also assumed responsibility for training aviation mechanics to maintain the school's aircraft and eventually planes in combat zones around the world.

TOM - BOMBIGATOR SCHOOL
Albuquerque, New Mexico, July 10, 1943

Dear Mom,

The enclosed is rather late but I hope it will help.

Our barracks bags and everything in them are believed to be in Sacramento. I'm holding on to some money in case I have to buy clothes. What we will do for athletic clothes and zoot suits, I don't know.

It rained a little last night and was quite something. I also spent a couple hours on my own poring over a B-24. I had quite a talk with the crew chief and learned a good deal. The bombardier has quite an office. The turrets were the same as we used in gunnery school so I was able to tell the Sarge a few things about them.

Today we had a physical exam and I measured 5 ft. 10 inches and weighed 159 which is not much change. Everything else is OK.

The mess here is wonderful and makes me wonder what they did with our dollar at the other posts. We do have meatless days but they generally have something good.

Our squadron from Santa Ana Army Air Base, which was separated when we went to gunnery, is now almost reunited. Our squadron is smaller than they usually run through here, but we are the first group of bombigators so I expect we'll get more individual training. All for now. Stiff inspection coming up.

Love to all, Tommy

"Bombigator" is Army lingo for Tom's projected rating upon completion of bombardier-navigator training.

JACK - MISSING CALIFORNIA
San Antonio, Texas, July 12, 1943

Dear Mom,
Not much to write about but I do at last have that package ready to send home. It is mostly letters that I want put away and saved for me. Naturally, there are some that I wouldn't let a lady read, but you know that anyway. The box itself is a checker game, but there is a .30 cal slug in there, two field manuals, rather technical in parts but sufficient to give you an idea of what the Army is like. Also, a pin I borrowed from Pat.
I don't know of anything else except some flying lessons and a bit of meteorology. I would like that put some place too. I doubt if it is very interesting to you but you are free to look at it of course. It is stuff I acquired in Emporia. It should be along any day.
Things are the same here with the prospects of leaving getting better each day. I expect to go this week but you know how it is.
We have gone on a few road runs with ditches to jump and we cross a small stream three different times. I pity the guy that falls in, as the stream is none other than the notoriously foul-smelling sewerage I have mentioned in other communiques. It is absolutely vile, as you can imagine.
The weather is about the same, with a few clouds now and then. I feel fine myself. I still weigh the same 145 with my clothes on. I am getting a lot of sun and a bit of a burn but it doesn't bother me any. I would sure like to get my burn on a sandy Southern California beach with a quart or so of 6% beer under my belt. It beats a sandy cow-pasture and 3.2 crap all to heck.
Guess this is about all for now. I will try again when I have some news worthwhile. Say hello to all and you be careful. I hope I move toward home. Bye now.

Your loving son, Jack
P.S. Chocolate is impossible to find.

Not yet knowing that Jack "wouldn't let a lady read" some of the letters he was returning home, I read them—just a few about girls from a childhood friend who was also in the service. I gave the boys editorial privileges in compiling this book, so as Jack "requested," I haven't included them.

TOM - THE JUNIOR CATERPILLAR CLUB
Albuquerque, New Mexico, July 14, 1943

Dear Mom,

Received yours today and cheers for the good news. Glad to hear that Frank is getting home. The idea of Bob and Jackie being there sounds good also. I guess Little Pat will be a big boy by the time I get home again.

Being guinea pigs has become our lot it seems, and systematic Army confusion reigns—if you can imagine such a combination. I can't say that the course so far is very hard—mostly review. By the end of this week I'll need a navigator to lead me around because I won't know where I am going. School ten hours a day does not leave much time for letter writing except right now.

Our third day of calisthenics was much easier. The obstacle race was not quite so fearful but most important of all, I am getting into good condition again. The program, though a little more rugged, is better than at any place I've been yet.

There is a war going on here with the lieutenant. He has some pretty strong ideas on how a latrine should be cleaned. It is amazing how clean and shiny that place can be and he still won't like it. So far I have been lucky not to pull the detail and by the time I do maybe he'll get religion or something and slack off.

It is quite a joke now to walk by the lieutenant's office and say to whomever you are with, at all times of the day, "Well, I guess I'll wash and brush my teeth now so I won't have to do it in the morning while they are cleaning up." The place is locked for cleaning up right after breakfast, of all times. Breakfast is at 5:20. It is even more satisfactory to say you are going to do your necessary morning body functions twelve hours in advance. A nice trick if you could do it! No doubt this will all get a rise out of the CO one way or another. Who will win, I couldn't say for sure but I've been in the Army long enough to guess. If you can overlook the above characteristics, he is not a bad guy. If.

I had a ride in a B-24 all arranged Sunday but at the last minute I discovered they would not be back until seven and with a formation at six, it was impossible.

Our desks at school are regular office desks with everything but a swivel chair. Our instructor is a redhead 2nd lieutenant from Brooklyn. If you shut your eyes you would swear it was Allen Jenkins of the movies who is quite famous for his Brooklynese. As most redhead guys seem to be, he is quite a wit and there is seldom a dull moment. When he gets his dander up however, he can be quite a wild man. Gradually he is getting nicknames for the whole class. We are his only students (our flight of 25 men) but he gets us all day long and must be congratulated on his patience. He has graduated from both navigation and bombardier school and possesses both wings. He wears his bombardier wings though just so guys can ask him, "What the hell are you doing teaching navigation?"

Yesterday was gas drill day and we wore our masks slung all day and on our faces to all formations—even calisthenics. This, of course, was cause for repetition of well-worn jokes such as, when a man has his gasmask off, "OK mister, you can take your mask off now," or conversely when a guy has it on, "You can put your gasmask on now." You can see this is all very unfunny and the fact that we have seventeen more weekly gas drills to go is not encouraging. If you or the boys have any suggestions for improvement in this rather corny banter, rush them along.

Did I tell you about all the equipment I have? If not, I may say I have everything from paperclips to a parachute. My name is signed to every item and I've got keys for briefcases, footlockers, my desk and no doubt there will be a few more.

The thought of having a parachute in the corner of your room sounds silly, but the harness has been tailored to fit just me and my fat, and the knowledge that, if I have to use it, I won't fall through the harness is comforting. At Vegas you either tripped over the straps or had to hold your breath and get a couple boys to help you into it. I also know when it was checked and packed last and that I am not going to burn a hole in it with a cigarette. This type is hooked on to my chest straps and if the ripcord fails, you just tear it open with your hands. They open pretty easily though.

One brand new bombardier was showing his to his wife (one is issued for personal use after graduation) and she didn't believe you could just "pull that little red handle and pop it open." The result was a very red-faced looey walking a couple miles across camp with his arms loaded with enough silk to keep the Rockettes in stockings for a year. About the silliest and most embarrassing thing a man can do is "open a chute without sufficient altitude"—on the ground, that is. My instructor at primary belonged to the Junior Caterpillar Club for that very reason. You get a big write-up on the bulletin board announcing your membership and seldom live it down.

Well, Mom, it is about time for school again. We have two more hours tonight and get back just before lights out. If I can get to a phone Sunday I shall try to phone sometime around noon or early afternoon. That is not a promise though because we may have classes.

It would be swell if Frank could get a little time at Albuquerque though I know he will want to—and should—spend it with Peg. There are such things as "delays en route" but perhaps he's used them all. Maybe I'll get a tactical outfit near him sometime.

I'm enclosing the insurance check and you can do what you please with it. I won't try to tell you what to do with it as you wouldn't anyway, and it is not a heck of a lot. I expect to stretch my dough pretty well here as the absolute only time we have to go to the PX is Sunday—maybe! Feeling swell and confident too. Things look pretty rough but possible.

Love to all, Tommy

JACK - MOM'S LETTERS ARE THE BEST OF ALL
San Antonio, Texas, July 14, 1943

Dear Mom,

As usual, I won't guarantee the text but will let you know I'm still alive, I think. We had a 22-mile hike yesterday. The cadence was quite fast and several passed out from exhaustion and shortage of water. I was OK for 20 miles but I sure thirsted. The last miles were terrible as we were in the limits of the camp but I had just finished my water and my mouth felt like it had a sandpaper lining. A few got water from mud puddles, whose source is none other than our trusted sewerage. I pity them.

I dragged my butt the last mile but I hit a barracks and drank a helmet full of H_2O. It isn't the right thing to do but I dood it anyway. We made it home by 2:30 and averaged about 3.8 mph. That is going some. The sergeant said he would like to do it again and he could set a record. (No thanks, sergeant.) We did well. We have a 30-mile nite hike coming up, I think. We all went to the PX and drank beer. It was 3.2, but good.

By now Frank is home. I bet he looks swell. Would like to see him. Be sure and take some pictures. I bet Peg is a reasonable facsimile of a balloon, not only inflated in front but also walking on air. I have every intention of writing her but with the weather as unbearable as it is, and this camp such as it is, I have very little ambition. I will make a supreme effort soon tho. I won't expect an answer tho as she might have trouble getting close to the writing desk.

Since reading *Turnabout* I often think of the state of affairs that would arise if Frank were to have the baby instead of Peg. I can picture the look on the grocery boy's face as he sees Frank with an open kimono, a pipe in one hand and a drink in the other, with his (or her) protruding midriff, and a masculine voice filling the air with violent cursings and condemnations. 'Nuff said! Too much!

After that bit of indecency, I had better see the chaplain.

Before I forget it, Johnny Corbett is being sent to the Pacific Coast fleet. He thinks it will be in San Francisco. I told him to be sure and get to LA and I invited him to stay at the house. He could sleep with Mark if he stays overnight.

The ration points have me worried, but you are free to draw on my money if you need to and *don't* hesitate either. It wouldn't be any harder than if it was one of us. If you deem it possible, I hope you will *insist* on his staying. He will be made at home, I'm sure.

Frank is doing swell. If he should need any money, mine is available. I owe Jackie and Bob a letter so I'll try to get it off now. Do write soon, as your letters are the best of all.

Your loving son, Jack
P.S. Pictures are swell. J.
P.P.S. If Johnny Routh hasn't gotten those stars yet, have Pat try an Army-Navy store that sells service ribbons. They have them for overseas service and battle engagements. Tell her to get six. Will you put the enclosed pictures in my book? J.

In an earlier letter from Emporia, Jack wrote, "Service Flags are everywhere." That term was not familiar to me so I researched it. Originated during World War I, and continued during World War II, families displayed a blue star on a service flag, or banner, in their window for each family member who had gone to war.

At this point, four Cahill brothers were in the service—Frank, Jerry, Tom and Jack. Planning ahead, Jack suggested his mother get six stars, to include Mark's planned entry in the Navy, as well as my dad Bob's potential service. In the event of the death of a service member, the blue star on the family's Service Flag was covered with a gold star. The organizations of Blue Star Mothers and Gold Star Mothers are still in existence today.

JERRY - WHOSE ROOM IS THIS ANYWAY?
Oxford, Mississippi, July 15, 1943

Dear Mom,

Just a quickie to tell you who my new roommate is. None other than Morton C. Tuttle of Concord, New Hampshire.

He was assigned to the room while I was at class, and on entering, the first thing he saw was Tommy's picture, so he went dashing madly out to see who the hell had the room. I didn't know him, he has changed so much, and I do mean changed. We are going out and have a few beers Saturday nite.

Got the papers and socks today, also your letter, one from Jack and one from Aunt Mary. Time for bed now. Will write again soon.

Your loving son, Gerald

Morton C. Tuttle, nicknamed "Tut," was the son of Mrs. Tuttle mentioned in an earlier letter. The Tuttles and the Cahills were good friends in Concord. At this time it had been six years since Jerry had seen him.

The "papers" reference: My grandmother sent the boys Concord's newspaper, "The Monitor."

JACK - ACCORDING TO DAVE RUMOR
San Antonio, Texas, July 18, 1943

Dear Mom,

Just a quickie to let you know I'm still around. I don't intend to be long tho. I'm on shipping orders now and expect to leave anytime. I may go to Madison, Wis., but that is a comment from "Dave Rumor." I don't expect I'll go to armament but no one knows around here anyway. I am glad I'm getting out tho as this joint is getting me down. I hope this is the last letter I'll write from here but I've a feeling I'll be back after radio or armament. They do more fooling around in this outfit.

I suppose by now you are all enjoying Frank's company to the fullest extent. I wish I were there. If I can get a furlough after radio, I will try but don't know for sure. It is as uncertain as the day is long.

Nothing has happened since I last wrote except that I got a swell letter from Tommy. Since he gave you his gunner's wings, I'll give mine to Pat, if I ever get them. I saw *Dixie* today. It was good but not like I expected.

I'll send a telegram if I can but will call you when I reach my next stop. I hope I can do both. This is a hasty but corny letter. I am pressed for time. Will see you later.

Your loving son, Jack

TOM - STRATIFORM AND CUMULIFORM
Albuquerque, New Mexico, July 21, 1943

Dear Mom,

It was swell talking to you Sunday and it sounded like Frank's homecoming made you feel much better. I wish I could have talked to him but that's luck I guess.

We actually have an hour free now. They fumigated the barracks today and we moved our toilet articles into an empty one and so will have no calisthenics. Day before yesterday it rained so hard that we had no athletics yesterday. I was so surprised it was called off that I went to the PX and just played the jukebox. I did go to the post office to mail that package but the box was not strong enough they said. Maybe I can find a box just big enough for the wings.

School continues and I think we are going to get half an hour knocked off the evening session. It seems that Taps is at 9:30 and at that time we are just getting out of school. Our "so important schoolwork" as they call it doesn't seem to be important enough to make us late for bed. We don't get enough sleep anyway but I guess nobody else does in the Army.

My average grade for the week was about 86. That is lower than I want in anything which requires such a thorough understanding as navigation. However, the weekend exam made clear to me just what I was weak on and that has all been corrected now.

So much of navigation—the logbook work—is quite like bookkeeping. The time past and the distance traveled must be the exact difference between the distance remaining to be traveled and the time estimated for arrival from the total flight time. Tolerances are about a minute or two on time and a mile or two on destinations, so if you have ten lines of entries you can't make any big mistakes or many very, very small ones. Our instructor is very conscientious. All afternoon one day last week he was bragging about the date he had in Albuquerque for that night. We were not catching on to what he was trying to teach, so instead of having our regularly scheduled instructor for that night, he came himself. He really did bust his date, the other instructor told us. Naturally, we are quite anxious to put out for him.

They have changed our schedule too. We were going to start flying next week but now we will have most of our bombardier classes just as we have had the navigation—all in two and a half weeks at ten hours a day. We will be getting out weekends by then, though, and the tension will be eased. I was thinking there might be a good voice teacher at the university and perhaps I could take some lessons. Not too strenuous but enough so that I won't get too out of practice. It will be relaxing in a sense.

The climate here continues to be swell. One thing I have noticed here is that my legs don't ache as they did in Las Vegas even though I get much more tired here. Whether it is the weather, calisthenics, food or my mind, I don't know, but it is a relief not to be bothered any more.

They have a great love for gasmask drills. We wore them all day Tuesday to calisthenics and all. Monday was a practice alert and the alarm came right in the middle of the biggest hailstorm I ever have seen. The hailstones were as big as mothballs, and in any weather like that, gas would not be a bit effective. It was a big laugh on the big shots though and we don't get many.

We have just started a study of meteorology and I don't know a better place to do it. At 5,000 feet altitude we are almost at eye level with the lower clouds and can see a big cumulus grow into a thunderhead. Cloud formations are something like mixing paints. They have basic classifications as stratiform, the long flat type, and the cumuliform, the fluffy snowball-like ones, just as primary colors. They are classified then for altitude, cirrus high, also medium and low, so stratus clouds forming into cumulus would be in a medium altitude altostrati cumulus and you can well imagine the possible combinations to be developed just from five classifications.

Unfortunately for us who study them, there are dozens of other combinations defined to a more exact degree. Actually classifying a cloud type perhaps won't find two weather men in perfect agreement though they both will be about right. It will be an interesting course but will take quite an understanding to learn very much as long as there are no definite classifications.

One thing that makes things pleasant here is the way they serve the food. It is cafeteria style and when they set out a tray of salad it is not just a tray of salad. It is decorated like a birthday cake with borders of fruit, designs on the top, and perhaps an orange or something opened in sections at the top for a centerpiece.

The mess hall is the most perfectly organized one I've ever seen. Nobody seems to rush around but you never have to wait for a thing. They never run out of anything and only rarely is something cooked too long. The boys can bring their wives to meals on Sunday, and you should see those girls pop their eyes at the food.

It is almost time to go back to school now. So I'll call this one a finished log.

However, I won't go so far as to draw a double line under the last entry.

Love to all, Tommy

TOM - THE PICKLE BARREL CONTEST
Albuquerque, New Mexico, July 24, 1943

Dear Mom,

Your cookies arrived today and as usual were devoured.

We have been so busy this week that I have been unable to write. Just the day after I wrote to you last, they changed our program and we are now studying the theory of bombing. Next week we will have no navigation classes but I think there is a mission scheduled for Friday. I am listening right now to the New York Philharmonic and I think it is one of the pleasantest hours of the week.

Today at the field they are having the fourth Pickle Barrel Contest. When the bombsight first came out you may recall boasts that you could drop a bomb in a pickle barrel at 10,000 feet. That is how it gets its name, and the trophy is a small pickle barrel and the highest award a bombardier can get. The target is a five hundred-foot circle, the bullseye being a thirty-foot "shack." The shack is really a cone but its name comes from the old buildings they used to use as targets.

Today from ten thousand feet, two cadets scored "shacks." They hit the bullseye. That is super super—shacks being rarer than furloughs. Students are graded on the "CE," circular error of the hit, the measured distance from the target. We are allowed an average of 230 feet—that is what I'll be required to get. If they did not have a telescope in the sight the bombardier would not be able to see the shack hardly. On the target range, one side was lined with bleachers, and half of Albuquerque came out to see the bombings. Just like a ball game, with programs, scorecards, pop and a band!

Those bombing planes are just a speck against the clouds, the announcer repeats the cadet's radioing of "Bombs Away!" and the crowd seems to know it takes about 25 seconds to fall from 10,000 feet and there are cheers and groans as the bomb hits. I think Albuquerque won today. Our instructors said they had better. It seems they have done pretty poorly in the past. If they didn't win this one, the instructors had their bags all packed because the colonel would be a hard man to get along with.

Along with the Pickle Barrel affairs are the visiting generals. The damn floor has to be mopped three times a day. The latrines are no longer useful, essential and a place for good fellows to meet, but sacred shrines where the glistening brass is more important than the comfort and relief which may be derived from their proper use.

I had not heard that Tut was Gerald's roommate. I wrote Jerry this week but have not heard from him. It is strange that they should meet while I'm just getting ready to visit Tut's relatives here.

I have pulled my marks up quite a lot since last week. I did one pilotage problem Thursday and got 100. They take from two to three hours to work out and as I told you, half-miles, half-minutes and half-degrees all add up to a successful mission. I think I got another bullseye Friday, and on the exam yesterday we had another pilotage problem, along with an hour of computer problems and an hour on aircraft instruments. By that, I mean that we located our position by landmarks on the ground and pinpointing them on the map. I finished the problem just under the time limit and arrived right on the nose. It is possible to arrive on time and still make mistakes though, so I won't know what I got for grades until tomorrow.

The theory of bombing is a deep but fascinating subject. Knowing the theory, it's possible to make the bombsight do all you ask and to make proper analysis of our errors. The hardest thing about the course is being as much on the ball Friday and Saturday as you are on Monday. It's a grind.

For the first time since I have been a cadet I'm enjoying athletics. Our program is still tough but I'm getting in good shape and play the games hard right up to the last whistle. Before it was drudgery but now I'm really enjoying it. This afternoon I may go out to play some tennis if I can influence Bohlman.

He and I pal around quite a bit. We always used to have little arguments as to who would go through doors first. I'd say, "After you," and he'd say, "After you," neither of us going in until brute force seized one of us. Finally we hit on a system. This week I went through all doors first while he respectfully held them open. Next week he'll go through first and I'll be a doorman, so it just goes to prove that every problem has a solution somewhere.

Well, I've about run out of words now. This week will bring on new things to do. As I contemplate that navigation mission Friday, I am trying to figure out all the different places I might get lost near. DeMent is in Amarillo about 200 miles away—probably where we'll go but won't land. Brad is in Bonham, Texas, in another direction. Krushot is down at

Deming, but I'm afraid Los Angeles is a little too far away—and they know I live there.

Your loving son, Tommy
P.S. Did you get the watch and wings? Perhaps the watch can be taken to Johnny's to be cleaned. I now have a GI Waltham, seventeen jewels. It has a large second hand which I will need in my flying. I also have an Elgin stopwatch down to one-tenth of a second. However, these are just loaned to me for my stay here, and I like my own watch, that didn't get any further in primary than I did.

JACK - PRIVATE FIRST CLASS
Sioux Falls, South Dakota, July 24, 1943

Dear Mom,
Well I'm now in Sioux Falls, So. Dakota. The camp seems to be pretty good but I haven't really seen it yet. My barracks is a tar paper shack but is clean. It is in a favorable location as the outhouse (king size) is just outside the door. Some have to walk a half a block to get there. My bunk is right next to a window and a stove so I get fair weather in winter or summer. The country here is beautiful and the weather nice. It is really a contrast to anything Texas has to offer.

If last nite's chow is a sample of the food here, I have a good chance of adding weight to my 20 pounds heavier body. I weighed 145 when I left Sheppard Field. Reveille is at eight a.m.

I just returned from breakfast, French toast and syrup, corn flakes, oranges, bacon and coffee. Last nite we had delicious meatloaf, potatoes, tomato sauce, corn, bread, butter, orange drink, pie, ice cream and seconds on anything.

The train trip was tough. We had chair cars and our previous passengers were said to have been Axis prisoners from the Afrika Korps. The train was filthy at any rate. I have never been so rotten dirty and unable to do anything about it in my life. The facilities were lousy. I took a nice but *cold* shower last night and slept like a baby.

I don't know just how long this radio course will last but I guess I can stand it, even tho I much prefer armament. We will go to school seven days a week with every 8th day off. Also off every nite from eight to twelve. The school operates 24 hrs. a day. We are to fly in Cubs a little too. We will supposedly get 15 hours to get practical experience in radio in-flight. 'S funny how I joined the Air Corps with hopes of getting a P-51 but I don't seem to be able to get past a PU-65 (Cub). I guess this is all for now. I am resigned to the task before me. Write soon.

Your loving son, Jack
P.S. PFC now.

TOM - BETTER BRING YOUR BUCKET
Albuquerque, New Mexico, July 27, 1943

Dear Mom,

The last two days have been pretty warm but not anything like Vegas. Today we saw the bombsight and have started to study it. About all I can say about it is that it is very ingenious and right now complicated but not baffling.

A thorough understanding makes the better bombardier so I'm going to study as much as I can.

Today we had the best news in a long time. Our instructor told us that the colonel wanted to keep washouts below 15% for our class. Every effort is to be made to get us through. While I have had a lot of confidence, this announcement was a boost to me and to all of us. We all have washed out before and know that just working hard was not always enough.

You may only need one break but, when you need it, it is priceless. So now we will work even harder because it looks like it will not be again in vain.

Before I forget it, you asked me a while back if I had received some snapshots of Patrick J. Well, I didn't, and certainly would like to have some. I keep the picture I have of him up on my shelf where it never fails to receive a compliment. He must be quite a big boy now.

What's this about Bob enlisting? If he must, I hope that he still has his mind on the Coast Guard or Navy but for God's sake stay out of the Army.

I suppose the grass is always greener on the other side of the fence. As a cadet I've definitely had good equipment, food and lodgings, but I would hate to be a GI. Frank and Jerry have done all right I guess but the Army is quite a mess from what I've seen of it.

Friday, we are definitely going on a navigation mission. I believe our flight is going to Winslow, Arizona, and back though we are not positive. We will fly in the afternoon when the ships are not used for bombing. It's too bumpy for accurate aiming but evidently not for navigation though they make no bones about telling us to "bring our own bucket." I've flown up to an hour and a half of bumps, upside down and all ways, but this will be three or four hours. I expect to be darn busy, but I'm going to try to have a good time anyway.

We are also learning some of the functions of the aerial engineer and co-piloting. Eventually we will have delved and dabbled into enough things to be Bombardier-Navigator-Gunner-Engineer-Observer-Co-Pilot. We will really get a good deal of stick time when we get to our tactical outfits. Getting passes this weekend so will go into Albuquerque. School now.

Your loving son, Tommy

TOM - FLYING TO A CORNER OF WINSLOW, ARIZONA
Albuquerque, New Mexico, July 31, 1943

Dear Mom,

We are just having a bull session over yesterday's navigation flight and I thought I'd drop out and give you the news. Yesterday we flew from Albuquerque to Winslow, Arizona—about two hundred nautical miles. It was a pilotage method of navigation. We didn't know the wind so we just flew the same heading as our course originally was laid out. When about sixty miles from destination, we were supposed to figure our wind—the difference between track and heading—work ahead ten minutes or so, and then using the wind we found, plot a new course direct to destination.

Going out, we had a tailwind, which carried us along like a bat out of hell. At first it was difficult to pick out landmarks because the terrain doesn't look much like the map. Anyway, while I was trying to figure out where I was, the instructor pointed out the side and there was Winslow. Well, I washed my hands of the whole thing right there and navigation looked plenty bad. However, I was the second navigator on the way out.

On the return trip I was to be first navigator and would direct the pilot. Brown and I changed places up in the nose, which by that time was knee deep with maps, computers, plotters, briefcases and God knows what else. Fortunately, neither of us got sick a bit or we really would have had a mess. Anyway, we crossed over the field, I gave the pilot a new heading and off we went.

Going back was a little easier. The checkpoints were coming up on schedule and all going smoothly. About seventy-five miles from Albuquerque, I this time figured my wind, worked ahead fifteen minutes and about five seconds before my planned time to turn, I handed the pilot a new heading. Just one half-minute early, we hit the field right smack over the middle. I was working so fast that I didn't fill in all my last three lines of the log, but I did have my course right and my estimated time of arrival within a half minute, so was quite satisfied. The next missions will be easier. I won't rush myself so much and will have things down to a system. I don't know when we will fly again but we probably won't have a mission for two or three weeks.

Some of the boys got sick. One hung his head out the camera hatch and the stuff blew right back in his face! Then he left the hatch open and the pilot's parachute fell out—that will cost him plenty. Probably won't have a chance to write until next week now.

Your loving son, Tommy

JACK - THE CODE SENDER
Sioux Falls, South Dakota, July 31, 1943, "Pay Day (for some)"

Dear Mom,

I am more than elated at receiving seventeen pages of type from you in two days. I know I can't even halfway meet that but I will let you know I am thinking of you.

School started Thursday and we have tackled about 17 letters in code. The reason for the king-size printing in this letter is just practice. It is required that letters be about 1/4" high.

As for the code, I think I'm learning something but I wonder. This morning I did pretty well but this afternoon it just seemed to go in one ear, vibrate around a while, and leave the other ear in a violent manner. I expect I will learn the alphabet soon but no doubt I'll use all twenty weeks to get sixteen words per minute. I read in the post paper where a guy from here took 72 words/min. While he was going strong the machine started to smoke and throw ink—what a man.

The food here is OK and the supply of milk is momentarily good. I had a quart for breakfast. We are kept fairly busy. From 10 'til 6 we have school and from 6 'til 8 we have physical training. Chow at nite is about 8:30 so by the time we go to town it is 9:30. There is usually something doing but not much time to do it in. Our day off is Wednesday. By that time you can fairly well guess that we are pooped out.

I had a card from Fr. Donnelly today. He is in Canada, on vacation I guess. I wrote him some time ago and knowing he was busy, I didn't expect an answer. It was a thoughtful gesture on his part. The card was pretty, a picture of "Manoir Richelieu" in Quebec.

I have a number of letters to write but have no time. I could get out a short one each morning but the last two days I have been reading your letters. I get them at 8:15 and start in. I just start them, fall out for chow, read them on the way, get my food, read and eat, and end up with both letter and food about nine. By then I just get time to clean up and go to school.

Actually nothing happens here except that Squadron 811 is picketing their orderly room because their CO restricted them for 90 days. That is grossly unfair and it should fairly well catch the major hell. He had no good reason to put out such punishment. The guys sing "Don't Get Around Much Anymore." It is really comical.

I will certainly write Faulkner soon. I imagine he gets more kick out of a letter than we do. I must write Betty R. too. We correspond more or less but I haven't written her since I was in Emporia. Her birthday is August 4th. I remember when we were in love, we had a fight the night before, August 3rd. The next day I didn't go to church with her as previously arranged. She cried like heck. Her mother got a kick out of it—boy, am I mean!

Guess this is all for now. Time for chow. Incidentally, did you forget to send the $5 or is it coming? . . . _ _ _ . . . (SOS) !!! Write when you can as yours are by far the best.

Your loving son, Jack
·_ _ _ ·_ _·_ _·_ ("Jack" in Morse code)

The seventeen pages of type Jack referred to were copies of his brothers' letters as well as a letter from his mother.

TOM - WEEKEND IN ALBUQUERQUE
Albuquerque, New Mexico, August 2, 1943

Dear Mom,

Payday rolled around Saturday and so the enclosed. I imagine you have use for it and I wish you would use some of it for a visit to Dr. Otto. Perhaps you know what he will tell you, but he might also let Grandma know that you can't wait on her so much. It is like having two people sick. You are the only nurse—and also the patient.

We are now having a lecture on the "Honor System." It is being *read* by an officer. I don't believe lectures on honor should be read. It is something that no one should have to have anybody else write about for him.

I had quite a time in Albuquerque over the weekend. Just so you won't have any illusions about me, I got higher than a kite Saturday nite. I had a couple before eating which gave me quite a shove. However, I don't recall being unreasonably rude but always just as happy as could be. For once I forgot temporarily about navigation and bombardiering. About every night since I have been here my dreams have been filled with navigation problems and despite the sleep, I get up just as tired as when I went to bed. Yesterday I bought *Random Harvest* (tried to get *The Robe*) and by reading before I go to bed, I can divorce my thoughts from the work of the day. We started operating the bombsight on the trainer today and I want all the sleep I can get.

Getting back to the weekend, I kept my cookies and had no hangover. Sunday evening I visited the Clarks. They said that Mr. Tuttle is in pretty bad shape and they are trying to get him away from the New Hampshire winters to New Mexico. As I am sold on this place I will add my plug for the country when I write. Mrs. Clark is Concertmistress for the Community Symphony Association and tells me that I can make some good musical contacts at the university.

It looks like we will have a two weeks' furlough after graduation. The big day is November 13th, and as things stand now, we will go to our overseas tactical outfits the first of the following month. I'd like to have you come down here then for a little rest anyway, or when I come home you can go someplace—Frisco maybe. The big obstacle will be money. If you can save any that I send home it might help.

Will try to write more later in the week. Went to Mass at Immaculate Conception Sunday and will go there every Sunday. It is right near the Franciscan Hotel where we are staying.

Your loving son, Tommy

I found another interesting note in Col. McHaffie's Kirtland compilation which, per Tom's letters, he and his buddies certainly corroborated: "With the base officially becoming Kirtland Field, and the buildup continuing, the citizens went through serious culture shock.

"The appearance of straight-backed, adventurous cadets in freshly starched khakis, on leave or a pass, attending local churches, cruising the downtown area and dating their women was mindboggling. Coupled with the southern skies filled with noisy aircraft, all this hustle and bustle indelibly imprinted in the minds of the Albuquerquians."

TOM - THE BOMBSIGHT TRAINER
Albuquerque, New Mexico, August 5, 1943

Dear Mom,

For a million reasons this will have to be short. Yours just arrived and am glad Pat had such a good time in Frisco. I hope that when I finish here you can have a trip too.

Our schedule has been again changed and the precious time I had before has been broken up in little pieces, and some of it is spent sweating out lines that hithertofore were better times.

Yesterday we flew another navigation mission. I'm catching on better now and next week expect to fly a perfect mission. We went to Winslow again. We would have gone to some place in Texas but I am in a new flight now and they went to Texas last week—hence the repetition. However, the wind was different this time so we drifted over a different course.

I have now had six hours in the bombsight trainer. It is boiling down to a matter of fine touches, so delicate you can hardly perceive the motion to watch it. However, the tangent of an angle from 10,000 feet will make awfully big errors on the ground. I may try to pick up some modeling clay in the art shop in Albuquerque. It will be a relaxation and also help my fingers.

I got a 98 in theory of bombing last week. I think it was one of the hardest exams I have ever taken. I did not learn any simple rules just by rote but have to draw diagrams for myself with the perfect bombing problem for the one they gave me, and find just what the target error would be. Seeing as I did have to work it out myself, I figure I know it that much better. I am now in the innards of the bombsight itself. Before this class it was so secret that students could not even take one apart. I still can't tell you anything about it though and you wouldn't understand it anyway.

I got my pass to the bomb vault today with a picture that looks like a police lineup.

I have finished reading *Random Harvest*. If you have not read it I'll send it home. I tried to get *The Robe* but couldn't. Is there a copy at home? Enjoyed the snapshots very much and will try to get some of myself for you.

Your loving son, Tommy

P.S. The "WC" in my address does not mean Water Closet, but West Coast, in case you wonder.

TOM - BOMBS AWAY!
Albuquerque, New Mexico, August 10, 1943

Dear Mom,

If I'm ever going to get this written I will have to do it during this study period. For the last couple weeks we have had lectures during our "study" periods, and so my own time in the barracks had to be spent studying. We had five exams last Saturday. In a test on oxygen and equipment, one other fellow and myself got 96s, the highest grade in the whole squadron on an exam which had about 15% failures. On the rest of the exams, I averaged about 90 which keeps my average up.

Yesterday was a black day. We got hold of a couple bombsights which were in terrible condition, and as I also was in another muddled condition, it all turned out to be a tough day. I couldn't even hit the "bug" at times. The bug is our target—about a foot square on top—propelled by an electric motor. The bombsight is mounted on a big tricycle affair ten feet high. As both the bug and trainer move slowly, it simulates an actual bombing run. The bug is run in different directions to present different problems. Anyway, it looked pretty bad that day. Last week for the last couple days I had a CE of between about 75 to 85 feet which I may say would be plenty good. So last night I fortified myself in the chapel, not that I haven't always been arming myself, but I was sure that today I would have to do extra well—I was due for my ten hour check.

Well, to make a long story short, I passed my check today with a CE of 96 feet. I felt pretty good about it. I will take little of the credit tho, 'cause I know Who makes or breaks me in all I do and hope that I never forget it. Our instructor (Joe Brown and I have the same instructor, so when I say "our" or mention "Joe" you will know what I mean) seems very pleased with us and so far we have comparatively low CEs. Saturday I had a hot day with five shacks out of twenty-seven releases. Joe and I are next to each other alphabetically so we sweat out lines together, fly together, work on the trainer together and so far our CEs are nearly the same. This is good because if one gets ahead of the other it is a strain on the fellow behind.

Tomorrow we are flying again. This time we will calibrate instruments. All instruments on aircraft have some slight errors. These are determined by flying at different speeds and altitudes, comparing with a corrected instrument, and then we can add or subtract the errors and obtain correct readings.

This noon I ate less than usual in order to stay awake in the afternoon. The boys will tell you that after a big meal it practically is impossible to stay awake in class. So after class tonight I was hungrier than ever. Just for the books, I ate one plate full of spaghetti, potatoes and carrots, a few crackers, a dish of Jello, two pieces of chocolate cake and drank a quart of milk. We had ground meat in the form of hamburgers and meatloaf for the simple reason that it was all they could buy. We usually however, have two different meats every day. This noon though was meatless and so was tonight, but meat or no meat, chow is something which nobody misses if they can help it.

Most of the notes we take in class are marked "Confidential," and some "Secret" stuff we have to keep in our heads. There are penalties for leaving a notebook containing confidential material in class after dismissal and for leaving the footlocker unlocked even if your buddies are left in the room. So we lock the lockers to visit across the hall, unlock when we want something out of it. Briefcases must also be locked. If you take off or land with the bombsight uncovered—though there may not be a soul within yards of it—they really jump on you.

Congratulate Peg for me on the new baby. When all the Cahills get producing it will really be a mess of uncles, cousins, nephews and nieces.

Tomorrow night the CO has arranged a dance for our squadron at the super sophisticated hot spot of Albuquerque known as Club YWCA. At least we won't have school that night and it might prove entertaining. Tell the boys I don't know when I can write but will try.

Your loving son, Tommy

JACK - MARY ELIZABETH
Sioux Falls, South Dakota, August 11, 1943

My brother, Little Patrick, referred to previously in these letters, held the baby limelight for the first two years of his life until others of my generation started joining him. In 1943, my dad's brother Frank was the first to issue competition when Mary Elizabeth was born August 7.

Dear Mom,

I was more than elated to hear of Peg's baby. It must be the topic of conversation in the House of Cahill. For a girl that is supposed to be anemic, Peg sure did a swell job. Eight pounds and six ounces is a big kid in any woman's language. Tho it was a girl, causing me to lose a fin to Jerry, I am still glad. Boys get monotonous after a while. Not that Little Pat is, because you know he is the cutest kid there ever was. But being a girl sort of introduces a novelty into the family.

I wish you would let me know what they intend to name her. It had better not be Betty because there are too many in LA now. If Betty R. doesn't like that, tell her we have two Pats, two Jacks and when the friends of the family are all with us and a name is called, no one knows who in the hell is wanted.

I like Jane or some simple and common but not too often heard handle. However, since Frank likes to be different, and he just showed that, she will no doubt get some different name. But if he has any ideas about operatic names that the kid would despise the rest of her days, I'll either shoot him or hang a decent nickname on the kid. After all, I am the Godfather!

Nothing would please me more than to be there for the Baptism. Maybe Bob or someone could stand up for me, but it won't be the same as my being there. I just hope I and all the rest of us get out of this mess well enough to enjoy the little lady's company and maybe have a bunch of kids ourselves.

I think I will have to spend my time making money enough to build a bunch of barracks to quarter our families in whenever we have a party. It will be out in the Valley so we won't disturb the neighbors and it won't be worth a cop's while to go out there.

I got paid yesterday and celebrated last nite. The barracks was well represented in town. I got rather tight but not disgracefully so. It will hold me for quite some time. Don't feel angry at me, Mom. I explained the situation a while back. We walked back to camp and I was able to pass the scrutinizing eyes of the MPs without being quizzed. Like I said, it will hold me off for quite some time.

I am enclosing $10 toward the phone bill. You can take the balance from my money in the bank. It will leave me with a clean slate.

I want you to make your plans for going to Tom's graduation. It is something no mother should miss. He has worked unbelievably hard and it will be just over a year when he gets out. He is in better physical condition and his mind is as keen as a razor, but a rest wouldn't hurt him in the least.

You are to use the money in the bank that I have, and if necessary, you are to cash in part or all of my bonds. I want to hear no talk about the latter being un-American or the former being absurd. I am not in the habit of giving you orders, but this is one case where only "yes" will be taken for an answer.

As for my getting home, that is too far in the future to think of. I'm sure when the opportunity comes I will be able to get there. Be sure to take all the money you can as I want you to have only complete enjoyment.

It will do you a lot more good than it will me and will make up for the trip to Emporia that you didn't get. So no matter what goes on at home or what Grandma will no doubt say, you are to go.

This is all for now. I have been getting all your letters. Keep 'em coming.

Your loving son, Jack

Jack mentions above the novelty of a baby girl arriving in the family. After his sister Patricia was born in 1912, the next children in the family, seven, were all boys. Little Patrick followed in 1941 to make it an eight-boy stretch. I haven't found any subsequent comments on how Jack felt about the name chosen for the new baby, but I do know he didn't shoot Frank. Though my cousin went by "Mary" into adulthood, Jack's concerns about her liking her name were prophetic. Later in life, Mary legally changed her name to "Liz".

JACK - DANCIN' THE NIGHT AWAY
Sioux Falls, South Dakota, August 14, 1943

Dear Mom,

Well, this is Sunday and also the Feast of the Assumption. It feels more like the latter because, even tho I went to church, I still had to go to school.

We had a check-in code today and I missed it by one letter. I know I have a good ear for it as I put down 114 letters and all were right. We have to take 8/min. for three minutes and are allowed five errors out of 120 letters. Under the old rules I would have passed as you only had to get 40 consecutive characters. I expect I will do OK tomorrow. We learned about radio vacuum tubes today. Next week we will meet the "Quiz Kids." They are a highly publicized bunch of characters who give oral exams to see you how dumb you are.

Last night being Saturday, we couldn't resist going to town. Andy and I went to the dance and we had a swell time. The strongest beverage we drank was coffee. So you know now that my eyes weren't deceiving me when I say I danced with a girl who is blond, a little taller than I and looking for all the world like Greer Garson. She is definitely a honey and I have a date with her Wednesday.

Did I tell you about the old time dance last Wednesday? It was a lot of fun and those old gals 40 and 50 years old really go to town. We had a dance "Promenade" or something where you keep changing partners and they fairly well tuckered me out. At one time they had a "butterfly" and I had two young kids (high school age) on that one. It was terrific. I was the only one of our bunch in on that, and the boys all cheered and laughed and got a big kick out of it every time I went by. I had on my new shoes and darned if I didn't slip right in front of them. It was a lot of fun tho.

How is Peggy and the family now? I sure wish I could see them. Guess this is all for now. Hope to hear from you soon. Say hello to all.

Your loving son, Jack
YOUR LOVING SON JACK A BIG KISS FOR YOU
-.-- --- ..- .-. / .-.. --- ...- .. -. -. --. / ... --- -. / .--- .- -.-. -.- / .- / -... .. --. /
-.- .. .. / ..-. --- .-. / -.-- --- ..-
P.S. Do you have a picture of me in uniform you could send to Jerry? I have none and he wants one. Take one from my book?

TOM - THE CALIBRATION MISSION
Albuquerque, New Mexico, August 16, 1943

Dear Mom,

Again I must write during class—study hall. I'll confess that I am so fascinated by *The Robe* that I read it during the little time in which I might write. When I can, I will send you *Random Harvest*.

Wednesday we flew the calibration mission I was telling you about. My position was in the nose. We were between 150 and 250 feet off the ground and made six runs past the ground station, each time increasing the speed until we hit 165. I had on my GI flying suit—really high-class overalls with zippers on the legs, sleeves, pockets and down the front—and my parachute harness. I just roasted up there under those circumstances.

Poor Joe was in the back checking the navigator's instruments. When I went back to see him he was really green. It was very bumpy and in the tail it is much more noticeable. One look at him and I was almost ready to go myself. By some rather corny jokes in an effort to make fun of the situation, and hanging onto the old breadbasket, we landed with all parts still inside—but plenty mixed up.

This Wednesday we are going on another pilotage mission. Where, I don't know. The most likely spots left are Amarillo and El Paso. Thursday we start our bombing missions. We won't take any bombs along this time but will practice procedure and teamwork with the pilot—which is all important.

Formerly the instructors flew every mission with the students. Under the new system, however, after the first few trips, we (Joe and I) will fly with just the pilot. That means Joe and I will take turns co-piloting.

At first it will be just lowering the landing gear, working flaps and out-of-reach switches but after a while we may get some practice on the controls.

I passed my ten hour check—think I told you that—and Friday my instructor wanted me to take my 17 hour. It is a more exacting test than the other, and part of it is done with one, two, three or all switches on the sight "off."

I had quite a bit of luck with it, but the flight commander ordered my instructor to have me wait until today. Today we had a lousy sight and so did not take it. Tomorrow probably we will and I think I can pass it all right.

The dance at the YW turned out to be a swell affair. All of us got telephone numbers and Yours Truly did quite well for himself, and so Saturday night I had my first date in about fifteen weeks. There seems to be no place to go but the hotel bar—where we can dance—and I fooled everybody (including myself) by staying very definitely on the wagon. I also had a swell time.

Sunday I went to Mass and Communion at Immaculate Conception, back to the base for the graduation review and then to bed and read part of *The Robe*.

I have not seen the Clarks since the first time but expect to go out this weekend. I'm going to rent a bike if I can and perhaps see more of the town.

Albuquerque won the Pickle Barrel at Big Springs yesterday. One of our boys had an average CE of 54 feet which is nothing short of amazing. I would give a lot to make the Pickle Barrel team.

Once selected, you are no longer under the command of the cadet detachment! No school! No athletics! Nothing but bombing. And if you win the meet and the colonel bests a few fellow colonels and generals out of a couple hundred skins—well, the sky's the limit to what you can have.

My mail still is unanswered including ones from Jack and Jerry and lots more but they will just have to wait.

Jack did say he got about four of my letters to you so the "system" is working and he knows at least what I am doing and vice versa.

Five weeks down and thirteen to go. It looks pretty good now but we are really just starting. After this week we will be dropping the real McCoy and every one counts, so remember me and my bombsight hand when you pray and I'll try to do the rest.

Your loving son, Tommy
P.S. (8/17/43) Passed my 17 hour check.

JACK - THE SOFTBALL GAME
Sioux Falls, South Dakota, August 23, 1943

Dear Mom,

It seems ages since I've written you and even longer since I called. How is everything and how is my niece?

I am now on 10/min. I passed my light word check with no errors yesterday. You could have fooled me when she said no mistakes. Ten isn't bad but you would be surprised at the difference in speed.

Tomorrow, I meet the Quiz Kids. I guess I told you of them. I expect to do OK. This last week class has gone fast but it cleared up several things of the days gone by that were a bit foggy. Tomorrow is our last day of circuit analysis. Next week we try and make a radio. We will go into this week's subjects in much more detail too. I am beginning to like it now and since we send for an hour a day in code we really have a little fun.

I have been playing a lot of softball lately. The left side of the barracks plays the right and we have some swell games. I haven't really played ball since we left New Hampshire and I had to learn all over. My throw to first base was nothing short of miserable, but now I can come about plus or minus four feet. I am playing my old spot, second base. We have lots of fun and we play in the cool of the evening. I really enjoy it and it affords wonderful relaxation after a hard day. Just now I am in a hitting slump but hope to improve.

Before I forget, the PX has an abundance of Hershey bars; the big ones. I will send home some come payday. Do you use semisweet or otherwise in cookies? Let me know as I will send them next week.

I had a wonderful letter from Jackie today and a picture of Little Pat. He sure is a big kid now. I will have to meet him all over again when I get home. I can't wait to see Mary 'Lizbeth. Be sure and send a picture when you can. Tell Jackie I will write her in a few days when the news is new and interesting.

What's doing with Aunt Mary these days? I have been a miserable correspondent on that score. I saw *So Proudly We Hail* last night. It is about the nurses in the Philippines and is truly marvelous.

I'll take a break now and hold this 'til tomorrow. I am about due for a letter from you.

Cont. August 24. Rec'd yours this a.m. This is the last day of the week and so I am a bit pooped out. It is awfully hot now, a dry heat but for the most part the weather is wonderful. I expect we will have an Indian Summer.

Our laundry is four days late and I am low on sweat sox. School starts soon and I am out of material to write about. Give my regards to all.

Your loving son, Jack
P.S. I was reading your letter in the chow line and a guy asked when was the book being published?

TOM - MY FIRST REAL BOMBS
Albuquerque, New Mexico, August 24, 1943

Dear Mom,

We are on a new schedule again. Reveille at 03:45, flight line at 05:00, ground school 10-12, chow, then two hours of school in the afternoon, athletics, chow and taps at 7 p.m. It is sort of a graveyard shift I guess you would call it.

Today I dropped my first real bombs, from four thousand feet and I had a CE of 60 feet on the first and 50 feet on the second. Converted to 12,000 feet it gave me an estimated CE of 88 feet which is not bad, 230 feet converted is needed to qualify. However, I have 148 more to drop and I only hope days like today will be the rule rather than the exception.

I have a new duty today, to take pictures of Joe's bombs. We remove the camera hatch in the floor near the tail, and with a 35mm movie camera, picture the bomb. It gets rather drafty there with some breeze coming from the hatch and a lot from behind through the bomb bay doors.

After I dropped my bombs (Joe had already dropped his) we had a little time to kill and my instructor told me to pick out objects on the ground and practice. So for about an hour, I was sighting on bridges, powerhouses, factories and most fun of all, trains. It is much more fun to aim at the real McCoy than just a circle on the ground. I had the pilot going all over the place.

Yesterday we practiced a few dry runs on the targets. On the way home the pilot asked me if I washed out of pilot school. Telling him "yes, primary," he let me take over the wheel and for about half an hour I was having a swell time. Later our instructor won't fly with us all the time and we should get more stick time.

Jack was swell to offer you his savings in order that you might come to graduation. I hope that I'll get home so you won't have to but I don't know just what will come up. I checked with TWA about flying here to save you the long train ride and it will cost just about the same from what I figure. I would like you to make the trip though.

Halferty, Davy and Amspoker, all from my old gang at Santa Ana and Hemet, arrived Sunday with the new class. It is good to see them as I knew them all quite well and we spent many weeks together.

In dead reckoning navigation class today the lieutenant happened to catch me sleeping. So I stood for the remainder of the period—which fortunately was not long. I knew all he was talking about backwards and he was just killing time 'til the end of the period. This DR will really be fun. We are not allowed to look out the window while navigating and must keep track of where we are on a chart.

I'll close this now so you will have some news anyway. Let me know where Jerry is and tell the boys I'll write when I can—perhaps this weekend. Keep your fingers crossed.

Your loving son, Tommy

P.S. If you see *Liberty* magazine for August 21st, there is an article about a bomber crew which got shot down. Lt. Dowart, the navigator, is in our squadron now. He's quite a boy and looks about as much like a hero as Lord Fauntleroy.

TOM - CHASING RAINBOWS
Albuquerque, New Mexico, August 27, 1943

Dear Mom,

Today has been really a day to write home about. As we happen to have an hour free due to exams this afternoon I'll try to tell you about it.

For three days we had been dropping bombs. This morning, for those three days, my estimated CE was about 153. Yesterday I had a 185 which brought it up and today we were to bomb solo—without an instructor in the plane. I had not yet dropped one outside the 200 foot circle and only 4 outside the 100 foot but my instructor told me I could do better and, for my skin, I had better. I had done pretty well, he said, but he wanted more than that.

This morning I was to bomb first and Joe would photograph. The lieutenant came out to the strip to see my preflight inspection and of course, I had to make a couple mistakes which he warned would be my ruin. When we were all set to go he left and I could see he expected the worst.

We were to bomb from 15,000 feet above sea level and 10,000 feet above the target. After takeoff I climbed up into the meat house and warmed up the sight. By the time we reached our scheduled altitude the clouds were only about 100 feet above us and part of the time we were in them. The first dry run over the target I couldn't even see it. The second time I saw it when we were right over it and the third time I spotted it in time to get my sight all set up.

We opened the bomb bays doors and Joe, back at the camera hatch, about froze. The temperature was not much above freezing. We had oxygen masks on too which made it rather awkward. Well, I managed to drop four bombs but the target was playing "now you see it—now you don't!" I'd be sighting on the darn thing and then I couldn't see it so I'd take my eye off and make a couple adjustments and back to it again.

As I've told you before, I pray out every bomb and today they really were answered—all four bombs landed between 50 and 90 feet of the target. Best of all Joe got pictures of them which will put them on record.

The fifth approach I was determined to get a shack. (Joe got one yesterday from 10,000 feet.) Everything was synchronized perfectly, racks open, trigger up. About three seconds before it would drop I couldn't see anything around me but snow! Even if I blew the shack to Kingdom Come we wouldn't have a picture so I dropped the trigger, shut off the switches and closed the bomb bay doors. The pilot meanwhile just dove her down and we were homeward bound.

Our instructor met us with "Where have you been?" Some of the fellows in our flight had come back before us and had dropped no bombs. Two other crews at the same target we were at didn't drop a bomb—and when we told him that I had dropped four and all within a hundred feet!, boy, he jumped up, grabbed my flight record and dashed into the flight commander's office. He was really pleased and now if I can just drop my qualification bombs as well, I will have nothing to worry about.

Flying solo was really an experience—I should say bombing solo—as everything was up to me and I had nobody to lean on for help. I had never seen the target before and with the weather the way it was I found out just what I was capable of. The pilot was a swell Joe, and when he gave the order to go home I had to climb out of the nose into the co-pilot's seat. He had seen where the bombs were hitting and he gave me a slap and mussed up my hair and said he sure wished I could have dropped the fifth one.

Then, as the bombs were all armed and dangerous for landing, Joe and I had to put all the pins back in them. Yesterday (not on our ship) one of the bomb shackles came loose, the bomb was armed and the instructor picked it off the rack and dropped it out the camera hatch. There is not much explosive in them but there would be danger of fire.

Tomorrow morning we are flying a dead reckoning mission to some place in Texas. Until now all our navigation missions have been pilotage—navigating by ground landmarks. DR is all instrument reading and plotting on a chart. If you look out the window and try to locate yourself you are likely to get a failing grade on the mission. Incidentally the highest grade you can get on a navigation flight is 85%. They claim that a perfect mission—split destination and on time—is the result of compensating errors, as navigation is an art and not an exact science. That 85% business is hardly anything to spur you on but you will flunk under 70.

This afternoon we had a 3-1/2 hour examination in DR and I think I did pretty well. I need to work faster in the air and I'll do alright. Our instructor told us if we dropped our bombs OK not to worry about us failing navigation. His name is Lt. Conniff and though he can make us real mad as the devil (and don't think we can't make him mad!—and don't think we don't!) he knows his stuff and is too exacting, if anything. However, I don't care how much he raves as long as I get through and can really bombigate.

Last weekend I made it two in a row on the water wagon. I blow hot and cold on this bombardiering so easily that I'm going to play it safe. I'm flat this week so Halferty and I are going to have a bull session at the PX tomorrow night. He will be confined for quarantine for three weekends so we can talk over the good old days.

Your loving son, Tommy
P.S. We flew right through a rainbow this morning. In the air they appear as circles.

TOM - FIBBER McGEE'S CLOSET
Albuquerque, New Mexico, August 31, 1943

Dear Mom,

Good things come in bunches I guess. Your letter and this month's pay arrived within five minutes of each other. Such good news. Frank's going to OCS—Jerry home—Mary Elizabeth—and that picture of Little Pat! I expect when I next see him he'll walk up to me and say, "Hiya, kid," and then break a few fingers as he shakes hands. Speaking of pictures, I have my camera fixed now and shall try to send you a few glamour shots.

The last few days have been loaded with action. Saturday I landed in Amarillo on a navigation flight. We had Maj. Rosenthal, director of training for pilots, no less. Tried to find DeMent but couldn't.

Yesterday I didn't drop any bombs but today I started on my record bombs. There will be forty in all and the average CE must be under 230 feet. So far they have all been practice bombs and I averaged about 135 or 140 feet CE which is a pretty fair score.

Today the automatic pilot broke down and we had to fly the mission manually. That is, with the automatic pilot I really fly the plane at the bombsight. The autopilot is much better coordinated and more sensitive than a human pilot.

Consequently on one bomb today, the pilot banked the ship just as the bomb went away. This, of course, threw the bomb out to the side. Ordinarily the force is in the direction of the plane, but this force plus the outward motion caused by banking the plane caused the bomb to hit out at 340 feet.

In 21 bombs so far that is the first one outside of 200 feet and the fifth outside of 100. In spite of that one bad bomb I averaged about 165 feet today on five bombs. Tomorrow with half a break I expect to really lower that CE.

It is these 40 record bombs that practically determine whether I get through or not. Twenty will be dropped at night but the first twenty will be dropped this week, I think.

Incidentally, tomorrow some fellow from the Air Inspector's Department will ride with me to see how they work things at Kirtland Field. I guess it is something to be chosen for this as they would not send anybody who would botch things up too badly.

We continue to visit with the Clarks. Tut would really be surprised if he knew his uncle rides me back to the base every time. It is always his idea too and not just Mrs. Clark's. We, Bohlman and I, were out there Sunday and they had a couple girls for us that were really OK. One's father was a bank president no less and I think this weekend we will follow up.

The Clarks are really swell to us and we feel right at home there. I'm going to buy some sheet music to work on out there.

Well, I've got a mess of junk to clean up now that has been accumulating for weeks—like Fibber McGee's closet—and I'd better do it tonight. Will write the boys tomorrow or next day.

Your loving son, Tommy

P.S. Instead of coming here for graduation (knock on wood) how would you like to go to Frisco? It would be less traveling and more time to rest. Maybe fly both ways.

P.P.S. Money order as soon as I can get to the post office.

Fall 1943

TOM - BOMBSIGHT MALFUNCTIONS
Albuquerque, New Mexico, September 6, 1943

Dear Mom,

This morning reveille is at 11:00 as we start night bombing tonight. Of course, we could not sleep that late this morning, but it was good to stay in the sack until about nine. After that I went down to get my parachute repacked. This is done every 60 days.

I hope my ears didn't deceive me yesterday, but you didn't sound so tired on the phone as you did the last time, though it hardly seems there is any change in the circumstances. Nevertheless, I hope somehow there is a letup.

There is not a heck of a lot to talk about right now. I have dropped half of my record bombs and by the grace of God I have kept the average under two hundred feet. I say by the grace of God because on all four missions we had trouble.

No automatic pilot on two missions, and on one of those two I was sick. I don't know what it was but I had chills and a fever and a headache, so consequently had difficulty sighting. My reactions were about twenty minutes behind and it is a wonder I hit the target at all. Anyway, I only felt that way for a day and feel fine now.

The other two days we had sight malfunctions—Friday there were three no less. As our bombs hit under 230 feet, though, we have to keep them on the record. As my instructor and I agree, the score does not mean anything when you operate with a bad bombsight. We both know what I am capable of and that is most important. This is about all for now. Will write later and tell you about night bombing.

Your loving son, Tommy

TOM - A DAY IN THE LIFE OF A BOMBARDIER
Albuquerque, New Mexico, September 9, 1943

Dear Mark,

I've been owing you a letter for so darn long now that I think I had better get on the ball. Mother says you are a great help to her and that is swell. You'll be quite a boy when I get to see you, what with working and all.

I received Mother's clippings from *Life* magazine and they are very good. Perhaps you'd like to know how we fly a mission.

This week for instance we are flying nights. The first thing is to dress warmly for our high altitude bombing. At 15,000 feet it gets to just above freezing. Over the bombsight you sweat but if you are in back taking pictures, the open bomb bay doors and camera hatch make it pretty miserable, and thoughts of California's sunny beaches are too much to bear.

Anyway...about fifteen minutes before the formation to go to the flight line, I start getting dressed. Over my underwear goes my athletic sweatshirt—suit—like basketball players use, you know. Heavy socks and GI shoes. Then my flying suit. This is not very heavy but is wool gabardine and quite warm. It only has two pockets, one below the knee and the other on the right breast—both with zippers. Into these I put locker keys, fruit drops (Beechnut!), Saint Anthony's medal, pencils, erasers, a flashlight and three paper bags in one—in case I get a sudden urge to get rid of my dinner (so far have kept them). Then goes my leather jacket, and with my bombardier's kit, I'm about ready to go.

Then, the bell, and we march off. It is of course, about 10 p.m. and everybody is wishing they were home in bed, but somebody usually starts a song and we sing all the way down to operations. Arriving at operations, we discuss last night's mission with the instructor and prepare for this one.

From the bulletin board we find which target we bomb, elevation, winds aloft, ship number and all the necessary data. We take turns being first bombardier. He gets his chute and oxygen mask, goes out to the ship, sets the altimeters and gives the sight a preflight inspection. He is also co-pilot on takeoff.

The second bombardier gets the camera, checks the oxygen supply in the ship, sees to it that all bombs are properly stationed in the racks, and after takeoff he removes the arming pins.

Climbing to flight altitude, the first bombardier has to figure the exact altitude to fly as pressure and temperature affect the altimeter reading. At flight altitude the second bombardier helps the pilot to adjust the automatic pilot. From then on the business begins.

Your first bomb is away and you lean way over the sight to see where it hits. Left, right, over or short, there is a reason, so while the pilot is swinging around to make another run, you check your sight for a malfunction and review every move you made and prepare for the next run.

This time the heading is different. That means changes in ground speed and drift so you have a new problem. After the second run the headings go back to the first and then the second again and so on. After five not so hot bombs, you start wishing the hell you never heard of being a bombardier. Hitler gets his share of the blame.

When you have a good night on the sight the cold doesn't bother you so much and you even try to sing through your oxygen mask. Nobody can hear you but you, and Oh! it feels good to have the CE go down for a change.

Sometimes your reveries are interrupted by troubles. A bomb won't release or the bomb bay doors won't close. You try to crank the doors shut by hand but it's no luck. So you hang on tight, reach down and pull the damn things up by hand.

Coming home is always fun. Regardless of your luck, the night is over. No matter how much you love flying, there is still no place like bed. The field at night has the runways illuminated by rows of lights with big red arrows. The pilots seem to land just as well at night as in the daytime.

Back at operations we turn in our reports and estimates of hits and go home. Chow may be anything from hot cakes to steak, and whether you call it breakfast or supper, it is still hot and good, and that sack is the next thing on the list.

Of course, everybody is telling everybody else what a hot bombardier they are. Last night at 4,000 feet we had ground speeds of 180 mph. Boy, that target was really coming at you. I had one 10 foot and one 15 foot bomb, and also a couple 200 footers!

And that's the way it goes. We love it but I guess there are times we hate it too. But who doesn't feel that way about a job? Stick at it, Marcus, and maybe we'll be seeing you come Thanksgiving.

Your loving brother, Tommy

Col. McHaffie noted in his compilation that Kirtland Field was chosen by RKO Pictures as the location for filming the movie, "Bombardier." Squadron personnel were selected to support the production, provide technical advice and recommend sites for particular scenes. The movie began filming in 1942 and was released the following year. It starred Pat O'Brien, Randolph Scott, Robert Ryan, Eddie Albert and Ann Shirley.

TOM - DEAD RECKONING
Albuquerque, New Mexico, September 13, 1943

Dear Mom,

Well, I can't say anymore that I have never been airsick. Outside of about three horrible minutes when I earnestly desired to die, it was all very funny. I shall always remember it as being funny. The story is rather involved so I'll go back a bit.

We flew nights all week long with good and bad results, then Saturday afternoon, in order to give us a little sleep, we had a combination bombing and navigation mission scheduled. I mean it was scheduled in the p.m. so we could sleep in the a.m.

It is very bumpy over rough terrain in the afternoon. We were to fly a pair of geographic coordinates in the desert and then fly a "dogleg" to Hot Springs, New Mexico. This by dead reckoning done by the first navigator, Joe. Arriving at Hot Springs he moved into the nose to drop a couple bombs on targets at the Deming School. Well, going down I never had such a rough ride in my life. I'd been carrying a couple paper bags in the pocket of my flying suit for weeks and never had occasion to use them—never having been sick.

Well, when Joe came up to bomb, I moved to the back and was almost gone then. However, I persevered for a couple minutes and then bang! I grabbed the bags, placed them on the floor between my knees and proceeded to cough up some of the best chicken a la king I've ever ingested. I must have looked like I was salaaming to Buddha or somebody 'cause my instructor happened to look around at that precise moment. He damn near died laughing, and made Joe stick his head around the instrument panel and watch the fun.

After the aforementioned horrible minutes, I knelt in the beautiful cool breeze coming through the open bomb bay. I had kept my bag all this time (not quite sure if I was finished) but by the time Joe was ready to drop his second bomb I waited with the bag and its contents poised over the bomb bay. As soon as Joe set up the dropping angle and let his bomb go, I let my missile go too. I don't know where it hit but I wish Hitler could have been at least near to it.

As I was supposed to be first navigator going back, it was high time to get to work. My instructor, still enjoying my previous exhibition, was nevertheless solicitous of my well-being and desire to navigate. As I was feeling fine by then I told him it was OK. Then we surprised the devil out of him by turning in 0-0 missions, that is, split destination and estimated time of arrival on the nose. I never did see where my bombs hit. They were water-filled bombs and not until an hour and a half out did we discover that the water was leaking out.

Coming back to the field it was a scream to see the boys with their buckets going out to clean up their ships. I didn't spill a drop, but they were less fortunate. Despite dozens of lectures on aerodynamics, some still tried the "direct approach"—right out the camera hatch. This results in one-half minute's pleasure at watching the stuff go down and then it's "Duck!" because straight back it comes and puts a delightful finishing on the top of the cabin unless you catch it in your face.

The more I think of the whole day, the funnier it gets. Everybody laughs at themselves and everybody else so nobody minds. I guess the only way to treat such a messy subject is as a joke.

Night bombing is terrible, cold, and consequently accuracy takes it on the chin. I only have nine more record bombs to drop and if I can keep them inside about 250 feet of the target, I will have an average of around 200 feet. I guess the Pickle Barrel will just have to be a dream for me, but with all the trouble Joe and I have, we are learning a lot of bombing, and the war won't be won at a Pickle Barrel contest.

We are only flying a couple days this week. We start dropping combat bombs. We fly evasive action up to 40 seconds from point of release then synchronize. From 4,000 to 6,000 feet the targets are about 125 feet square and from 10,000 feet about 200 or 350. They are refineries, docks, convoys, battleships, etc. and are scored singly as hits or misses. We are required to get 23% hits. After a week or so to see how I'm doing, if things are going fairly well, I'm going to start getting fitted for my officer's uniform. Oh, happy day! My instructor (we are getting a new one for combat procedure) says that our work (Joe and I) is good, and if we just keep it up, we should have nothing to worry about.

Saturday night in town I ran into Johnny Robinson who was with me at Santa Ana and Hemet. Also in town were J.R. Lewis, Broderson and Sherman. Out at Kirtland, Davy, Amspoker and Halferty—from the old gang—heard they were in town and we had a swell reunion. When your outfit gets broken up you just figure that the Army will send them far enough away so that you will never see them again. They were certainly a swell bunch, and the week after next they and others that didn't come this time are coming back and we expect to really paint the town.

Also, Saturday night I took my date out to the Casa Manana. There it seemed almost like being at a club affair as I knew everybody there, the old gang from Hemet and the present bunch, and it was quite a welcome change from going every place and just knowing your own party. I was also on the wagon through it all. My date was very attractive (a widow of all things) and very lively so I did not need anything else to have the best time since I left Los Angeles.

This morning we were having a lecture on bombing probabilities. From thousands of bombs dropped, tables have been compiled telling just how many bombs it takes to do certain jobs allowing for dispersion and probable errors. For instance, you might want to bomb a bridge just badly enough to delay the enemy—maybe only for six or eight hours. Well, by looking up in the tables the size of the objective, etc., you come to the conclusion that seven bombers will do the job.

At this point somebody always wants to know why they don't send about a dozen bombers and really wipe it out completely? Well, the instructor argues that it isn't necessary to demolish the bridge, that they only can afford to risk seven airplanes and so forth, to no avail.

Finally, Lt. Purick gave us a parable that no one will forget. "Suppose," he said, "I tell you that this girl Lulu you have a date with, will, from my own experience, become mellow on only one beer. But, though I have proven one beer to be sufficient, you don't wish to take any chances and so buy her champagne. Now, I ask you, comrades, why the hell waste all that champagne when one beer will do the job?"

There is one thing about Lt. Purick, you never sleep in his classes. He knows his oats too. We are now studying the D-8 bombsight made by National Cash Register Company. Of course this brings up the old gag that if you don't get a shack, the sight rings up "No Sale."

Enclosed is a picture of the ships we fly in. They are supposed to be the best training planes the Air Force has and the pilots here seem to agree. That's about it now.

Love to all, Tommy

TOM - IGNORING MR. BELLAMY
Albuquerque, New Mexico, September 20, 1943

Dear Mom,

It is 06:30 and so far the teacher has not put in an appearance. Monday is always horribly confused. The other days are just confused. We fly today and tomorrow at noon, Wednesday and Thursday at night and

Friday in the afternoon. So far there is no flight scheduled for Saturday which is a break. The instructor is here now and I shall try to finish this in snatches.

Today we started having wing staff officers who are cadets. Big cheese in this stinking mess is the worst example of a cadet and male biped homo sapiens, B.P. Bellamy, Jr. I have been in the same squadron with him ever since I have been a cadet and nobody knows him better than I do. Somebody gave him a swell shiner about two weeks ago and I don't know of one person the least bit sympathetic.

The worst thing is we are supposed to salute these jerks by order of the major. So, starting today, we are going to avoid saluting Mr. B.P.B. as much as possible and we will, as much as possible, salute fellow cadets because of their "rank"—that is latrine orderlies, room orderlies, squad corporals, table monitors and just plain cadets.

Spent a quiet weekend due to a collapse in my financial structure. Sunday afternoon Cassidy, Booth and Bell were in town and we came out to the field and I showed them all the ships on the line. We also went through a Curtiss Commando. They are cargo carriers and you wouldn't believe the size of them. The pilot has to have twenty-twenty eyesight just to see the wings—they are so far back. Inside, the ship looks like the Hollywood Palladium the morning after.

We have completed ten weeks here and there are actually about five more weeks of work. Last week we only flew two or three missions and my total bombs dropped did not increase very much. If we only get past this week I will feel much better. We have had such poor bombsights that I don't know what I can do with a good one. My instructor tells me it is in the bag and not to worry but, with all the dough being spent in this war, they would do us a great favor to buy some new bombsights. They cost $15,000 each but I would like to figure the cost of a mission which we fly and don't drop bombs because of the sight or bombs which are thrown out because of malfunctions.

You mentioned something about Pat selling the car. The only thing I own in it is the rubber seats and they will be a selling point. I don't know what Jack owns of it but I think Bob could handle it as he sees fit, though I would speak to Jack about it first.

I've been checking with TWA and I can fly to Los Angeles in four hours. As soon as I know exactly when we leave here I'll make a reservation. I can hardly wait to get home and will leave here the minute I can.

It is getting cold now around here and I hope it does not get too bad. The colder it is on the ground, the colder it will be up there, and at 15,000 feet it has been just about zero centigrade.

Your loving son, Tommy
P.S. Dropped five more record bombs today. Only four or five more to go and I can't miss converting under 230 feet. Don't stop praying 'cause you should have special influence and I must now get about 25 combat hits.

TOM - TOM'S BLACK EYE
Albuquerque, New Mexico, September 25, 1943

Dear Mom,

For three days now we have been weather-bound. This morning it looks worse, if anything. We canceled a navigation-bombing mission yesterday, bombing called off Friday night, but Thursday night we somehow found a patch of clear sky at 15,000 feet and I dropped the last of my qualification bombs. The general feeling here is like school days as a kid when snow canceled school. We are still going to school but we are having a little vacation from flying. Right this minute, outside looks just like when you fly into a cloud.

As I mentioned above, I have dropped the last of my qualification bombs. I now have about 75 or 80 more to drop but they are combat type on specific objectives such as docks, wharves, railheads and convoys. I'll be required to get 30% hits on these which should not be too difficult.

We were ordered to have our uniforms by two weeks and so yesterday I was fitted for a blouse and one pair of dark green trousers. Next I'll order a couple pairs of pinks and shirts. Also I'll get a couple dark green shirts. The reason for ordering so early is to allow time for tailoring— even the shirts. Some of the fellows are buying trench coats but I think they are rather impractical in wartime and that a short coat and raincoat can be obtained for the same money. We are also getting two shoe stamps which will make the wardrobe complete. So far most of the stuff I've bought has been Hart, Schaffner and Marx and pretty good.

I hope to have some money left from my uniform allowance to spend on that time off. I also hope to be able to get you a new dress. After all, if it wasn't for you there might be one less 2nd lieutenant in the Army. While most of the boys will agree that less shavetails wouldn't be a bad idea, for my part, I am grateful for the opportunity.

There is another Pickle Barrel contest tomorrow at Midland, Texas. Our boys are at a disadvantage this time because we have only been bombing for about five weeks while all other schools are graduating their entries next week. I think they will throw the meet anyway because if we make it four straight there will be an investigation as to why we win all the time and that will mean trouble. They made the colonel a brigadier-general because of the Pickle Barrel.

Mark deserves a pat on the back for the idea of sending me Babe's picture. I happened to open the letter in class and five navigators began plotting courses to LA. If we should come in a body, they want the necessary data on the girls in the background.

The major is trying to get us to sing at all formations. We flew a couple nights this week, and while we were sleeping at 7 o'clock in the morning, the other classes went to school singing loud enough to wake the dead—and us gadgets. Consequently, when we fly again from 22:00 to 02:00 there is going to be very little sleep in Borecky Square when we come home.

In honor of our new cadet wing commander, I wrote lyrics to the tune of "Around her neck she wears a yellow ribbon," He struts, he struts, just like the Little Corporal, And we must all salute him, And bow before his sway, Hey! Hey!, And if you ask us, why the hell we do it, We do it for the pair of bars so far, far away. Far away, Far away, Oh, we do it for the pair of bars so far, far away.

And so it goes, never a dull moment.

I'm staying in tonight to attend a camera class—and so is almost everybody else. As I have told you, we take pictures of each other's bombs. Once in a while we don't get all the pictures. We don't see the bomb, not awake or sometimes, intentionally miss taking them.

Now, when Joe accidentally drops one way the heck out of the pasture, I don't take a picture of it, he estimates low enough to convert under 230 feet and that is that. He would do the same for me. Fortunately, we have actually had only to do this once or twice. Then too, you have camera jams, fail to sight properly, so miss pictures that way.

Some of the group have been getting by because they missed so many pictures and estimated their bombs much lower than we have. In this situation, Joe and I find that, comparatively, we have been much too honest. While I as a rule can't compromise with any such goings on, nevertheless, you can understand our position and that we should not cut our own throats as the standards to graduate actually are not what the school sets up—but what the student does himself. So now we will probably start taking two pictures of each bomb to allow a miss later.

I know that I can bomb well above the necessary standards, my instructor agrees (he's coaching the Pickle Barrel team), and what the actual figures are do not matter.

Other than this one circumstance, the honor system works pretty well here. On some subjects I have done very well, others around 80 or 85%. In no case have I had to resort to anybody else's work, but in fact do a little "tutoring" in the barracks.

We are still getting all the stuff they can throw at us. Yesterday they announced that 90 hours of navigation and bombing have been dropped from the course for the following students and we are the first, last and only class to go through this grind. I know that we get dead reckoning ratings, which our underclassmen won't get. They won't have Mercator flying (that is flying on a Mercator chart by trigonometry and logarithms), radio navigation or astrocompass. I'm personally glad to get all this but I've been a cadet for an awful long time now.

My old gang of pilots graduate October 1st. There are some of them coming to town tomorrow and we will have another reunion.

With all this shortening of the course, we are led to believe something is definitely in the wind and once we leave here there won't be much time wasted. I'm trying to get B-25s, but the pilot is doing most of the bombing in them now and a B-24 will be our "medium" bomber, so I shall have to be satisfied. We may get a chance to drop a few from a B-24 before we graduate. I hope so. I'll send you some money after payday. Fingers crossed.

Love to all, Tommy

P.S. We are now playing soccer instead of volleyball. We only wear sneakers and shorts and I think it is going to lead to bloodshed. Everybody is getting mad at everybody else. So far I have one black eye (in exchange for a few bruises) and future games should simulate combat conditions. XXXOOO

TOM - THE PARACHUTE JUMP
Albuquerque, New Mexico, October 9, 1943

Dear Mom,

Received yours today and I'm sorry to have been slow in writing but several things have happened to upset things. In the first place I flunked an exam last week probably because of letter-writing between periods and during the "least important" parts of the lectures. In the second place I've had a cold which grounded me a couple nights and rendered me not quite up to a decent letter.

The most important subjects have now been covered in ground school. Remaining now are code (hi Jack!), aircraft identification (duck soup), naval identification (I like it very much and perhaps might shine on sea patrol if I get hot at it) and other odd stuff.

I've dropped about 100 bombs now, have about 1/3 of my required hits and should get the rest next week. And so it goes in a more or less downhill fashion. And so goes my morale. The hard grind is almost over. Eleven months as a cadet (ask Frank how it would be to go through OCS three times) and I can't wait to get through.

I'm no longer "eager," after months of lecturing on being on the ball by officers who are misfits and must be assigned to tactical jobs.

I can't quite believe I'm almost finished and perhaps that is because I'm not yet. I've surprised myself a lot of times by doing things I never figured I had the guts to do. What I'll do on the Big Job we don't know yet, do we? Right now, just let me get home for a few days and from then on let's not waste any time. Anyway, it all boils down to about two more weeks of putting up with the inherent confusion attached to any authority around here. I'm just going to keep on praying and "sweating it out."

Tonight (Saturday) I'm CQ, charge of quarters. This is not too bad as my date went out of town this weekend and I'll be able to have a good weekend following. After that, on Saturday at midnight (the 23rd), we go on bivouac. We'll do a little bombing there and if I have my hits in I hope to experiment with a little "skip" bombing. We'll also drop a couple real demolition bombs just to get the feeling of having our butt blown up around the ear drums.

Also, tonight I've borrowed a radio and it is worth staying in to hear some of my favorite programs—Saturday Nite Serenade, Koussevitzky and the Hit Parade. I'm looking forward to coming home and having a little jam session. I sing whenever I can with results no better than ever but I enjoy doing it.

Before I forget it, Bobby mentioned—or rather you did—about him perhaps getting in the Air Force. I don't know what he intends, air or ground crew. About the latter, I can't tell him much about cadets. The deal now is to also have aviation students, some training as cadets but former enlisted men, drawing pay at their former rank plus for dependents, etc., plus flying pay. I'm presuming that if a civilian wanted to join he would also draw for dependents. This was the main motive for the change—to enlist those who would transfer if they could get allotments for dependents. Up until now, it has been $75 plus food and no dependents. Bombing and navigation is interesting, offers "swift rise" to a young man and the future is a little brighter since they put a gunner in the nose of B-24s.

Bobby likes mechanics a lot and maybe that is what he meant by Air Force—another good racket and a little more to come home to after the war. However, right now, I prefer him as the guiding hand with Jackie in my fast growing nephew, Patrick Joseph.

Had a letter from Tut this week and I guess he is on his way, shipping out.

Mark will do well in the Navy. If I couldn't have made a cadet that is where I would have gone. I know that the grass is always greener in the other guy's backyard, but that is how it looks to me.

Today we made a dry run on a parachute jump. They have a platform about 20 feet high out there with a chute harness on a rope—a weight on the rope. You buckle the chute, holler "Geronimo" and dive off. If you jump off you have to do it over again. As I was CQ I had to get it over quickly and get back again.

All the boys had on zoot suits but I didn't have time to change. I got up to about fifth position in the line. First was Terry who used to be a paratrooper. It was more fun than a barrel of monkeys everybody hollering up, the guy in the chute solemnly shaking hands with everybody on the platform.

Before I knew it I was being buckled in, and, as in such matters, the longer you wait the harder it is, the boys got quite a kick out of the way I did it. Not wanting to have to get chewed out for anything approaching a jump, I dove off with my feet definitely above my head. Wow! It seemed funny as hell to be just going head over heels but not for long. I used up the slack in the rope, the weight picked up and there I was hanging there. If that is all there is to a parachute jump they won't have to order me twice to abandon ship.

Incidentally, don't worry about a chute failing to open. These chest packs open very easily and, the normal means failing, you can rip the darn thing open with your bare hands.

And that is the way things look from here as the radio commentators say. Had a letter from Eleanor Hunt yesterday and she says she has her 500-hour pin for working at that Army Plane Spotting Headquarters. That is a lot of hours for spare time. Don't worry about a thing. Regards to everybody.

Your loving son, Tommy

P.S. *Flying Aces* has an article about cadets at Kirtland you might read. The bull is pretty deep but when I get home perhaps I can give you the real story. If it was as tough as they picture it, I would have washed out long ago!

FRANK - A CHOICE BIT OF FLUFF
Monroe, Louisiana, October 19, 1943

Dear Ma,

Just a few lines and an enclosure about the school which I thought you might enjoy. It will give you an idea why I haven't written much and then only to Peg.

Of course, a lot of this OCS stuff is baloney, as Tommy or Gerald can tell you. The papers make it sound tougher than it is. They do occupy a lot of your time here tho.

We have a general coming in tomorrow and are putting on a review. Also we are moving tomorrow. The worst thing about this place is the food, anyway.

In case Tommy gets sent into New York, or thereabouts, be sure he gets the address and phone number I've enclosed for Alice Belbey. She is the sister of a friend of mine who came down here in our group from the Gap.

I spent the weekend at his house before we came down, and believe me, this kid is some dish. About as choice a bit of fluff as there is. Tommy would be very welcome there, so tell him to be sure and use that address should he hit that vicinity. It's just across the river from New York City.

There isn't a great deal doing here; next week we go on the range from 4 o'clock Sunday morning until the following Sunday. Live in tents, etc. However there will be no book work which will be a relief anyway.

Peg said something about Gerald going to Idaho. That is probably the world's worst place to spend the winter.

I don't know where I'll go, although I am going to try to get a California assignment. It would be nice to be able to come home for a change once in a while.

This isn't much of a letter but I guess I had better get back to my studying.

Hope all are OK.

Love, Frank

TOM - BOMBARDIER WINGS
Albuquerque, New Mexico, October 22, 1943

Dear Mom,

There remain 20 days, 17 hours and about 15 minutes until graduation. By the time you get this I will probably be on bivouac—roughing it! Hubba Hubba!

Today we got a taste of being a soldier when we were issued a blanket, canteen, helmet liner, mess kit and a piece of canvas with ropes attached to it whose purpose I am hardly able to guess. We also have been getting weather reports which say it will get colder if anything. Already overcoats are the thing for breakfast and the air temperature gauge in the ship reads zero before we get off the ground on these dawn missions.

My friend Kay, a native of these ol' parts, says that one of the coldest spots in all New Mexico is Santa Fe—and that is where we will be. Fortunately it warms up around noon and as we will do all our bombing at night, perhaps we will sleep through the coldest part of the day. We are leaving razors at the barracks and I'm bringing my camera so I should have some good pictures.

I'm brushing up on my card game. It has been a long time since I've had time to play and as I have so little to lose, I shall play with a certain vim which has been lacking in our hithertofore sporty games.

Our mess kits are beautiful. The silverware does not have "H" for Hilton Hotels on it but it would be much better than Hilton's in hand-to-hand combat. The rest of the service set is rather in need of cleaning and it grieves me to find that there is no partition for salad. If they will just serve spaghetti up there it will be OK with me. However, as beans are also quite fluid, and as we will be on field rations, you can guess at least one third of the menu.

There was an awful discussion as to whether or not we could bring our winter flying clothes. They are very bulky and quite a problem to the transportation department. Well, it finally developed that we will bring them and chances are they will win a great reputation as a sleeping bag. They have zippers all over and you can just lay down and zip yourself in.

Of course, most of us have had some preparation for this at Santa Ana last winter sans heat and hot water.

Your cookies came, were seen and were conquered. Needless to say, they were up to and perhaps surpassed your usual high standards. I say perhaps because just your usual would be difficult to surpass, and second because they are the first home cooking in so long that comparison was difficult if not impossible to make without prejudice.

For a couple weeks now we have been on field rations rather than the usual cadet mess. While this is probably the same food that the rest of the boys are getting, and I certainly don't deserve any more than they do, it has been rather a strain on my just-getting well-regulated digestive system. While I am not starving and enjoy enough of the food to be fairly content, nevertheless, the sight of one GI giving me one piece of butter (and another standing there to make sure he didn't give me two) tells me definitely that "The Country Club of the West Coast Training Command" is no longer a country club. I ventured to ask for a second piece of cake the other day, but unlike Oliver Twist, I got it without getting a thrashing, though the man-at-the-cake took a quick look to see that the sergeant was not watching. Hubba! Hubba! I'm really at war now!

We had planned a dinner dance graduation week really formal and all that, but we can't get the ration points so nobody knows what we'll do.

I've got most of my bombs dropped now. I have only dropped one more since I phoned you but got a hit with it. It was a rough ride though, 8 below. Connors dropped nine bombs and I was on the camera. He broke the tube connection on his oxygen mask so I let him use mine. Then I'd hold his together, take a couple gulps and go back to pictures. It doesn't hurt any to be without it at 15,000 except that you tire very easily and eyesight goes haywire a little. I'm all finished with that high altitude stuff now and have some 500-foot bombs to drop. If we don't bring a camera along I'm going to try some skip bombing.

Albuquerque lost the Pickle Barrel Contest last week. We had it well in the bag when one of the boys had an accidental release which ended up around 700 feet. All the rest of the bombs were swell. I think if we won one more meet there would have been an investigation.

I also have bought all my uniform except a raincoat. Nobody seems to have them so I'll try LA or the PX at Santa Ana. Anyway, the stuff is beautiful, and after bivouac we will no longer wear our cadet clothes except our insignia. Also, I bought a pair of bombardier wings. They are made of cloth and rhinestones or something—anyway, they look much better than the metal ones (which also keep punching holes in the blouse) and I have left you the dubious privilege of sewing them on when I get home. Don't think I'm getting a "hot bombardier" complex, but for a whole year now everybody has been telling me what I can and cannot wear and how I should wear it. While I'm still subject to certain regulations, on this little point I am having my way and when you see them (the wings, hot cha!) you will agree.

Tomorrow we are also going to fly our last navigation mission (so they tell us). It will be an air plot and should be lots of fun. The pilot flies out a while on one heading, then turns on another, and so on four or five times. The navigator (if he hasn't bailed out after about the third change of course) keeps plotting these headings on the chart and how long he flies them. After about an hour of this sort of stuff the pilot says, "I'll give you ten minutes (maybe 15 or 20, I don't know yet) to find out where we are and tell me how to get home." As you are not yet a lieutenant (and he may be a major or captain) you can't tell him to go chase himself but must go to work and figure this mess out.

The navigator in the nose also has fun. You can fly for a long time in this country and never see anything but desert to give you a checkpoint. So I have figured, mathematically, that if we have a wind of 500 knots by true air speed on true heading I'll be some place within an area of 48 square miles on the first leg and after that keep multiplying. After about four legs, I'm someplace within a couple hundred square miles of God knows where. Very simple.

Won't know about the furlough until graduation. Meantime, take care.

Love to all, Tommy
P.S. Can't send any money payday but will have some when I get home or if I don't get home will mail some. Should get home though. XXX

TOM - THE FEATHER MERCHANT
Albuquerque, New Mexico, October 25, 1943

Dear Mom,

I'm afraid that this son of yours would not have done so hot as a soldier in the field. I sigh for my dear, warm barracks and GI bunk. Of course one gets adapted to these things and learns the tricks which mean little comforts. These tricks are well known to Joe Brown who is in our tent, and without him I don't know what us feather merchants would do. The feather merchants include Walt Clark of Pasadena, Ed Connors from Michigan, Cassidy and Cherry from New York. What we know about pitching a tent or making it habitable after somebody else puts it up might well be summed up in one word—nothing.

We left Kirtland in the dark early Sunday morning by truck for Santa Fe, about sixty miles north. I found my barracks bag in the truck, dug out my blanket and managed to exist throughout the three-hour ride.

There was one helluva wind coming down from the north so the first thing we did was to put on our fur-lined suits and boots. The next four hours we spent putting up tents. At the last moment they abandoned the idea of pup tents and we set up six-man affairs. I found out by using my bean a little I was able to suggest a couple short cuts and we were one of the first to finish. By that time we were able to remove part of our flying suits and get back to just ODs.

Eleven-thirty we lined up for chow with our mess kits and the food was as good as we get now at Kirtland since we went on field rations and better than at Las Vegas. Of course, I have a 1917 mess kit without the new partitions and everything flowed together. Being extremely hungry it was quite enjoyable. Best of all were some slices of onion, about 1/2 inch thick which were eaten just as is.

In the afternoon we helped the officers set up their tents and at 4:30 they had Mass down on the flight line. The altar was the elevator of an AT-11 ship that I'd flown in before. If I get a chance to fly in it again, I expect to have a swell mission.

Also in the afternoon, the wind died down to a whisper, but with the setting of the sun we could just feel it getting cold again. We were not scheduled to fly last night so we got ready for bed. I had a half shelter canvas on the ground, a raincoat, my fur pants over them and a blanket. On top of that I had two more blankets and a quilt. To the boys who have no doubt done some tent sleeping this may be quite a lot of comfort, but to this feather merchant it looked like a cold night ahead. I wore my sweat suit and sweater for pajamas. About midnight I put on my fur-lined boots and thus endured.

We were up at 05:30 and all I cared to manage was a cup of coffee. Then we found out our squadron was not scheduled to fly. So, back to the sack this time, fur-lined suit and all, and that is the way I'm going to sleep tonight.

We did not even bring razors with us so I'm just relaxed to the idea of getting good and filthy. Sack time will be logged in quantity. One athletic instructor came with us, and the last I saw of him, I don't think he was enjoying himself. Whether he will take it out on us or rediscover that heart he lost some time ago, I don't know. We will have a couple hours of school also. The rest of the time will be spent playing cards, writing letters and sleeping.

The City of Santa Fe is northeast, and above it the mountains are snow-covered. The elevation here is 6,300 feet which helps keep the place cold. The latrine is about a quarter mile away and when the sun is high enough to shine over the canvas wall, I'm a-goin' down there.

We will have gas attacks by AT-11s sometime during the day and also a few flour bombs.

Saturday I did fairly well on my air plot mission, and the bombing was more fun than I've ever had. I was scheduled for 500-feet bombing with the D-8. The D-8 sight is nothing more than two pieces of wire set at different dropping angles. I could make one myself. Anyway, as the bombs were instructional the pilot and instructor and I were all anxious to have some fun. So, the first three we dropped from about fifty feet. On one of them we "snuck up" on it from the rear as the pilot said. There was a hill to the right of the target, behind it two smaller hills. We came buzzing along at 195, around the hill then between the two little hills. "There it is!" and bang! knocked the hell out of the target, a bridge 50x100.

The last bomb he said, "Want to dive bomb?" I, of course, was all for it. So we climbed up about 3,000 feet. "Hang on!" and down we went. He pulled up a little too soon I think 'cause we hit short but it was sure fun. I hope I can specialize in that stuff. I think my touch of rheumatism will be uncomfortable at high altitudes anyway. It doesn't bother me now but it might.

That is about it now. All in all, we are having fun and will be back at Kirtland Saturday. I have my uniform all bought and Saturday night I put it on. Hot cha!

Love to all, Tommy
P.S. The dread news has just been posted. "Calisthenics at 12:45."

TOM - BIVOUAC RECAP
Albuquerque, New Mexico, November 1, 1943

Dear Mom,

I started to write to you Friday on bivouac but was rather rudely interrupted. At about 16:30 Friday we put up a smokescreen over the field. Bombers from Kirtland were to try to teargas us through the smokescreen—providing they could find us—and if they couldn't, I'd recommend washing them all back to cadets at least. Anyway, the wind shifted making our screen utterly worthless except in the area of the latrines. The smoke had all cleared away and still no planes, so we figured they were weather-bound at Kirtland as the weather in general was bad.

Figuring as everybody else did, that there would be no gas attack, I left my mask in the tent and set out to wash. About twenty-five yards from my tent I saw three planes hell-bent for leather coming at our area about treetop high. As our own planes had been buzzing the field all day, I decided to get a picture. I crouched down and snapped just as they were over me, noticing at the same time two apparitions under the plane whose only purpose I knew was spraying gas.

And I was right—but too late.

I caught a whole snoot full of the stuff and I thought it would burn holes in my face but the after-affects proved to be harmless. At that moment, however, it was far from harmless to me. I dashed back to get my mask and by that time the stuff was all over the place. My mask kept out any more but the stuff inside was strictly tearjerker. I just had water running out of my eyes and nose in a steady stream. At the place where we were to evacuate to, I found more of the boys in much the same condition and looking at each other just streaming tears. It was really funny. After a bit, the planes moved out and I went back to wash my face which by then felt pretty good.

The boys will tell you that teargas in Army nomenclature is classified as a "lachrymator" and "non-persistent," the latter meaning it will dissipate in a few minutes. The former description is undoubtedly true but under the circumstances we were in, I would never call it "non-persistent." It had been raining during the day and it was quite cold. So the gas hung over the ground and would not clear up for love nor money.

The tent refused to let it go, so with gasmasks and flying suits, we went to the outdoor movies never minding the rain, as we knew what it would be like back at the tents. But as all earthly things must do, the show finally came to an end. Back at the tent the stuff still hung about a foot off the ground. We ventilated all over the place. Then we built a dozen little fires of paper to perhaps lift the gas out with smoke. This did little but add smoke to the mess and giving the whole thing up as a bad deal, we went to sleep with masks. By this time, also, the novelty of living "in the field" (brother, is that word "field" descriptive) had worn off and we were all glad to tear the tents down in the morning.

All in all, bivouac was not bad. We logged plenty of sack time—that is, those of us who had dropped a lot of bombs, and the food was much better than I ever dreamed it would be. The pilots were all for getting to and from the targets in a hurry and guaranteed to give us a good buzz when we got back to the field.

Speaking of buzzing, today it will delight civilians I'm sure to learn that we ran at least twenty pounds of good beef off an animal this afternoon. We "snuck up" over the hill and there he was all by himself and the temptation was too much. With a "Hi Yo, Silver" our pilot peeled over after him and we sent him galloping. There is a gasoline shortage here and so any extracurricular activities have to be done on the trip out and back. Now that we have our hits, all we go out for is fun. Dive bombing and stuff like that. The tension is off and it certainly feels good.

I still don't know where I'm going from here or if I'm getting furlough. As I told you we won't know definitely until a couple days before graduation. Chances are fair of getting a lift on a B-24.

Wednesday we go into our officer's uniforms while our cadet clothes go to the cleaners. A week from Wednesday night we are having a dinner dance and all the instructors will be there. Wednesday Don Hendricks is getting married in the chapel and Dick Frodl and I are going to serve Mass.

Just wrote to Frank but not since receiving the address of the "fluff" in New Jersey, which sounds pretty good. You know with Jack, Jerry and Frank traveling all over the country I should be able to build up a pretty good address book with the proper cooperation. I in turn will turn over my meager findings. Meager, except for one deal here in Albuquerque.

Enjoy your letters immensely but don't worry about cookies. Send them to the boys as I may be able to have some soon, right from the oven.

Your loving son, Tommy

JACK - RADIO WAVES
Sioux Falls, South Dakota, November 5, 1943

Dear May,

Just a line or two to let you know that I am alive and well, except for a cold. I can't say much more than that due to the fact that there is nothing more to say. I owe a bunch of letters.

School is of course as usual and we have taken up the very high frequency command set. It is a wonderful chunk of mechanism, and is really an ideal set, for the most part. It employs "pushbutton" tuning which makes it easy for the pilot. It is used extensively by the RAF, and is said to be one of the main reasons for the British winning the Battle of Britain. Without going into deep technical facts I will try and give you a few reasons why.

Radio waves can be controlled, and on the lower frequencies, as on the radio at home, the waves go thru the air and along the ground. They can go only so high until they hit what is called the "ionosphere." This causes them to bounce back to ground and again be refracted to the sky, etc. This manner of transmission is common.

Now on very high frequencies, there is no refraction to speak of. That makes it impossible for the enemy to pick it up. This is called "line-of-sight" communication. On the ground the range of it is only 10 miles. At

10,000 feet it will go 100 miles and at 20,000 it will go 200 miles. Even this has a formula to figure range.

On the VHF there is no refraction to ground, so even if the enemy knew the frequency, they couldn't pick it up.

I hope it is clear to you but if it isn't, I'll tell you all about it when I get home. Maybe the price will show you what a fine quality it is. The total cost, transmitter and receiver, is $16,000. It is really a sweet job and a modified version is expected to go a long ways after the war.

After reading this over, I doubt if you will understand it. However, if it is OK with you, I will swap you "easy-to-understand" lectures on radio fundamentals for some good old home cooking.

If I can, I may go in for radio after the war. I have a pamphlet showing possibilities for the postwar world.

We are doing OK in code. I'm still on 18 but whittling it down. I honestly expect to pass twenty per before I get out. That will give me an 80% for code.

This is the 15th week and our last radio to learn. We have two weeks of maintenance and in the second week of that we go to the Quiz Kids. I have a multitude of notes to take a glance at between now and then. It is surprising how fast the time has gone by. It won't be long now.

The weather is a bit cold and it snowed a little bit today. It has been trying to do it for a long time, almost like the snow clouds were constipated you might say. I expect it will be covering the ground shortly.

Today we had a bit of excitement. A Lockheed commercial plane came in with his wheels up. The pilot realized it in the nick of time, and I saw the plane suddenly pull up into the blue again. I guess it surprised the passengers, but if he kept on coming they would have been more surprised.

I went to the old-time dance Wednesday and it was a barrel of fun. I had a hot time doing the "butterfly" with two girls from Iowa. It was really groovy! The square dance got me tho. I was one-half of the fourth couple and I kept getting mixed up. The older people there understand tho, and they are always giving you words of encouragement. I get a big bang out of it!

Overheard in the barracks column: There was a monk in Siberia, Whose days grew wearier and wearier, He done to a nun, what he shouldn't have done, And now she's a mother superior.

Well Mom, I've said enough and maybe too much! I'll close now and hope to hear from you soon. Say hello to all.

Your loving son, Jack

TOM - THE GOLD BARS
Albuquerque, New Mexico, November 7, 1943

Dear Mom,

It's Sunday morning and all is peace and quiet. Most of the boys didn't come in last night which leaves me the place practically to myself. I'm waiting to go to Mass at the chapel at 1:30 and it's a good time to bring you up to date.

You have probably received my graduation announcement by now. Walt had one left over and I thought you might like to have one. They have to be ordered months in advance so I didn't get any. It's just as well, too, because expenses seem to be mounting and there is some little thing I must buy every time I turn around. There are some things which I will leave go in the hopes of buying them in LA.

One of the best buys I've made so far has been three pairs of gold bars. This afforded me considerable pleasure as you may understand, and after a year of waiting the cost in money meant nothing.

I am at present working on a deal to ride to LA in a B-24. There is nothing definite as yet. I may have to leave so suddenly that I can't wire you. However, I should know by Friday or Saturday and tell you whether or not to expect me.

Yesterday, our class, including this feather merchant, received the Good Conduct Medal. That is the red one with white stripes. We are all quite agreed that it should have been a campaign ribbon for being cadets so long. But it's all over now, so who cares?

By some generous buck-passing, Walt Clark, my roommate from Pasadena, and myself find that we are in charge of our graduation dance Wednesday night. It will be held in the gymnasium and Capt. Shipkey has given us from Wednesday noon until the dance in the evening to clean the place up, build the checkroom and ha! ha! decorate the place. In order to do anything we have to get permission from captains in charge of this, that and the other thing. The main problem is to get the lights somehow dimmed, fix up the checkroom and steal some furniture for the colonel and his wife and numerous other colonels and majors, etc.

As master of ceremonies, I got Lt. Languinetti to agree to give out in his own inimitable style. He is a graduate of Santa Clara, witty as all get out, makes a big hit with the ladies, and knows enough about military customs in social life not to pull any boners. He will be the biggest factor we have to make the affair a success.

Lt. Lawrence is dishing up a buffet supper. Everything is so last-minute that we won't even have the invitations until tomorrow. For decorations we are going to ordnance and try to borrow a few empty bombs. They are painted blue and would be converted into a number of different things.

We are all finished school now. This week we are supposed to get class passes which means we only have to be on the post when we have a formation.

Happy birthday to Patricia. I have a pair of bombardier wings for her that I'll bring home or send if I don't come. Also happy birthday to Bob and isn't Little Pat's birthday this month?

Thursday morning Don Hendricks is getting married and Dick Frodl and I will serve Mass.

I hope to be able to ease Gerald's financial situation but not right away. It may be six weeks before I get paid again after leaving here. An officer has to pay cash for so many things that I've had just handed to me that I don't know just what I'll do.

I'll make about $245 per month with flying pay, and it will cost about $100 for a room at the BOQ and meals plus insurance and dues at the officers' club, and after that we can start figuring. I should be able to take most of the burden from both Jack and Jerry.

All for now.

Your loving son, Tommy

At Kirtland and other training schools around the country, aviation cadets' leadership and organization skills were polished, and their ability to perform under pressure was evaluated. Trained to be officers first and bombardiers second, a total of 53,000 bombardiers graduated during the war.

In his Kirtland compilation, Col. McHaffie quoted Major General Eugene L. Eubank, an early base commander, on the responsibility vested in bombardiers: "The greatest bombing planes in the world take him into battle through every opposition, and in thirty seconds over the target, he must vindicate the greatest responsibility ever placed upon an individual soldier in the line of duty."

This is Tom's last letter from Albuquerque. He graduated from training and received his commission as 2nd Lieutenant (and those gold bars!) on November 13, 1943. He then had a short leave home in Los Angeles prior to departing for operational training in Columbia, South Carolina.

TOM - CAROLINA IN THE MORNING

Columbia, South Carolina, November 29, 1943

Dear Mom,

I hope you will forgive the delay but things have been so upset and uncertain that I just couldn't write. A postcard or short note might leave too many things unexplained that no news was perhaps the best.

The trip was quite eventful. It was impossible to get a wire to DeMent and I only had a couple minutes in Amarillo. During that time I phoned him but they called for takeoff before I could get him to the phone.

Arriving in Kansas City I was welcomed by lovely gals in the employ of TWA whose sole occupation was meeting planes as they came in, finding what rides were available and putting servicemen on them. I just missed a plane to Nashville by a couple minutes so spent the afternoon waiting around. I had not opened Bob's candy and that afternoon seemed like the ideal time, so with the girls and another fellow waiting for a ride, I shared the candy, which incidentally tasted swell.

In the middle of the afternoon I rode to town with a couple of our hostesses, delivered a couple captains to a hotel and toured downtown Kansas City. As it began to look like there would be no ride that day, when we got back, one of the girls made a reservation for me at a hotel. Then I got my baggage at the terminal and the station wagon was waiting at the door to take me to the hotel. What service! Unfortunately, the girls were on the evening shift at the office so I was still without a date for the evening.

I stayed at the Continental, had supper there and proceeded to see the town. I had two or three drinks in the bar there with a marine who had just been discharged and the place was lousy with women. However, as some of the women were rather lousy too, I moved on to the Muehlebach, I believe it was. There I swapped lies with a couple liaison pilots from the artillery. They left about ten to "catch a train" so I adjourned to the coffee shop to wallow in my beloved chocolate cake and milk.

Fortifying myself with some black coffee, I, by some fast talking and throwing my rank, convinced my waitress that I would leave Kansas City with a very unfavorable opinion if I had to continue my tour solo. Being proud of her city and not wishing me to have an unfavorable opinion of KC, she accepted my offer and now I have left there with a much better opinion. As she had to work the following day (Thanksgiving), I had my turkey at Fred Harvey's, alone. The turkey was very good, but turkey is not what makes Thanksgiving.

That evening, I boarded a chair car to Birmingham. I shared a couple seats with a pair of privates returning from Fort Riley. One slept on the floor and then we took off the backs of the chairs and flattened them out to make some sort of bed. There was not quite room enough to do this however, unless the guy behind did it, and finally the whole row from our seat back was flattened. Despite these efforts, I didn't get much sleep.

The next day we were rolling through hillbilly country. Some of the sights I saw made me rather ashamed of my country. Here we are supposed to be an example to the world (and we think we should be too) and yet we allow such conditions to exist. While even at our worst we are perhaps much better off than conditions are, say in India, nevertheless, the rest of our country lives so well that I don't think such conditions should prevail. The term "the South" seems to cover a multitude of sins also.

From Birmingham we changed to another coach to Atlanta and Greenville, South Carolina. At Greenville we changed again (2 a.m.) and were on the last lap to Columbia.

I forgot to mention earlier that I also tried to go to New Orleans by air hitchhike and see Frank. Wednesday night my friends at the field called and said they had a ride for me to Monroe, La. However, consulting a map, I found that the time I would have spent visiting would have been taken up going from Monroe to New Orleans as I had figured things pretty closely. So I had to turn down the ride.

The next morning there was nothing immediately and, as the weather began to close in, I decided not to put in any more time waiting, but would take a look at the town by daylight. If I had known I was going to be there so long I would have looked up some of Clyde's friends, but I didn't take any names from him for that reason.

My impressions of Columbia are not quite collected, as yet. The sun was out Saturday morning but I have not seen it since then. There seems to be a perpetual pall of fog or smoke or some form of "hydroscopic nuclei," as we used to say in meteorology class, hanging over the city.

Sunday, Bill and Dick (my roommates) and I took a walk through the town and the university. The girls at the university have a curious habit of driving by and, seeing us (or anybody else perhaps), would hang out the windows, wave, shriek and holler in a manner which we immediately interpreted as "Southern Hospitality." However, they would keep driving like mad, and as all their actions seem to conflict with each other, I feel that their quaint goings on need closer investigation. We will have two nights a week out overnight and every night until 23:30 providing there is no flying or classes. After I get my bills paid will be time enough though.

After describing everything but this field you are no doubt saying, "Well, he's holding the best for last." That, Mom, is putting it mildly.

For a year as a cadet, among other things, I dreamed of the officers' club and living in the BOQ (bachelor officers' quarters to you). At Kirtland, the BOQ made Peckets on Sugar Hill look like a hot dog stand. Though I was not working just for the glamour of the commission, there were certain favorable aspects of the deal which could not be denied.

Now, I am at last in the BOQ!

There are sixteen of us sassy seconds living in a long low structure, divided into four rooms, with the walls, ceiling and floor beautifully covered with charming black tar paper. We have in each room one potbellied stove and one locker just about big enough to hang a change of underwear in. The latrine is communistic, an affair nestled in a gully about 75 chilly yards from the door. And, when it rains, the water rushes down the sides of the gully in rollicking rivulets which form a delta right around the entrance. Directly west of us is Branch #2 of the officers' club which does not open until eleven a.m., serves only sandwiches, and so a hike to officers' club #1 on the hill is necessitated. Otherwise it has only to boast of a nearness to the PX and laundry office.

On top of it all, we are going to earn a couple new ratings here. Not content with making us amateur radiomen-gunner-bombardier-and-DR navigators, we are now informed that the new B-25s which are coming here don't use a bombardier but a celestial navigator who in turn loads a beautiful 75mm cannon mounted in the nose. This means no bombing by us and we must learn celestial navigation.

Whether we ride astride the cannon or sidesaddle, nobody seems to know, but already we are trying to find our new name for our trade. "Cannoneer" had a brief spurt of popularity. "Bazooka Boys" is coming up fast.

"Cannigator" is a dark horse, but most popular of all is one which I cannot repeat to you, my mother. We are designing a new pair of wings with crossed 75mm shells rampant on a field of dividers and protractors.

And there is the Air Force. The reason, I guess, that "Nothing can stop the Army Air Force" is that nobody knows where it is going next—even the AF doesn't know.

Love to all, your confused son, Tommy
P.S. Tell Frank that by giving out with a smiling "Good Morning" to snappy saluting WAACS, you vastly improve the spirit of comradeship between officer and enlisted feminine personnel.

P.P.S. Also, expect to get paid about the 10th and enough to cover all outstanding debts. If this is too late, let me know. Have you seen how two second looeys greet each other? Shake hands with the right hand and then throw the left around the other guy's neck at the same time polishing his gold bars! What a life! Keep me posted on the boys' addresses will you? Will try to write them this week. Went to the dentist today for a couple small fillings and had my bridge re-cemented.

A few times in these letters, the boys mentioned "WAACS," as above in Tom's P.S. notation for Frank, but I also knew of the acronym "WACS." Research clarified that WAACS was created in 1942 as an ancillary unit, the Women's Army Auxiliary Corps. In 1943, it was converted to full status, thus WACS, Women's Army Corps.

JACK - NASOPHARYNGITIS
Sioux Falls, South Dakota, November 29, 1943

Dear Mom,
　　I'll try this again and hope it is worth sending on to you. Just now I am in the hospital again. This time it is nasopharyngitis. I guess to the average person that means head cold, severe. To say the least, it is severe. I expect I will be over it soon tho.
　　I came in here Thursday. The sickness on this post is terrible. I think some 600 went to the hospital yesterday and today it was worse. We have beds down the aisles now. In the last three days, 10% of the field's students went in. The reason? Physical training in such bad weather and those **!!??** Mackinaw jackets. It was the same last year and no one does anything about it.
　　The place is in a bad way here. I could no doubt leave here tomorrow but I don't want to; I am not ready. I will rest up a bit first. I think Classes 8 and 7 graduate together so I will join Class 8 if I can. That will make it around the 27th when I graduate.
　　I have a swell innerspring mattress now and I slept beautifully last nite.
　　I haven't shaved since Thursday and I feel a bit messy. I will do it tomorrow tho because the captain will be over with my pay. They pay you in the hospital by coming to you from the squadron. I think I will be in bed just for spite.
　　The Thanksgiving Dinner was terrific but I just didn't feel well enough to get it down. The best I could do was nibble. When I couldn't eat a meal like that, I decided on the hospital.

I wish I had my pen. I'm not used to this one. It belongs to the kid in the next bed. I will write a better letter soon. In the meantime, don't worry. I am OK. Be careful and say hello to all.

Your loving son, Jack

Winter 1943

JACK - STOCKING THE LIQUOR CABINET
Sioux Falls, South Dakota, December 1, 1943

Dear Mom,

Let me warn you that this letter will not be so hot. I was released from the hospital. I should not have been, as I wasn't ready, but countless are sicker than I. Six of us from 1116 were in at one time and I must say, at least six more should have been. At nite the barracks sounds like a TB ward. Mother, it is pitiful and so little has been done about it. I hope I don't get back there but will if necessary.

I have many letters to answer but I guess I will wait. Yours today was swell, and so was Tommy's picture. I will keep good care of it. I am enclosing one of my "Kansas Gal." The dogface is her brother; he has spent many months in Alaska. Put this some place, in my book or something. I would like a pic of Frank in uniform. Any around?

Well, Mom, this won't go any sooner so I'll end it manana.

Cont'd. December 2. I feel a lot better today and I expect I will live thru school tonite. We will still have a month to go. I hope I get Class 8 because a lot of the boys I know are in that since washing back. It is surprising, the ones that did, Jimmy Campbell, Tom Carroll and then some; all smart and consistent in code.

I put $20 in the bank today so it brings my total up to 40 bucks. I hope to have more before I get home, so if I can keep it up, and if I don't get home 'til after gunnery (which is very probable now), I will have 80 to 100 simoleons. We can have a lot of fun on that don't you think? Better get rested as much as you can 'cause you're in for a big nite. What a whopper we can throw on that. I suggest that Pat start putting in a supply of liquor. I am getting on in years you know and am almost old enough to drink.

I have not "had a bag on" in a long time, 4 months. I think it nice of me. Don't think me a soak or anything of that sort. I am, when I indulge, very moderate and can recall on the next day even the slightest of my actions, the spending of my money, and all in all, I am a good boy and no source of worry.

There is a shortage of whiskey up here and rum and brandy is beginning to become scarce. If any money is needed to stock our liquor cabinet, my bank account (in LA) may be tapped. It will be my share of Christmas cheer to the family. I can't do much more and do not want as much from you. As I said, I don't need a thing. I hope that Bob and Jackie and Peg understand.

I will be sure to fix up the young ones for Christmas. I couldn't forget them you know. I wanted to get Little Pat's birthday present but circumstances prevented. I have not forgotten him tho and will see to it soon.

Your cookies, my dear, were wonderful. They far surpassed the turkey dinner and so I feel that I am far ahead of the rest. Needless to say, they went a damn sight faster than any part of the turkey dinner could have.

Guess I will get this in the mail now. Hope you are all in good health and spirits. Say hello to all.

Your loving son, Jack

TOM - THE GREEN CHRISTMAS
Columbia, South Carolina, December 4, 1943

Dear Mom,

We got a partial payment today and the enclosed will take care of Grandma's check. The balance is up to you. I don't remember just what I promised Pat—the bonds could wait she said.

If Pat doesn't need this for the house, you use it on yourself. No bonds, no nothing. Go shopping if you can—take a cab. I'll send more next week when I get my travel pay.

Nothing doing here. No school 'til next week.

Going to town for some shopping now. Went to Confession Thursday but missed the First Friday. Don't worry. More later, but all for now.

Your loving son, Tommy

P.S. It doesn't look like we'll have to pay rent as the bachelor officers' quarters are not "adequate." It will be a green Christmas, I think.

TOM - FOLLOW THE LEADER
Columbia, South Carolina, December 9, 1943

Dear Mom,

I started to write to you on the 7th but since then so much has happened that I abandoned the first project. As there is quite a lot to write I'll use both sides of this paper. If you just lay it flat or any way that the light won't shine through, you should have no difficulty in reading it.

Yesterday morning I was scheduled to fly a mission labeled "Congaree Maneuvers." Nobody knew what it would be but I was to be navigator anyway. We took off about 11a.m. in a B-25-G (a la cannon) with a pilot, co-pilot, engineer, radio-gunner and Yours Truly.

We circled around this neighborhood playing follow the leader, I thought. In reality the pilot in the lead ship was looking for Congaree Air Base. It turned out to be about 20 nautical miles from Columbia and as yet had not been put on our maps. We landed there and a captain called the pilots into the briefing room, "And bring your navigators, too." (Actually we have not started school yet and were flying just to get our flight pay—"navigator" was just something to put on the records.) There, with dozens of maps, he explained our job.

The troops at Fort Jackson were having maneuvers and we were to act as support of the Blues and to make-believe strafe and drop flour bags on the Reds. The maps were made by the engineers at a scale of about one mile equals three inches. As we were always doing at least three miles in one minute and the maps were not very large, they really were not much help. Anyway, we took off and for a while just flew back and forth buzzing away.

Somewhere along the line I got curious about camouflage and troop movements and things of that nature which I was not required to learn. Little tricks like knowing where certain weapons are of the most strategic value, and looking for them first in those positions rather than all over the country, helped me find lots of things my pilot didn't.

This paid off later when the radio in Bill Bohlman's ship gave out. He had been in the lead ship, and we moved up to that position making me actually navigator for all three ships. At that time our next job was to bomb a few bridges with flour sacks. We were in the locality of the bridges but needed a pinpoint to come in on in order to have some element of surprise. So I told the pilot that the only place for our bridge was at the end of the road leading to the river, and as long as we were known to be coming let's come out of the sun and get some protection that way. So we did and we busted flour all over the bridge and let a few go at some civilians who were standing around.

Then I gave him a heading back to the field (which I put on my map when I learned its location). We got there OK, then after more gas (if the civilians could hear these pilots casually saying, "Oh, a couple hundred gallons will last me a few minutes"), more orders and off we went again.

There really wasn't much navigating—that is telling the pilot where to go. All our flying was in a certain area, but at all times I had to know just where we were, just how to get home or wherever we might next be ordered. For instance, the bridges were up toward Charlotte. Our ground speed averaged about 180 and ran from 160 to 200. I don't think we ever got more than 500 feet above the treetops—usually about 200 feet and that meant our visibility was quite limited for such a speed. (You could fly over a town and not know what it was because you could not see any other place in *relation* to it to be sure.)

As I told you, we are not on a regular schedule yet and these B-25-Gs do not have glass noses and, as yet, no good place for the navigator to do pilotage (navigation by recognition of landmarks, etc.). So the navigator has to crouch, half-sit, stand, scrunch or whatever you want to call it, between the bulkhead and the pilot and co-pilot's seats. This space is the width of the plane and is from a foot to a foot and a half, front to back. With nothing but breakfast in us and a candy bar we picked up, we were flying or getting orders again from 11 a.m. until 6:30 p.m. We actually logged 5 hours, 40 minutes flying time, and when we finished I was tired. This morning I was lame all over. Being tossed around there all day really took it out of me.

There was some compensation though. I flew almost enough to get in my flying time for November and December. If I don't fly anymore this month, it will mean that I made at least $125 for that day's work which is not exactly hay. I also learned a lot about troop movements and the efforts of these boys to conceal themselves; trucks and tanks were terrible but the artillery boys were excellent. It also gave me more confidence in my navigation at high speeds.

Today I figured on getting some sort of a rest but instead drew an assignment to the celestial navigation trainer. It is really colossal and represents about one quarter of a million bucks worth of bonds. It combines line trainer, which was developed for pilots to practice instrument flying, with the navigation instruments and equipment, plus a sky full of stars plus a movie of terrain going below the ship which I use to take drift readings on. I direct the pilot, he flies it, and in another room, our course as we fly it is drawn on a chart. At the end of the mission they compare where we went and where we were supposed to go and grade accordingly.

It is just like flying. The thing turns and banks and climbs and glides and does everything but make you airsick. They also have full radio equipment and today I had to take a couple of bearings which I have never done before. I finally ended up 2-1/2 miles to the right of destination but my estimated time of arrival was right on the nose. They gave me a 91 on it which pleases me a great deal.

I'd like to spend more time in the trainer and also really learn some celestial. There is about six weeks of theory before you can study celestial though and it's not part of the course here. These trainer flights last from two to four hours, incidentally, and the main thing is keeping calm because you can get rattled just sitting there sweating out ETA.

My other check came today. What I will do for Christmas I don't know. I won't get my flying pay until January 1st. Food runs about $60 a month including a few meals in town. No liquor or girls as yet to drain finances, but my old debts are paid up in part. I still have to buy another set of sheets and pillowcases, a pair of dividers and some woolen OD clothes to work in. I don't have a surplus of pinks and greens and will have less if I keep wearing them on flying missions.

This is my plan for Christmas. I'm not going to Richmond to see the Lowrys as I mentioned earlier. Transportation will be too crowded and cost too much money. Walt Clark and his wife have a house here and I've accepted an invite there for the holiday.

I've had some pictures taken and may get a few printed by Christmas. For gifts I'm going to send money orders to Jack, Jerry and Frank as I think that will be best. You know anything I send them is just something else to carry and the dough may help them get home or at least have a good time. For the rest I can only send my regards.

To you, I'm going to send something after my January 1st pay about which I am telling you now there will be no argument. As for me, saving any money, don't worry. The opportunity to do things I have wanted to for so long is so good that I can't turn it down. A month or two won't make much difference.

Reading Jack's letters makes me feel quite unworthy of such pulling for me as he did. To have the disappointments he has had in the Army and still wish somebody else so well, even his brother, is something which I hope I shall never forget or underestimate. It is still a thrill and with a feeling of pride that I go about my business of trying to be a good officer, but there are times when I can only thank my lucky stars for the break. There are so many worthy fellows who just didn't get that break.

Also at this field is Joe Callahan, pilot, from Concord and St. John's. I think he used to deliver the *Monitor* to Aunt Mary. I called him Tuesday and he is in my squadron but on the other schedule so that when I'm flying he's at home and vice versa. We're going to get together Sunday I think when I have the day off.

In the 426th Squadron is Ted Mulligan, also from Concord. He's a bombardier and I'm trying to see him. He's on the same schedule as Joe is so it's difficult.

Let me know if you need any money or if Pat does 'cause I can get hold of some from Bill or Dick. Incidentally, Bill and Dick and Joe Brakora room with me here. Bill and Dick were my buddies at Albuquerque, and Joe was in my flight for a while. Joe Brown is in the hospital having his tonsils out, but he and Walt are also in my flight, and so we have what you might call our own little gang together.

Your letter was nothing short of tremendous, as also the enclosures.

I still can't quite realize that I traveled about 1,000 miles yesterday, but I can realize that there are lots of swell places and people within a thousand miles that we didn't see. C'est la guerre!

This about winds it up I guess. I'm afraid there is not much continuity to this letter but I'm about due for chow so I'll buzz off.

Your loving son, Tommy

"St. John's" (St. John the Evangelist Catholic Church), mentioned above, was the church the family belonged to in Concord. It was also the name of the high school where my father graduated in 1934 and Tom graduated in 1937, just before the family moved to California. The youngest children, Jack and Mark, finished school in Los Angeles at St. Agnes High School.

TOM - FINANCIAL DRIVEL
Columbia, South Carolina, December 14, 1943

Dear Pat,

And how goes it? To my nicest creditor I should be a better correspondent but the situation here is rather SNAFU and I just don't seem to write.

The shock of finding that the enclosed money order is not for you will, I hope, not be too great. I tried to make my situation clear to Mom in my last letter and seemed to meet with approval. I'm on extremely thin ice right now but Bill always has liquid assets and can meet most of my emergencies. I think next month I'll give him my money and let him put me on an allowance. We go everywhere together and it would work OK. This you may count on.

After payday, the 1st, I'll send you a money order for $50. The slight difference between that and the debt accrued will be chalked up to interest, goodwill, Christmas—in fact, on the whole, I think I'm being pretty cheap about it. So start shopping for the coat.

This Christmas will probably be the screwiest one I've ever spent. Walt and his wife have invited me to dinner that day—if we aren't flying. Bill and I had a couple girls lined up but being university students they are going home for the holidays leaving Friday. However, as there is hardly any liquor around, just the general slant of things indicate that anything may happen.

A number of people will be neglected but I'll try to catch up after the first. I've had to spend about $50 for a flight jacket, pants, bed sheets, etc., other items not counted on beforehand.

But enough of this drivel about finances.

I'm going to write Tom and Monette (long overdue) and will mail it to the house where they will get it. Also the money order for Jerry, as I expect he will be there.

The weather today has closed in and all they are doing is instrument flying. I wasn't scheduled this morning, and hope I'm not tonight as I'm going to Joe Callahan's for chicken dinner.

I finally saw Joe Saturday at the parade and Sunday noon went there for dinner and a swell bull session. He said he flew up to Concord and couldn't believe it was so small. Then he flew between two church steeples, which kinda put the town on its ear. He married Mickey Rogers of South Street. Ted Mulligan from Concord is here but I haven't seen him yet.

Tell your friend at work that he doesn't need to worry about me bombing his hometown. At the rate we are going here, the war will be well over before I leave here.

That's about it for now.

Your loving brother, Tommy

JACK - DEAR MARK
Sioux Falls, South Dakota, December 18, 1943

Jack was two years older than his brother Mark, who entered the Navy in December 1943 at the age of 18. He was the fifth of my grandmother's sons to enlist.

Dear Mark,

Just a little one to wish you a Merry Christmas and the best of everything in your Naval career. I would like to give you a little something but I hope you will understand how it is. This will be a crummy Christmas for you and the rest of us, but it will damn sure make us realize what it really means, and when we are together in better times, we will not find it hard to get back in the groove. Of that I am certain.

It would be swell if you could go to San Diego because judging from here, Idaho will be plenty cold. Being close to home would be a snap too. I had hoped to see you before you left but just now it is SNAFU.

I won't lecture on what to do. That you will find out as you go on. But just be sure of the friends you pick. That is all important. Let your conscience be your guide and remember that uniform carries a lot of weight these days.

The first few weeks will be lectures and drilling. You will get tired but you will sleep "honestly." Pay attention and stay on the ball. There will be a lot of guys you will want to slug—that doesn't go. Keep quiet and take it. Don't stick your chin out—someone will knock it off, maybe.

You've been out in the plant working long enough to know how to do your share. You do that and you will get on OK. We are all in back of you and damn proud of you before you start. I know you won't let us down.

It will pay to have a lot of socks, shorts and handkerchiefs. I have over two dozen of the last and I just get by. If you think I'm kidding, wait 'til you hit Idaho.

Well, guess this is it. Be good and take care of yourself. The first year or so is the hardest.

Take along about 40 bucks if you can but take it easy on it. It will go like hell if you don't watch it, and it is a long time between paydays.

Best of luck and we're with you.

Your loving brother, Jack

JACK - FIRST CHRISTMAS AWAY FROM HOME
Sioux Falls, South Dakota, December 19, 1943

Dear Mama,

Just a note to keep you posted. I sent one to Mark this p.m. so you will be posted up to date.

I wish Pat hadn't told me in her letter to let my tongue hang out as a package was en route. It keeps hanging out more and more each day and hour. I think I looked rather odd with half of it stuck in my Mackinaw pocket as I walked along Phillips Avenue.

Kidding on the square tho, it has me guessing. I guess it will get here tomorrow. I will send a box home this week but believe it when you see it. I am awful lazy about such things you know.

I have a little something for the kids and the rest of it will be on the priority line. I hope the "little ones" like what I bought for them and I sort of wish I could wear them myself. They are about all I could get and are not like I used to have when I was a kid. I remember mine as clear as day and I sure got a bang out of them. One box, Little Pat's, is not wrapped. Could you take care of that for me? I only wish I could see him open it.

I tried to call you tonite but there is a four-hour delay and this joint closes in an hour or so. I wish you could get me word if Mark would be home on Wednesday nite. No doubt he will be busy shopping, but if I called after school, 9 p.m. your time, could I reach him? It would be swell if Bob, Jackie and Peg and all could be there, and Jerry, if he is home on furlough (that bejeweled hunk of paper!), I could cut him in. It will be a lot harder to get through Friday, Saturday or Sunday, if not impossible. Talk it up and I will see what I can do.

The little lady up front says I can put in my call Wed. morning for such and such a time but it may be subject to delay like the others. I will do that then and expect it after nine some time. Here's hoping.

Say hello to all, Mom, and if I don't get another line your way before the 25th, don't worry any. I will try and write soon tho. Take care of yourself and I sure hope you have a nice Christmas.

You are doing a lot more than millions of other women by letting the five of us go to this damn war with such courage and hope for the future. I wish I had as much of that as you have. Don't worry as I will have a good time and make the most of everything. It will do me good to be away for once and with the swell guys in 1116 and surrounding territories, I will have a lot of fun.

It will be harder for you than me, but I know you will make the most of it and remember the Christmas we will have in the future. Boy, won't that be a dilly!

With love and kisses,

Your loving son, Jack

TOM - NAVIGATING CHRISTMAS
Columbia, South Carolina, December 21, 1943

Dear Mom,

Just why I seem to be unable to write I can't understand, but the fact remains that I have done very little corresponding. I guess it is our "schedule" that does this. We have either nothing to do or we get our work in bunches.

Last night I was navigator down to Savannah and back and the trip was more or less without incident. Coming home I had a pleasant feeling inside to know that, with not even a board to write on as our position in the plane is now, I can still get a ship to where the pilot wants to go with reasonable accuracy, be it by day or by night, and over unfamiliar territory. Best, though, is to have the pilot just take his directions without question, and trust in your judgment.

There are times at night when I'm not quite sure of our position, and then I have to keep my fingers crossed "sweating out" my original plan or make some arbitrary correction based on only my limited experience and judgment. With a quarter of a million dollars' worth of equipment depending on my computers and dividers, there can't be any mistakes.

And that I guess is my Christmas—that feeling after all the months of wondering what will ever become of me, I now have a very small niche in the war picture. There are thousands of other guys doing as much and a lot of them more. It is a pretty good Christmas present, even if it is not exactly what you had in mind for me those other Christmases, when looking forward to the next one was not asking too much.

As Pat so well put it in her letter, this is not a Christmas with a load of gifts under the tree, but it is Christmas just the same whether we are all together or scattered about the country, which is now of such great concern to us. Here in the South, though, we'll have to make our own Christmas, with "goodwill toward all men" as not just a slogan to decorate greeting cards and department store windows.

As I told you, I have not been able to do much for Christmas as yet. I have not even written letters or sent cards. After the first of year, I will try to make up a bit. I had some pictures taken which are only so-so, and won't be ready until after payday anyway. I don't like to send them as gifts anyway because it seems like a helluva nasty trick. We'll call them a sort of report on the development of one Lt. Cahill, Thomas D., 0-760099A U.S.

Getting back to my "schedule," we as yet have not started school. We report to the flight line once a day and generally have nothing to do. I flew last night and today had a mission on the celestial trainer, which was

"Very Satisfactory" with a 95. I got a 91 the last time and without boasting it is the best work in the flight. I'm scheduled to fly tomorrow morning, but I don't yet know where to or anything else about the mission.

The most regular thing we do here is get "shots." Every week we have been getting two or three, either new ones or boosters on our old ones. Tomorrow we should get the last two. You would think that with so little to do I could accomplish a great deal but that isn't so. We used to go to town quite often but simultaneously my funds ran out, and we became exceedingly peeved at the prices, as well as the general hooking that our uniform, which we are so proud to wear, seems to invite.

There are no nightclubs in town. (What a clipping they could give us!) Theaters are fair, crowded and offer no special rates to servicemen. I don't expect a special rate myself as we are commissioned and considerably better off than the enlisted men, but they should get a break. True there are an awful lot of soldiers here but that should be more reason for better treatment. Girls are still a problem, the parody here being, "They're either too young or too cold."

They say if we really want to go, we can get in a crew now but without the ground school. Much as I would like to, I think it would be an injustice to myself and my crew to enter such a serious business if there is any chance of me being incompletely prepared. As it is, it will be only a month or so's difference, so I'll wait.

There will be no flying Christmas day and I have an invitation to have dinner with Walt Clark and his wife. Walt moved in with us yesterday. That makes the roster now stand with Joe Brakora (Brown is in the next room), Bill Bohlman, Walt Clark and Dick Frodl. Joe is the only one who is not an old buddy and is rather pedantic, and is a good target for some of my nastiest cracks. I, of course, get some in return. We both mean most of it, but realize that it will be a long war and so try to pass all remarks off as being humorous.

Bill and Dick are from way back, and we hit it off swell. Walt is the oldest of the group and really keeps things under control. He was group alert officer last night. I left my watch out in the ship and as they are dispersed all over the field it meant a long walk. So Walt gave me a couple boys and a jeep and I got the watch, and then they let me off right at my door. I roomed with Walt and Connors at Albuquerque and, all in all, we have the best gang from the class.

I took your advice and started a pinup collection on my wall. Just to be cynical (and to show that my interests are not entirely women) I have among pictures of the girls one still life of a bowl of fruit (no cracks from the boys) and the posterior of a hippopotamus, which I got, of all places, on the back of a Christmas card.

Well, I hope this reaches you in time for Christmas. You can be sure I will be there in spirit, and I'll think of you all at Midnight Mass.

Your loving son, Tommy

JACK - THE NIGHTS BEFORE CHRISTMAS
Sioux Falls, South Dakota, December 23-24, 1943

Dear Pat,

I'll start this tonite because some rather humorous things are going on. One kid has on his "John L's" and a pink and white flannel nite shirt. He is a funny picture and all the wolves are whistling, flirting and making passes at him. He is far beyond description and I burst out laughing every time I look at him.

About five little code-senders are going out, and in about two seconds a barrage of shoes is going to go in five different directions. You don't know what it's like 'til you've gone code happy.

Now Broz, our night-gowned boy, and Allen are harmonizing on "My Gal Sal." They are OK and Allen has an excellent voice.

Two other guys are brewing hot tea on the stove and this goes on every nite. If a shot of rum or whiskey is handy, it goes in too. Unfortunately (?), none is handy just now.

The customary "snow jobs" are going around and Albino, a Brooklynite, is far ahead on a standpoint of volume but a bad loser on common sense.

Jimmy Campbell, "the kid upstairs," is busy breaking in a new pipe. He just remarked about Broz, "He wasn't born, he was issued!" One of the Okies is busy with "Dare Devil Aces" and he should take off any minute.

The food is abundant in this barracks and I guess everyone is lousy with sweets.

For a while, this bks. was going card happy. J.P. Brown is a keen amateur magician and he has a lot of tricks. He showed a few guys the secret of a couple of them and for a week you couldn't turn around without having a deck of cards thrust in your face and the words "Pick a card" rattling in your ears. This went on in such "distant" places as classrooms, chow hall, the PX and the snack bar. The novelty has died down for a while tho.

The remnants of the 1118 moved in here the other day and you would think it was another civil war. Carroll is still griping about the cadets. When you say, "If you're so good, what are you doing here?" he pipes down. Gad, what a mess.

Well Pat, I'll lay off 'til tomorrow, time to "board the sack." G'nite.

Good morning. It's Christmas Eve Day. This barracks is sort of quiet now. I netted one box of cookies from Jackie and a card and letter. The card was from the Sisters and Boys Sodality of St. Agnes. It was very pretty and had a line or two from some of the nuns.

The letter came from Emporia. I told the young lady about "my banana girl" and so, not to be outdone or something, she said that she too will send me some. She works in a grocery store so she will have no trouble. Hot damn!

Like most everyone else, she had the flu but is back again on her feet. It is very cold there, 5 degrees below for a while. A minus 5 there is worse than a minus 20 here, and I know.

Did I tell you she may go to LA this summer? If I'm in the vicinity I'll bring her around, maybe. Tonite I go to see the **!!!***!!! "Quizlings." I'll knock them off or know the reason why. Next week will be rugged as our exams are then. That means study so I'll have to do just that.

Jackie's cookies incidentally are long since gone. They were good and naturally didn't last long at all. The silver bells she included are now adorning the barracks' rafter and with a Christmas tree (nomenclature—TREE, xmas, green, cardboard, M-1) we found, it is our total effort toward decorations.

If I didn't know better I would say that Frank, Tom and especially Jerry are hogging the furloughs for the Cahills. This is a hell of a branch to get one in anyway so I can't complain.

Well, sis, it was swell to talk with you, Mom and Mark the other night. I'll be glad when we can do it free of charge—face to face.

Since last adding to this I have had a bite to eat, a *swell* letter from Mom and I've been to Confession. We are all going to Midnight Mass in the theater. School gets out at 11 and at 11:30 we sing hymns, etc., before Mass.

I don't quite dig Tommy's jive. He seems to think that he doesn't deserve his commission and all that, and that just 'cause I didn't get a shot at cadets, I was robbed. Maybe yes, maybe no. I don't mind so much and I am satisfied as a GI. If anyone deserves it, he does. I've learned to watch out for JWC a lot and still have a heart for the next guy. But if I hear him say that again, I may violate an article of war when we next meet. That sharp uniform and fair pay is much too little for the stuff he has to go thru, and from what the guys here as instructors with 50 missions say, he hasn't even started yet. It is no bed of roses up there. Flak is *too damn* accurate all the way to 23,000 feet.

I hope to get a new shirt or two next payday and have this OD one altered. They are quite ill-fitting and I would not want to come home in such a condition. Guess this is all for now. I'll try to get a line home after Christmas.

Your loving bro, Jack

MARK - FIRST NIGHT IN THE NAVY
San Diego, California, December 30, 1943

This letter from Mark struck me. I knew him as an adult of course, but I can totally imagine him saying as a grownup what he wrote in this letter at a the age of eighteen.

Dear Mom,

We hit San Diego last night and had chow. Hit the sack at 9:30 and got up again at 10:00. Some of the boys were cutting up so the CQ got rather mad. We got all dressed and he gave us H - - -. As far as we know, he doesn't like guys from LA. So, we all discovered that we were from anywhere but LA. Me, I'm from New Hampshire again.

We came here by bus and had one loud time. We all go by nicknames. There are Curly, the Deacon, Dick and Yours Truly. Due to the fact that the Burkes called me "Little Duke" I am now just plain "Duke."

You should see the haircuts. I'm about the only one that got a good one. We had two shots today. Boy they just throw them at you.

Don't know where we go to but I wish it was quick. I gave the Deacon half of my paper. We just had time out for chow. It wasn't half bad. Don't know when we get our Blues. Right now we are in our civvies. We should hit boot camp by tomorrow. Will write again soon but this is all right now.

Love, Mark

JACK - SWEATING IT OUT
Sioux Falls, South Dakota, December 30, 1943

Dear Jerry,

Please excuse the paper and pencil but since I am in code and we are not supposed to write letters, it is obvious that a pen would look bad.

I am now in the process of "sweating it out." By *it*, I mean a spot check in code and a test on hand-sending. The suspense is terrific and I'm not just woofing. If I flunk it will mean three weeks more in this dump. I do know that I passed the test, the guy all but told me that. Also, I think I passed sending. I was unbelievably nervous and so were a lot of others. I made seven errors but got thru with about 15 seconds to spare. That counteracts the two extra errors. When you are shaky as hell, and there is less than 1/32 of an inch between contacts, it doesn't take much to put in an extra "dit" that will cause an error.

But the sweating comes in the code itself, like I said, I was tense as the devil. Eighteen words is quite a clip but I can, under normal circumstances, take it rather easily. There are only seven errors allowed. This includes those you left out, if any, the mistaking of one letter for another, those printed illegibly and any other reason they can think of. From the copying standpoint, I think I passed. From the legibility side, I wonder. The same goes for 16 words per minute. I will let you know in due time tho.

Tomorrow is New Year's Eve. I can truthfully say I don't know what I am going to do, but I can say, I have a faint idea.

Christmas was merry as could be. A few of us went out and eventually met up with Sgt. Dashielle. He is one of the best non-coms I've met. He spent 18 months in China, Burma and India with the ATC. We all got bagged to the general vicinity of our ears, but it prevented, for sure, homesickness with which you are a little more than vaguely familiar. But we had fun—egad!

I think you and Tom and Frank are taking care of all the furloughs for the family. If I was in Class 8, I might have gone to Fresno and be on my way home right now. (Maybe.) If I go to gunnery, I won't be home for about two more months at least. If I go to a line outfit, I will get ten days off. It is said that delays to gunnery are to start, but that is from stool no. 9, a very unreliable information bureau. The best thing to do is believe it when you see me, so don't raise any hopes for a while yet.

I sure hope you get in on that warrant officer deal. It means a lot more to go up thru the ranks. But I am satisfied as a GI. Three officers, two sailors and a GI is a good average—the proportion is about right.

If I go over as a 1st radio operator, I will be a Tech./Sgt. If I go over as a 2nd RO, I will be Staff.

You should see this joint—civilians run this school, work in the orderly room and supply—civvies—civvies—civvies. I was one once!

You should see the one in back of me—my teacher—wow! (Need I say more?)

Well, old boy, get a few shots down the hatch for me, and I'll drink to all of you from here. I wish I could see you all but "c'est la guerre!" Etc...

I will "QNW" for now but may "QMG" again manana. (We have hundreds of these "Q" signs to learn.) "QNW" is close down your station. "QMG" is open up. To be polite, I would send you "INT QNW," may I close down? If you were a good Joe you would say "QNW QPZ," yes, you may close down. Blub! Blub! Blub! Gurgle! Gurgle! Gurgle! (Code doesn't affect me, does it?)

Your loving (but code happy and theory weary) brother, Jack
HAPPY NEW YEAR!

Jack's projection above of his family's service members' futures refers to Frank, Jerry and Tom as officers, Jack a GI, Mark Navy, and Bob possibly Navy, Merchant Marine or Coast Guard.

MARK - HAPPY NEW YEAR, MOM
San Diego, California, January 1, 1944

Dear Mom,

HAPPY NEW YEAR! It is now 5:50 a.m. What a Navy! I have been up for about an hour. We have an inspection this morning before nine.

The "Deacon" did me dirt this morning. He had cubicle guard from 4 until 6 so the first thing he does is come to my bunk and start hitting my head with his club. He told me last night that he would.

You know the Navy isn't half bad after all. I don't mind getting up at 5:00 a.m. because I go to bed at 9:30 p.m. and I'm really pooped out. We march to chow and come back any old way. I expect to go to Mass today about 6:15. I may see if I can get on the altar again. Got to go so I'll close now.

Your loving son, Mark

JACK - THE CAREER PATH
Sioux Falls, South Dakota, January 2, 1944

Dear Mom,

Only a line or two to let you know that I am in good health and spirits in spite of my New Year's celebrating. I welcomed in the new year in a typical Cahill manner. The remnants of 1116's "charter members" threw a bit of a binge. It was a good deal of fun and was tremendously enjoyed by all.

Well—I think that in a short while I am going to be of service to the U.S. I prayed, went to Mass and Communion, studied and sweat and I did pass my exams! I am glad of that because since my waterloo at San Antone, I have been wondering of my value to the cause. I knew what I wanted to do but radio operator was not it. However, this will make me a little more valuable than being a "career" gunner and so I'm happy.

I suppose I will be off to Yuma in a few weeks and after that I will get B-17 or 24. I would like B-29 but I think that is out. Actually, I would like most a spot on the A-26 in preference to all others—but better yet a B-25, as long as Lt. Thomas D. Cahill was the navigator.

However, I may not go to gunnery and anything can happen. This is all jumping at conclusions tho, and I just hope that no matter what comes up I can handle it.

I will say that if I don't go to gunnery you can expect me home, *maybe*, within three weeks. Otherwise, it won't be until March. Don't put any hopes on it and just expect me when you see me.

I had a card from Sister Archangel today. She is in Boise, Idaho now, and I think as soon as I get Mark's address, I will forward hers to him. She asked to be remembered to you.

Guess this is it for now. I am sure relieved at getting through this course tho.

Your loving ("Big Time Operator") son, Jack

MOM - MOM'S NEW YEAR'S RECAP
Los Angeles, California, January 4, 1944, to Tom (in Columbia, South Carolina) and Jack (in Sioux Falls, South Dakota)

Dear Tom and Jack,

I know you will not mind if I write part of this letter in duplicate as there is much I would write to you both anyway, and by doing this I will probably get the letters done so that the mailman may pick them up.

Well, four days are already on the way out of this new year, and I only hope that when the last day of it has come it will be nearing the time when you will all be home once again.

As you may know, I am glad that Mark is in San Diego for we will get to see him once in a while, and it will not be quite so bad for him as it was for you Jack when you had to go so far away for the first time.

Frank got home New Year's morning and looks wonderful. He has lost all that excess weight he carried before he went in the Army, and his uniform fits him beautifully and becomes him, and as I said of the rest of you, he becomes the uniform. He doesn't seem to have changed any so I guess the statement Jack made, there being at least two good lieutenants (2nd) in the Army, is true. I think he will be good and considerate of those under him for he has been through the mill himself and knows what it is all about.

He and Peg came up for dinner New Year's Day and brought little Mary who is fat as a butterball and cute as can be. Bob and Jackie came with Little Pat and he is so cute. Patricia says she has never known anyone cuter. As he has some cute tricks and is learning to talk fast, I don't need to say how enjoyable having him around is, but he can run you ragged. Everything has to be out of reach, and you have to be about three jumps ahead of him in everything. Then Frankie and Kay came with little Johnny and it was pretty lively. He had Pat to play with and they got along fine. Both kids like beer.

Gerald was here with his buddy Ed Haley (incidentally he is the hungriest man I ever saw for meat) so we had a full table. Mae Guerra called up to say that she wished us a happy new year, and when I told her Frank was to be here she said she was coming up, so she had dinner with us too. Ben went to the Rose Bowl game. We didn't see him at all. Well, the dinner went off nicely and I guess everyone had a good time, but we missed the rest of you. You were spoken of often though, so it was not only Pat and Gerald and I who were thinking of you.

Mr. and Mrs. Slaven were over Sunday morning to see us and an old pupil of Pat's had dropped in. He has all sorts of ribbons on his chest. He had been in Africa, England, Ireland and Scotland with the Air Transport Command, and is now at Santa Ana as an aviation student as he wants to be a pilot. Because he had been in Scotland, he had a great time with the Slavens.

He was telling about the kid stuff at Santa Ana, but said after what he has been through overseas he can see why they do it—if you can stand that which irks you so much, you can stand about everything, and it is really more nerve training than a desire to keep kids down. He is crazy about Fr. Clasby. He says he has met any number of chaplains, but of them all, Fr. Clasby is the best.

Saturday evening another pal of Gerald's, Sgt. Blum, telephoned. He was in Pasadena and said he was coming over. Betty Reeder was over both evenings and they cooked lunches anywhere between two and four in the morning so Sgt. Blum stayed all night. He and Ed have both gone.

Gerald is here but not for long. He called up camp yesterday to see if they had kept out his pay as he was going down to get it, and the sergeant told him the lieutenant said he is to leave Camp Callan the 7th for Fort Douglas, Utah, on a special detail and only a PFC is to go with him. Doesn't know how long he will be gone this time. Says he guesses he never will enjoy a full furlough as this is the second time this has happened. So he will be leaving on Thursday.

Frank has to go back to Indiantown Gap on Wednesday, and whether he will stay there or not he doesn't know as he in a replacement group. However, he intends to have Peg with him as soon as he finds out when he will have to leave there and to where, if he does. There is a chance he may be at the Gap but probably for only six months, and then probably it will be overseas for him.

As you may see from Mark's letters, I guess he is doing all right. At least he doesn't show any signs of homesickness in his letters and I am glad of that. Probably after the new wears off, and he begins to get the real grind of it all, it may be different.

Our Christmas tree began to shed so much I had to take it down. Every time anyone passed it, the silver went on the floor and the balls were a great temptation for Little Pat. He helped me dismantle it and had a great time taking the balls off, pulling out the little pins you hang them up by and then giving them to me—if he didn't break them first. He is so cute though, and has that infectious grin when he does anything, so you really can't get mad at him.

It was raining this morning and I thought we were in for another gloomy day but the sun is trying to come out, and if it succeeds it means the washing machine for me. Went to dinner last night with Frank, Gerald and Peg and enjoyed it a lot—particularly because I didn't have to get it.

Pat is still working hard at her job and taking her music lessons as usual. Bob had a new engine put in his car, and it ran just like new but the rear end fell out the other day, so it looks like he is going to have almost a new car. He has heard nothing from his draft board as yet but you never know. It might be anytime now.

Well I guess this is all of the general news so I will devote the next page to each of you.

I only found Jack's individual page in our collection, not Tom's. To Jack:

Well, Jack, got your letter yesterday. Sorry you got robbed on one of your exams but hope that things work out all right for you and that you too may have a delay en route when you finally finish. I am proud of the way you have managed to stick things out even with so many disappointments, and know all these things are going to be beneficial in the long run even if they don't seem so pleasant at the time.

Don't know whether you sent your package or not. If you did, I have not as yet received it. Will let you know when I do. Will be sending you some cookies soon. Couldn't send them as I promised as I had Little Pat to watch while Jackie was sick and believe me, he is a handful. He will be glad to see you when you get home and he is so cute you are just going to be crazy about him. You will fall for little Mary too. She is like a little butterball, she is so fat, but she is cute and loveable.

Guess this is all for now. If there is anything you need that I can get you I would love to get it, for I don't feel right about not having sent you and Tommy something for Christmas even though you both said you didn't need anything. I feel that everyone else in the place must have been getting something but you two.

Loads of love, XXOO Mother

TOM - TOM'S NEW YEAR'S RECAP
Columbia, South Carolina, January 7, 1944

Dear Mom,

I had a letter all ready to go but I got off on a tangent and so decided not to mail it. This one will of necessity be brief.

We have been going to school this week, Sundays and all, and though it is all a review, we have to attend just the same, and with flying it leaves me again short of time. However I like it better this way, and the less time I have, the more things I seem to be able do.

As I mentioned on the phone, the money orders are enclosed. Thanks a lot to Pat and to you. I hope you'll have some fun on it. I don't know what, but do at least a couple "foolish things." I'm going to be rather short myself for a while this month but as it now stands I don't owe anybody a cent and that is a swell feeling.

Just what my financial future is, I don't know. For the next couple months in this country I hope to save enough for you to make the trip east if I can't go home or to make a trip anyway. Then there's a couple of other things which have been hanging on for years such as Dr. Mullin's bill, and perhaps Jerry would like to square up with Ralph Kenisten. I had a Christmas card from him by the way.

New Year's Eve was comparatively expensive but on the other hand, the preceding month was pretty lean. What I might save in the next few months for myself is not much. Overseas I'll have an allotment sent home as fat as possible. If I'm around to spend it later, well and good, and as I said before, these first months won't make a difference to that sum. And if anything should happen, money will then be the least of my worries and you'll have insurance and stuff like that.

Stan Gerry and Larry Evans, of my old Santa Ana and primary days, showed up here this week. Gerry was sent to the 426th and we'd like to crew up together but he is being transferred to a pool squadron and it will only be by luck that I'll get him later. I think I have a snapshot of Gerry in that bunch from Hemet. He's the guy with the ears sitting under the palm tree drinking beer. I also found out that Floyd is up at Charlotte and I'll try to get in touch with him. On the missions we've been flying, the navigator picks the fields to go to and it should work out.

Later on we will have an RON (Remain Overnight) to Reading, Pennsylvania, which is not far from Indiantown Gap and when we do I'll wire Frank. It probably won't be for a month at least though. Joe Callahan and Bortz are up there now and Joe said he was going to sneak up to Concord if he could.

Speaking of Joe, I had Christmas dinner at his place and had a swell time. Night before last I started to make up for the meals I've had at his place by taking him and Mickey out to dinner with me—and a friend—and dancing afterwards. I'm certainly glad they are here.

Had some pictures taken and will try to mail them tomorrow. The hat isn't cocked quite enough but it is too late now. Better close now so this will get mailed.

Love to all, Tommy

MARK - PLEASE SEND COOKIES
San Diego, California, January 7, 1944

Dear Mom,

Your son is rather tired and hot. I think that I may have a fever. We got a double typhoid shot yesterday and the boys dropped out. Some went to sickbay. Others hit the sack at six o'clock. I was too busy putting guys to bed to worry about it. The Deacon and I spent about two hours helping the boys get to bed. Some of them could cooperate with us—the others went out just like a light. Boy, did we sleep after that.

By the way, do you know a fellow by the name of Beggs? He used to know Dad and Maurice and he is a good friend of Mary Brooks. Well, anyway, he bunks right next to me. He is a darn nice guy.

I now have 138 dollars' worth of clothes. Three suits of white, three blue jumpers counting my dress, two blue pants, two shoes, etc.

How are the boys? I haven't had time to write them so I guess it will have to wait. I realize that you forward all these letters so I hope they will excuse the lack of penmanship. Also, I hope that you will pardon same. When I write these I'm in rather a hurry.

Today I only ate six times. We had KP and all the food we could eat (if you want to call it food). On top of that we had an hour or two of rifle drill.

All of that was on top of the double typhoid. Some fun. The boys can tell you what those shots do to you if you don't know now.

Say hello to Leona and all the rest of the folks and tell them I'll write when I get more time. When I get out of "Detention" I should have more of it. Time to hit the sack.

Love, Mark

P.S. Please send some COOKIES if you get a chance. The Deacon, Lucky and I can take care of them.

MOM - JACK THE GRADUATE

Los Angeles, California, Letter to Jack in Sioux Falls, South Dakota, January 10, 1944

Dear Jack,

Congratulations on passing your exams. I am very pleased for you and with you, and know that it must be a great relief to you to have them over. Now, the next thing is your newest assignment, as yet unknown to any of us.

If it is to be Yuma, maybe you can get a delay en route. If not I think that it is near enough to LA so that a three-day pass if available would be of help to you. When you have had nearly a year it seems to me that you are due for a few days at least, and you may be sure we are all looking forward to seeing you. I expect that you have changed a lot.

Well, Gerald is on his way again. He left last Friday for Fort Douglas, Utah. He was one of twenty chosen out of one hundred and fifty men for special duty. Whether it is now that he has been made a permanent personnel auditor I don't know, or whether there is to be any sort of a promotion in it for him. There should be, though I suppose it is one of those things that we never can tell about. He doesn't even know how long he is to be gone and I will not either until he writes me from there. As soon as he has a more definite address I will send it on to you. I should get a letter or something from him today.

Haven't heard from Mark for a week but Babe had a letter from him in which he said there were too many buttons on his uniform. Well, he had seen them before, and knew what to expect, but I imagine that was put in his letter more for effect than for any other reason.

My hands are very cold today. Can't seem to get them warm and somehow, though I was going to just do what I had to today then write letters, I can't get in the mood for it. Maybe if I get letters in the mail, I will feel more like doing my other things.

Tommy telephoned last week and said he had mailed a letter, but it has not come as yet. There were two money orders in it too for fifty dollars each and I am a bit worried about it. I don't know whether or not he could get it replaced particularly if he didn't register it or send it special. One hundred bucks is a lot of money to lose at one whack. I hope for his sake and Pat's that it isn't lost. My part of it would go for bills anyway, so I don't mind so much except that it is rather necessary just at this time. Company makes inroads on your pocketbook, particularly when it comes in bunches.

I just had a letter from Mark, and will make a copy of it before I mail this so you will be up to date on his activities.

Bob and Jackie were up with Little Pat last night for a little while. Bob is working outdoors though and gets pretty tired so they didn't stay long. Little Pat is so cute. You will be surprised at his progress. Bob called the house the other day and Little Pat answered the telephone. Bob told him to call his mother so he yelled, "Jack!" His hair is almost white it is so blond and he has such a darling infectious smile. You can't help but love him.

Little Mary is a sweet baby and very bright for her age. She has grown faster than Little Pat did at her age and being a girl seems a little different type but she is really lovely. I don't blame Peg for raving about her. I know Frank is crazy about her too, but you know how calmly he takes everything, so he sort of disappointed Peg by not going into ecstasy in saying what he thought of her.

I wrote you earlier about New Year's and all the company we had. So far as having a crowd was concerned, that seemed sort of like old times, but we surely did miss the rest of you. When that New Year dawns that has no more war, it will really be perfect if we are all here.

All for now dear. Lots of love and hope you will be home soon.

Yours, Mother

P.S. You remember Milly Chadwick, the Maryknoll sister who was interned in Japan for three years? She came back on that ship and had two weeks with her folks, went back to the mother house in New York, and two weeks after that she died, I guess quite suddenly. She was a lovely girl. M.

TOM - THE FLIGHT TO NOWHERE
Columbia, South Carolina, January 12, 1944

Dear Mom,

At last we are definitely on a schedule and I seem to have a place in the scheme of things. Sunday we started regular school for Phase 1 as they call it, with a talk by Col. Nedwed, group CO, who was kind enough to hold up the lecture until I got there, as Yours Truly was very much in the dark about the schedule. As it now stands, we will have four weeks of straight school, a week to organize our crews and then six or eight weeks of operational training, OTU. That means about early April I'll be moving out.

Incidentally, we fly to wherever we go to, either Europe or the Pacific Theater. In the formation will be a celestial navigator in the lead ship but if anything should happen to him or we run into bad weather, the business of getting there will be up to me. So I'm really brushing up on my navigation.

I flew a 385-mile trip from Rome, Italy, to Sofia, Bulgaria, the other day on the navigation trainer, and was only three miles off course with ETA zero and controlled ground speed at that. By controlled ground speed I mean that a time is set for me to arrive there. Every time the wind shifts a little, this changes my planned ground speed and I must correct all over again. My last mission on the trainer was controlled ground speed from Port Moresby, Australia, to Rabaul, New Britain, in the Southwest Pacific. It was 327 nautical miles which was again only 3 miles off. Leaving there we had to follow the pilot and then dead reckoning back to the base north of Moresby. Then I was eighteen miles off which was still considered good for a trip that long. My pilot caused half the error so I don't feel too badly about it.

Saturday night I was alert officer. I let Bill take my date to the officers' club dance and I established my headquarters there. Between drinks and dances the sergeant of the guard would pick me up in the jeep and we'd go out inspecting. He made me drive once just to prove to me how easy it was, and with the help of the Canadian Club Bill was supplying, I had quite a ride, and without mishap—except that Bill is dating my girl tonight and I had to get another.

Did the money orders arrive OK? If you have any suggestions in line with what I mentioned in the letter, let me know.

I have been transferred from B flight to A flight now. Checking the schedule last night I found my name was not on the A flight roster yet, so I'm just going to consider school as keeping me busy enough. I need a half hour more flying time to get flight pay for this month, but if I don't get it I can make it up next month. As long as I'm going to try to have you save it, it won't matter whether I get it this or next month. Chances are that I'll get it though.

That's about it for now. I wrote Mark last night but I have about two million more letters to write so I'll get on them now. I can do more in my lunch hour now than I could all day on the old schedule.

Love to all, Tommy

TOM - FIRST PHASE TRAINING
Columbia, South Carolina, January 25, 1944

Dear Mom,

Your most welcome letter arrived yesterday, and this being about the fourth letter I have started in a week, I'll make an extra determined effort to finish it.

Just what makes it so difficult to write anybody I have not yet been able to figure out. It is not that I am worried about anything—in fact, that may be the reason—not being worried. I guess as long as we are "sweating out" a pair of wings or something, there is a tendency to keep as many contacts as possible—to keep reminding ourselves that our friends are still there and behind us. Now that the tension is off, those letters do not seem so necessary. Then, too, once something becomes routine in your training there is a tendency to forget that writing about it might make it as new and exciting to your reader as those same events were to you at first.

We are now in the third week of regular First Phase Training. Each week gets a little tougher. This week we are going to school out of flight, that is, we are scheduled to fly in the morning and/or evening today and so school is in the afternoon. It rotates like that. There is not much flying for us just now, as the regular crews are using the ships most of the time to finish up their missions.

Sunday night I flew to Florence, Charlotte, Greenville and home. We spent quite a while trying to find old buddies there in Florence (unsuccessfully I might add) and so it was finally about 2 a.m. before we got home. That doesn't help getting up for school in the morning. I think we will have one more week of school, then a week to organize a crew and tidy up loose bits of training and then start working as a unit for a couple months. As yet, I have no pilot. While in the 377th I got to know most of the pilots and selecting one of them (also being selected) would have been relatively simple. Now I must nose around and try to get the jump on the rest of the boys.

Sunday is just another day around here and only tends to make the weeks without beginning or end. There is no school on Saturday; weather permitting there is a review in the morning (07:30) and then flight line 20 minutes after.

The MO arrived in time and I can see the end of the month coming. I'll return to you the same plus 50 or 75 more for laying away. While on the damn subject, don't worry about what I said last time regarding my future, financial or otherwise. Incidentally, this month I'm going on a budget and will probably have Bill put me on some sort of an allowance after sending as much as I can home. Perhaps you didn't notice on the photo envelope but it was addressed to you and Grandma. Of course, if she doesn't want it you might give it to Bob and Jackie. I was going to have some more made for them next month but they can have that.

I'm so glad that Jack has graduated from radio, and the package he sent home merely proves a point which I have become acutely aware of lately. In one swoop he has shown more thoughtfulness and self-sacrifice than I have in a year with all the good things I myself have had. I'll just have to get on the ball as I have been extremely selfish and neglectful in just about every department.

Had a letter from Mark which I must answer and it appears he likes the Navy very much. Glad Jerry is getting a break and I hope that Bob can start having things come his way for a change. I may be getting up Frank's way in a month or so. We can now land almost any place within a thousand mile radius—subject to group approval—instead of just certain 3rd Air Force fields. That might mean Concord some time. Joe Callahan is going to try to make a trip and get me on it. I was scheduled for an RON (Remain Overnight) to Monroe, Louisiana, Friday but it was canceled. Some of the fellows here a week ago are now in India. Boy, would that be some navigation! There is also a training mission to Battle Creek, Michigan (RON) and that would mean a blowout with Allin and Theda.

Last week we went out to the range to qualify on the carbine and .45 automatic. I didn't qualify the first time on the carbine, but the second time I got a sharpshooter rating. I qualified on the pistol too. One of my targets had twenty-two holes in it for fifteen shots! Luck of the Irish! I think the guy next to me must have been cross-eyed.

My roommate, Connors, and I have considerable difficulty in getting up in the morning on time. Casserly and Fisher were proud possessors of an alarm clock and used to call us when they got up. However, they moved out and now call us on their way to breakfast. This, of course, makes it too late for us to go to breakfast, and a close shave just to make the flight line. Connors is in town now looking for a clock—he says. As he didn't take the half-pint I have in my locker, I presume he is doing just that. The reason for the liquor is that you can't buy mixed drinks here so we must carry our own.

Connors is quite a character. He is about twenty-five and one of thirteen kids. He has a degree as a mining engineer and knows Colorado, Utah, Nevada, Arizona and those parts like the back of his hand. He was captain of his football team in high school and at college in Michigan, and to prove it, has a nose which he says has been broken four times. I think he must have forgotten a couple other times. I've seen cauliflower ears that looked more like a nose than his does. Anyway, we hit it off in great style.

He thinks I'm crazy. I disagree with him on everything from women on down (or up—depending on what you think) but I somehow understand him having his viewpoints (though not necessarily his viewpoints). That, I think, is something worth noting. I think if you know what makes a fellow believe what he does, you can, while not agreeing with him on the point, not be antagonistic about it. He, on the other hand, accepts my ideas with much the same attitude so everything works out fine.

We have good teamwork about keeping the place in order (did I say "in order"), borrowing each other's things, etc. The payoff is in little things—viz: when I have to fly at night he'll pick up a cake or candy bar at the PX to keep me from starving when I get in late in the morning. I do the same thing for him and it is all without a conscious effort on the part of either of us.

I'm sorry to hear about Betty's trouble but am glad that she is going to Los Angeles. That will be a break for all of us, and regardless of what might have happened, for my money, Betty can do no wrong.

That, "Mamacita," is about six pages more letter writing than I have done in weeks. While it is only as it should be, it might have drained me for a while. In any case, if I don't write as often as I used to, don't worry. The hardest thing I have found to do here so far is write letters and lose this weight I've put on—so you see, nobody is picking on me. Will try to write more often though in the future.

Your loving son, Tommy

TOM - THE INVENTION
Columbia, South Carolina, January 30, 1944

Dear Mom,

I have just come from the matinee at the movies where I saw *Madame Curie*. Very good and thank God there was no propaganda in it. It is the first afternoon I have had free in a long time. The fact that it is Sunday has nothing to do with it. I flew last night until 2 a.m., this morning went to school and calisthenics before lunch, but talked them out of any further activity today at the flight line.

Last night's flight—about 500 miles in all or maybe a little more—was quite successful from a navigational point of view. However, I wasn't expecting to fly, didn't feel like flying and had no supper. The pilot picked up a bag of popcorn for me in Savannah but I was too busy to eat it while it was fresh. It seemed that the whole state is one big brush fire. At night in the distance they can easily be mistaken for towns and are a great help in getting you lost. Doing 220 or 240, you get lost very quickly too.

Connors and I have been working on a combination straight edge and time-speed-distance computer. It is being etched on celluloid by a fellow in the school headquarters and might be a great help to our navigation if it is found convenient. There just isn't time to figure in the air. In two minutes working on a problem you can be seven or eight miles from where you were when you began to figure. In bad weather that might not be so good.

Did I tell you I may have found my pilot? He's a fellow named Coombs, 19 or 20, from New Jersey. Not definite yet but maybe confirmed this week.

Remember Floyd whom I used to mention in pilot days? He was here yesterday for about three hours. He's flying A-20s up at Charlotte and we hope to get together more often. He and DeMent and I used to pal around together all the time.

Had a letter from Jack the same day as yours arrived. He was running short so I sent him ten and will try to repeat tomorrow if I can get my check cashed. Also will send you some. Exactly how much I don't know but as much as possible.

This last week in school we have been studying radio equipment and taking code. I checked out on 12 WPM and got an idea of what Jack has been up against. That's about it, Mom. May be able to write more later but I'm going to try and log plenty of sack tonight.

Your loving son, Tommy

TOM - HEAD UP AND LOCKED
Columbia, South Carolina, February 2, 1944

Dear Mom,

The enclosed is this month's effort to balance the budget. I was going to send $120 but am sending another ten to Jack. I again don't owe anybody anything, but this time I also have bought enough meal tickets to last me through the coming month. I didn't leave much for spending but don't expect to have much time for play as I am now crewed up. Next month I should be able to send you as much at least and probably more unless something unexpected shows up. Anyway, the fifty is yours personally and the sixty you can also spend if you need to or put it away for later.

We have no idea as yet whether we will go to the Pacific or Europe. If the former, I should get home for a few hours at least, as San Francisco is the usual port of embarkation. How much time I have will depend entirely on the weather.

This is the last week of school now and concerns mainly gunnery and armament. I have been assigned a pilot who is at present on leave so I'm going to try to work a little deal and get the pilot I want. He is a good friend of Walt's and Bill's pilots and we'd all like to stick together if we could for as long as we can anyway. Next week will be spent shaping up the enlisted part of the crew, getting rid of any misfits before serious trouble can develop and organizing the final little details.

There is a possibility I might get up to Concord under a new setup they have here. I'm going to try anyway. Incidentally, the field at Reading, Pennsylvania, has been closed to Army traffic so I'll have to try something else up that way to see Frank.

Connors and I have now almost finished our navigational gadget—the one I mentioned. We are keeping the idea pretty much to ourselves around here as it may have a future. Without getting too technical, I'll try to explain what we have made. First there is a long Plexiglas rule. This is graded in miles to work on Lambert-Conformal Charts (most used in U.S.). Over this we have a Plexiglas cursor—like on a slide rule—graded off in miles per hour, conforming to the range of a B-25 (may be designed for any range).

By some mathematics we figured out time lines which we etched in the back of the rule. For instance the five-minute line would begin at the top of the rule at 15 miles (180 mph or 3 mpm). Therefore, any place on that five-minute line that crosses our cursor will give us on the cursor our speed in mph and in the top of the rule, the distance in miles that we have traveled.

The rule is pivoted at the point of departure so that it may be swung right or left measuring also miles off course so with one little gadget we have eliminated the use of dividers and our old computer and speeded up computations by about 400%.

We are trying to find out just what types of charts are used in the Asiatic and European theaters. So today we are going to show it to Jake (Jacob P. Ascola, captain and navigation officer for the 426th). If he likes it, we will see about having a more exact one made and perhaps something will come of it.

Yours arrived this afternoon and also a swell one from Jack. He expects to be moving soon.

I am no longer in the 426th. I fly out of the 426th but am attached there from the 309th Combat Crew Section. I started this letter yesterday, and since then we have made a little progress toward getting crewed up with the pilot I want. However, nothing is assured yet so I'll just have to wait.

In the business of moving from the 426th to this other outfit, the 426th came around, took all our pillows, coal shovel and bucket, orderlies to see that there is hot water in the latrine and, all in all, Connors and I are so damn mad that the situation is no longer funny. How this Army and all its red tape and "head up and locked" attitude manages to win the war I will never, never know. I have seen the waste of time and material and I hope there is not the same disregard for human lives. So, before I do any more griping, I'd better buzz off. Going to the show tonight in an effort to forget it all.

Your loving son, Tommy

P.S. Your letter was postmarked February 1st midnight and arrived February 3 sometime in the morning. Not bad after all.

TOM - THE NEW HAMPSHIRE TRIP
Columbia, South Carolina, February 13, 1944

Dear Mom,

Here I am, back in Columbia after three swell nights in Concord. As I don't have much time now for letter writing I hope you'll make copies of this for the boys and I'll try to make this report more detailed than I could if I had to write each one.

It all started about 5 p.m. Wednesday night. There was a notice on my bulletin board that Joe Callahan wanted to see me. As that always means something doing, I didn't waste any time getting in touch with him. When he told me we were going to Concord, I could hardly believe it. After seven years, I had just about abandoned hope of getting back there. So, of course, I told him I would be ready in the morning after I got permission from my navigation officer. Jake was all for it and the next thing to do was plan the trip. I have never made a trip with a radius of over two hundred miles and could not afford to leave anything until the last minute as this I knew was at least eight hundred miles from the base. I had a date that evening and I told her I would be late so she would not be waiting.

Joe told me that he would like to fly a straight course to Concord but, as it might be difficult to get a clearance for that trip, I had better plan an alternate route, through Raleigh, Newark, New York, Hartford and then direct to Concord. It was 824 miles as a B-25 flies and slightly farther by the alternate route. In any case, four hours was what we figured it would take. The weather at Columbia was not too good but Joe had an instrument rating and so we got off before the rest of the field. What a crew we had! Callahan, Kelley, Sullivan and Yours Truly plus a couple of foreigners named Hamilton and Getchell.

It was not long before we found out that the radio was acting queerly, the drift meter was out of line, the oil pressure on one engine was slightly low and to tie it off, we were encountering stiff head winds. I got a look at Richmond for the first time in my life.

We turned into the air lanes to Washington and there was the heart of this war effort—the mechanical heart. It is absolutely forbidden to fly over the White House and other such vital spots, and after they put all the restrictions we had on the map, it looked like you couldn't navigate unless you got low enough to read the street signs. We pushed on to Baltimore and Philly and landed at Newark.

The wind had been slowing us down considerably and Joe wanted to have more than enough gas. We got a couple hundred gallons but that was hardly a drop in the bucket. As it would be some time before they finished gassing some cargo planes we decided to push on to Hartford.

At Rentschler Field in Hartford, Joe made a beautiful landing onto a 3,000-foot strip. A B-25 needs at least 3,500 feet for a fair deal. No gasoline there so rather than use the short runway again, Joe took off catty-corner on the grass. At Bradley Field, just below Springfield, Massachusetts, we finally got some gas after showing curious colonels the fine points of the B-25-H. This H, by the way, is what I'll ship out in. I ride in the co-pilot's seat, and with a few minor changes it will be an ideal set up.

At about 5 p.m. we hit Concord. We circled the field several times while Joe radioed the tower that he was going to land at Manchester in order to have some repairs made. Then we buzzed the town a couple times to wake up the place and landed at Manchester. We were rather provoked at the slow time we made flying up (about 180 min.), but that was nothing to what we felt when it took an hour for the bus to crawl that eighteen miles from Manchester to Concord.

At Manchester I telephoned Mary Waters. She was the one person I could be certain of to know just how to reach Aunt Mary after working hours. She sent Jack to meet us at the bus and just as I was getting into his car I caught a glimpse of what I thought was a familiar face. It turned out to be Rita Donahue and she asked me to come to Nora Donovan's if I could. I then went to Mary's and it seems Aunt Mary was out for the first time on a Thursday in weeks. Leaving there I went to the Puritan Restaurant for a quick supper then took a cab out to the Tuttles'. It was great seeing them and at the time it did not look like bad weather would keep us in, I only stayed a few minutes. When I came out the cab driver was sleeping and I began to think of the fare.

Back to the Waters' for a visit and to see if Aunt Mary had been found yet. No Aunt Mary, so I decided to try Donovan's where I thought I might kill a lot of birds with one stone. Ann, Nora and Franny Burke were there, and after coffee and cake Rita drove me up to Slattery's, and after that to May Whittaker's where I did see Aunt Mary. While I was there Celia came up. We had quite a talk but finally I had to call it quits because the next day looked like a lot of work. Taking Mary Waters up on her offer, I stayed there where I was certainly treated like royalty.

The next morning it was snowing! Joe and I took the train to Manchester and at the field they told us there would not be clear weather for at least 36 hours. This was great news so we went back to Concord and I established headquarters at Waters' again.

Took Aunt Mary to lunch after visiting the Green Front (what a paradise that is these days!). Paul Sullivan was chauffeuring Joe and I all around town and at his house I decided I had better shave which I did. I brought my maps with me to work on them so there would be no delay in taking off when we finally had to go. After lunch, back to Waters' to work on my course home, phone you, and also make a few appointments. I stopped at the rectory to see Monsignor. He was not in but Peg Crowley was and again it was old times revived.

From there I took a cab to Betty's. She is still Betty, lost a little weight and looked pretty swell to me. As I had all the dope, she pumped me about Los Angeles and the way things were in California. The whole trouble Betty has been up against is that she is just too far ahead of Concord, must put up with all the small time gossip, and all in all, the situation is unbearable. The Cahills, she said, were the only ones who ever understood her, and that since Patricia has been gone there has been no one else with whom she could really be at ease and happy.

We had supper at Angelo's—figuring that it would give Concord plenty to talk about—and Della Paine (Mrs. Messier) waited on us. She was asking about Bob and the rest of the Cahills and says that George will be coming home soon. Tommy Berryman is home and from all reports he is a wreck. After supper Betty let me off at Rita's and we stopped at Peg Crowley's for about an hour and a drink. Peg is as lively as ever and we had a sweet time.

We went back to Betty's and Ted Forsberg and some other girl were there and we played records, danced and Betty gave out with some singing that was really terrific. I hope she can do something with her voice in Los Angeles. I know that she can do plenty with mine and I also think she'll see Mrs. Miner about lessons. Betty is really looking forward to seeing you all, and I think you'll find she is still the same Betty, which I don't think any of us would care to change.

I forgot to tell you but that same morning before we left Manchester Joe and I went to Sacred Heart Hospital to see Fr. Kenneally. He was just recovering from an operation and again the surprise was terrific. We stayed with him for two hours which was about three times longer than we had stayed with anybody else, as we tried to see the whole town at once. He's just about the same and asking for everybody. Fr. Donnelly is now in Laconia so we couldn't see him.

Saturday we went down to check the weather again, but it was still snowing. We stuck around though until afternoon thinking it might clear up. Finally back to town and Joe went with me to Mary's for a shower and supper. What a time we had then! Mary got out a bottle of Canadian Club and we were on our way. Went to Confession and saw the Monsignor. I started to cover everything in this letter but at the rate I'm going I'll never finish. So I'll try to sum it all up.

The snow was beautiful, though I'm no longer able to put up with the cold. Everybody I saw was anxious to know about all the Cahills. The war has hit Concord terribly hard with over 2,700 in the service. Saw one of the Rosens—the older one I think—and he recognized me right away which surprised me and was asking for all the boys, especially Jerry and Bob.

While I was gone, Connors took our invention to Col. Sorenson, group CO, and he was easily sold on it and backs it 100%. Monday, I think, Maj. Bradley is going to fly Connors to Wright Field and that will be the final test. Looks good. I used it yesterday with Capt. Ascola riding with me. I was lead navigator in a three-ship formation and we hit everything just about 0-0.

Last night I went over to see Joe and Mickey. Mickey made a colossal chocolate cake, and as she knew I liked it, I made a hog of myself with her permission.

That's it for now. You probably read about the crash we had yesterday. It was pretty tough but nobody I knew was on it. This is the first accident in Columbia since last July which is pretty good.

Love to all, Tommy

P.S. Didn't send the dough to Jack 'cause he was moving. Don't have it now but you can send him some of what I sent. More about the trip east next letter.

P.P.S. We flew over Concord Sunday morning—right down Main Street—and exactly four hours later we were over Columbia Army Air Base. That's speeding but we also flew around New York and Mount Vernon sightseeing.

AUNT MARY - ACCORDING TO AUNT MARY
Concord, New Hampshire, February 13, 1944

Aunt Mary Cahill wrote quite exuberantly—charmingly small town—to Tom's mother about his surprise visit.

Dear Mary,

Oh, all the excitement since Thursday night!

I went to the movies with Kate McDonald to the first show, then to the Puritan where we stayed 'til ten and she drove me home. When I got in the phone was ringing and I answered, and somebody was answering upstairs. I kept on and found out it was Mrs. Shook of the *Monitor* who said Tommy was at the Waters' house and she wanted to talk with him so I said for her to call him then I would. Then I went upstairs and one of the girls had left a note on my bureau saying that Mary Waters had received a message from Tommy for me to meet him at the Puritan at 7:30, but of course nobody at the house knew where I was. Then Miss Brown came out from her room and said that Tommy and Jackie Waters had come to the house looking for me but Tommy would make other calls and come back later.

Then Mary called and talked a long time. No it wasn't Mary that time. It was Mrs. Buchan who was down there and she said she'd called Mrs. Shook to get the story (they are great friends). She said Tommy looked simply grand and that he would be up later as he was still trying to find me. Then Mary Waters called and said to be sure to stay up because he would have to leave at 6:10 in the morning and would stay at her house, and she would be up bright and early and get him a good hot breakfast. She raved and raved about him, how nice he was, and how grand he looked, and how smart he must be, etc.

Well, it turned out that they parked the plane (he and Joe Callahan the pilot from Concord) at Grenier Field in Manchester and he phoned Mary from there and she had Jackie meet him. The first one he ran into after getting off the bus was Rita Donahue and she said she and Frannie Burke were going to Ann Donovan's on Grove St. to sew and for him to come down there as soon as he could so he did. He also went out to the Tuttles', who live almost out to the school and kept the cab waiting about 20 minutes.

Mrs. Tuttle called the next morning to see if he had found me. She said he called her up and said, "Hello, this is Tommy" and she thought it was Tommy Roy who was fixing Mr. Tuttle's car, but when he said "How are you?" she wondered and said, "What Tommy is this?" and he said "Tommy Cahill." Well, she said she never was so surprised in her life and when he called she was just thrilled. She said he was just the same as ever, and she had often told her husband that next to their son Morton she thought more of Tommy than any other boy in the world. Morton is at Hawaii, but has applied to take up aviation in this country and she is very much worried, but Tommy said, "Wouldn't you rather he would fight from the air than from the foxholes?" So, I guess she would in a way.

He finally arrived at the house at 11:30 p.m. and I was glad to see him. He looked grand but found it very cold in Concord. Said he would pray that the weather would be terrible so that they wouldn't have to go back the next day. We sat downstairs in the library and Mrs. Whittaker came in from a party and was so glad to meet him. About midnight the doorbell rang and it was Celia and Frannie so we visited a while. He stayed until after one and we said goodbye. He left at 6:10 a.m. but returned and phoned me during the morning that the weather was bad, and they would have to stay over until Saturday when they would leave Concord on the 9 a.m. bus.

We went to the Puritan for dinner and Joe came in and everything was lovely. Joe is a little younger than Tommy. Tommy was the navigator and had to go back to Mary's in the afternoon to work about an hour and a half making out his route. He said he was planning something with Rita and would not see me that night which was all right with me as my club was meeting at Nora Donovan's.

He came to the office Saturday morning to say goodbye. How all the girls raved!!!

The day was worse than Friday, and I didn't hear any more until after supper when Mary called and said that he had phoned her around six that he would be back and brought Joe, and she hustled around and got him a good steak supper. They both had supper and then Tommy said he and Joe wanted to go to Confession and to the barber for a shave and Joe took a shower.

I haven't heard from Tommy since, but yesterday morning, I was walking to church for the 10:30, and I saw this plane over my head going very slowly and very low over all the buildings on the right side of Main Street, past Lysters, etc., and I said to myself I bet that it was Tommy and Joe, and I found out today from Irene that it was. Irene's brother is married to Joe's aunt and they said it was his plane.

I am anxious to see Mary and talk it over. She was thrilled to talk with you over the phone and it was very thoughtful of Tommy to connect the two of you.

Love, Mary

FLIERS BLOW IN FROM SOUTH TO SEE HOME FOLKS
Lts. Callahan and Cahill Find Concord Climate Too Cold Now
From the *Concord Monitor*, February 11, 1944

A B-25 gave the local airport a "buzz" late yesterday afternoon, then winged its way to Grenier Field. In it were Lt. Joseph Callahan and Lt. Thomas Cahill, Concord aviators, on a special mission from their base at Columbia, South Carolina.

Leaving their home field at 9 yesterday forenoon, they stopped twice en route in the course of their 1000-mile flight. The 8 o'clock bus brought them to Concord.

There was a happy reunion between Lt. Callahan and his young wife, Marion "Mickey," who lives with her parents, Mr. and Mrs. Homer W. Rogers, 23 South Street, and with his parents, the Joseph Callahans, 75 Perley Street.

Lt. Cahill, son of Mrs. Mary Cahill, Los Angeles, and Patrick Cahill, late of this city, was making his first visit to his native Concord in seven years. He had a hectic night, taxiing hither and yon to contact boyhood friends and trying to find his aunt, Miss Mary Cahill, 234 North Main Street.

A resourceful youth, he soon discarded taxis in favor of "a girl with a car and some gasoline."

"Nevertheless, it's pretty dead around Concord," said Lt. Cahill, at the same time admitting he was having a wonderful time.

Long months in gentler climes had not prepared them for the rigors of a New England winter night.

"Gee, what a place," was their mutual verdict as they shivered mightily. "This isn't the kind of Chamber of Commerce weather I'm used to," declared Lt. Cahill, the Californian.

The officers left this morning on the 6:10 train for Manchester. It was understood that their flight back to the base was delayed by more of the weather they found so distasteful.

JERRY - PUTTING GERMAN POWS TO WORK
Ft. Lewis, Washington, February 24, 1944

Dear Mom,

Did I ever write to you before without giving a half a dozen different addresses and times of departure? It seems as though the Army is just trying to confuse me or you.

Our little trip back here was for the purpose of interviewing a bunch of German prisoners that we have in camp. It is a new idea dreamed up by the War Dept., and I guess they are planning on placing the prisoners in work similar to what they did in civilian life.

These prisoners were captured in Tunisia about the 10th of May last year and were members of the "Afrika Korps." One of them told us that they were short of equipment and Rommel told them there was more on the way. He told them the British had it at the time and all they had to do was take it away from them. Well, they tried and now the war is all over for them.

Others were in the hospital at Tunis and were taken there. I guess the credit was equally divided between the British and Americans. Each man has a record showing his home address, birthday, etc., and also shows who nabbed him. It was surprising to find so many men who gave their religion as Roman Catholic. Guess Hitler figures they can fight too though.

For the most part they were pretty much like our own Army. The same run of ages, looks and occupations. A few of course were professional soldiers and some were pretty rugged characters—but far from supermen. The air corps—like ours—were the cockiest.

We'll be through with them tomorrow and will leave for Seattle again Friday. You had better still write to Ft. Lewis though. You know this Army.

Will write again soon, but right now I'm pretty well pooped out. Write when you can.

Your loving son, Gerald

JACK - CHECKING IN FROM YUMA
Yuma, Arizona, February 25, 1944 ("40 days from home")

Dear Mom,

We have had a few exams on the machine gun, sighting and code. On my nomenclature exam on the .50 cal, I got 100%. On part functions I made 92, on sighting and harmonization I made 100% and on tactical procedure I made 95%.

I've passed an exam on radio maintenance but I don't know the grade. Code and blinkers were OK too. So, I am doing OK all around but the worst is yet to come. The exams I've had so far were simple and any one that flunks them is a potential moron. These marks count 25% of the final grade so I intend to make hay while the sun shines—my days take on a cloudy outlook soon but I'm not worrying.

That .50 cal is a swell gun. It shoots from 700 to 850 rounds a minute and can kill a man 4 miles away. It is a smooth chunk of medicine and the amazing part is that it can be disassembled to the greatest necessary detail with only a big nail or a cartridge as a tool.

Tomorrow we go up in a B-17. It will be about a two-hour ride for the purpose of acquainting ourselves with a big ship. The weather looks forbidding tonite tho so I don't know.

I am enclosing ten that will do a bit toward knocking off the phone bill. I hope you can get it cashed. Well Mom, take it easy and I'll see you in 40 days. Say Aloha to all.

Your loving son, Jack

TOM - FLIES IN THE OINTMENT
Columbia, South Carolina, February 27, 1944

Dear Mom,
I hit the jackpot today with letters from you, Pat and Dave Miner. Dave is in Africa flying in some Navy ships. He told of talking with a pilot over there who had just had a narrow escape. When asked how he felt at the crucial moment the pilot answered, "I just moved over and let Jesus have the controls." I've found that pilots are about the most expressive group of individuals on earth, better than all the authors in the world.

Before I go any further, thanks a million for the cookies, film, etc. The cookies went in style. Bill Bohlman, my pilot and Vance all came up to my place and I decided that was the ideal time to open a quart of precious Bourbon that I'd brought down from Concord. We got just mildly loaded. It was raining, no flying and an unexpected letup in an otherwise rough week.

About your trip east. I had originally planned for you to come here toward the end of March. The money I'm sending this month plus what you have would take care of the trip here and a little more. Then at the end of the month I would have enough to route you up through Richmond and Concord.

There are a few flies buzzing in the ointment—with fighter escort. First, it is fairly certain—99 and 44/100 per cent at least—that I will go to the Pacific. That means Los Angeles or Frisco as a port of embarkation. But that is where the certainty seems to end. I may be sent to Florida for torpedo school. This would mean leaving here a couple weeks before my crew and being in the country another month or so.

Another variable is how do we get to the Pacific. I have just heard that some have been going by boat from California. Whether this allows any time out there I don't know. It should but I can't tell. So, now the way it stands I don't even know where I'll be by the end of the month. Maybe here, maybe Florida, maybe California.

Nothing must interfere with Jack's homecoming. In the last analysis I'll either get to Los Angeles or get you to Frisco. In any case you will not be hampered by lack of funds for a trip to Frisco. However I still want you to make the trip to Concord and Richmond later. Perhaps Jack will be on the East Coast and it will be an opportunity to visit him.

This month I'll have to buy a few suntans and other clothes necessary for tropical wear. I still hope to be able to send you about $115. That's to do as you please with. When I'm overseas you can start saving some for me. I'll send a $100 allotment beginning April 1st. When I see how much I need over there I'll no doubt increase the amount.

Also you might tell Mark to be a little more careful with his phone calls but on my account he need never hesitate to make one. Just a suggestion of causing a financial inconvenience might prevent him from making a call just when he needs a touch of home. However, he should not be too much in the habit of calling home because some day he may be too far for phoning.

Not to throw a damper on things, I think Jack should plan on his trip after graduation being his only one. They told me I'd get another leave, remember?

I've been reading a very thought-provoking book called *Declaration of Interdependence* by H.A. Overstreet. He really seems to have some ideas. For instance, he says that we are a nation of specialists, doctors, lawyers, etc., all devoted to one particular phase of living. Because we are specialized ourselves, we leave all other jobs to specialists in that particular field, and the field of running our government we have left to a group of specialists known as politicians.

At the same time, in our daily speech, the word "politician" is assumed to be a shady character full of goodness and promise around election day, but otherwise a four-flusher and not at all the type of person we really should place in such responsible positions. Of course, there are exceptional men but on election day, as Frank has said, you don't vote to select one candidate but you vote to keep the other candidate out of office—the lesser of two evils.

Then, too, Overstreet says, we are a slave to platitudes. Unemployment is only natural as "The poor ye have always with you," though no one is lending a hand. "Where there's a will, there is a way" for the unfortunate, and that's about all the help they get. You know—the "rugged individualism stuff."

The whole country needs plenty of housecleaning from sharecropper to holding companies. The President started out to do a good job and I think he had the right idea but now the home situation is so bad that I don't know what will happen. Neither does anybody else either, I guess, but the only thing anybody seems to worry about now is their own postwar business or future, and not much of the nation as a whole.

Well, I've got my Sunday sermon off my chest so now I'll buzz off. I hope I've covered all the things you wanted me to in the first part of the letter and I guess I'll just have to wait until I find out more. I hope you'll get a chance to look at the book I mentioned.

Your loving son, Tommy

Above left, Mary and Patrick Cahill with Patricia and Maurice (standing), about 1914. This family with two children increased to nine children by 1925.

Above right, Patrick's sister, the children's beloved Aunt Mary Cahill.

Left, the Cahill children's maternal grandparents, Frank and Nellie Wardner, early 1900s. Nellie is "Gram" referred to in Tom and Jack's letters. She owned the Los Angeles home where the family landed after moving to California.

In many of my family's photos, it was dizzying to determine identities of the boys who looked similar. Luckily, in most group pictures, my grandmother lined them up in birth order. Top, Grandpa Wardner with, from left, Billy, Bob, Jerry, Frank, Patricia and Maurice. Lower left, Frank, Patricia and Maurice, driving. Lower right, from left, Jerry, Bob and Billy doing that hand-on-the-shoulder-of-the-kid-next-to-you-for-spacing thing. Mom on the porch with Tom (barely visible) in her lap seems to be directing this shot.

Above, children are not lined up in birth order, but, by the time I saw this picture, I knew the boys' different but similar looks. From left, Jerry, Patricia, Billy, Frank and Bob, some looking happier than others, late 1921. There are several photos like this where Patricia is sweetly mothering one of her younger brothers. All were close to her throughout their lives.

Middle left is Tom, about 1924. Love the hands in pockets, looking happy and confident, like the young man he grew up to be.

Bottom, Mark left, and Jack, late 1920s, on the car's running board. So many of these pictures capture moments in time. Jack and Mark were the two youngest children.

Upper left, my grandmother wrote "Tom and Jack, Easter 1927" on the back of this photo. Tom almost six years old and Jack three and a half.

Upper right, Jack in elementary school. It doesn't get much sweeter. I love this picture.

Bottom, Maurice, standing, with friends. He was a bandleader, but it looks like he had a day job also, maybe as a sign-painter—paint splotches on his clothes. License plate, enlarged, reads "1933" above the plate number.

LIVING IN LOS ANGELES

Left, the Wardner/Cahill family home in Los Angeles, about one mile from USC. My grandmother and the children loved the warm weather, sunny beaches and abundant live entertainment.

Right, my brother, called "Little Patrick" in the letters, with our dad Bob. Tom said in a letter he was quite proud of his "uncleship" to Patrick.

Below, from left, Jerry, my mom Jackie and Tom. This picture has me questioning: Who is taking the picture and what is my mother laughing at?

Top left is the second born and only girl of the nine children, Patricia. She was a concert pianist and played often to entertain our family. Tom was a singer and he wrote in a letter to her he was "recalling the patient hours you have spent playing for me."

Lower left, not sure who Jack was thumbing his nose at, but this picture sure captured his funny personality.

Below, Mark, left, with Jack, in the front yard of their Los Angeles home.

Above left, "Dear Mom," Mary Wardner Cahill, late 1930s at the family's Los Angeles home, to which all the letters to her were mailed. After I was born in 1945, my family lived in this house also, with her (then "Nana"), Patricia and Gram.

Above right, Hubba! Hubba! My handsome Uncle Tom in 1937, duded up for a date I bet. Pretty slick for a sixteen-year old.

The cartoon strip, below: I'd say Jack (in white shirt) started this fracas, but it looks like Mark emerged victorious. Never a dull moment for my grandmother!

At a Los Angeles area beach on the Pacific Ocean, Tom, left, with Frank in the late 1930s. I bet the young ladies in town were happy to see the Cahill boys arrive from New Hampshire. Multiple choice brothers.

Bottom left, Jack, about fourteen years old. His mother captioned this picture "Happy Jack." Jack added "Slap" so the revised caption was "Slap Happy Jack."

Bottom right, are Mark, left, and Tom. Tom and Jack were both good older brothers to Mark. Away from home in the Army, each wrote a letter to Mark with congratulations, encouragement and a bit of advice prior to his entry into the Navy in December 1943.

THE WAR YEARS

Mary Wardner Cahill, "Dear Mom"
Wearing Army Air Corps
"Sweetheart" Aircrew Wings

Army Air Corps
Lieutenant
Thomas D. Cahill

Army Air Corps
Technical Sergeant
John W. "Jack" Cahill

FRANK: *Frank was married but scouted girls for his brothers. From a letter to his mother, "In case Tommy gets sent to the New York area, be sure he gets the address and phone number I've enclosed for Alice Belbey, the sister of a friend of mine. I spent the weekend at his house, and believe me, this kid is some dish. About as choice a bit of fluff as there is. Tommy would be very welcome there."*

Frank Cahill, U.S. Army

JERRY: *I enjoyed this excerpt by Jerry about Bob Hope's appearance at the San Diego Army Base: "I went to see Bob Hope when he was down here a couple of weeks ago. Because we waited so long outside while the broadcast was going on, he said that he would give a little longer program, and he certainly kept his word. It lasted about an hour and a half and was really good. He certainly is clever and he does more of these extra jobs than anyone."*

Jerry Cahill, U.S. Army

MARK: *Barely eighteen in December 1943, Mark entered the Navy. I remember Mark as a funny guy, always laughing. From a letter to his mother, "We hit San Diego last night and had chow. Hit the sack at 9:30 and got up again at 10:00. Some of the boys were cutting up so the CQ got rather mad. We got all dressed and he gave us H - - - -. As far as we know, he doesn't like guys from LA so we all discovered that we were from anywhere but LA. Me, I'm from New Hampshire again."*

Mark Cahill, U.S. Navy

Crewmembers of Squadron 486, Bomb Group 340, Corsica, France, 1944. Tom is back row, second from left. His good friend Angelo Adams, also standing, is fifth from left. Squadron pet Jocko, who has a recurring role in Tom's letters, is front row, center.

On July 10, 1944, Tom sent this photo to his mother: "The enclosed photo was taken about six weeks ago. The characters are, left to right, Wells Morris, Jr., of Westwood, Yours Truly, a couple enlisted men, and on the right Lt. Angelo Adams. I don't remember where he is from but I think he married a girl from Santa Ana. The picture was taken by the group public relations man wanting something of 'typical' combat men. Morris, Adams and I at that time had flown exactly NO missions."

Left, Jack at Emporia State Teachers College in Kansas where he was stationed for four months in 1943. He often wrote how much he enjoyed the town, the welcoming people and the social activities they arranged for the soldiers. This is my favorite picture of Jack.

Below, Jack's telegram to his mother telling her of his arrival in Emporia.

WESTERN UNION

1201

SYMBOLS

CLASS OF SERVICE

This is a full-rate Telegram or Cable-gram unless its de-ferred character is in-dicated by a suitable symbol above or pre-ceding the address.

DL = Day Letter
NT = Overnight Telegram
LC = Deferred Cable
NLT = Cable Night Letter
Ship Radiogram

A. N. WILLIAMS
PRESIDENT

NEWCOMB CARLTON
CHAIRMAN OF THE BOARD

J. C. WILLEVER
FIRST VICE-PRESIDENT

The filing time shown in the date line on telegrams and day letters is STANDARD TIME at point of origin. Time of receipt is STANDARD TIME at point of destination

IKA53 40 NL COLLECT=EMPORIA KANS 28

MRS MARY W CAHILL=

2949 1/2 VAN BUREN PL LOS A=

1943 MAR 10 AM 5 35

=DEAR MOM AM IN AIR CORPS DETACHMENT KANSAS STATE TEACHERS
COLLEGE EMPORIA KANSAS THIS TOWN IS REALLY NICE FIND I NEVER
SAW SUCH ACCOMMODATING PEOPLE. WISH GRAMMA A HAPPY 86 FOR
ME LETTER WILL FOLLOW SOON YOUR LOVING SON=

JACK.

86.

THE COMPANY WILL APPRECIATE SUGGESTIONS FROM ITS PATRONS CONCERNING ITS SERVICE

Tom was artistic like his landscape painter mother. He had several art books as well as supplies that he shared with squadron buddies on Corsica. He sent home this sketch, left, of the tent ("the dump") that he shared with good friend and fellow bombardier Bill "Willy" Mravinec, who was from Pennsylvania. I especially like where Tom labels for his mother "your picture," the "settee" and "Poets' Corner" with the typewriter on which he wrote many of his letters.

In August 1944, Tom received the Air Medal for "meritorious achievement while participating in aerial flight." He wrote his mother that many men received awards that day, "so don't think I did anything extraordinary."

Left, the back side of Jack's shaving mirror, a collage he made of his family to take with him when he joined the Air Corps. It explains a few old pictures I found with heads cut out of them.

Below, with his crew, Jack, back row, far right. In 1944, they flew this B-24 Liberator bomber around the country for three months, then left Topeka, Kansas, on July 23, to ferry this ship to England via Labrador, Ireland and Wales.

Left, another photo of Jack at a favorite spot, the lake in Emporia, Kansas. The dark corners of this picture are scorch marks from the fire at my grandmother's house in 1964. That is how close we came to losing Tom and Jack's letters and photos.

Below, future radio operator Jack practiced Morse code sometimes in his letters, as in this sign-off to his mother.

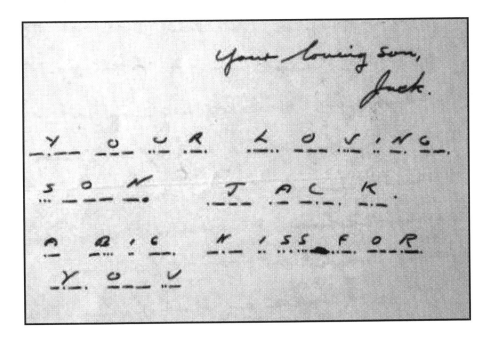

Upper, Tom wrote home, "The enclosed picture was taken before Christmas and the scene is our squadron officers' mess. I am right behind that pipe and under that mess of hair. The wall decorations were all done by Willy. Comrade Adams is to my right. Hearts I think was his game."

Lower, congratulatory photo issued to fliers of 12th Air Force B-25 Mitchell Medium Bombers, 340th Bomb Group, Mediterranean Theater, when they helped make bombing history with 100% target hits in a full month of operations.

*In August 1944, Tom sent this picture home, writing on the back,
"Smitty and Hill brought this one back. My airplane, but I wasn't
flying in it that day." He had just returned from leave to Rome and
wasn't yet back in the missions rotation.*

*Tom's friend Willy took this picture of him and Jocko. It's my favorite
picture of Tom. I'm sure glad it survived the fire.*

Three of Tom and Jack's brothers, in uniform. Upper left, Frank with wife Peggy and Mary Elizabeth ("Liz") born in August 1943. Peggy wrote beautiful letters, two of which I included in the book. Tom said he would re-read her letters for "sheer literary satisfaction." Upper right, Mark with my brother Patrick, about three years old in this picture. Below, Frank, left, and Jerry, both in the Army, stateside during the war.

This postcard is the only communication from Jack from England that survived our family home's fire. There are other postcards, but none with writing. It was confirmation that Jack went to London on leave at least once.

THE KING WASN'T IN TODAY,
SO NO COLORFUL GUARDS
WERE OUT. THE BIG
STATUE ON THE RIGHT IS
THE QUEEN VICTORIA
MEMORIAL. TO THE FAR
RIGHT, OBSCURED BY
THE TREES, A BUZZ

BOMB HIT. NO SE-
RIOUS DAMAGE THO.
BUT THOSE BOMBS
PACK A WALLOP.

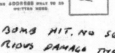

In a 1944 letter, Tom told his mother he sent her some money for her birthday, April 12. It arrived in this envelope, which seems to have had quite an adventure getting to Los Angeles.

HOW THIS BOOK GOT ITS NAME

This book was named by my grandmother, Mary Wardner Cahill, in a letter she wrote to Jack in 1943. In a collection she called "Dear Mom," she kept copies of all the wartime letters available for family and friends in Los Angeles to read.

Prior to seeing this letter, I had begun to think the letters should be compiled in a book, at minimum for my family. The moment I read this letter I knew what that book would be named.

Jack sometimes called her Mamacita, thus her signature in response.

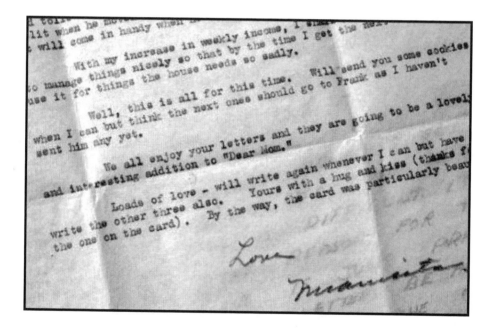

Spring 1944

JACK - THE TWENTY SPOT
Yuma, Arizona, March 3, 1944 ("32 days from home")

Dear Mom,

Received the latest communique from 2949-1/2 Van Buren today. It was really a swell letter, as usual. I do feel a lot better and I must be gaining a little weight too. God knows I eat enough. I have a bit of a headache tonite but not bad. I have so much to say that it is hard to start in.

First off tho I am doing OK in school. I have an average of about 96.5. My final exam on the machine gun netted me a 96. Tomorrow will tell the story tho.

We have to strip and reassemble the .50 cal blindfolded. I can do it but if my time doesn't improve I won't get such a good grade. Sighting etc. has been simple and I made a 96 on my final in it.

Basic deflection (skeet) is a lot of fun. I was no. 2 man in our group today with 33 for 50. That is lousy but better than a lot of them.

I received a letter from Tom the other day which I will answer soon. He extended the use of his "mazooma" to me on my trip home. I will most likely take him up on it—gently if possible. But with that valuable asset in sight I will enclose a 20 spot.

I wish you would pick me up a fountain pen and send it on. Don't pay over a couple of bucks for it as I may lose it as I did my other one. You can't buy one for hell or damn here. Of the rest of the money you can buy yourself something, maybe a shampoo and a wave, or send it to the telephone company.

I doubt if I will get to the East Coast. It will be Salt Lake City or Fresno. If things pan out OK I will see Tommy.

Guess I don't have so much to say after all. I am sort of tired and I hear my sack calling me. All for naught and I'll see you in 32 days. Take it easy.

Your loving son, Jack
P.S. Don't forget the pen.

TOM - THE SQUIRREL CAGE
Columbia, South Carolina, March 4, 1944

Dear Mom,

This will be a short one for the purpose of the enclosed. Do whatever you want with it. Today I applied for an allotment of $100 per month beginning April 1st.

It is Saturday night and there is not a damn thing to do. Bill is in New York. Dick is out somewhere. Connors is in Ohio with our gadget and My Boy is going to the Chatterbox with his frau. Due to a mixed up schedule I have had to break two dates in two days (the first ones I have even had time to make in two weeks) and now I'm stuck without anything to do. I've a million letters to write but I'm darned if I can do it tonight. With all the griping on my mind, they won't be very pleasant so I'll skip 'em for now.

Yesterday we were down to Myrtle Beach and I fired from the top and tail turrets and waist guns of our B-25. Incidentally, our B-25-H has more machine guns now than a B-17 and that's not counting the cannon either. We are gradually cleaning up our missions and this week we will probably make our Bahamas trip. It's an eight hour flight and over water most of the time. We're going to try to weekend in Pennsylvania too so I might get to see Frank.

Jack's notice about one and only one furlough is just what I told you so I guess the trip is settled for now. With the dough you have you might send some to Jack to fly to Los Angeles—will give him an extra day and will still leave enough for you and Pat to go to Frisco if I'm up there—or go anyway. I still want you to make the Concord trip though 'cause God knows you need a vacation.

Pat is really in the war effort and I hope it won't be too much for her. There is a fellow here who plays the piano during meals at the club. He can make me so homesick that I could bawl all over the place if I didn't keep my mind on my business. He doesn't use a scrap of music but from his technique I know he doesn't play by ear. The guy before him used to read a newspaper while he played but was not nearly as good. Best of all is his selection of tunes. He'll have medleys of all the songs from one show or operetta. Then a batch of Gershwin or Cole Porter plus some light classics. I can't wait to hear Pat get hep on her grand.

The crew is shaping up pretty well now. They know what to expect of us and vice versa. It's quite a job though as we have to be father, mother and banker to them: See that they get fed, keep them out of trouble, go to bat for them when they get in trouble, prevent squabbles among them, be human with them and at the same time draw that fine line which will assert itself in a critical moment when just a word is a command. That's the hardest part.

We go to classes together and naturally get to know one another pretty well. Plenty of kidding but still we have to keep them on the ball. In the last three weeks I've found out why I'm an officer and so far I guess I've held up my end of the bargain. The pilot has had a couple difficulties. I've been lost a couple times. We understand each other pretty well now and cooperate without ever a suggestion of what to do. Keep your fingers crossed.

Your loving son, Tommy

P.S. I sent a package to Little Patrick the other day—the 29th, so let me know if he doesn't get it.

P.P.S. In this and future letters "us" means my pilot and/or crew, and also "My Boy" means pilot. I think we'll name our ship the "Squirrel Cage" for obvious reasons. Tommy

JACK - THE FAST-TALKING LADY
Yuma, Arizona, March 13, 1944

Dear Mom,

I've got some new stationery so I will give you the first letter on it. The picture is the McCoy of one I sent you at an earlier date. I intend to buy a leather insignia for my jacket similar to it and will have Pat change the "YAAF" (Yuma Army Airfield) to "JACK" if she has time. It is a Disney design I think and is rather clever.

Today we fired the .50 cal and the .30 cal. It was a lot of fun but from tomorrow on out, our firing is for keeps. Today was practice and orientation—thank God. I got only a few hits with the .50 cal but the average was only about six. I am more acquainted with the fast-talking lady now tho and hope to do better on the morrow.

If I can duplicate my performance on the turrets with the .30 cal, I will be happy. I got 53 hits out of 100. That was good but I hope to improve it if I can. Both guns are mighty lethal and I would hate to be on the wrong end of them.

If you stopped to figure it out, you would find that a plane like Tommy's could dish out around 11,900 .50 cal slugs a minute. That is a lot of lead!

We started learning malfunctions today too. It is interesting and beneficial. We have an exam on them Saturday but I expect no trouble.

Tonight finds me just 21 days from graduation and better still, only 23 days from home. If all goes well, I will be there sometime on Wednesday morning, and on time for Easter and your birthday. Believe me, it is seeming longer everyday but is getting closer every day, actually.

Well, Mater, I've padded this enough. I am on my way to the PX for a cup of coffee and then the sack. I will be glad when I get home and get some good coffee! Take it easy and remember me to all.

Your loving son, Jack

TOM - EXPLORING THE COASTAL CURVES
Columbia, South Carolina, March 13, 1944

Dear Mom,

It seems like ages since I last wrote to you and to be truthful, I can't remember exactly when it was. I remember sending you the money orders, which, by the way, have you received? And I hope you heard from me at least once since then. One day or week I am so busy that I do not even have time to eat, and other days (rare ones!) we are grounded by bad weather, and before I can realize what has happened, my day is gone and I'm back on the treadmill.

The last week has been different only for the fact that Thursday we flew down to Florida by way of Jacksonville, West Palm Beach, and then landed at Drew Field in Tampa. We spent the afternoon there and came back that night. Going down we hit for the beach at Jacksonville and followed the coastline—every inlet was explored and every curve followed—until we hit West Palm Beach and then we cut across the peninsula to Tampa. The water was an unbelievably beautiful blue-green and the beach made my mouth water. We were flying quite low and every so often seagulls would blur past us.

Tampa itself was rather a disappointment but for the first time since I was in Kansas City, Thanksgiving eve, I sat in an honest to goodness bar with leather upholstering, soft lights and the bar just about high enough to hang your chin on. The drinks got better as they came and went along and it was certainly a change from bringing my own liquor (when it was available and I was off the wagon). However, as we still had seven hundred and some odd miles to fly that evening, we were careful not to have too many and believe me it took a lot of patriotism to do that.

I made up for lost time last weekend and had three dates in a row (two different girls). Oddly enough, the week before I was so busy flying that I had to break three. Previous to that I had not even been able to make any but now we have Sundays off so there is some hope of relaxation. Friday night we went to the only place in town open on Friday night—namely, the Elk's Club—and in deference to my date I drank straight Cokes. Being slightly tetched to begin with, I still had a lot of fun but Saturday morning I had a terrific headache.

Saturday night, not having to fly as I had figured, I agreed to aid one Lt. Mike Miles of Harvard, North Hollywood and other points of the globe, and squire a date, which was till then dateless. The occasion was a gay nineties dance at the officers' club. I can't explain it in a few words, to be worthwhile, but I had made a reservation in advance and then thinking I was not going, I gave it away to a half dozen people who "might go" but weren't sure. It finally ended up with a dozen of us at my original table for four. (We had to remove a few name cards from neighboring tables to handle the job.) At the door, they were giving bows for the ladies and handle bar mustaches for us men. Well, with the aid of Johnny Walker's Deluxe and my handlebar mustache trimmed a la Hitler, I must confess that whether I or anybody else could have done anything to prevent it, I became for a while the life of an already lively party. Some of the GIs put on a swell floorshow with a barbershop quartet, a bicycle-built-for-two and fitting costumes.

Sunday night was the final spree in my little social life and consisted of Coke and pineapple juice at Pat Salley's house, a walk to the theater where we couldn't get in, Coke and coffee at Walgreens, and back to Pat's to listen to the radio. From Frank to Mark, the boys will no doubt be snickering that I just listened to the radio, but so help me, it is the first time I've been able to listen to a radio since I left Santa Ana. Despite requests otherwise, we listened to Schubert, Beethoven, Mozart and Tchaikovsky. The whole evening cost me ten cents, believe it or not, and I felt "at home" for the first time in Columbia.

I've stopped trying to look into my immediate future but I think my last letter still covers the situation pretty well. I had hoped to be able to see Frank but that looks out now. The whole crew has tried to decide where we will go on our RON and it did not seem quite fair to go where just one of us preferred leaving the rest to maybe not such a good time.

So, if anything is possible, we'll either go to New York City or Miami. Most of us have never been to either place and if we go to the former I hope to perhaps hear a concert or something; if we go to the latter, I'm going to spend a whole day just sleeping on the beach.

They told us today to be ready for the Bahamas trip Wednesday, weather permitting. The whole trip is about 1,400 miles and in three or four legs. It will be the final test for my navigation (they send along a celestial man to make sure all goes well) and I hope we get off the first attempt. Sometimes weather will delay takeoff a half dozen times. As it is now, to me, it is just another trip but a couple postponements might bring on a sweating.

Connors got back from Wright Field with good results. The colonel in charge of instruments and navigation for the Army Air Forces has approved the idea and recommends it to be tried out at Central Instructor's School, Monroe, Louisiana, so now we are waiting to hear their verdict.

As you may have read Hendrik Willem van Loon died the day before yesterday. I have read so many of his books that it seems like a personal loss. It always gave me some reassurance to know that somewhere in this crazy world was a man who seemed to know what was going on and could offer any decent solutions to its problems. Just a couple of hours before I read about him in the papers I had bought a copy of his *Story of America* which seems to be better than all his other works.

Incidentally, just by chance, Sunday I met the editor of the *State*, the local morning paper. He invited me to drop in on him sometime for a talk and I certainly am going to. There's a lot of things that puzzle me about this part of the country and maybe he can at least give me another slant. That's all now.

Your loving son, Tommy

I tried to find out if Joe and Tom's navigation "gadget" was approved and used. Couldn't find anything.

TOM - GET A GUY FOR HER, OR ELSE!
Columbia, South Carolina, March 20, 1944

Dear Mom,

There is really a lot to write about but I just can't seem to do it. While on my way to the Bahamas, I imagined myself writing a detailed account from my preflight briefing to landing. But after nine solid hours of trying to read drift, giving position reports, and wishing I could stretch myself for just a minute, and to take more than one step without tripping over canteens, emergency equipment or bumping into the walls of my "office," the thrill of flying over water and being a big shot on the trip became decidedly monotonous and not something to write home about.

My navigation down there was not spectacular (in fact, it stunk) but we did hit the field coming back after a straight leg of five hundred and some odd miles. Going down we went first northeast to Cape Lookout and then out to sea to a pair of coordinates and then to the islands. Getting shot at will at least offer a little diversion from just drift meters and computers!

We are still trying to wrangle a ship to take to New York for a brief break in this South. There's not much time left. And that brings us to a quite important matter.

It is fairly safe to say that we will ship out before the end of the month. Probably to Savannah and then out from there. What I want to get across to you is that there will no doubt be times when I cannot write, wire or phone—that may be in about ten days, say. I'll keep you informed as to where to write as much as I can.

I may need some more cash which you may have. They say we will have to have $200 before we can ship out to cover a long trip or delay in pay, etc. I'll get paid before I leave, of course, minus $100 sent directly to you but I don't know how I'll stand. I'll have to buy summer uniforms, that is certain. Not a blouse, but shirts and slacks. I may or may not get to Los Angeles. I'm sure you can understand that. But if I do! Oh, boy! You'll probably have to put up the whole crew (5) but that will be nothing!

This week sometime, I'll send you whatever personal papers I have here. Some will concern you and there will be nothing "private" about any of them, as I don't get that kind of mail anymore. As Jack has been informed, his furlough will probably be the one and only. So April belongs to him—though I'll try to do my damnedest to join him.

What I would like you to do, if you can, as quickly as possible is: (1) Don't worry; (2) Let me know how much, if any, of that money I've sent home there is available in an emergency; (3) Let me know exactly how to reach Jack at Yuma if I should get a chance (tho it is highly improbable); and (4) Be sure that Jack has enough money to travel better than coach, which he no doubt would buy for himself. Maybe even fly from Yuma.

I'm trying to get all these things straightened out as quickly as possible as I'm going to be quite busy these next few days.

I must confess that in spite of the above preparations I am actually making more important considerations for coming home than leaving. I've been trying to find out as much as I can about this country so that I won't go bragging about a lot of hooey. Van Loon's *America* covers the subject very well for this lad's hurried reading. Articles here, there and everywhere are also taken in, and though it may sound funny, my latest book is *The Importance of Living* by Lin Yutang!

It's funny but the closer we get to combat, the less we think of it and the more we think of the country we will come back to. I haven't thought much of it as to my personal future but that of all of us. This is not necessarily as altruistic as it seems as the welfare of all of us has a direct bearing on our own, but the old politics of prewar days are thicker than ever now and they are trying to decide the peace before they get it. But that is an old argument of mine and you've probably heard it before so I'll let it go.

Saturday night we had a party at the Carrolton Club. Thinking our old gang was going to be split up soon we figured on having it while the having was good. (Looks like we'll all go out together now.) A couple days after the ball started rolling (no pun intended) Dick got orders to leave before the rest of us. As you know, Dick and Bill and I have been together almost a year now. We are different as 1-2-3 but somehow we always got along.

Dick had a disappointment a la femme while at Vegas and never quite got over it I guess, as he never went out with us except stag. He's a pretty sharp lad too which made it more extreme. Bill has always sort of been neutral on the subject and at times would even get slightly spiffed and would go on a date only if it was somebody I knew real well. As you know me, I am always in favor of a party so the only real problem was Dick.

For ten months it was no soap. Finally after three solid days of persuasion (I had never seen his pending date but was taking Pat's word for her) he agreed to come. To make a long story short, he had some sort of an accident with the cannon. No other word than that. It was Saturday night and we had an extra girl. Every guy I knew had vanished. Finally, Pat says, "Get a guy for her, or else." Well, I got two guys! So we had our party without Dick, toasting him whether he was alive, dead or wounded. It finally turned out that he got a bad bruise and nothing more except that it may be enough to keep him here long enough to go out with us. So, perhaps it was for the best though we still kid him that he did it on purpose.

Wednesday night, I'm supposed to go to Pop Clark's for supper and his wife swears I'll make a cake before I can eat.

Well, I'll write again as soon as I can. If you can take care of those items, I'll certainly appreciate it. As for the rest, you'll just have to rely on my judgment.

Your loving son, Tommy

TOM - PREPARING TO SHIP OUT
Columbia, South Carolina, March 28, 1944

Dear Mom,

I'm trying the second time to write to you. With all the beauties of spring about me I get off on a million tangents from my usual GI griping to the world situation. To any reasonable extent, I am helpless to do anything about them, and all it seems to add up to is a confused crackpot letter, which if I can't make head nor tail of, I certainly should not expect you to. So this will be a brief one as much to the point as I can make it.

To parody a popular song, it's "No leave, no nothing" unless something turns up at our next stop I can only hope to go to Frisco and drop in on the way. I have been "alerted." The orders are in and the 31st is the day. Today probably as you read this we will probably first go to a port of embarkation on the East Coast here and from there to wherever we are going. What you must understand is that chances are I will be unable at times to communicate with you in any way. It will not necessarily mean that I have left the country but simply that they don't care to have anybody know where we are. So don't worry if there is silence for a while. I'll make every effort possible to contact you and I'm still hoping to land at Burbank or Glendale.

The last few days have been spent buying equipment (money order received OK and thanks) and saying goodbyes. I don't have many friends here except the fellows I came with. Connors and I were over to Pop Clark's the other night for dinner. Pop is going with us. I've been with him now since last April and his wife has named me heir to his equipment, etc., and he is always ready with any help or advice when I need it. Lillian, his wife, will probably call on you when she gets home to Pasadena.

Then we have our little stag gatherings. Sunday night we had my pilot's instructor so tight that he couldn't make the flight line in the morning. He, the instructor, has been to combat, bailed out of a B-25 over Sicily and as one old Irishman to another, we had some mighty sessions. He gave us a lot of good advice too. He's so fed up with this red tape around the States that he is going back to combat next month.

Tomorrow night I'm going to dinner at Joe and Mickey's and Thursday night it's a date with Pat Salley. Incidentally, Joe is going up to Concord again Saturday, but of course, I won't be able to go.

Well, I'm afraid that is the limit now. I can't wait to get going and I only hope I have a chance to see you all once more before I ship out. The picture of Little Pat was terrific and he is now quite well known here at the base. Keep your fingers crossed and you'd better get some V-Mail.

Your loving, leaving son, Tommy

JACK - HOME IN EIGHT DAYS
Yuma, Arizona, March 28, 1944

Dear Pat,

Just an answer to your short but relieving note. I was glad to hear that it was merely company and broken glasses that prevented Mom from writing. I was afraid it might have been sickness and that would be too bad in more ways than 5 or 6. She has been under a big strain and it will be bigger before long.

Yesterday was a big day—long and hard. We were up at 3:30 for breakfast, cleaning up, etc. and then to the flight line for a briefing on camera missions. It was seven before we got off and we went out to the air to ground range. It was beautifully clear and the mountains, while being actually small, would rise abruptly and in a beautiful contrast of color from the barren and miserable desert wastes of this so-called state.

The targets are set at various distances from the plane, and tho it seems strange to most people, you aim in back of them, and on some, a large distance in back. We had no limit-stop on our waist gun and it surprises me that we returned with a whole empennage section on our ship. Some of the boys get pretty much absorbed in their work and hold the triggers down for a longer burst than they should.

One guy in particular does this often—he has long since acquired the names of "Snafuperman," "Carrots," "Typhoon," and at times, words no woman should hear. He is the screwiest character I've met since joining this Army. He is torn between two problems. He admits being afraid of combat, and he'd like to be an instructor. There was a call for volunteers for instructors school but he didn't sign up. He can't decide which is worst—combat or Arizona. I say Arizona.

The last two hours were a camera mission. We have a movie camera mounted on a turret. I managed to get a few hits plus a beautiful bunch of sky and a good picture of our tail section. A lot of the others knocked out some nice shots of the other B-17s in our flight. The idea was to have an AT-6 fly at you as a fighter would and you must nail him. It is lots of fun but I doubt if we will go on any more rides like that. I still have to fire five or six hundred rounds at air-to-air targets.

I hope you appreciate my effort in writing this. I am on the flight line bucking a stiff wind to say nothing of the dust raised by the planes.

We were on the go until 10 last night. We had a two-hour exam (final) and it covered everything we've learned and lots we "didn't learn." It was rough to say the least.

I'll be home in eight days so I'll kill time until then and we can have some good fun and long, delayed talks. Guess this is all so I'll see you later.

Your loving brother, Jack

JACK - HOME IN SIX DAYS
Yuma, Arizona, March 29, 1944

Dear Mom,

The time by my new watch is 18:58:43. We were issued our stuff today and the two favorites are the 17-jewel Elgin wristwatch and the B-4 traveling bag. They are both swell and no doubt you saw Tommy's B-4. We also got an A-3 bag which is sort of a square barracks bag with handles and zippers for our equipment and flying clothes. I think we are required to take them home with us so you will get a firsthand look at what the well-dressed gunner will wear. I intend to throw some laundry in too.

Today we went on a high-altitude mission. It was only to 15,000 feet but my feet got damn cold. The whole thing was to get experience with the mask. I did some firing at a target and got off 200 rounds. If my shots went where I aimed, I got a lot of hits—I will know tomorrow. That leaves me with 300 rounds to go and I hope to accomplish that on Friday.

We went down to about 300 feet and fired air to ground. It is out on the desert that we do this during the hottest time of the day. The heat comes up from the ground and really knocks that B-17 around. My stomach is still a bit upset but I didn't get sick. We had straight sights on our gun and I really raised the sand around those targets. I really go for that gun! I have a few slugs that I will bring home as souvenirs of this dump. They are empty so no danger is up.

I had another "scare" today. This time those dopes wanted to make me an instructor! Can you imagine, me an instructor? Not me. Some guys get drafted into it but I turned it down. Of course, I would be safer there, etc., and not such a worry to you, but teaching SNAFU gunners isn't my idea of how to fit into this war. With Tom and Mark into it, I can't see it. I know you will savvy my feelings and realize that I am just silly enough to stick my neck out. Like Tommy says, "As long as you must stick your neck out, you may as well have fun doing it."

I've had most of my final exams and passed OK. I made 93 in radio mechanics, 94 in code and procedure, 96 in aircraft recognition. These were easy compared to our final comprehensive and that was really rough. I made 86 on it and answered 129 out of 150 OK. We have a test on turrets Saturday and that's the last.

This is it for now and I'll see you in a little more than six days. Say hello to all and I can hardly wait to see you.

Your loving son, Jack

FRANK - THE STUBBORN LITTLE WENCH
Lebanon, Pennsylvania, April 2, 1944

Dear Ma,

I don't know whether this will be much of a letter; it's rather late in the evening and not much of anything is happening around here except that Mary squalled for the last two hours after we put her to bed.

She's a stubborn little wench, and seemed determined not go to sleep. She's quiet now, though, and will, presumably, sleep through the night.

As a rule, she is a very attractive young lady and seems to be quite strong, alert, and intelligent. She seems to have grown even since she came here, and can now stand up and is making efforts at self-propulsion. Putting her on her stomach is no longer a guarantee that she will stay that way, and we have had to lower the springs in her bed for fear that she would pitch herself over the railing. We got her a Taylor Tot and a playpen which will be delivered tomorrow.

Peg seems to be quite happy here, although she gets a little lonesome during the day. At least I think she does, although she hasn't said anything about it.

Soon, though, she should get acquainted around and I think then she'll be busy during the day and not quite so all alone.

We were fortunate in getting a rather nice house here. It's a stone place, French Provincial walls about 2 feet thick and rather well furnished with the exception of the dining room which is rather shabby.

There is a grand piano here which Pat would love and a radio which isn't too bad, although radio reception in these hills is poor to say the least.

The back of the winter has been broken and the trees seem to be budding. There are four specimens of bulbous plants coming up. One I think is crocus and another iris, but I'm not sure. Anyway Peg is all excited about them and is waiting with as much patience as she can muster.

There isn't much else doing here. I hope you are all well at home. Peg says she will write to you this week.

Love, Frank

PEG - THE SECRET LIFE OF AN ARMY WIFE
Lebanon, Pennsylvania, April 3, 1944

Dearest Pat,

It was swell to get your letter this morning. And I can well imagine you are holding your breath waiting for Jack's arrival. I had a letter from him a few days ago in which he can neither talk nor think of anything other than his homecoming. I wish he were going to see his Goddaughter, but I guess the picture of her will have to do for a while yet.

I do wish Ma were going to get away for a while. It's wonderful to have the boys coming home, but I can't help but feel that as much as home means to them, getting away from the constant care of Grandma and the daily grind in general would mean even more to Ma.

I wish Tommy would be leaving from the East Coast and that Ma were coming up here and going to relax and visit everyone she knows in this vicinity. Wouldn't it be swell if right after a wonderful long visit with Jack, she could get ready and leave for a grand trip to visit with Tommy first and the rest of us by turn later? It would do her worlds of good.

You should see what progress the baby has made in the past two weeks. She can turn over from her back to her tummy and vice versa, hold her bottle, and stand up in her bed. She's so proud of herself on accomplishing this last that she bounces up and down and grins between the rungs of her bed like a mischievous elf.

Frank is a wonderful father. He is crazy about the baby and is convinced she shows promise of great beauty. In fact, right now he amazes his friends by interrupting their conversations with such exclamations as "Isn't she a knockout!" "Did you see her teeth?" "Look at her now!" Naturally, I'm tickled pink and his friends are very indulgent.

I guess your new stove will help a lot. It will make more room in the kitchen and will be an attractive and useful addition. When you get your nice tile sink, I'll bet Ma will feel like a different woman.

We have such a nice kitchen here that I'm almost as much inspired by it as I am by an appreciative husband to dream up the best meals I possibly can. I'm having a good time fulfilling Frank's special requests for desserts such as your chocolate fudge pudding, custard like Grandma used to make, chocolate prune cake and lemon pudding. Frank even had the cupboard full of the necessary ingredients for chocolate prune cake when I got here.

Now to describe our new abode: It is very old and very homey. The landlord told me it is over one hundred years old. It is up on a little hill all by itself. It is right in the middle on the highest part of the hill and the lawn slopes down all around. There is a circle drive with a few benches on either side. It seems to me to be a sort of private park or maybe a small estate. I'm of course exaggerating now, but it really is a lovely big yard. There are quite a few large trees around the house too. A duplex, both occupants have complete privacy from each other. The walls are so thick, no sound travels, and we can let our daughter howl herself to sleep with no thought of disturbing the neighbors.

Best of all, we are soon going to have loads of spring flowers. I don't recognize the eastern varieties so Frank has pointed the ones on our grounds out to me. We'll have violets, crocuses, daffodils, freesias and iris. Later in the season we will have roses galore and bridal wreath. I can hardly wait to see what the crocuses are like and to smell eastern violets. The house itself is stone bricks with white wooden shutters and a huge white paneled door with a large brass knocker. I think it is very good-looking. It is French Provincial architecture, so our landlord says.

It has pine floors that have been waxed I guess because the dust mop slips over them easily. It has white woodwork and two deep bay windows in the living room and two in the dining room. Besides our beautiful baby grand piano, which is quite a dust catcher and also a temptation to me to try out my memory on my two recital pieces, there is a darling loveseat that separates whenever we try proving its right to its name. It is upholstered in blue. There are two other chairs to match. There is a blond wood coffee table, a light maple lamp table, and an antique rocker of light maple.

There is a huge brick fireplace in one corner of the room and two steps, then a white paneled door which opens on to the rest of the stairway. The dining room has a pretty antique buffet, a wreck of a dining room table and a stinker of a chest that looks like Pandora's box. I feel much as she did too because it's locked. However I put a pretty cloth on the table, and a doily and a figurine on the chest, so the room is not too bad. The kitchen has everything: a beautiful electric range, a nice white sink which looks like those movable ones you get at Sears, a good electric refrigerator, and a pretty white cabinet with a built-in flour sifter.

Upstairs is the bedroom and the bathroom. There is another bedroom which is being used as a storage room. The bathroom is all right; nothing special, just the usual equipment. The bedroom is large and has two bay windows and a great big closet. There is a light maple set in it which is quite good looking and then, of course, the baby's bed. Her bed is very darling and of red maple with a little fawn and a bunny on the foot of it.

Now, I don't think I overlooked a thing, do you? Oh yes, we have a cellar and a little Dutchman with a bay window belly, strictly in keeping with our house to tend the furnace. He is very attentive and even more talkative, so I usually hide from him so I'll have enough of the day left to get my work done.

Next time I write I'll describe our new friends and the city of Lebanon, such as it is.

Lots of love, Peg

JACK - STRICTLY CHEESECAKE
Colorado Springs, Colorado, April 4, 1944

Dear Mom,

Your picture came today and it was marvelous! Thanks a lot, Mom— it filled a big gap in my life away from home—bigger than I thought it was. I couldn't guess what was in the package and the surprise was terrific. The popular guess among the crew was *45 years* so you see you apparently haven't aged much in my lifetime. It is strictly "cheesecake."

I am enclosing my will and I hope I have the privilege of tearing it up in a year or so. I am just about finished processing now. Today I went to the dentist and had one filled and one "patched." The last had broken off a bit so the tooth is now half tooth and half filling. I did a stretch of KP too and that can hardly be called processing. It is a bad mark on my mental service record but I am none the worse for wear.

Tomorrow I am supposed to fly but things are so "FUBAR" here that I doubt if we will. I am anxious to try the 24. It is faster than a 17 but it wasn't designed with personnel comforts in mind. It is redlined at 355 mph and that is OK for a big ship.

We are all strangers to the ship. Lt. Quinn, our pilot, has 150 hours on it but on a lighter model minus all the weight of turrets, etc. Also he is used to 90 octane and that makes a huge difference on instruments. The engineer is likewise in the dark and the co-pilot has never even been in one. All of our turret gunners are unfamiliar with their turrets, and so that leaves the bombardier, familiar to his bombsight, and myself, semi-familiar with my radio, but both of us in the dark about our ship.

That makes us all about even, and we have so far gotten on fine. Lt. Quinn got sore because we hit KP and investigated the matter and raised hell. It won't happen again. He looks a lot and acts a lot like Frank but is not so well built. Incidentally, I had a super letter from Frank.

I hope we start school quickly because the colonel wants to inspect us. If we get to school before the 8th, we will foil him.

I would like very much for you to come here soon. First, tho, I want to get some cash saved and it would be best if I get a line on things. We might even move to Montana or Wyoming in June so I don't know.

By the way, do you think you could pick up a silk or rayon *white* scarf someplace? It would be a very useful birthday present and I could put it to use often. Silk is preferred but scarcer I guess.

Thanks again for the picture—it is swell. See you later via airmail.

Your loving son, Jack

Comparing dates between this letter (April 4) and the last (March 29), it is evident that the leave Jack was counting down to was canceled with little notice. I'm sure he called his mother to break the news.

TOM - LITTLE PATRICK'S GIRAFFE
Savannah, Georgia, April 6, 1944

Dear Mom,

Well—sometime I'm going to begin a letter with something besides "well" but just now I don't feel very original—here I am writing you again and I'm still in the good old U.S. (even if it is still Dixie). Due to a couple military secrets I've been in Savannah a little longer than I planned. They have given the OK on writing from here so I'm taking this chance to bring you up to date.

The crew is all well and ready to go and today we took up our ship for a test hop. It is a beautiful silver job with dual controls. So now I'm a co-pilot with more to do than just pull up wheels. My Boy is giving me all the stick time he possibly can without endangering our lives (that is not endangering them so much) and now I can fly for fifteen minutes or so without making everybody in the ship sick from losing and gaining altitude! Whether we'll fly in this type of ship over there remains to be seen but in traveling halfway around the world I should learn something about flying. (Take no hints from "halfway around the world." Almost any place is that far and as yet I have no idea as to where I am going.)

Naturally I am excited at the prospects. You know how I have always wanted to see the world and it looks like I'm going to. I have not seen as much of this country as I would like to, but still quite a bit of it. Everything looks rather strange now, the people, small talk and things like nice clean bathrooms, officers' clubs and bars are a source of constant wonder. It is not with any feeling of sacrifice that I'm leaving them, but rather to make myself a right to those privileges. I've learned that conditions are only bad when you yourself are well off and hate to think of how other people can stand them. I guess none of my living conditions so far have been really rough, but in each one I have been able to adjust myself.

On bivouac the food was plain, without any individuality when heaped in a mess kit. You had your opinions as to whether it was good or bad but still you ate it. At the officers' club, in comparative luxury, you can heartily like or dislike the food though even at its worst it was probably still far better than that on bivouac. But in the final analysis, you got along anyway and it was really not so bad after all.

So that is the way it will be with me. I'm going to catch up on long overdue letters to the boys, Grandma, Betty and lots more. I will probably be able to quote my pocket edition of *Shakespeare's Five Tragedies* from beginning to end. For sport I'll practice with my .45 and a charming little hunting knife I now have. Spiritually I should have a wide-open field with the teachings of all the world's old beliefs, plus the added fact that I'll probably leave here on Good Friday. And finally, I expect to have a wonderful time growing all sorts of beards! Van Duke, goatee, handlebars! The field is practically unlimited—except for the slight difficulty I have in getting much past the "five o'clock shadow" stage!

Tomorrow I hope to grab time enough to phone home and talk to Jack. Despite nothing definite it now looks like California is out. I wanted to see him—and you all—just as badly as all of us here who now at least can look forward to no more partings—only the great homecoming day. But in case I cannot phone, you do know that you are very much in my thoughts and your birthday which is practically now will be a little delayed in my celebration.

Before I forget it, there are a few "business" matters I'll have to cover. I have just found out that your allotment will not begin until April 30. I got my full check and thinking it was a mistake, it came as a windfall this month when I need it and could easily be corrected next month when I won't need it. So I'll try to get to the post office tomorrow and get a money order in this letter. Don't expect any of my things to be sent to you from here. I managed to pack them all in my two bags and they will be less trouble to me than to you. You'll get a card with my new address from the War Department as soon as it is known and can be told.

Also, did Little Pat ever get the giraffe I sent him? In case he didn't you might write to Belk's Department Store, Columbia, S.C. It was bought February 29th and should have been shipped from there.

I'm pretty well supplied with everything just now but if Pat or somebody could send me the lyrics to "The Surrey with the Fringe on Top" from *Oklahoma!* I'd certainly appreciate it. It's driving me nuts to learn the words and I've paid for at least a dozen jukeboxes in a vain attempt to catch them all.

For the first month or so over there I'll be a student again. This may make me actually busier than when we start flying our missions and hinder writing. In any case it is the time for the least worry. After that, there is still nothing to worry about but you won't be convinced. I'll try to drop you short ones by V-Mail to let you know how things are, and longer letters if I can without violating the censorship I must apply to myself with more to tell.

By fate, coincidence or I don't know what, pretty near all my class from Albuquerque showed up here when I did. They came from four different fields, which was more amazing, and each day has been just a series of reunions, "Good luck and maybe I'll see you there."

Oh, yes, I have taken up smoking—the pipe. There may be some long hours ahead and a pipe looks like a good deal. With a short haircut tomorrow, nobody will know me.

So, I'll be seeing you sometime, and I'll tell you what the rest of the world is like—just further proving there's no place like home.

Your loving son, Tommy

I told my brother, "Little Pat," about the giraffe mentioned in this letter, and my sister-in-law Susan said, "We still have that giraffe. It's in your mother's trunk." I was stunned. My mother had saved it all her life, among her favorite things. This giraffe, purchased in South Carolina on Leap Day 1944, is now on display in my home.

PEG - HAPPY BIRTHDAY TO MA
Lebanon, Pennsylvania, April 7, 2944

Dearest Ma,

I hope our little birthday remembrance will reach you on the proper date, but in case it doesn't, this will let you know we're thinking of you.

We're all doing splendidly here. You'd be surprised at the progress the baby has made just since we arrived. I think I mentioned her latest accomplishments in my letter to Pat. Anyway, whenever I take her out (which is about every day) she attracts a great deal of attention. It's always windy enough here to require the baby's blue coat in addition to a sweater and her leggings, so she really does look like a little doll. We bought her a Taylor Tot and she stands up in it most of the time and reaches out toward everyone passing her. Her cheeks are terribly chapped, but they look like red apples and are very becoming.

All of the children I've seen up here are pasty-looking and chalk-white. Frank says it's because they stay indoors so much. But they don't look like babies who have had proper diets or health habits.

Tonight will be the first time Frank has had to be away since we landed. He is duty officer tonight, and won't be home until tomorrow at noon. He is through at noon Saturdays, has all day Sunday, and is home about 5:30 every evening. He draws duty officer about every two weeks, and will be gone overnight. He will have to stay at camp one weekend out of every two or three months.

We know sooner or later Frank will have to go over because the President issued some sort of ruling to the effect that officers can only stay in the States a certain length of time, but we are trying to live just in the present. And right now the present is all that could be desired.

I guess you're happy as a lark having your Jack home. And I'll bet he is tickled to death to see everyone after an absence of fourteen months. Has he changed much? I imagine he seems much older and more mature. He's been so completely on his own that he would have had to grow up, although he had accomplished a lot in that respect while he was "the man of the house" the last few months before he left. Give him our very best wishes and all our love.

If you get a spare second, send me Bob and Jackie's address. I am enclosing with this letter one for you to give to Jack when you see him.

The baby just nearly knocked her brains out. She was pulling herself up in her playpen and slipped. She is surely active.

Lots of love, and I'll write soon again, Peg

JACK - THE LEAVE THAT DIDN'T HAPPEN
Lincoln, Nebraska, April 9, 1944

Dear Mom,

First I had better say "Happy Easter" and by the time you get this it will be "Many happy returns of the day." I feel pretty disappointed because I didn't get home for both occasions, but this war has suddenly grown bigger in my eyes and been dropped in the general vicinity of my lap. I guess that a lot of guys have discovered that the war isn't running itself; I know that I have. Just now I am sweating it out but may leave here in a week or so. Don't give up hope of my getting home because as long as I'm in the States I stand a chance.

I have been rather busy of late and have a formation to make soon. It smells very much like nite KP, but I'll know soon—too soon maybe.

Our position here is simple to explain. We are here to be processed and assigned to crews. The first is completed and I must say, the field is plenty efficient on that score. The assignment to crews is where the sweating comes. ("Sweating" isn't the right word for this place—it is cold as hell here.) There are four things that must be done, also. I've fired the pistol and have been paid to date so that leaves more first aid and another ride in the pressure chamber.

The radioman is also "amateur surgeon and doctor" on a big ship. We will be sent to B-17s or B-24s. I wanted medium bombers but that is handled by the Third Air Force. "The only way to get out of the 2nd AF is to die." (Almost a motto in these parts.)

There are many ex-combat men here for reclassification. My hat is off to any one of those guys. One good reason is that several of them declared open season on MPs last nite and knocked a fairly good number of them silly. In consequence, I think that "the curfew shall not ring tonite." That curfew is a pain right where it hurts the most.

I got a new issue of shirts here and a new pair of shoes. Also, a steel helmet, musette bag, overcoat and a few other items. We may be issued a .45 pistol too, but I don't know for sure. This camp is doing OK for the *tremendous* amount of men it must handle. It is at a good deal more than its normal capacity and many are bitter over the furlough cancelation incident and therefore not any too cooperative.

I would have called today but I've been busy as heck and the lines are crowded pretty much with guys that haven't talked with their folks in a lot longer time than I have with you. I will try to call on your birthday, but if I don't you will know that I'm on KP or something. This covers everything up until now so I will sign off. Say hello to everyone and I'll write as soon as something comes up. Be careful.

Your loving son, Jack
P.S. Mass was beautiful this morning with "Panis Angelicus" by post choir. The ten is for *you*, not the telephone company. Happy birthday. J

TOM - HAPPY BIRTHDAY, MOM
West Palm Beach, Florida, April 10, 1944

Dear Mom,

Couldn't find a thing at the PX so you get yourself something with the enclosed. Can't tell you anything just now other than all is well. Went to Mass and Communion Easter so feel pretty capable of anything right now. Mail will be delayed a few days until I have arrived at wherever I am going. So don't worry a bit. Happy Birthday and Easter, and I hope I'll be with you to celebrate the next one.

Your loving son, Tommy

TOM - THE DELAY
West Palm Beach, Florida, April 10, 1944

Dear Mom,

This morning in lieu of a birthday-Easter present I sent you $25 registered special delivery airmail. Money may be sent immediately from here after censoring but this letter and other mail will be held up a week or so to give us a head start out of here on any information which might have leaked out. I tried to get you something at the PX to give a more personal touch, but they just didn't have anything.

Saturday I took out an allotment of a bond a month to you and me. I tried to make it for you and Pat but my name has to be on it some place as long as it comes from my pay. I didn't know before that we were drawing pay for travel and rations as long as we are en route to our destination. It amounts to about $7.50 a day so I should get a head start on my finances. I'll probably take out more money in bonds when I see how it is to live over there.

Finances out of the way, will try to give you a little news. Easter was beautiful and warm. The chaplain gave a sermon which just seemed to hit the spot. I don't like to get sentimental about this business but it was nice to spend Easter in the States.

We should have gone sooner but we had a slight accident. My Boy stuck his head up through the hatch Friday when we were unloading baggage and our tail gunner's GI shoe caught him right in the teeth. It knocked two teeth clean out and cracked two more which had to be pulled. So, it meant a delay while he got a plate made. Colonels and majors on down all worked on him at the dental clinic to do a good speedy job.

So, today, when we were at the club eating, I kept noticing everybody at a nearby table looking our way. They were all pretty high ranking and kept me trying to figure out if I was in the wrong somehow. We finished our soup, then the waitress brought My Boy a plate of liver and onions. At this point the officers all got up to leave and one captain left the group, walking toward our table. Noticing then he was a dentist I began to put 2 and 2 together. He then put his hand on Whited's shoulder and said, "Well, boy, we were all watching to see if you would get through the soup. I guess you'll do all right now." I've seen everything now.

Well, we have a briefing to go to now. Don't worry if you don't hear from me soon as mail will be delayed. Write hello to all the boys.

Your loving son, Tommy
P.S. Now have short haircut and am starting a cookie duster. Will try to send pictures later.

JACK - THE LOCKET
Lincoln, Nebraska, April 13, 1944

Dear Pat,

Just an answer to your morale lifter of the 4th. As usual there is nothing to report so this will be a bit on the dull side.

Today we finished all of our lectures and our trip in the pressure chamber. That makes me eligible for shipping out of here now but I was ready for that a week ago. The trip in the chamber lasted only an hour but it was worth a fortune to me. As usual we went up without oxygen and stayed for about ten minutes. I volunteered to go up to 18,000 feet without oxygen.

A guy can't last long up there without the stuff and it is supposed to be like a "cheap drunk." You get dizzy and unsteady and your senses are dulled. You notice it but like a drunk you insist that you can do anything just as well. You laugh at the silliest things. You write on paper anything that comes to mind and when you get a bit "lit up" the instructor says to write your name and serial number.

As it happened this was the last thing I remember. I am enclosing the paper and you can see how my writing fell off. When you pass out you don't even notice it—just like going to sleep. A stream of oxygen brings you to and without realizing it you continue to do what you were last told, in this case it was writing my serial number. It is a funny sensation and best of all this "drunk" has no hangover trailing behind.

It was a valuable lessons tho because I will know what is going on if my air line is messed up or someone is stepping on it. It was worth the effort but definitely. I had a lot of trouble clearing my ears, now they are OK.

I don't know anything new so I will sign off. Take it easy. Before I forget I had some pictures taken tonite "al-a-moustache"! They are only 3-1/2 x 5 but will be OK to keep you posted and suitable for the boys.

Would you do me a favor and send me a snapshot (suitable for a locket) of myself? A certain young lady wants one and I would be glad to give this certain young lady one. Make it one of me as a GI. Thanks a lot.

Your loving brother, Jack

TOM - SOMEWHERE IN BRAZIL
Somewhere in Brazil, April 15, 1944

Dear Mom,

I'm writing this at a desk about three feet from a radio which is currently offering John Charles Thomas singing "Flow Gently Sweet Afton." It is the first good music I've heard in some time. However, it will probably be of more interest to you to know that I am "somewhere in Brazil." Just now it is getting ready to rain—but on the whole, the weather and atmosphere is not unlike good old California.

Yesterday I bought a pair of boots for which Brazil is now world famed. It seems that almost everybody in the Air Force has them. The equator is quite prompt about giving a tan and with my mustache (well, it will be some day) short haircut, pipe (now well broken in) and boots, you'd hardly know me. Everybody on the crew is well, though Whited is having trouble with his teeth—or lack of them. Bill Bohlman is also here along with lots of the old gang so we manage to keep things lively.

My address is temporary but I'll let you know when it is changed. Also despite the new 8 cent airmail rate you may write to me for 6 cents per half ounce and vice versa. Will try to write a longer one later.

Your loving son, Tommy

JACK - SALUDOS MAMALITA
Lincoln, Nebraska, April 16, 1944

Saludos Mamalita,

Madre caro, come sis ta questo giorno, son stato molto content de recivato tuo letter, e molto content de recivuto el addresse del Marie Margaritta, et Lieu Thomas. Questo giorno son nolto stank e un poco de giorno ci scruiari un lettra. Canco son stato picare de sentira de tuti genti, son a casa, ma son ci, e molto displeased. Magara un noltra, vergo casa, e guerdo questo giorno vina, e then son molto contento.

I guess it isn't enough for you to have to make copies of letters from us all—I make you half nuts with mine as it is. It will take an Italian to figure this one out. If Tom goes over by Italy maybe he can get it translated.

What I say tho is how are you, I received your letter today and was glad to get Peg's and Tom's addresses. It also states that it displeases me to read in the letters about what a swell time I am having at home (which I ain't because my leave was canceled). The last is that I hope those letters come true soon. Then, when I am home in my casa I will be "molto contento."

You can see how scarce news is here when I rely on foreign languages to pad this with. I will write Tom and Peg Tuesday when I get my pictures (Joe Carbonatto—my translator—says I look like Errol Flynn! Keee-rist!).

Absolutely nothing has happened and so I'll close now. I'll let you know if anything comes up. Saluto et millions de baci.

Tuo Spusa Figlio, Jack

TOM - AT WAR WITH THE MOSQUITOS
West Africa, April 19, 1944

Dear Mom,

Just a few lines to let you know I am well and have not forgotten you. I am now in West Africa which is quite a ways from home. The days are hot and busy and the nights are just one big battle against mosquitoes. By now I should be used to mosquito bed nets but I am not and don't care for them very much. They'll keep the little devils out but you have to go to bed an hour early to get out any that might have stowed away. It is cooler tonight, however, and I should be able to get a good sleep.

There is not much to tell about. Africa is alternately incredibly rich or incredibly poor but it is consistently big and hot. Some of the natives are exceedingly Americanized. Nine times out of ten if you start trying to get across an idea in sign language or pidgin English, they'll come back with some of the sharpest Brooklynese you've ever heard. The boys shoot quite a game of craps and they talk to the dice just about like you'll hear in any lively game.

One kid yesterday was showing us a sample of handwriting. It was a good hand and he said he'd been schooling for four years. Work a while, then school, work and more school. We asked him where his home was and he said, "In the bush." "How far?" "Well, if you walk it takes one week." As there is no other way for him to get there I guess he is about as far from home as we are. There were a surprising number of them going to school and I'm sure that when they grow up they'll not be pushovers for fifteen or twenty cents per day.

Yesterday, just to prove what a small world it is, I ran into a guy named McClure who was with Ralph Miner at Palm Springs and Long Beach. We had quite a talk and he told me to pass along a "hello" if you should contact the Miners. I'll probably write to Ralph after I get settled down. I've run into lots of guys, some even my old upper classmen from pilot preflight at Santa Ana.

Well, think I'll buzz off to the show now. It's Monty Woolley in *Holy Matrimony* and should be good. More letters later.

Your loving son, Tommy

JACK - CREWLESS, CARELESS AND PENNILESS
Lincoln, Nebraska, April 23, 1944

Dear Mom,

This will hardly be a worthwhile letter but should serve to keep you posted as to my health, unhappiness and nonsuccess. As yet I am still crewless, careless and gradually growing penniless. On the last I should say that my money has held up nicely this month but three trips to town dealt my purse a ghastly blow. At this stage of the game, I have nine bucks, and with payday still an uncertainty, I would appreciate it if you stood by in case of need. I will let you know if I need it.

The weather here is absolutely lousy. It has rained all month long and part of March too, so there is no fun gained in the long run by those culprits who violate the curfew and resort to the fence as a means of re-admittance to this no-good joint. This is an oft' practiced trick and to my knowledge has never backfired but has ruined many a good shoe. I abstain from the whole thing tho as it is no fun to traipse knee deep in mud, and a few extra hours of sack time can always be fitted into my curriculum.

I had a very good time last nite with my friend Rudolf J. Bryan. In spite of the surname, he is still a Polock (sp?) and calls himself a bohunk to cinch the deal. We drank several beers and at one time we had 5 beers in 5 different places, downed to the tune of a polka and all within 25 minutes.

I have a standing invitation to go to Trafford, Pa., at any time and he is going to take me to one of those Polish picnics with all their gayety, color and quaint native dress. He says they are terrific and I find a polka is a good chunk of music to drink to. It inspires one to bigger and better beers. Likewise, if he comes to LA, we shall have to have a plain old knockdown and drag out Irish binge.

He is a good egg and a lot of fun. When Joe Carbonatto and Bryan and I go out to dine in town, the waitress gets rather sore at us. You see, we talk the menu over, Joe in Italian, Bryan in Polish and myself in combined bits of Latin, Spanish, French, Pig Latin, double-talk and anything that comes out. We had one waitress thinking Joe was from free France and Bryan and I were from "Tres Rivers" in La Canada. We don't know what the others say and sometimes we ourselves don't know. It is silly as hell but affords a lot of fun and occasionally induces a smile out of the young lady, which is a scarcity in this town. Women and smiles are both sort of scarce.

We had a swell sermon in the chapel today and it really was down to earth. I went to Confession this morning so I think I will receive at the 17:00 Mass tonight. We have some good chaplains here and occasionally they drop over to the soldiers' club to chat with us while we goldbrick. They are the only officers allowed in the place and are very jolly and stand in nicely with the boys. In fact, a few cups were "borrowed" from the mess hall for them and have been designed as permanent fixtures for them there. One has a definitely priestly look on him and the other has unruly hair and could pass for a wrestler minus the usual cauliflower ears.

Well, I have padded this enough without resorting to foreign languages so I shall close. Can you send me Jerry's and Mark's addresses? I want to send them a picture, the one I sent to you (kindness of Bob) could be given to Pat if you consent. You have the big one of me and I don't think she has any. OK? This is it for now. I'll write again soon. "Cum millioni de baci."

Your loving son, Jack

TOM - HAVING A WONDERFUL TIME
North Africa, April 24, 1944 (V-Mail)

Dear Mom,

Just a few lines to say "hello." I'm in a recreation room in North Africa listening to a few classical recordings which the Red Cross is providing. I've not yet settled down enough to have any mail so in answer to the inquiries I'm sure you have written, I'll say I've never felt better in my life.

Things are going smoothly and despite the fact that since I've left "the States" I've been having all sorts of thrills—and boredom—there is not much to write in just a V-Mail. I'm not worried about violating any censorship regulations—for once regulations do not seem silly—but am waiting until I can make a halfway interesting letter. I'm spending otherwise loafing time playing poker and trying to pick up my French. I'm having great success—knock on wood—with the former and if I could only get hep to the parlez vous, all would be rosy.

They are now playing "Barcarolle" from *Tales of Hoffmann* and I remember that night we all went to see Eliene in that show. So far we've been getting good radio programs here. Anyway, having a wonderful time and "hello" to everybody.

Your loving son, Tommy

JACK - TRUSTING YOUR WOMAN
Lincoln, Nebraska, April 26, 1944

Dear Mom,

You will get a telegram before you get this and I hope you get the mazooma to me before then, too. The beautiful truth is that I am at long last on the alert. They say we leave in three days, but also said we would only be here 3–10 days, so your guess is par with mine.

I signed the payroll the other day but have no idea if I will be paid before I leave. However I shall reimburse you as soon as I can. Next month I should make about $99 so I'll be better off.

I am, as far as I know, first radio operator on crew #5266. I haven't met any of them yet but should soon. There are several of us going but I only know a few and they are ROs too. Staff Sgt. Cahill is one so we have some good times in store. I don't know if we get B-17s or 24s, but I hope it is the former. The 24 has several features that I don't like, but if I get one, I expect to swear by it once I get used to it. After all, what good is a woman if you don't trust her?

I have no idea as to where I'm going but don't expect a base in California. Kansas is likely but still I don't know. I will give you a buzz when I get there tho—will write you when I know I'm leaving.

I am in the service club now. It is pretty nice and just reeks with maps and pictures. They are all done by GIs, and several large maps show where we bombed last nite, where the Air Forces are hanging out, and how much land someone's got where. It is a nice joint but an unhealthy place to be when you're not supposed to be. The CO has a bad habit of playing "Gestapo" over here.

I'll be very happy to blow this joint and get on with the war. It is really chicken here. OTU is supposed to be better. Here's hoping! All for now. I'll write again when something comes up. Say hello to all.

Your loving son, Jack

TOM - A FROG OF A DIFFERENT DIALECT
North Africa, April 27, 1944

Dear Mom,

For the first time since I left the States I feel really clean. I am at the officers' Red Cross club this evening and the best thing they have is a shower room with honest to gosh hot water. With a good deal of scrubbing, I gradually got rid of a black ring which had been collecting around my neck despite daily ablutions with whatever facilities were at hand. The shave was a real pleasure. I really cause myself some trouble trying to trim this would-be cookie duster with cold water. They aren't hardships by any means because after the first day you are used to circumstances or resigned to them, I don't know which—but anyway, tonight will be a red letter day as I look back in the days to come.

This particular hostel is located downtown about a block off the main thoroughfare. It has a little theater, snack bar, games, reading and writing room and all sorts of comforts—but the best is still that shower downstairs! The walls are decorated with scenes from New York City and the girls at the snack bar are French but can talk more English than most of the local stuff.

As you know, all I can tell you is that I am in North Africa. That is hardly what you would call pinpointing a location, but for as much as we all know about North Africa, that is good enough. The predominating language spoken here is French and I'm trying my best to catch up on it. I can read it even better than I thought I could, but speaking it or hearing it is a frog of a different dialect.

We have had occasion to visit some of the cities and they are at once beautiful and appalling. From the air they glisten and appear to be the cleanest places in the world. They have few if any factories to soot up the buildings which saves them from being really terrible. Some of them in the downtown section look like the pictures you see of Paris—smart shops, open-air cafes and tree-lined streets.

They have innumerable parks, large and small, all well designed and at this time of year, blooming at their best. We are only allowed to eat in Army messes in town, which is all right with me, though we can help relieve the cafés of their beer, wine, cognac (ooh la la!) and in some spots, brandy. This cognac, we learned too late, is very potent stuff. It goes down like 100 octane with seemingly no effect until a couple hours later the world is on a merry-go-round and you are supplying the music! Enough is too much, we discovered. My present is Muscatel and orange pop—when it can be had. Mravinec has some John Haig Scotch, which is being saved until after that first mission. Don't get the idea that I am running wild over here, I'm just telling you the setup.

Of course, it's spring here now. Everything is so green that it just can't be Africa—but it is, 'cause I know I don't navigate that badly. The mountains are beautiful and the hillsides are terraced perfectly. Each little town with its glistening walls and streets and red roofs looks like a picture you might paint or something an architect would put on paper, but never dream it possible to build a place like it. The whole thing looks rather fantastic tho. A bearded, dirty, incredibly large Arab, in incredibly dirty robes, will come jogging along on an equally incredibly small donkey, while down the opposite side of the road will come clanking the biggest damn tank you'd ever want to run head on into with a bicycle.

Most items like candy, cigarettes and stuff at the PX are rationed. After seeing the abundantly stocked PXs in the States it seems rather odd. They say after you get to combat it will automatically cancel rationing, but that remains to be seen. I brought along a couple bed sheets that I had to buy in Columbia and from the looks of things they will make your son Tom one of the wealthiest men in all Africa. I'll never sell them if I can possibly use them but it's nice to have a couple bed sheets for a rainy day!

Well, guess I'll go up to the snack bar and see what's cooked. I'm getting fatter, tanner and still coming out at least even on the poker. Will write again when I can, and "hello" to all.

Your loving son, Tommy

TOM - WAXING PHILOSOPHICAL
North Africa, May 1, 1944

Betty was the family friend Tommy took to dinner, "to give the town something to talk about," when he flew up to Concord in February. She relocated to Los Angeles shortly after he saw her.

Dear Betty,

For a month now since I have left the States, your letter from Arkansas has been in my letter kit waiting to be answered. In all that time however, each evening was either a relief after a long flight or a relief after a series of them with a blowout in whatever town we happened to be near. In any case, I never seemed quite relaxed enough to write more than a note to Mom saying I was still on the move. Such information to you would only be a repetition of what you probably heard from Mom.

You really can't write about what you are doing, have been or plan to do without possibly revealing something or other which somebody or other wishes nobody else to know. My signature in the lower left corner is my own censorship—though still subject to censor—and I try to live up to what is expected of me.

Your letter was a model of thoughtfulness and more kind than I deserve. But rather than try to deny what you say (with a modesty which I would have to assume for the occasion) I take pleasure in accepting your judgment and drawing from it some much needed self-confidence.

I've seen considerably more of the world since I last saw you and have been filled alternately with amazement and disillusion. I was still in the States Good Friday and through Easter, gaining a spiritual lift which was quite welcome embarking on what is easily the greatest project of my life. More and more, though, I am concerned with what to do when I come home. It is not homesickness, but with the job at hand, it is a good far away thought to occupy my idle moments.

I feel certainly that I must express something or other. Singing most likely but what type?—not opera, definitely not—and Mrs. Miner agrees with me on that. I sing to myself by the hour and can imagine any accompaniment from the Pied Pipers to Kostelanetz. I expect to have some free time here, and if I can find a spot where I won't be interrupted, I'll try to brush up on my diction with my *Shakespeare* that I carry.

I'd like to see *Shakespeare* on the stage—I never have, it's funny—if only to see how they do it. I can read it and not miss a word and generally get the more subtle points, but each speech wanders off into so many little similes—and I think in grammar they are called hyperboles or something—that I wonder how an actor could keep the train of thought before the audience.

I should complain about *Shakespeare*...when I can't start a letter without branching off onto a dozen unrelated topics. In fact right now I can't even figure out what I started to say in the first place.

I will say, in a fumbled effort toward a conclusion, that I can now see things much clearer than I could, say, in February. I have thought, argued and observed, and have managed to get a somewhat clearer picture. If I only could have had some purpose or a little more guidance in my teens, I am sure I would be much better off today. Of course, a fellow in his teens is not generally expected to be pondering the problems of the world around him and generally has enough to do looking out for himself—if he does that much. With a bit of realism for my mess of idealism, I might have done things with my imagination which I believe is vivid to say the least. But all is by no means lost. I still will bet anybody that I have a future, and with the help of God I'll make something of it.

I have not had any mail since shortly after your letter and only know that you have arrived in California. (They tell us not to expect any mail to catch up with us until at least our next destination—whenever and wherever that may be.) I can imagine what your opinion is but how about Charlie and Signe? They are pretty young to notice a real change yet but no doubt you are aware of the possibilities and can now fare for them without any outside influences.

You've no doubt met Bob's boy Pat. He is really the apple of my eye, and despite the fact that he has four other uncles, I take quite a special pride in my uncleship—to coin a word. It's fascinating to watch a child just growing up. To see in him his mother and his father and to imagine what he will grow up to be. Not an opportunity will you deny him to live his life better than you did.

This constant improvement with each generation has been both the doing and undoing of America. Each generation has been dissatisfied with what the preceding one had—progress! But each generation tried to make it easier for the following. What the father earned by his hands, the son had given to him, and he started from there. So many fine things so hard earned were commonplace and cost nothing, and were taken for granted and lost the respect really due them. The Frigidaire, the car and the four-bit cup of coffee in a swanky spot were goals. I think the families lost the battle, but I can find a dozen people who will say they say the same thing about every generation, and I am put right back where I started.

I always seem to be right back where I started.

I am now in North Africa. My ideas of burning sands, etc., are now well down the drain. At night it is frigid here. Just to cinch matters we are now living in tents. However, they are still much better than foxholes so who's complaining?

Have you met Mrs. Miner yet? I am anxious to hear from you about her and perhaps of your own intentions toward singing. She is pretty busy with her war work though, and with her two sons in the service she is certainly doing her part. I've been owing her a letter for some time so I think I'll write her tonight. I'd better do it in a hurry though as it is now quite cold here and if I resort to some of this so-called champagne to keep warm, I shudder to think of the letter I might write!

Incidentally, Mrs. Miner has some recordings of mine upon which I would welcome a detailed criticism. Your viewpoint would be fresh. You would see the degree of development—if any—rather than just "an improvement over the last one" which was very encouraging but not quite conclusive. Do not worry about discouraging me as your frankness will make it all the more believable.

I think that is about all for tonight. I have roamed over a number of subjects and hope there are not too many loose ends. It is wonderful to be able to write to someone and just ramble. It is almost a conversation as I try to imagine your answers or remarks generously allowing you two or three different viewpoints on each subject. Best regards to Charles and Signe and that's all for now.

Sincerely, Tommy
P.S. My Gad, six and a half pages! What patience you have to get this far!

Tom was an old soul, far more mature than the twenty-three years he was about to turn a few weeks after he wrote this letter. Betty shared this letter with my grandmother to type for the family. I'm glad this one was captured. Thank you, Betty.

TOM - THE LAST MINUTE HUDDLE
North Africa, May 1, 1944

This is a letter from Tom to his brother Jerry, based in the States.

Dear Jerry,

As I write this, it is your birthday so congratulations! I put the ball in motion today for a money order for the occasion. I say, "put the ball in motion" because it takes two or three days to get one here. Why, I don't know.

The word "here" may raise the question "where?" and it's a good question. Of course, you know I can't say where except North Africa. It's a pretty big place, Africa, so take your pick. As you can see by my address, I am at a training squadron again. I thought all the training was in the States, but this, I guess, is the last minute huddle before we go into the game. How long I'll be here I don't know—but do care.

I arrived here after what seemed like an age of one-night stands. On the whole it has been extremely interesting, but wearing the same clothes day in and day out, and buying clean underwear in order to change, is hardly the Life of Riley. However, it may prove to have been better than what I now encounter, though this is by no means to be construed as a complaint. After seeing what some of the boys here have gone through under conditions which they say are comparatively good, I can never complain—at least not for a while.

Actually, since we hit Africa it has been quite a celebration. After a couple rather rugged nights I can now better judge what my capacity for champagne, wine, cognac or brandy is, whiskey being just an old burp around here. This stuff is really quite rotten but after a while you can't tell.

It has not been all riotous, of course. I spent quite a few evenings at a couple Red Cross clubs eating cake and doughnuts and stuff, listening to the radio and writing letters. They had a dance one night which was good fun but knowing little French I was rather up a creek. There was one really gorgeous American girl there. She was just a civilian, though she wore a snappy uniform and had lived here seven years. She was just the type which magazine covers choose as the "typical American girl," "the girl who is waiting for you at home," etc. I guess I danced with her fifteen times but never got more than three steps. What a war!

There was one place in a town (Algiers) where in the evening the French "baybees" would drum their little trade. There were all types—all prices—all tres expensive. For 2,000 francs in American money you should get something good. In the States they couldn't get a tenth of that but over here money does not mean very much.

I think I've spent about twenty-five dollars at the most since I left Brazil, not denying myself, buying meals, etc., but with the meals only 5 or 10 francs it goes a long way. I have not been paid since March, and for once don't really care to rush the paymaster.

I am writing this in the officers' club which in this case is just a big Nissen hut with a bar at one end—beer and wine—a felt lined table with walls for crap games and a few tables. I'm going to write a couple more letters then hit the sack.

Hitting that sack will be something. We are now living—pardon me, existing—in tents. If there is a colder place on a spring night than North Africa, unless it's where you were in Washington, I've never seen it. Tomorrow, if we get ambition and do not freeze to death tonight, we will build a stove—the kind Ernie Pyle writes about—with 100 octane gas, no less—and no doubt an explosion or two.

Well, Jerry, many happy returns. By the time you get this it will probably be my birthday and I'll accept your congrats too. Incidentally, my mail has not arrived here and I don't expect to get it until my next stop. So, if questions you write me are unanswered, assume I have not yet got the mail. We had our original destination changed too which should really SNAFU things. Have a double shot for me and take it easy.

Your loving brother, Tom

JACK - JACK'S LAST LETTER
Lincoln, Nebraska, May 2, 1944

This is the last letter we found from Jack. All original letters from him and his four brothers, from May-November, 1944, were destroyed in the fire, probably stored chronologically. For Tom, though we don't have his originals during that time, we do have the file copies of the ones my grandmother typed to forward to the other brothers. Though this is the last time we will hear Jack's voice, my amateur sleuthing unearthed interesting information about his activities after he shipped out. As we follow Tom's escapades during combat, Jack will not go unmentioned.

Dear Mom,

Just a few lines to say hello and tell you a little of "what's new." It is a first-class blizzard outside so I'm staying close to the sack.

We have a crew of nine now. The pilot is Lt. John Quinn, a New Yorker. About 25 years old and with 150 hours of B-24 to his credit. He seems OK tho it is still early in the game to tell, and his prowess as a pilot is as yet unknown to us.

I'm not sure of our co-pilot's name, as I've only seen him once. I think it is Lt. Simmons tho. He is just out of cadets and has a total of zero hours on the 24. He has his car here and he is from Calif. but I don't know what part.

The bombardier is Lt. Hibbett and he is from California about 80 miles north of LA. He went to the line this morning and went through the B-24. He is about 27 and a lot of fun. He was in pilot training but washed out in basic. He was in 43-16 bombardier class but not in the same place as Tommy.

We get a navigator later. So the rest of the crew is Cpl. Pietszch (Peach) and he is funny as hell. Cpl. Todd will no doubt be 2nd radioman, and Cpl. Hoyal is a Texan and the old man of the ship. Cpl. Tillotson is the engineer and a good old Irishman, Cpl. Flaraty (sp?) finishes it off. We get on fine. Of course, I'll keep you posted as to our doings as we go along.

The 24 is a good ship I guess and it has four power turrets to keep the Focke-Wulfs from our doors. I will be firing a waist gun I think, and from the looks of things it will take nine of us to make a gunner go into the Sperry ball turret that is under the ship.

The radio room is not much more than a cubbyhole. It is just in back of the pilot and has a Martin turret on the other side to make it worse. The ship for the most part is crowded. In the nose are a turret gunner, bombardier and navigator. It is a tight squeeze and a major problem to get there to begin with. The waist is very spacious with only one man to use it most of the time. The bomb bay is twice as large as a 17s in length.

Just over the last part of the bay is a big ledge. It is for general storage purposes and some inconsiderate engineer put my spare transmitter, the pilot's radios and a lot of other stuff way up in there. So, if I have to get any of it, I go through a hole, under the top turret, thru another hole, thru the bomb bays, around a turret and up to the ledge. After tossing junk for a half hour, I find what I want and return thru the obstacle course to my post. The pilot no doubt gives me hell for taking so long and the flight surgeon wonders why I have flying fatigue. Then I curse the B-24 and wish I was on a B-17 where everything is at your fingertips, no one is crowded and you are king of all you survey. I guess it will be OK once I get used to it tho.

I meant to tell you on the phone to have Jerry get me a pen. I dropped mine—it is a total loss. They have none here.

Now the snow has stopped, almost. This camp is OK and the mess hall is a "chow-hound's dream." Not only is the food good but we have two halls to choose from plus 24-hour service. Reveille is governed by the times of classes, etc., and there is no one blowing a whistle every time you turn around.

The town is infested with infantry and they don't love us any. If they went to see *Memphis Belle* they might see that we live no dream job when in flight. I haven't seen it yet but hope to. You and Pat should take a see at it. The radioman in that movie is an officer now and we saw him at Yuma where he is stationed.

I have to go now but, before I forget, would you send me my notebook on radios. It is the small black loose-leaf one. I could sure use it pronto and if you have any cookies around, let me in on them. They won't go unappreciated I assure you.

Guess this is all for now. I will be processed again tomorrow and will make out my will I suppose. I have nothing to will, my clothes won't fit Mark, my airplane data and material is Greek to all but me, I have no mushy love letters to get a kick out of and no money at all. I expect to save some cash soon though and if my number should come up, you're my attorney. I doubt if it will but it is something you can't tell about. I hope to have a big wad saved up by the time it is over and the law will play hell trying to stop the fun in Cahills' house that nite. All for now so I'll close with much love to all.

Your loving son, Jack

TOM - HAPPY MOTHER'S DAY
North Africa, May 6, 1944

Dear Mom,

Another Mother's Day is just about here. I'm extremely fortunate in having such a wonderful Mother that I do not need a calendar to remind me of how much I owe to you. But perhaps I do need somebody to remind me to tell you so.

So many kindnesses over so many years unfailing might be remembered only for the more outstanding events—the thousands of little thoughts being overshadowed and received as a matter of course. Now, so many long miles away, having received no written word from you due to military circumstances, I can still feel your thoughts and prayers for my well-being, still be inspired to carry on whatever task I may be assigned.

It is impossible to find anything here worth sending home to you; also I have not yet been paid for April and probably won't be for a couple weeks. At that time I'm going to send about fifty dollars with which I want you to get something *for yourself*. Don't think I'm extravagant or stretching my own resources as everything is rationed here and my luck at poker is holding.

While on the subject of money, did you get the allotment? There is supposed to be a bond too but I don't know whether it will be taken care of this month or not. Also could you send me the addresses of Little Pat and Mary.

It is getting warmer now and the nights are quite comfortable. Yesterday going into town we rode with a major general and a lieutenant colonel in a staff car. Just now I can't seem to write a thing. Oh, yes, Willy and I had our pictures done in watercolor by an artist at the Red Cross. They were profiles, as that was his idea, and not too sharp, but I'll send mine along as a souvenir just to show you.

I'm really tired from doing nothing and will certainly be glad when they give me something to do. Just now, I spend most of my time wondering what's coming in the mail. Never did hear from Tom and Monette while at Columbia though I can't see why. That's all now.

Your loving son, Tommy

P.S. Could you have somebody send me a new pipe? Mine is broken and there are no decent substitutes here. Maybe Frank could get it if you send him the dough—about five should do it. A good pipe, nice lines and reasonably convenient to carry. XXOO Tommy

TOM - DON'T WORRY A BIT, MOM
North Africa, May 8, 1944

Dear Mom,

Yesterday, May 7, your letter dated April 19th arrived. You mentioned not receiving any mail and I wondered if you received some cash I sent about April 10th from Florida, registered, special delivery airmail. I also wrote once before that and several times since.

I think now that I will number my letters so you can keep track. This will be number *one*. Later I'll try to figure how many you were previously due.

Jack seems to get all the tough breaks, and I do hope he gets home once or yells loud and long. I feel sure that while the Air Force commits numerous oversights there is somebody there at his post who will go to bat for him. In any case by June 1st or sooner, you should have enough money to visit him no matter where he is and you may call on me for any more needed.

Nothing much in the way of news. Hoping for more mail as it seems to be coming through faster than I expected.

Don't worry a bit. Having a swell time, and all in all, much better than expected.

Your loving son, Tommy

TOM - IT'S A SMALL WORLD AFTER ALL
North Africa, May 11, 1944

Dear Mom,

It's been a couple days since I last wrote to you so I'll try to bring you up to date. Haven't been doing much since Whited has been in the hospital. Did I tell you he got burned? The boys pilfered a steak and were cooking it one night when suddenly Whited's leg was on fire. I wasn't there but the final result was second degree burns and a week or so in the hospital.

They had a USO show here the other night, which was different from the rest in that it was made up of concert and light classical numbers. They had a girl from Los Angeles who really played the violin. She was soloist with Stokowski's American Youth Orchestra on its South American tour. Quite nice too. Then they had a girl with a voice who insisted upon acting coy and playing up to the boys with some sex appeal she didn't have, thereby spoiling the voice that she did have.

A baritone who couldn't find any place to keep his hands made up the rest of the vocal department. Also had an excellent cellist and the accompanist was from Pasadena. On the whole tho, it was better than this eternal jive which, while entertaining, is hardly what you would call soul-satisfying. The movies here are rather beat-up but they pass away the time.

Day before yesterday I really ran into an old-timer. We were having a bull session with some of our reunited brethren from Class 43-16 when a guy who looked like Genghis Khan for his beard approached and was addressed by one of the guys as Soldati. I took another look at him and remembered the first game of football in 1936 when Bill sent *me* in to see what *I* could do with *Soldati!* I remember a gorilla crouched across the line with his right hand menacing for a knockout blow and telling me to, "Step aside, kid, I'm coming through!"

I asked him then if this was the Soldati of Somersworth High in New Hampshire, and sure enough, it was. All the old enmity was forgotten and we had quite a talk. He is a gunner on a B-26 now and almost the first thing he asked was, "How is Fr. Kenneally?" All of which goes to prove two things. It's a small world and, in that world, Fr. Kenneally stands head and shoulders above millions of his fellows.

Pretty near all of 43-16 is here except for a few who went to other theaters. So in a few weeks, after we get into combat, you can know when you read the papers of medium bombers hitting the Nazis, that all my buddies and I will be doing the sighting. It certainly makes the future much brighter (it was never dull though) to know that I'm flying with such a good gang of boys.

I also ran into a fellow who took his cadet exams with me that memorable day on Ardmore Street, April 22, 1942. I was going by the tents when some guy hollered, "Cahill! What the hell are you doing here?" I'd seen the guy only once since then and how he remembered my name I'll never know. I recognized him right away and another session was in order. Despite what scarcities there are of some items here, there is no shortage of friends and old acquaintances.

I found Dave Miner's address finally and have written him, but I don't believe we will be able to get together.

Everything is fine here and I never felt better in my life. The mail has not come through yet but I'm expecting some in a couple days. One thing I don't have is reading material. As soon as I get to a permanent APO I'm going to get a subscription to the overseas edition of *Time* but I would appreciate it if you could send some books.

I like any good historical books and would like van Loon's *The Arts*. Perhaps if Pat could look around and get a line on things by the time I have a permanent APO I'll have sent home enough money so that it will impose no undue burden upon yourselves. Outside the above suggestions, I'll leave other types of books to Pat's and your judicious tastes.

The food continues to be good and that covers a multitude of minor discomforts. Will try to write the boys tomorrow or this afternoon, if I don't go to the hospital.

Love to all, Tommy
P.S. Don't send any books or stuff until I get my permanent APO.

I remember hearing the name "Fr. Kenneally" all my life. He was a priest at St. John High School, mentioned earlier. In addition to Tom's visit with him in Concord in February, here is his name once more. I recently found a 1971 letter from, by then, Monsignor Kenneally to my mother after my father's death. Our family had stayed in contact with him all that time.

TOM - DESTINATION CORSICA
Corsica, France, May 14, 1944

Dear Mom,
    In case you didn't get my earlier letter regarding today, Happy Mother's Day. Your mail caught up with me with a bang, also letters from

Frank, Jack, Bob, Jerry and others outside the family. Enjoyed all the news excepting Jack being unable to get home.

That means only that now you *must* visit him and if you don't have enough money this month, you certainly shall next. No ifs, ands or buts, and I'm taking the liberty of appointing Pat and Bob to see that you do. I think he'll be in OTU long enough that you won't have to make an ill-planned trip. But also, don't wait until it is too warm.

As you can see, I have a new APO number. The location is now Corsica and it looks like I'll be here for a spell. The boys know there is a war going on here and there is absolutely no formality and everybody is more friendly and cooperative than any place I've ever been. Already I have been told that I'm in the best squadron, in the best group, in the best Air Force in the world. We have a wonderful record and I'm certainly going to do my damnedest not to spoil it.

Now that I have a final APO, and my stuff won't pass through 50 million post offices, I'd sure like you to send some books and some of your extra delicious cookies and possibly fudge. Speaking of fudge, Mary Waters' package has not arrived, and as the mail I just received went from March 26th to May 2nd, I doubt if I'll ever get it or that it was sent. Also about the pipe, perhaps I'll write Frank too and have him send one.

I haven't written in the last couple days but yesterday I did order a couple bonds. They will be cabled by the finance department to Pat J. and Mary E. Pat's will go to him and Mary's will go to you and would you please forward it. I didn't have her address with me.

Everything is fine and am settling down for a good time. Swell gang, including Willy Mravinec, so morale should stay up there. Pat and Mark's snapshots from Bob were wonderful and now well known throughout the camp.

Your loving son, Tommy

MICHELLE - TOM'S TRIP OVER
Savannah, Georgia, to Corsica, France, April 10–May 12, 1944

Sixty flying hours. Thirty-five days. Thirteen thousand miles. One-fourth the distance around the world.

After departing Savannah, Tom's crew received directions to their final destination one leg at a time. Even when they were in North Africa, Tom wrote in a letter to Jerry that he still didn't know where the journey would end. This long unknown destination was the French island of Corsica, southeast of the French mainland, west of Italy in the

Mediterranean Sea. He was in Squadron 486 at Alesan Air Base, attached to the 340th Bomb Group of the 57th Bomb Wing, the Mediterranean Theater of Operations.

There were several times while compiling this book that information came to me before I knew I needed it. One of those times happened when I met Sterling Ditchey, a WWII veteran who lives a few miles from me in Southern California.

In August 2012, Sterling saw an *Orange County Register* newspaper article I wrote compiling excerpts of some of Tom's letters. Sterling emailed me to say he was stationed on Corsica at the same time as Tom, though he didn't know him. They were both bombardier-navigators, but at different B-25 airfields, twenty miles apart. Primarily "bridge-busters," they warded off German supply and munitions transportation in Italy and France. Arriving on Corsica as second lieutenants, both were promoted to first lieutenant during their tour.

Several days later, Sterling emailed me to say he was looking at his shipping orders, and he and Tom with their crews shipped out from Savannah, Georgia, in the same formation in April 1944. Sterling was happy to reconnect with history, and it was exciting for me to see his scanned copy of these orders with his and Tom's names and crew lists on the same page. Sterling subsequently found a second "original" of these orders. He sent it to me to replace the same item of Tom's memorabilia that was lost in our family's fire.

In Tom's letter titled "Little Patrick's Giraffe," dated April 6, 1944, he wrote to his mother about looking forward to seeing the world as he always wanted, though at this point, he didn't know where he was going. Following this letter, he wrote two letters from Florida, then nine letters headed vaguely "Somewhere in Brazil," "West Africa" and "North Africa."

Sterling emailed me links to logs he kept detailing his Trip Over, which he ultimately summarized in an autobiography for his grandson, *What Gramps Did in WWII*. With this information, I identified Tom's likely flight legs and landings, subject to adjustments due to weather, mechanical or airport issues. Both Tom and Sterling flew as co-pilot/navigators, ferrying new, twin-engine B-25s from the States to war locations.

Sterling's diary documented the crews' departures from Savannah, Georgia, to West Palm Beach, Florida, where the ships and men received a traditional blessing by the Catholic post chaplain. All crews received shipping orders in sealed envelopes, were given a compass heading southeast to Puerto Rico and told not to open the orders until they were airborne for one hour.

Using Sterling's logs, the landings were at Georgetown, British Guyana; Sao Luis, Brazil; Natal, Brazil; and Ascension Island. Stops in Africa were Monrovia, Liberia; Dakar, Senegal; Marrakech, Morocco; and Algiers and Telergma, Algeria. Tom's crew then flew north from Telergma to Bizerte, Tunis, up the coast of the island of Sardinia to Alesan Air Base, Corsica, France.

Sterling wrote about this "once in a lifetime experience," which was full of excitement, hazards and beauty: "It was a long circuitous route, supported with only the most meager of radio and other navigational aids, one being half a clipboard.

"The flight depended almost entirely on dead reckoning navigation, that is visual sighting of landmarks via computation of air speed, wind direction and speed, ground speed and compass headings. No ground controllers monitored the flights, except on landings and takeoffs at the airstrips themselves."

One airfield where they landed had been recently hacked out of the jungle. It was a beautiful setting, doused by tropical rain every afternoon. Other airfields had obscured terrain and dangerously illogical landing approaches. Weather delays were lengthy. At one field, some ships received sabotaged oil, prompting emergency landings.

But there was also beauty. Of flying over the Amazon Jungle, Sterling observed, "It was such a brilliant green that it looked as though there were floodlights shining up through the foliage."

En route from South America to Africa, the crews experienced 1,455 miles of the emptiest stretches of the South Atlantic Ocean. This landless void of sky and water separates Natal, Brazil, and Ascension Island. Sterling wrote, "Over these seas roll swift-gathering storms. In them abide schools of ravening sharks. We were aware of our chances of rescue if we were forced to ditch in these waters." Sterling quoted *The Rime of the Ancient Mariner,* "Alone, alone, all, all alone, alone on a wide, wide sea." Of spotting Ascension Island, he wrote, "What a thrill to see the island, seemingly, all of a sudden, rise out of the ocean after seven hours of flying over open sea."

Next came another one-day flight of 1,250 miles over water to Monrovia, Liberia, on the west coast of Africa. The following day's flight was a change of scenery from the vastness of water to the greenery of the lush coast to Dakar, Senegal.

I also learned from Sterling that the change of destination Tom mentioned in his letter to Jerry related to Marrakech. The original destination was to be Casablanca, Morocco, but a switch to Marrakech was made verbally.

Sterling's log continues, "En route to Marrakech from Dakar, over 1,000 miles of utter barrenness of the Western Sahara, we flew through a storm that at times was so violent that we were encountering sand at 11,000 feet flying altitude. We had an aircraft that was painted olive drab green, and the leading edges of our wings were sandblasted clean, down to the bright aluminum underneath.

"At our next radio checkpoint, Tindouf, Algeria, we were cleared to Marrakech. The trick, though, was to get through the Atlas Mountains— they were too high for us to fly over. We had good maps and pretty good photographs, but there was only one pass—all other entrance canyons were dead ends. We flew up one, turned around, and found the right one the second try. Then it was easy from there to Marrakech.

"When we landed in Marrakech, we sure got our eyes opened. We thought we were big stuff in our B-25 medium bombers, but on the field, landing just ahead of us were several squadrons of B-29 super bombers, en route to India, then Burma and China. They were *so big* that we could park B-25s under their wings.

"It had taken us 16 days to reach Marrakech. The B-29s had flown in overnight direct from Wichita, Kansas."

With any luck, Tom got lots of "stick time" as he wrote in an earlier letter to his mother, "I can now fly for fifteen minutes or so without making everybody in the ship sick from losing and gaining altitude."

Tom's last letter during his Trip Over was to his mother from North Africa, dated May 11. He arrived on Corsica May 12, and wrote his first letter home on May 14.

Within hours of Tom's arrival, at 3:30 a.m. on May 13, the Luftwaffe made its final attack on the Mediterranean Theater, smack in the middle of the 340th. Sterling remembers being up most of that night, watching the fires from his base a few miles south. Among the dead and injured were soldiers who had arrived with Tom and Sterling the day before. All received Purple Hearts, and those seriously wounded were sent home with total combat zone time of one day.

Without Sterling's help, I would have known only what Tom described in his letters—the people, food, entertainment, sites, etc.—as he explored these new places. I would have known none of the actual locations and nothing about the logistics of traveling there.

Thank you, Sterling Ditchey, for filling in the gaps, helping me to learn more about Tom's thrilling adventure, his Trip Over.

TOM - THE 486TH POKER SOCIETY
Corsica, France, May 16, 1944

Dear Mom,

The enclosed is a little surplus I had this month. Also contributing was the fact that I was introduced to the 486th Poker Society and I came out fifteen bucks ahead. Knock on wood, Mom, your boy is keeping out ahead!

There is not a heck of a lot to write about. Yesterday we moved out of the tent we were in and pitched a double one with Mravinec and his pilot, Morrison. I dug an addition (or should it be a subtraction?) to Mravinec's foxhole and that work was really rugged. There is not an awful lot of room in the tent as is, but we expect to make an extra veranda with our shelter-halves.

Lt. Stout, one of my old instructors from Albuquerque, is here and he really has a swell setup. It takes a lot of work to make a deluxe hangout but there is not much to do. The tents all have the names of the occupants plastered all over the front along with other such names as "The Rainbow Room," "Panther Room," "Savoy Plaza," etc. You can pitch your tent any place, anyway you please.

There's no "chicken" at all here and when you are not scheduled for a mission, nobody cares where you go. Everybody is friendly and full of advice on how to judge ack-ack, pitch a tent, build a stove and everything under the sun.

This squadron has a great deal of pride and tonight there is a ball game against the 489th. They want some lusty rooters and we all expect to go. Should be a bloody battle.

The food is pretty lousy but at present we have a carton of K rations that we got from our ship, and between meals and before bed we have some pretty classy snacks. Canned meat and cheese, biscuits, coffee, bullion, fruit bars, chocolate bars, gum, cigarettes and stuff like that there. We are gradually depleting our stock, however, and are all looking for those packages from home.

As I said before, reading matter and home cooking are the most desired items in the world.

Haven't forgotten that Thursday is Ascension Day and Willy and I intend to make it to Mass and Communion someplace. Chaplain will probably come here or at group.

Have not been on any missions as yet and probably won't for a week or so. I will be able to tell you when I do, though nothing about them.

Use the money for whatever you want. Sometime I would like an idea on any that you might have saved. Let me know if you get the allotments.

Your loving son, Tommy

TOM - READY FOR ANYTHING
Corsica, France, May 18, 1944

Dear Mom,

This is my second anniversary in the Army of the United States. By coincidence we had chicken (tough), chocolate cake (half-baked) and all in all it has been quite a day. The AF Public Relations boys were around and five of us got our pictures taken. May be in the local papers. Welles Morris, bombardier, from Los Angeles is also in it. So keep an eye out.

Being Ascension Day we had Mass and I got to Confession and Communion so now feel ready for anything. Still haven't been on any missions but no doubt will have by the time you get this.

Went to the ball game tonight and our team lost. It was quite a game though and the GIs rode the umpire all night long.

No more mail since the last batch and we are told not to expect any for some time. In case this beats my other letters, note my new APO number.

Your loving son, Tommy

TOM - WHAT MORE CAN A GUY ASK FOR
Corsica, France, May 25, 1944

Dear Mom,

There has still been no mail since that I wrote of, about the 12th of May. "Any day now" is about all we hear. Of course we were forewarned and know that "somewhere" there is mail for us. Being in the dark as to things at home, my efforts in the literary line are pitifully inadequate. Added to this is the fact that I'm getting very, very lazy. The way things have been going though we can't stray far from the camp as there may be a mission called.

I now have two missions to my credit. I have some idea what the score is, making the future much easier to look forward to. I've been good and scared but I am over that as much as anybody will be here. It is really a swell deal here and I couldn't ask for anything better.

The officers are building a club for themselves, and I have worked a bit with pick and shovel digging the foundation. We'll use it for mess too and I think the food will be improving. Movies about every other night, candy ration ample, I managed to pick up a fair pipe, and what more can a guy ask for?

Your loving son, Tommy

TOM - THE RINGSIDE SPECTATOR
Corsica, France, May 27, 1944

Dear Mom,

Your letter dated or rather postmarked May 5th arrived here today. Since that 16029 APO I have had two new ones. This 650 being my latest and relatively permanent. It also means that there is a flock of mail at the other APO which accumulated before I could tell you of this one. But nevertheless, it is the opening trickle which I hope will develop into a man-sized flood.

The enclosure of Peg's letter was a boon and she certainly has a style of her own. With her talent and Frank's combined, Mary should develop into an Ilka Chase or equally successful feminine author. The enclosures that arrived in North Africa were prizes. It doesn't surprise me that by now Frank should be a 1st Lt. and develop into a captain. For my own part, the best I can hope for is possibly a 1st after 50 missions. Don't really care.

At the time of this writing I have four missions completed. Not an impressive number to be sure, but enough to make my job routine enough so that I can attend strictly to business.

The first mission I crawled right up inside my helmet but now I feel like a ringside spectator.

Tomorrow is Sunday and I guess the padre will be around. The week just breezed by, it seems.

I had hoped to have the good omen of a first mission on my birthday but didn't make it. I'm afraid I'm getting superstitious. The pin from a bomb on my first mission hangs from my jacket zipper and all, stuff like that.

Company is in the tent now so I'll close. Try to write again tomorrow.

Your loving son, Tommy

TOM - GETTING THE LAY OF THE LAND
Corsica, France, May 30, 1944

Dear Pat,

Welcome today was the arrival of your V-Mail of May 8 and your letter of April 25, both sent to APO 16029. It seems that V-Mail is quicker than airmail. However, it is hard to tell as nothing as yet has reached here directly to this APO. Once you get over here, it doesn't matter how long it takes the mail to get here once it comes in a steady stream. I'll stick to my old system of V-Mail when pressed for time or news and regular letters when feasible.

I guess you are way ahead of me on letters and I'm afraid I'll never catch up. You know, of course, that I write mostly to Mom and in that way reach the boys and you too.

This is the first evening I've been able to write at night as our electric lights are now installed. They (the bulbs) are soldered right to the wires as we could not get sockets but have a switch which shuts them on and off, so it is now quite the life.

Yesterday I got ambitious and expanded the side of our tent, thusly: Lift up the side, put shelter-half around the sides and the space is increased immensely. We have two tents fastened together to accommodate Willy Mravinec, Morrison, Whited and me. We are raising the other side and will have the biggest tent in the place. Furniture is gradually being collected. Mosquito nets are up for the summer.

We have eaten one case of K rations in two weeks. That is rations for twelve days for one man. It has all been consumed in "snacks." Canned ham and eggs, cheese, canned pork, chocolate bars, crackers, etc. The old rations, which we have left, have the same contents except the crackers are not so good. We either put so much stuff on the crackers you can't taste them or throw 'em away. Once you get the lay of the land here, it's not bad.

We found a family to do our laundry. Whited went up to pick the stuff up and was invited in for wine, etc. We now have a PA system for the squadron area which provides various programs—good and bad. The best deal of all though is the coffee and doughnuts and the shot of rye, now it is, after a mission. I now have five. I guess I eat from six to eight doughnuts each time.

The baker at the mess hall is from Manchester and makes very good cake. Can't think of his name. We now have a new mess hall going up. Had a tent but it wasn't big enough and so the new one.

Well, I was going to make this longer but it looks like our whole tent may be flying in the morning so I'm going to sign off, check the schedule, and hit the sack. Can't be going to sleep over there.

Bang out "Pathetique" and "Appassionata" on the piano for me, and I'll try to make a little noise for you over here.

Your loving brother, Tommy

Summer 1944

TOM - JOCKO THE BOMBER MASCOT
Corsica, France, June 2, 1944

Dear Mom,

It's 6 p.m. here now and a rebroadcast of Fred Waring is just beginning. Said rebroadcast is via the new PA system, which for a change is turning out some decent music. My day is not yet over, as I have to go down to the bomb trainer from seven to eight. Willy thinks I'm being groomed for lead bombardier but I think that is a long way off. I had a practice mission leading the second element today and was scheduled for another this afternoon but it was canceled. Taking advantage of the break, Willy and I went down for a swim.

We have a nice swimming hole here. One of the rivers runs down to the sea but at low tide it is separated by a narrow strip of beach. So with a freshwater hole on one side and saltwater on the other, we are in a unique position to be choosy. We had a life raft floating around and as a couple enlisted men from our crews were there, we were ganged up on. The boys gave us some dunkings which they've probably had pent up for some time.

I think once before I mentioned Jocko, the dog next door. Since his master went home on leave he has been rather down in the mouth but is gradually getting over it. The other day we decided to bring Jocko along on a mission. He has about eight or nine missions already they say. Taking off, I stood as always behind the pilot and co-pilot with Jocko in front of me. When it came time for me to crawl up in the nose, Jocko was in my care for everybody else was at the controls or up in the turrets. He didn't want to move from where he was but also didn't want to be left behind so he practically pushed me all the way to the front.

Once there Jocko peeped briefly through the Plexiglas and climbed behind the ammo box in the corner. With time on my hands for a while, I wrapped him in my jacket as he was shivering a little though I was plenty warm. After a while, he got a little braver and put his head and forepaws in my lap and a while later he was ready to come out entirely. After that, 99% of my attention was engaged in keeping him from rubbing against the salvo lever.

Once the bombs were gone, I could relax a little and we spent the rest of the time watching the water underneath. When it came time for landing, we moved out of the nose and this time I was doing the pushing. Jocko was pretty glad to hit the ground again, and since then he has been quite affectionate and trusts me quite implicitly. He certainly made the time go by faster.

Yesterday afternoon we jeeped up to town for our rations. I don't recall exactly how this island was taken but there was considerable bombing in the deal. For the first time I've been able to see a more exact picture of what a bomb does other than that puff of smoke. Magnifying what I saw many hundred times gave me some idea of what the blitz must have been like, and multiplying again many thousand times, I could guess what Berlin has received. I'm glad I believe in my cause for I don't know how I could do it otherwise. Up in the air it is quite impersonal but on the ground again, you sometimes look up and wonder.

Your letter about Babe's death came yesterday and I did my best to write some sort of a note to Leona. That is a subject here on which you gain rather complicated ideas unless you ignore it entirely and the latter course is as difficult as the former.

So far I have not been worried except for that first mission. I think I got all of me up in my steel helmet that day, all because I didn't have any idea what I was up against. When I got back I felt quite foolish. I've told you before not to worry just as we all don't want you to worry whether or not we worry ourselves, but I've seen just about all phases of this business now and can speak more knowingly—and the advice is still the same.

Can't think of a thing to send me other than the reading matter. Candy ration is ample. I got a new pipe but would still like another if you can get one.

Tomorrow if I can get to the post office I'll send $50 or $60 dollars to help on a trip for you to see Jack. With the allotment, etc., it should be ample and I wouldn't count too much on his getting home. You'd better go to him, then if he should get a chance to come home, he'll have two visits.

Just thought of one thing you might send. That would be airmail stationery—at least two or three packs of it. The only paper available here is what I am using and it's not very good.

One of the gunners that flies with me all the time is named Schmitz and he is from Hawthorne. Just a half-pint but he had twenty-six missions in the Pacific in B-17s. The other day waiting to take off, our ack-ack boys started firing their machine guns at a red balloon they use for a target. Missing it completely before it got out of range, they sent up another one. By this time Smitty had climbed into the top turret and shot it down on the third burst and got the second balloon on his second burst! The amazement, to say nothing of the chagrin of those ack-ack boys, was terrific!

Stan Gerry, with whom I went through preflight and primary, is here but in a different squadron. The old gang from Columbia is pretty well split up. Pop Clark went to the South Pacific. Bill Bohlman, Dick Frodl and Connors are all in India so we'll probably be civilians when we meet again. I'm enclosing Pop's address and phone number—Walter E. Clark. You might call up Lillian and see if you can get a line on him. I'm going to write but it will probably be months before I get a reply.

The weather continues to be swell, pilot and co-pilot fly with the windows open but the breeze is too stiff coming head on for me to do it. Have a vent up there so I keep cool enough.

Let me know of arrivals of allotments, bonds, etc., so if they are not coming through I can start checking up.

Well, we have some "work" to do so I've got to get ready. Enjoy all the letters immensely and will be seeing you. Love to all.

Your loving son, Tommy

TOM - MILITARY SECRETS
Corsica, France, June 5, 1944

Dear Mom,

Another day is coming to an end. Jocko is honoring us with a visit, lying at the entrance of our tent wagging his tail, making us aware of his presence and therefore our privilege. It looks like I'm going to ignore him for a while with this letter, so he is showing two can play that game by going to sleep on the spot.

He is gradually getting combat-wise, and on our second mission together, he got the idea that getting between my legs and under my flak suit was a nice place to be, especially near the target. Coming home, he is brave once more, and from an ammo box near the side of the greenhouse, he surveys the formation with a commanding and critical eye, while the boys in the other ships do all sorts of silly things to attract his attention.

He is gradually getting over the absence of his master who is on leave in the States, and he's beginning to take an active interest in the life of the camp.

This afternoon Willy, Morrison, Rahatz and I went down to the beach for a salt and fresh water swim, a short snooze, and I believe there will be evidence of a sunburn later in the evening.

Did I tell you I now have a down sleeping bag? A few came in and I got remarkably ambitious and went to the line and got one—in a jeep, of course—but the effort caused not a little comment around here. I've been using an ordinary bedroll which was some help but this is the real McCoy.

Incidentally, Whited says that in Naples they have real silk stockings so if you'd send me yours and Pat's sizes, and Jackie's too while you're at it, I'll try to send you some. I don't know when or if I'll get over there, but Whited has to fly over on business once in a while and could pick them up.

While swimming today I suddenly got the idea of finding a chunk of wood and making myself a sailboat. Shades of White's Park!

I'm darned if I can get into high gear writing tonight. There was no mail today and what came in was direct to this APO so I suppose I still have some being forwarded from the old places.

It is still supposed to be a military secret how I got here. Why, I don't know as most of the magazines in the States know more about how we would get here than we did ourselves. I'll never understand. Oh, yes, for your information, I am in the First Tactical Air Force of the Twelfth Air Force. *Time* magazine covered it a while ago when the Tactical and Strategic Air Forces were formed in the 12th.

We don't fly in the same ship each time and therefore never did get around to naming one. *Battlin' Betsy* happened to be a special favorite of mine. The crew chief named it, I guess. The more I fly in them, the more I'm convinced that the B-25 is the best ship in the Air Force and you can trust it to perform miracles.

That seems to be all I can think of now. Had a letter from Allin and Theda. He's a sergeant now and she is giving lectures in fashion and design in Battle Creek—in dress shops, schools, clubs and places like that. She certainly gets around.

The MO is earmarked for you to spend on a trip to see Jack. Don't wait too long. Buy some new clothes, and be sure to make the trip. Spend every cent I've sent you if you care to. Be sure to let me know if the allotments are coming through OK, and I'd like to hear from you in envelopes postmarked Colorado or wherever he is.

That's all for now. Have eight missions now and having a great time in general. Never felt better in my life physically and spiritually. Will try to write the boys tonight or tomorrow. Love to all.

Your loving son, Tommy

TOM - YANKEE DOODLE DANDY
Corsica, France, June 11, 1944

Dear Mom,

It's Sunday evening and a beautiful sunset is bringing the close of another day. There's a cool breeze blowing but I'm writing outdoors to save our hard-to-get bulbs. There are still planes from all over flying around, and every so often some playful guy comes sailing through to buzz the hell out of the tents. Whited and Henthorn are debating how many seconds an airplane would last inside a tremendous cumulus nimbus coming this way.

Across the way there is a pot-limit poker game going on which I am now glad I'm out of. I weathered it through the afternoon breaking even but it is pretty rough now. Jocko is stretched out sound asleep in front of the tent.

The boys are now placing bets as to how long it will take the cloud to pass over the field. Henthorn offered to bet a drink out of his bottle of beer against one from Whited. Whited has refused as the stakes are too high. It is the first good beer they have had for a long time. Jocko's love affairs are now being discussed, and that is the scene here tonight.

This morning, with nothing to do, I went down to the beach for a couple hours for sun and a swim. The afternoon was spent in the aforementioned poker game with Mass and Communion at four.

There is not a lot to write about as I've told you all the general information about the place and anything else comes under the heading of military information.

On my last mission, No. 10, I moved up to fly as lead bombardier in an element of three ships. Whether or not the eighteen men had stuck their necks out in vain rested upon me, and I'm sorry to admit I didn't do very well. There were certain unfavorable circumstances, which lessened my own mistakes but I know now how most of them can be avoided in the future. Nobody criticized me, perhaps 'cause it was my first trip in that position. Anyway, they are keeping me there and I think I'll make good. I've learned a heck of a lot from the other more experienced bombardiers.

Don't get the idea that this is a promotion for any outstanding ability, but is a normal increase in responsibility due to my experience on previous missions. At bombardier school I was bombing constantly under the pressure of the washout that would come with a failure. Actually, the stakes are much greater here but that old pressure is no longer necessary. That was my old trouble—trying too hard and underestimating my ability even such as it was.

Our cloud is now directly overhead and black as night, while to the west it is clear. I'm glad we didn't run into any of these babies in South America. I have never seen such bad weather as they have down there. Every noon there is a rainstorm and everybody does all their flying as early as possible. Thunder and lightning, now, and the wind is coming up. I hope it doesn't get too strong as our tent has been extended to almost double its original size and I don't know how much it can take.

I think in a while Jack will be really fond of his Liberator. Those babies can take a terrific beating and still get home. First impressions of ships are not very accurate. The only ship I've flown in that I still don't like is the Lockheed Ventura, yet the Navy and Britain swear by it. The B-25 is still tops for my money.

We may start flying in a certain ship every mission but as yet I don't know which one is mine. *Yankee Doodle Dandy* is a swell one. The crew chief used to go to Cushing Academy and was Ray McLean's roommate. I think he went to St. Anselm's too. The boys are very proud of their ship and the silver ones are kept as shiny as a new dime. You never have to worry about the maintenance and no adjustments are too fine.

It sounds like hailstones hitting the tent now. They are usually found in nimbus clouds and it looks like a good time for me to close and climb into that super sleeping bag. Your mail is coming through OK from Africa and should be coming direct from the States soon. The next letter will be to Patricia.

Your loving son, Tommy

TOM - MISSION 12-B
Corsica, France, June 16, 1944

Dear Mom,

Your letter of May 22nd arrived today and yesterday came the first one direct to this APO dated May 31st. So it looks like the mail situation is pretty well in hand tho the packages have not yet arrived. Glad to hear the allotment arrived and be sure to let me know if it stops. There is also supposed to be a bond a month and I sent one from Africa to Little Pat and Mary. I also have receipts for money orders of $50 May 16th and $75 June 5th. I guess it's too early to hear from you on that as yet. I think that covers the whole situation to date for mail received and expected. Oh, yes, the "Surrey" letter received, and also the snaps of Little Pat from Bob.

Life in Corsica goes on as usual though today I am rather tired from working and not the usual reason of loafing. I'm still flying in an element lead with nothing exceptional and a new order today relieves a great deal of the responsibility. However, it is still a good spot to move from into squadron leader. They say as soon as you lead you are recommended for promotion but I don't care.

I have passed my 13th mission, or as we call it around here, "12-B." Willy flew his on the 13th and that made him extremely popular with his crew that day. I seem to be doing more training than ever now with a practice mission every day after a usual combat run in the morning. It's better than hanging around though, and if I ever do lead, I'll be that much better prepared. I've gained a good deal of confidence the last couple days by improving, but I felt like a pretty big jerk for a while and still owe Jerry a couple missions that might have been better. Well, I'd better get off the war or I'll be slipping up on my censorship.

Night before last I saw Bing Crosby in *Going My Way.* Perhaps you've seen it or it's played around LA some time ago, but if you haven't and get the opportunity, don't miss it. Bing plays a priest—very well, too—but Barry Fitzgerald steals the show. He gave the best performance I've seen in a long time over here.

The movies all seem to be musical—some are OK—and war pictures. Once in a while we have a short—like Pete Smith showing why everybody should turn in their old scrap—and since I left the States—one cartoon. I went to a public movie in Algiers once. American pictures plus cartoon both in English but with French translations on the screen. Those Frenchmen laugh in the darnedest places!

I thought I'd have a lot to write about but that doesn't seem to be the case. I haven't been to the PX and Red Cross up in the town for two weeks and most of the happenings here are of a military nature. Speaking of the PX, I get most everything I need here and you might as well keep the soap for yourself as I've got a couple bars of Palmolive and one seems to last about three weeks. As you may gather I'm not washing more than once a day. It is so much trouble getting khakis clean that a dirty neck kinda blends with a dirty collar.

I would like a couple jars of Noxzema Face Cream. Not the shaving cream. I use it under my lather and it makes cold water shaving as easy as any shaving will ever be. That sort of stuff is generally saved for the nurses if they get any in. If you can't get hold of it, send some money to one of the boys and they can easily get it at the PX.

Corsica is still as nice as ever. We had a lulu of a storm—I guess I wrote to you about that. The sequel was that our tent, with all its annexes and patchwork, really took a beating. The old drainage ditch that used to be outside the tent ran right under Morrison's and Whited's beds and it looked like the Mississippi for a while. Willy had just two of the Great Lakes under his bed while I by some miracle escaped complete inundation. Morrison was visiting a couple tents away when the storm broke. Rather than soak his clothes he left them in the other tent, and if anybody was dumb enough to be out, they would have got a kick out of him running down the company street clad only in God's Issue.

For some reason the liquor usually served after missions has stopped flowing. The last time I saw any, I had Schenley's Bourbon after weeks of rye. Of course, that was the day I forgot my Coke bottle so I don't suppose I'll see any more bourbon 'til the States. For the last six or seven missions, I and the rest of us have had to settle for just coffee and doughnuts. What I'm wondering now, if after six or seven missions more with a dry welcoming committee waiting for me, may I apply for a quart or so to kinda even things up?

More important, will I get it?

Oh, yes, Smitty, in the next tent, is also from LA. He gave me his wife's phone number and is sending yours to her. We thought you might like to hear from somebody besides ourselves that all's OK. I've never flown with him but Whited has and he says he's a pretty good boy. Her name is Virginia, by the way, I've enclosed her phone and address. We have quite a gang here from LA but the best deal is the bartender at the group club. He's also from LA and though I don't get there very often, when I do, as a fellow Angelino, I get the best stuff in the house.

The other day one of the boys buzzed the field just when the adjutant was in the latrine. Said latrine is on the crest of a little rise and there the captain was staring right into a B-25 coming toward him at about 300. The fact that the captain was in a favorable location to be scared to his very bottom does not alter the fact that if he ever finds out who did it, there'll be a devil of a row!

Buzzing is quite popular here and nobody seems to mind. If we buzz another field in the morning, they'll raise the dust around our tents in the afternoon. I actually met a fellow (pilot) in town late one afternoon, and after he got through bragging about how he had said "hello" to the 340th,

I told him how we damn near blew his tents down that morning! He said they just couldn't let a thing like that go unnoticed.

The beach is still the best spot around here. After a practice mission yesterday afternoon, McMillan and I hitched a ride down and had a quick dip. I have never seen such clear water. It never seems to be the same shade of blue or blue-green. Every minute of the day, every different altitude we fly over it, and every depth seems to have its special color.

I think that really winds it up for tonight. I'll try to write Grandma this week but don't promise her. Be sure to see some shows with the money you have. Take Jackie and Bob and both Pats, and try to go once a week or at least every two weeks. Patricia mentioned that she wants to make some recordings of her piano playing. I think Mrs. Miner still has her machine and would really enjoy having her use it.

Your loving son, Tommy

TOM - BOMBING MISSION EMOTIONS
Corsica, France, June 17, 1944

Dear Pat,

Your letter of May 31st and Mom's of June 2nd arrived this afternoon, earlier than usual, and served to brighten this rainy day. Your letters have been arriving OK, and as I have answered Mom's in far greater proportion than yours, I'll start now to even things up. Of course, all the letters go into the family pool, but I enjoy hearing directly from the boys a little more than the carbon copies, but I am sure we all get more mail under that system.

I have not written the boys much here and when I do I'll mail them to Van Buren Place. I don't have Mark's new address, Jerry is chasing all over the place, and I don't know whether I have Jack's or not. Mom's report as to letters received sounds about complete. I did not write much en route as my address was always changing. However, I have received no packages yet though letters only take about two weeks to get here. I noticed too, she mentioned that they were officially censored. Was anything cut out?

The mail situation is really funny today. Whited got a letter from some old flame who wrote, "You are still one of the swellest fellows I've ever known." We countered that she didn't say he was *the* swellest fellow. "Well," he yelled, "you can't expect her to write that with her husband sitting right there, do you?"

The selection of books sounds swell. The government has printed in pocket book size a number of good new books, and old favorites. These are supposed to be distributed by special services, and there seems to be about one copy of each and they are rotated throughout the camp.

Good reading is pretty essential. Morale is very high here, but sometimes three or four hours after a rough mission, a reaction sets in that might be bad. Before, during and immediately after, there is an excitement that is tingling and a funny situation can be made out of whatever you happen to be in. It is quite amazing, really. But as I say sometimes, a while after, you find yourself saying, "My God! Did I just do that?" The best remedy I know of for that is a good book, a horizontal position on the old sack and some of the week's candy ration still at hand. Come supper time and it's just another day.

I don't sing much or get much chance for that matter, but I do manage to keep up with the songs. With the aid of an Army "Hit Kit," I learned the words to "Besame Mucho" while going on a mission.

Jerry seems to be getting quite involved. Can't say as I blame him.

I have fourteen missions now. Having successfully passed "12-B," I won't have another worry until I get up around fifty or sixty and start thinking about going home. The boys on the ground in Italy are moving so fast that I'm amazed. What after Italy? is the question.

It's almost time for supper now so I'd better close. *Knickerbocker Holiday* is at the show tonight if the rain doesn't cancel it. Thanks again for the letters and take it easy.

Your loving brother, Tommy

TOM - THE RANT
Corsica, France, June 19, 1944

Dear Mom,

Yours arrived yesterday (the June 6th one) and I'll just dash off a short one now.

I think you have done wisely regarding Jack. I don't think any of us would really object to being shipped overseas without a leave if it would actually help the war. Unfortunately, it does not work that way, and days wasted here and there add up to ages which might have been spent at home, rather than just hanging around the base doing nothing.

At Albuquerque I was ordered to be at Columbia November 27th. No later absolutely. Several articles of war were read and as a final emphasis, we were informed that it would be impolite to arrive after five p.m. on the day designated. Arriving there as ordered, and as you know at additional expense to get there on time, we were informed by the reception committee that we were by orders five days too early and by circumstances six weeks ahead of their training schedule.

In view of the gigantic increases made in the training program, some of these delays are pardonable, but beneath it all, there is such a disregard for personal feelings that is in itself inexcusable. We are no longer human beings or it seems even citizens entitled to some consideration, but serial numbers with classifications just as any field piece or vehicle has following its nomenclature.

This is more noticeable in the reputations of each Air Force, group and squadron. Each presumably operates under the same regulations as the other, but why is, for instance, Las Vegas Field such a hellhole compared with say Kirtland Field? It is not the climate. It is the personnel who, by reason of their U.S. Army uniforms, we are led to believe are fellow Americans, but by their treatment of us, have a classification not fit to be written here.

Well, I have a practice mission to fly now so I'd better go.

Your loving son, Tommy

TOM - THE SUNDAY SING-ALONG
Corsica, France, June 19, 1944

Dear Mom,

It's Monday morning and GI hot cakes were cause enough for me to beat it to the mess hall before they closed at 08:00. While the weather is not threatening, it is cloudy enough to make bombing today impossible. So a "stand-down" has been announced and this afternoon I hope to go to town for some rations.

I'm writing this on a broken down GI cot in the back of the tent where I am absorbing Vitamin D whenever it beams this way. I have just finished reading the May 1st edition of *Time* which I fished from a dump barrel. Dump barrels are never just passed lightly but are quite thoroughly inspected. It is amazing what useful things you can find. A piece of string, a cigar box, magazines, bottles are veritable gold mines. A suddenly available supply of lumber has put ideas into the more industrious heads in our outfit and building is going on apace.

I am not very ambitious in the building line but our tent has been expanded and I think I'll make some sort of a table. With our added room and furniture I'll be able to play host to a poker game and expect to have a regular housewarming. We have a few characters from Sardinia making us bricks out here for our own club.

Last night an "order" came over the loud speaker for all officers—with their mess cups—to report "immediately to the mess hall." There with elaborate care and ceremony a barrel of beer was being tapped. It guess it came from Naples. I expected it would be beer—which I still can't drink, though I think I've tasted everything by now—but went along to be sociable. There was still beaucoup cake left from supper and so I lit into that.

The beer foamed and frothed and before long a mellowness was affecting the boys which only beer and miles from home can accomplish. This was followed by a burst of song accompanied by Capt. Meyers, adjutant, on the accordion and Lt. Pierre on the harmonica. Some song about Georgia was inspired by Capt. Shealy, and a couple other crackers retaliated with "Marching through Georgia" by us damn Yankees. "Texas is a helluva a state, parlez vous!" followed, and then the party started to get rough.

"I used to work in Chicago—I did but I don't anymore" stole the show for the evening. This was put over by a newcomer, Cooley—Brad Slaven with brown hair—and the irrepressible Snogles. It consists of a number of verses ranging from subtle to vulgar but all producing a riot. "Sweet Adeline" was frequently requested but the old hands at beer fests kept putting it off, as it was to be the last song of the evening, and it was too early now to break up the party—and besides there was still beer left in the barrel.

By eleven-thirty I was hoarse, the cake was gone and bed looked pretty good so I went home. An hour later "Sweet Adeline" was heard, and as predicted, the party ended.

I found out yesterday that I can write about flak and fighters though give no specific instances. No doubt you have been wondering about them. Missions are generally classified as "milk runs," "beaucoup" and "beaucoup-beaucoup." Beaucoup means in our parlance flak. Flak can generally be evaded as you can see it coming—one—two—three and don't be around for four. The colonel says it's just a "harassing agent," but when I'm the guy being harassed it makes the cheese decidedly more binding.

Enemy fighters are few and the escort generally takes care of them before we even see them. The fact that Jerry is on the run helps considerably, but as their positions keep moving, a flak-free target yesterday may be Hitler's hideout today. Of course it works the other way too. We generally know what we are up against which helps a lot.

For my money, any trip you come back from is a milk run, so don't worry about that stuff anymore. A real milk run comes frequently enough so that you don't get the idea you are personally getting the whole German artillery thrown at you.

We had an American artillery officer go along for the ride one day. On the ground he always "bracketed" his targets. One over—one short—and the next one right in there. Jerry works up to you. He didn't know that and when he got bracketed he damn near died expecting the third one. Actually if the second one is over so will be three and four.

Incidentally, I am now flying my missions with Lt. Johnny Moyer from New Jersey or as I call him "Moyer the Boyer."

Willy Mravinec has been working on a new insignia. It is "Dopey" of the Seven Dwarfs looking right at you with that wistful dopey expression as he is dropping a bomb with his right hand—not seeming to care where it goes. We have one of Bugs Bunny throwing a bomb which is supposed to be the official insignia.

Willy has real talent and I keep telling him he should go to art school after the war. His cartoons are original, refreshing and with a simplicity of line which is amazing for a fellow with no training at all. He draws perspective unconsciously well and never omits a necessary detail. I harp on him going to art school every day, and perhaps by the duration plus six I'll have him convinced.

It's almost time for chow. It is generally bad with beans served in various forms every day and often it is the main course. Bread and jam and canned fruit are the filler-uppers. We get real butter often enough. Once in a while we'll have a feast of hamburger, native onions, potatoes, peas and cake. The next meal we'll have not a darn thing. I wished they'd spread it out a little bit. That's my griping for today—I'm getting fatter daily so I guess it's not killing me.

Your loving son, Tommy

TOM - OLD MAN WEATHER
Corsica, France, June 24, 1944

Dear Mom,

Today I received your letters of June 14th and 15th, also one from Gerald arriving in a record eight days, also letters from Peg Crowley, Aunt Mary, Bill Bohlman's mother, Dick Frodl's sister, one from Babe and yesterday yours of June 12th. Also arrived, the fudge from Mary Waters.

The package was in fair shape but the contents had aged a little in three months. I don't believe it would have taken that long if it hadn't gone to so many post offices. It was originally sent to Columbia so it has really been around. Despite its condition, it is still good and makes my tent quite a popular place. I expect your packages will be here in a week or so.

I have been expecting the picture of you as they were mentioned by all the boys and Aunt Mary. I think it is still a bit early for me to expect it but when the delay seems too long, I definitely want you to send the other. Wait until I write tho.

Enclosed you will find a minute picture of me. The civilian zoot suit is a military secret but don't go getting any wild notions about spying and such. It shows "the lip" just enough so that I doubt if I can shave it off now if I want to.

There is not a heck of a lot in the way of news. I have sixteen missions now but Old Man Weather has not helped much to increase those. *Battlin' Betsy* has been grounded, and I never did fly much in it. We all have a ship of our own with the bombardier's name near his compartment, pilot's next to his window, etc. So far I have never even flown in mine and don't even know if the name is on there yet.

The letter from Capt. Steel about Jack sums the situation up pretty well, but the idea I had was the delay before and after a phase of training is completed. It never seems to fail. If I know Bridges, there might be a devil of a row but that might be just what is needed. I was pretty mad when I wrote the other day and hope I didn't write the wrong thing, but I don't know where I've ever seen such manpower wasted as in the service.

Don't worry about the stockings. If I can get them it will probably be through the PX and quite reasonable. I've been rereading your letters trying not to overlook anything. Willy took a picture of Jocko and me, which I'll try to forward, also a couple shots of us in our foxhole. Morrison, Whited and Willy all endorsed a V-Mail to you requesting cookies as per your suggestion.

We have few dull moments here and since we don't have to fly with each other we seem to be getting along better than ever. The day I accidentally shot the cannon at Columbia scaring Whited (and myself) to death, my mistakes in navigation and some of his landings are told and retold.

Whited is now disturbed by the fact that an old girlfriend of his read a letter she received from him to his wife's sister! Yesterday he was telling (exaggerating a little of course) of how his wife first saw me. It was at the Carrollton Club outside of Columbia and I was doing figure eights in an effort to reach his table. "Here comes my bombardier!" he told her. One look and she says, "Wring him out a little bit so I can see if it's human!" It seems every time I met her, it was at a party and I, of course, would be doing my best to keep things lively.

I'm waiting for Whited to come back now. The group is opening a new officers' club tonight. The place is located just across the road making the trip home fairly simple in almost any condition. I haven't had a drop now in over a month and think that sort of thing has gone on long enough. Anyway, when he comes in I hope to borrow a clean shirt (56 nurses are going to be there they say—a second looey might even get to dance with one) and let him use my beer ration. I myself will be fortified with a can of orange-grapefruit juice which will make most of their stuff taste bearable.

Tonight we had chicken for supper. This time Willy and I got eager and being about 30th in the line, managed to get a fair hunk. Last night they had hamburger. We got there all primed for it at 17:15 (they started serving at 17:00) and by then they were serving hot dogs. I, of course, hate the latter. These two suppers are about the best meals we've had (or almost had) in a couple weeks. It runs in cycles of good and bad foods with a steady stream of beans, which has a well-known cycle of its own.

Speaking of cycles, some wag put a picture (in oils) of Capt. Shealy, our executive officer, up in the latrine with a note stating that for various stages of constipation various numbers of looks at the picture were sure cures. He's a pretty good Joe and is also the boy that forwards applications for promotions so you can see he can take quite a ribbing.

About the package under eight ounces, I am quite well supplied with socks and handkerchiefs and can easily get them at the PX much cheaper than you can. However, those "Pocket Books" come under 8 ounces—I think they can be sent for three cents for that matter. You might see if you can find Pocket Books #195 *History of the U.S.* and #1 *Lost Horizon*, and darned if that isn't all they have up to #219 that I care about. The rest either don't interest me or we have them. There is actually darn little you can send under eight ounces so don't worry about it.

I'm enclosing a couple snaps taken at Albuquerque graduation day. One is of Dick Frodl and me and the other of Dick and Bill. I don't have any of Pop Clark, but thought you'd like to have these anyway.

I seem to be just about out of news now. Glad to hear the boys are getting along so well. I would like to beat Frank to his 1st. If I do, OK. When I start leading it will go right in but if not, it will probably wait a while. Don't really care but do like to keep up a little competition.

I'll now place my formal request for cookies, or whatever you can send this week in that line, send them. Whited just came in so I'll start duding up. It will probably be a couple days before I'm able to write again, so don't worry. Love to all.

Your loving son, Tommy

TOM - THE COOKIE PETITION
Corsica, France, June 21, 1944

Dear Mom,
   Can't say much but hope this note will find you in the best of health and happiness. We are sure having the time of our lives over here. They treat us wonderful and try in every way to help us to enjoy ourselves. We have quite a time with Tommy though. Yes, Mom, we sure would appreciate some of those cookies if it would not be too much trouble to send them.
Yours truly, Manley J. Morrison

Dear Mom,
   I wouldn't mind a few, myself.
Ditto, William F. Mravinec

Dear Mom,
   It seems like you have become quite popular all of a sudden. I think I could appreciate a few of those cookies Tom has been telling us about. Sounds good to me.
Yours, V. E. Whited

MICHELLE - JACK: OPERATIONAL TRAINING, June 1944

As I mentioned earlier, our family has no letters from Jack after his May 2 letter from Lincoln, Nebraska. They were lost in our family's fire. To keep up with his story in the absence of his letters, I weave in his missions and other likely activities during that time.

   Staff Sgt. Jack Cahill, radio operator-waist gunner, belonged to a ten-member crew of a B-24 Liberator bomber. The other crewmembers were: 1st Lt. John Quinn, pilot, New York; 2nd Lt. Melburn Simmons, co-pilot, Illinois; 2nd Lt. Sam Agin, navigator, New York; 2nd Lt. Robert Brooks, bombardier-navigator, Tennessee; Tech. Sgt. Patrick Flaherty, flight engineer, New York; Staff Sgt. Bennie Tillotson, nose gunner, Iowa; Staff

Sgt. Lewis "Red" Hoyal, top turret gunner, Texas; Staff Sgt. Frank Pietszch, Jr., ball turret gunner, Texas; Staff Sgt. John Todd, tail gunner, Indiana.

Shortly after Jack's May 2 letter, the crew embarked on operational training, referred to as OTU (Operational Training Unit). They flew around the country for three months—to Tennessee, Texas, Colorado, Nevada and Kansas—becoming familiar with their ship, practicing their individual duties and learning to work as a team.

TOM - ONE LESS MILK RUN
Corsica, France, July 2, 1944

Dear Mom,

Today was quite a day. For Sunday it was unusually busy and I now have 19 missions. For lunch we had some *fresh* onions which made the hash bearable and for supper we had steak with more onions! But that isn't all.

After supper the mail was handed out and your brownies, pipe and picture came. The picture is swell, Mom, and has the top spot on my cabinet. It is swell to have it.

Just a few minutes before, I was talking to the flight surgeon about pipes. He had just picked up a couple Dunhills in Rome and I told him how long I've been waiting for mine and he said, "Oh, it should be here about now." By a happy coincidence it came soon after. Morris here used to work at Bullock's Wilshire and told me the pipe was a good one—not that he had to, as I was smoking it then. The brownies were in perfect condition and surpassed the usual high standards.

"Junior" is visiting us now trying to teach Willy Italian. Junior is the major's Number One Boy and is decidedly a character. He's learning quite a bit of English, is smart as a whip and takes quite a ribbing from all the boys.

It seems like quite a while since I last wrote to you. There wasn't a thing doing for a week but then after that I got in three missions in a row to make up for lost time. I'm still flying with Johnny Moyer and we've flown enough practice missions besides the regular ones that our teamwork is now pretty smooth.

A bunch of the boys just got back from a day in Rome. They say it is the cleanest place they've ever been to overseas and looks untouched by the war. I'd like to go over for a day and I think I'll look into it. By the end of this month I'll probably have enough missions to go to rest camp at Capri or someplace. Everybody goes to rest camp usually between 20 and 30 missions. They have hotels with regular beds, clean sheets, breakfast in bed and good liquor.

Relaxing in style, I hope, will be better than this loafing we've been doing. After a week of inactivity, when we did have a mission I was as jumpy as on my first one. The next one was easier and the last one was as "normal" as they'll ever be. You've probably been reading how the ground forces have been moving forward. We can appreciate it even more when we hear of a town being taken from the Germans, and can say, "Boy, I'm glad we don't have to bomb that place again." Or sometimes, "Well, there's one less milk run we'll have." It is all a very pleasant feeling though.

Well, Mom, the mosquitoes are out in force tonight and coming in with fighter escort. As I'm rather behind on my sleep I think I'll quit now. May be able to write more tomorrow but this will be better than no word. Thanks again for the swell stuff.

Your loving son, Tommy

P.S. I sent Aunt Mary the money to even up Doc Mullin, so I guess that is all square now.

P.P.S. Let me know when the June allotment and bond arrive.

Once Tom and Johnny were assigned a mission and the target was known, they flew a practice mission to rehearse the bomb run. On the actual mission, near the target, the pilot handed control of the ship to the bombardier who flew the plane through the bombsight as he dropped the bombs. As soon as the bombardier yelled "Bombs Away!" control of the ship returned to the pilot who got them the heck out of the area. These flight control switches between pilot and bombardier had to be precise, thus the ongoing practice.

TOM - MENTAL QUIRKS OF COMBAT
Corsica, France, July 5, 1944

Dear Mom,

This letter may be rather snafued due to the fact that I have not done any typing for a long time and this machine is a little different from any I am accustomed to using. Willy and I being especially alert this morning (a phenomenon in itself) happened to be within hearing when Lt. Wheeler remarked that he was going home for thirty days and did we know anybody in the market for a typewriter? We told him that we would buy it, so after a brief preflight, thirty bucks was produced from nowhere, and we are now proud possessors of a German make "Continental." All in the spoils of war, I guess.

As I go stumbling through this, I am at a loss as to whether my forthcoming letters will be longer or shorter. You have to use the shift key for numerals, periods and a few things are backwards. However I use a tough system—at hunt-and-peck speed. Perhaps after a while I will become mediocre at least. It is a pretty good machine though and finished in red enamel, and I think we would have bought the damn thing even if it didn't type—just for the color. I am rather tired tonight after a fairly rugged day which may account for about 1% of my difficulty.

I am glad to hear that you got in touch with Smitty's wife. I can't figure out why he has not told her how many missions he has flown. Since I wrote to you about him I have flown with him on a couple lulus. I now have twenty-one, by the way, and I would say he has at least that many.

Today I received yours of the 26th and 27th, enjoying every word. I have already received a couple of Peg's but read them again for sheer literary satisfaction. One of Frank's reads just like a page out of the *Officer's Guide* and it gives me an idea as to which one of us will remain a second looey the longest. I should be getting a lead spot one of these days, and if I can come within a gnat's eyebrow of the target I'll get recommended. When I get saluted over here, I have to take my pipe out of my mouth, reach for my field manual covering the proper rendition of a military salute, and by that time the guy is past me.

I passed up a couple colonels in Algiers one day and they asked me, "Aren't you saluting today, Lieutenant?" "Pardon me, Sir, I was distracted by a couple nurses that just went by in that jeep." "That is good enough for me," he said. And that was good enough for me too.

The question has been raised as to when I am coming home. Despite 21 missions, it seems like I hardly got here. However, the poop now is seventy missions or one year overseas to apply for rotation. There is also a possibility of going home on a thirty-day leave after about 50, taking at least a month to go each way (regardless of how long it actually takes) and then coming back to this same outfit which I happen to like. If I went on rotation, I could still be sent over again, perhaps in heavies which does not appeal to me at all. The ruling power though is the flight surgeon. Maybe I'll get a little flak-happy before seventy or even fifty and I'll go home for good. Nothing serious but just not up to the fitness required for combat. So far, the only thing that really bothers me is a layoff of more than a couple days. Even that is not so bad if I have something do, but just now, the only thing I am thinking about is hitting the right keys on this machine.

We all have our opinions on how to keep the right mental attitude in this business. I try to think only of the mission at hand or the one tomorrow. The ones past are milk runs for my money—not that they were at the time—but for the simple reason that they are over with and will never have to be sweated out again. Each one looks tough to me until it is entered in my scorebook.

I always had a very vivid and strong imagination, which when trying to relax, is not the best thing in the world, but so far, I have been able to keep going. I don't know how I got off on this subject of the mental quirks of combat but it will not hurt you to read it and might be of some help to Jack.

These guys you hear about flying over a hundred missions are all fighter pilots and it generally boils down to so many combat hours. Heavies have flights about four times as long as ours and fly one fourth as many.

Incidentally, there is nine or ten hours' time difference and usually when you are getting up in the morning, I'm going to the movies—the day's work (or loafing) is done.

Well, the boys want to go to bed now so I'll knock off. Everything is under control and things look pretty fine ahead.

Your loving son, Tommy

TOM - POETS' CORNER
Corsica, France, July 8, 1944

Dear Mom,

This morning, due to a stand-down, I find myself with time on my hands. So I've tried to give you a little idea of what the dump looks like. I can't picture the dust and debris.

The perspective is poor, but it can partially be attributed to the fact that the tent is on a slope, and that it leans precariously in the wrong direction.

The name "Poets' Corner" is partly my own invention. Since acquiring the typewriter, everybody kids us about being war correspondents. Also, the occupants of the original "Poets' Corner" in Westminster Abbey are marble or granite statues and everybody also agrees we have just about as much ambition as they do.

Have a practice mission now so better close. May write this afternoon.

Your loving son, Tommy

TOM - THE PUBLICITY HOUND
Corsica, France, July 10, 1944

Dear Mom,

Just received yours of June 21st and 23rd, also one from Eleanor Hunt dated June 30, so you see the mail is still irregular though speedy at times.

I believe I have had later letters from you than the ones mentioned above.

Nothing doing all day today. Now we are waiting for it to get dark and then we'll go to the show. Today our duffel bags, which were sent over by boat, were finally picked up in Naples by a ship from our squadron. So for a few minutes there was a little excitement as we emptied the contents. We all had a couple pair of winter undies, which are now waving in the breeze from the "veranda." To passersby, they are the new M-1 flying suits and cause considerable comment about how lucky we are to have them.

The enclosed photo was taken about six weeks ago. The characters are, left to right, Wells Morris, Jr. of Westwood, Yours Truly, a couple enlisted men, and on the right Lt. Angelo Adams. I don't remember where he is from but I think he married a girl from Santa Ana.

The picture was taken by the group public relations man wanting something of typical combat men. Morris, Adams and I at that time had flown exactly *no* missions.

I don't believe we look any different now and I certainly don't feel much different.

Just this evening, however, I don't feel so hot and think this is about all for tonight.

Don't worry if there is no mail every time you go to the box or even for a couple days as you see your letters do not reach me in proper sequence.

Willy and I have started nosing around to see about going to Rome at the end of the month, in which case there should be plenty to write about. Until then, I'll try to keep you posted every other day or so.

Your loving son, Tommy
P.S. Pat might take the picture to Mrs. Miner as I think she'd like to see it. They said it might appear in the local papers too.

TOM - TOM AND WILLY'S BOOK
Corsica, France, July 13, 1944

Dear Mom,

Well, after sweating out this afternoon's schedule of practice missions, I find that I am not on it and can devote all my attention to this letter. Willy unfortunately was chosen and I can only foresee more of them for him. I think I have flown as many practice missions as I have combat—to date, 26—and the practice missions are definitely one of the hardships of war. (The foregoing is the most botched up paragraph I have ever botched up and this typewriter is gradually destroying whatever hopes I might have had for some day learning to pay the piano or to do anything which requires dexterity.)

Things have been going pretty much as usual here. We are quite busy flying due to the beautiful weather we have been enjoying. As I mentioned above, I now have 26 missions to my credit. In fact, it is getting to the point where I am contemplating whether to ask for a 30-day leave at 50 or fly more than fifty and go home on rotation.

In a letter a week or so ago, I tried to explain the situation here and give you some sort of an idea how this business has affected me. It seems now to be a regular affair. I have been able to take off on a mission without being overly apprehensive and dismiss the flights from my thoughts shortly after they are completed. We generally have a good idea of what to expect from briefing, though there are usually a few surprises.

We were the subject of a newsreel outfit the other day, and I must admit they got a good show, and the theaters back home saw what a pretty rough day's work looks like. I found myself constantly wondering what the civilian reaction will be. Is everything on the screen fantasy a la Hollywood, or do they actually realize what is happening is true? Things which happen here sometimes come up in print very excitingly written. They are the subject of conversation for a while, but by the next mission something else has happened and the other incident is forgotten.

Out of about 89,000 decorations given in the Air Force, we read that some 80,000 went to the Eighth Air Force. The figures sound pretty fantastic, but it would not surprise me. Since I have been here I have not heard of anybody getting anything but the Purple Heart. I don't want that one or any other for the matter, but some of the boys here certainly deserve a reward.

I have my first theater ribbon, coincidentally with one star on it for the Rome campaign. When they get up to Florence I suppose there will be another star. Personally I am content to just roll along here, flying my missions, and going home in the same condition I arrived here in. Nobody wants to be a hero, that is a cinch. And there are no heroics uttered. Nazi is a word we only hear over the radio. I don't believe there is very much hate generating here either. Naturally we object to having our normal living disrupted and endangered, but I think that the fellows we are bombing are thinking just about as we are—why all this!

One of the fellows wrote a poem about his thoughts while lying on the beach, all peaceful and quiet, then he gets thinking about flak. It was really a riot the way he wrote it, but there was plenty of truth in it when he said how, up in the plane, he was looking down, praying that the enemy ack-ack boys would not hit him, while down on the ground that ack-ack battery was hoping that our bombs would not drop on them. I expect that after the war there will be reams written about the war, its causes and effects just as there is so much being written now, and before our time since Cain killed Abel, so I'll not pursue the subject any further.

It looks like Mark is really going someplace. I have as much faith in his ability as I have in the whole Navy, and I think that the world is U.S. Navy-conscious by now. Sometimes when I get pretty griped at things here I find myself wishing I had gone in the Navy. I know that after this is over, if I have any money, I'm going to buy a little sailboat and see if I can't work up to a nice big yacht.

I guess it would be asking too much to see Mitchells and B-24s at the Douglas plant, but I think you will find, in the current and later issues of *Flying* magazine, good pictures of our business office.

My subscription to *Time* has started to arrive and it is swell to have it coming regularly. The mail has been good lately though running rather in spurts. In one day I got a swell letter from Peg, and also letters from Tut, Johnnie Hardiman, Frances Slattery (telling me Johnnie would write), Mrs. Estabrook and Hal Burkhard. Hal was with me in cadets until I washed out of primary and is now in England flying P-38s. He is from Glendale or Burbank, I never could remember which. Also had a V-Mail from Allin who is in Camp Beale, California, and it looks like he'll be going overseas.

Did I tell you I cleaned up Dr. Mullin's bill finally? I am now broke with nothing to buy anyway and feel rather satisfied that it has been taken care of, and I have been thinking that if there are any more old accounts to be straightened, now is a good time. For instance, Mary Waters. If you could give me some idea of what it is, I could send you some to forward. Just now use my allotment as you have been doing and try to get ahead at home. Later when things get straightened out, you might be able to save a little more for me. I have been reading that the government might finance college for vets and I might be half-interested.

Don't disown me for saying so, but I have become increasingly aware of the political stink, and its cure. Other sociological problems interest me to the extent of sticking my neck out to do something about them, but so far, my main interest is still in singing. I tried to start a GI correspondence course in history, and also something in writing, but can't seem to gather any concrete plans for applying. I do a little drawing now and then but don't show any improvement. Willy does some excellent cartoons, which for point, simplicity and expression can't be beat.

He did one of Lt. Tipton, the operations officer, coming around to our tent scheduling for a dawn practice mission. Morrison is on his knees pleading—with tears and all. Whited is hiding under the bed trying to shoo Jocko away who is not letting Whited's position remain secret. Willy, with a cunning expression on his face is sneaking around the tent for a getaway, and it appears that I was caught first, as I am pulling my hair and letting loose with one of the screams which in our house always resulted in a flying slipper from Frank. It made a great hit on the bulletin board, but alas Willy is this afternoon on a practice mission!

Willy and I have contemplated collaborating on a book. I would write it, he would do the illustrations, and the subject matter we would supply jointly. We have had some funny times together, and in the proper mood, some day we might accomplish something.

So far, other than the pipe package and your picture, which I told you arrived a couple weeks ago, there have been no arrivals. So still very far away from home cooking, I wish you could send something along. The brownies were swell and I believe they keep better than anything else. As for Noxzema, I had another bottle in that duffel bag which came and so am temporarily well supplied.

As for books, I don't read mysteries very much and there seems to be an abundance of them anyway. I do like good biographies of all types of people. I'm going to try again to take one of the courses I mentioned and hope thereby to keep occupied. However, things are going OK and I'll just get along with what I have at hand. If you should see any newsreels with 25s in them let me know how you like them. That's about it for now.

Your loving son, Tommy

P.S. Smitty just found out that Mary Waldo, now married, lives right next door to his wife, further proving it is a small world.

P.P.S. Last but not least was an incident which happened the other day. We were coming home from a raid on what must have been a pretty important Jerry target because they threw everything but the kitchen sink at us. Anyway, we are all feeling pretty gay about the whole thing, shooting the bull over the interphone when the radioman said, "Switch your earphones to the liaison set and you'll hear some sweet music." So I did and this is what I heard. They were playing the last few bars of somebody's concerto which I could not identify, and then the piece ended. In perfect English a beautiful feminine voice came through with, "You are listening to 'The American Hour' dedicated to all the brave fighting Americans today, particularly those in the Mediterranean Theater. The next program today is Radio BERLIN'S news broadcast. Come in Mr. So-and-so." All the comforts of home.

TOM - ON THE BEACH
Corsica, France, July 18, 1944

Dear Mom,

I'm not even sure of the date today and though it has not been long since I last wrote, that "You'd better write while you have the time" feeling is on me.

It's about 09:30 now and I'm at the beach. I have a particular spot which I always come to now where it is quiet, private and there is a smooth sandy bottom of the sea. The first duty upon arriving at the beach is to rub yourself liberally with "Scat," a GI issue which keeps the sand fleas away. They are the only things that at all mar the enjoyment of my surroundings. It takes a bit of energy to walk down here but it is always well worth the effort.

This morning we had a dawn practice mission. It is wonderful here in the early morning (once you get up) and despite the lost sleep, which I seem unable to regain during daylight, the sun rising over Monte Cristo was breathtaking and almost distracting from the business at hand.

The mail situation has been terrible for over a week now. Outside of a V-Mail from Bob, there has been little else. It seems that nobody else is getting any either so I can't very well complain. On my part, I have not written very much as the typewriter has been on the blink and I have been pretty tired.

The responsibilities of being a lead bombardier are infinite but the satisfaction of a successful mission more than outweighs the worries involved. When you hit the target you are happy for a number of reasons. There is, of course, the thrill of coming through, but the personal uplift is decidedly secondary to other emotions. You've led the formation to, over and off the target with your best judgment for their safety. A target destroyed is one that you won't have to come back to, might save a few boys on the ground the task of wiping it out, or may hold back a trainload or even just a truckload of German ammunition and supplies which may at some hot spot turn the tide. Then, too, it is another mission completed and one more closer to being home.

Unfortunately—at least with all the bombardiers I've ever known—you don't bat a thousand and sometimes miss. Often it is a bad break, but the fact that some miscalculation on your part might have been responsible for the failure always leaves a guilty feeling—slight or great. Right now that is my biggest problem.

Paradoxically I sweat out an easy target more than a hot one. I have some excuse on a hot one. On the whole, however, I have done well, they say, and better than I had hoped.

I'm much calmer than ever and added responsibility gives added confidence. I like to take a backseat whenever I can, being built on the lazy side, but I like to see things done right even if I have to do them myself. I don't worry half as much.

When I get back to the tent, I'll enclose a couple poems I found in Art Barron's class book from Childress Bombardier School. One is serious but the other takes up the problem of the postwar bombardier. By examining all the jobs in the Air Force, one of the least likely to be of benefit to a civilian life is that of bombardier. And so there is an endless supply of jokes on the subject.

The poem is one of the best. Once these appeared in a magazine, an advertisement for something or other went at great length to write about the "first bombardier."

According to them he was (illustrated) some sort of prehistoric man who hit upon the charming idea of mounting a prominent hill and stoning his enemies as they tried to advance on him. (Somebody wrote "Staub's Grandpappy" under the illustration and caused a riot. Staub is about six foot three or four and is dignified with the nickname "Bubbles." He is also the best bombardier in the outfit.)

This business of stoning by centuries advanced to the art, which has now made Sperry and Norden almost household words. What these advertising agencies won't go through to sell something! I shudder recalling at one time that I had ambitions along that line!

I hope you don't mind my writing so much of my own affairs. It seems rather pointless to inquire as to how many teeth Little Pat has or how everybody individually is.

I say "pointless" because your letters seem to cover every phase of life at Cahills and their in-laws and friends and neighbors that such questions are superfluous. And I don't believe it is necessary to demonstrate with questions how much you are all in my thoughts and to return to you is my biggest hope. Since being overseas, I have censored quite a lot of mail and most of the letters seem to be just a session of questions.

Well, the "Scat" is beginning to wear off, and so I think I'll have a swim and go back to the tent. I'll try to write the boys this afternoon and that's all for now.

Your loving son, Tommy

When Tom mentioned his "Norden" above, at first I thought he'd forgotten his censorship. This was the highly secret bombsight he referred to, though not by name, during bombardier training in Albuquerque. Its secrecy was reduced during the war, thus his ability to mention it in this letter. The sight's innovative key features were its ability to constantly calculate a bomb's trajectory based on flight conditions, and its link to the plane's autopilot that let it react quickly and accurately to wind or other effects.

TOM - BOMBARDIER VERSE
Corsica, France, July 21, 1944

Dear Mom,
    Didn't get the letter mailed yet. There has been no mail for anybody here for almost two weeks now. Anyway, here's the poetry.

"The Last of the Bombardiers"

On a lonely road thru a cold black site
A miserable beggar trudges thru the night
The people whisper over their beers:
"There goes the last of the bombardiers!"

What was a bombardier? No reply!
For men turned silent and women sighed
As a breath-like silence fills the place
With the gaunt grey ghost of a long lost race.

It's hard to explain the catch of breath
As they seemed to sense the approach of death
Furtive glances from ceiling to floor
'Til someone or something opened the door.

The bravest hearts turned cold with fear
The thing at the door was a bombardier!

His hands were bony and his hair was thin
His back was curved like an old bent pin
His eyes were two empty rings of black
And vaguely he murmured, "Shack, Shack, Shack."

This ancient relic of the Second World War
Crept 'cross the room and slouched on the bar
No one spoke but they watched thru the glass
As the beggar produced a Bombsight Pass!

And with hollow tones from his sunken chest
He demanded drink and only the best.
Glass to his lips, they heard him say
"The bomb bay's open—Bombs Away!"

Then speaking a word, he strolled to the door
And the bombardier was seen no more.

People still wondered at his strange last words
'Twas the strangest phrase they'd ever heard
But all thru the times the phrase has stuck
When they say "Bombardier," they say
"Ha–ard Luck."

(Author Unknown)

The second one follows—

God of the evening
God of the dawn
Help us to fly 'til our bombs are gone.
From high in the heavens let there be
A trail of fire down to the sea.

God of the darkness
God of the night
Give us the strength that we may fight.
And if it's thy wish that we may die
First let us flame against the sky.

God of the morning
God of the light
Keep our engines strong in flight
And then, O Lord, if it's thy will
Let us know nights when we need not kill.

(Author Unknown) .

Both of these poems appeared in the Childress Bombardier School book for Class 43-15. Guess that's all now.

Your loving son, Tommy

TOM - NOTHING TO WRITE HOME ABOUT
Corsica, France, July 24, 1944

Dear Mom,

There is hardly a thing to write about. Haven't flown anything but practice missions for a week now and it makes home seem farther away than ever. A few little items are worth noting however.

We had a new arrival in the squadron yesterday in the person of Lt. Graber. He, you may recall, was my navigation instructor at Albuquerque. His assistant there was Lt. Staub who is also in this squadron. Staub is about ready to go home on leave. He's a character. He is also one of the best bombardiers this outfit ever had and has taught me a lot of things here though he likes to kid me in the midst of giving serious advice.

Once when telling me how to pinpoint flak positions (if we know where the enemy guns are you can fly out of their range except at the target). Anyway, it got to be quite a detailed talk and I was all ears when he slipped in the suggestion that the best thing to do was to, "Watch the leaves on the trees rustle after the gun fires. Then you are really pinpointing it." All that is supposed to be seen from 10,000 feet and I, your son, swallowed it, hook, line and sinker.

There is never a dull moment with Staub around. Everybody calls him "Bubbles" (he's about 6 feet 3 inches). So now Graber is here and we've really been giving him a line about fighters and flak. The payoff is going to come if he ever is my navigator! Boy, he'll be keeping a log, double-lined at all the turning points, five-minute entries and all that stuff he hammered into us as "ironclad rules." Very rarely a cadet has a chance to give his instructor a workout!

I tried to sign up for a correspondence course but found it will be at least three months before I can receive the first lesson so that is out. I have got hold of Walter Lippmann's *U.S. Foreign Policy*—very good, too. Any books of historical or political nature, Patricia's suggested book on the theater sounds good, so if you could, send me any books on history, politics, musicians, and I would not mind some plays either.

Your letter and Pat's of July 5th reached here the 21st so you can see the mail is slow, and I have given up expecting your packages. There hasn't been a package arrive here for anybody for over a week. This whole European war is just too big to accommodate such things as home-cooking and books. If it will end any quicker I don't mind though.

Seems like I'm forgetting something but can't think of it now. I did sign my papers for my promotion to 1st looey today. So, unless somebody gets lazy and leaves it laying around, I should be a 1st looey perhaps by the time you receive this. Just to keep up the competition I hope I beat Frank, but I think after 1st he'll leave me behind. That's about all for now. Keep me posted on Jack's and Mark's whereabouts.

Your loving son, Tommy

TOM - SOMETHING TO WRITE HOME ABOUT
Corsica, France, July 27, 1944

Dear Mom,

Jackpot today! Your package of June 1st—with cookies and chocolate in perfect condition—arrived today with your letters of July 15 and 17, one from Bob and Jackie, two from Mrs. Miner, one from Bill Piekaar, one from Theda and one from Pop Clark. So, after the dismal trickle of mail which has been our lot for the last couple of weeks, we have a flood. For some days here, there has been no mail whatever for the whole squadron.

It is just coincidence that you should advise me to take a rest when I get tired. I was planning to ask to go to Capri after payday but now my rest has been settled. Johnny Moyer, my pilot, got a pretty bad head cold and so the flight surgeon is sending us both to Rome for three nights, leaving tomorrow. They have a rest camp hotel there and I expect to be shocked by a few luxuries like beds with sheets, ice cream, a big city. Just so the shock won't be too great I have dug out my last clean sheet I brought from the States, snow white and still smelling faintly of the laundry. I'd hate to lose a night's sleep in a bed just because I'm no longer used to sheets, so tonight I'll try to get back in form. If I can I'll try to send some postcards or something. I expect the whiskey situation is a little better there, and so may not be much for writing immediately, but Sunday at St. Peter's should be something to write home about.

Things on Corsica are just about the same. I haven't done much letter-writing as the typewriter spoiled me for the Palmer method. The machine is undergoing repairs now and should be ready shortly. It has taken me two hours to write this much as there is a constant stream of visitors, all sampling the cookies, all talkative, and I try to be the host.

I've got thirty missions now and am flying in the lead all the time. I have really been successful in the lead, far beyond my expectations. I've only led four times but if I can continue half as well, I'll do well enough. I don't mean to blow my own horn, but I'd like you to know that I have gained some badly needed self-confidence which will be of value not only in this business but after the war. I know now that I can do a job as well or even better than the next man. I never believed I was a bombardier except in rating, until my 30th mission. I've got more to learn and perfection is my goal. I'll never reach it, but if I just keep improving little by little, there will be no difficulty.

The lead bombardier is responsible for the success of the mission, and as much as is in his power, for the *safety* of all the men and ships in his formation. So it is not just twisting knobs. I'm sure that you can take plenty of credit for any success I might have for the simple reason that you have made me conscientious. Johnny and I have put in plenty of hours flying to perfect each detail of the run. All this for just one minute's work.

Well, I've got more missions ahead of me and God willing we should continue to do as well. We get a complete day off after a mission now which is something in itself.

My whole outlook has improved—having my life in my own hands seems to be much better than leaving it to someone else. Actually, lead is the best spot. It's safe enough so that you try to keep the rest of the guys from getting hit and not vice-versa.

Well, that's enough about that. I try to make you understand as much as I can of what I'm doing. I think it is best and I don't believe I have held out on you. Usually only the technical facts come under censorship and those you wouldn't understand and I couldn't tell them anyway.

Well, want to get up early and be off to Rome. Will write more later.

Your loving son, Tommy

MICHELLE - JACK: LIFE OF A RADIO OPERATOR, July 1944

After touring the States during operational training in May, June and July, Jack and his crew left the country from Topeka, Kansas, on July 23. They landed for fuel at Goose Bay, Labrador, flew to Ireland, then Wales, before reaching their destination in England on August 1: Station 125, Flixton Airfield, Bungay, Suffolk County.

Bungay is on the east coast of England, about 100 miles northeast of London. His crew belonged to the 706th Squadron of the 446th Bomb Group, and became "Bungay Buckaroos." The 446th Bomb Group's motto was "Voler, Venger, Vaincre" (Fly, Avenge, Vanquish-Conquer).

Jack's job of radio operator/gunner was different from other crewmembers, as veteran radio operator Raymond "Ted" Tate wrote for *The 446th Revisited*, by Ed Castens. With Ted's family's permission, I paraphrase, in part, from its reprinting on the 446th Bomb Group website.

During combat, radio operators continued to attend ground school to keep up their Morse code skills. On the day of a mission they attended main briefings with the pilots and navigators. A separate briefing followed, specifically for the radio operators, where that day's frequencies were disseminated and codebooks were issued and signed for. The loss or misuse of a bomber codebook was a court-martial offense.

Most crewmembers had additional responsibilities on the aircraft. Radio operators, stationed on the flight deck, also had the responsibility to clear any stuck bombs in the front bomb bay. Using portable oxygen, the radio operator would crawl on the catwalk above the open bomb bay doors, and by hand, work to release the bomb.

Per Jack's letter of April 9, 1944, "The radioman is also 'amateur surgeon and doctor' on a big ship."

TOM - TOM'S TRIP TO ROME
Corsica, France, August 1, 1944

Dear Mom,

Since I last wrote, many things have happened and I hardly know where to begin. First, as you can see, the typewriter has been repaired, and I am also using some of the paper which you sent me. The books *Lost Horizon*, etc., also came with the fudge and all in good shape and well received. Everything arrived while I was in Rome which is always the way.

I am also sending a package your way as soon as I can get it mailed. I bought a scarf for Pat in Rome. I don't know much about materials but it did not look too bad and makes at least a fair souvenir of Rome. For you at the Vatican I bought some rosary beads and, shortly after, went to the audience with the Pope where he blessed them and even touched them with his own hand.

This all started when my pilot Johnny was grounded due to a bad cold. Rather than have him hanging around the camp, the flight surgeon put him on orders to go to Rome for rest leave and I was to accompany him. We arrived just before noon and were billeted in the Albergna Savoia, which is a ritzy place with most of the original Italian help, with GIs in some jobs.

Morrison and Whited flew us over there, and they came to lunch with us. The dining room is out of this world with fine silverware, clean table linen, chinaware that matched and above all, splendid service. Most of the waiters spoke anywhere from a little to fluent English and we had no difficulty securing our needs. The meals were included in the price of our room, $4.50 for three days, honest. The food itself was GI originally but by the time those Italian chefs got through with it, it was something that you read about in *Good Housekeeping* or a fancy cookbook. Accompanying the meals was music by a pianist and violinist who played everything we wanted.

After lunch we set out to see what we could of the town. As you know, Rome is built on several hills—not very big ones but it gives the town winding, sloping streets and always holds the secret of what is around the corner until the last minute.

As far as the war is concerned, Rome has never seen it. The shops are smart and streamlined, well stocked in some items, low in others. Sidewalk cafes and open-air bars do a bang-up business all day though they keep odd hours. What this was before the war I don't know— perhaps a shopping center like at the Ambassador—anyway it is an ideal setup for its present purpose. Twice a day they served ice cream, which was the first real ice cream I had since Easter, plus pastries which I thought were out for the duration all over the world.

Not quite knowing where to go, we started walking downhill which seemed to be the easiest thing to do. We did not go very far though, as we were pretty tired and planned to take a Red Cross tour in the morning. Johnny did not think he would do anything but sleep, so I thought it would be a good time for me to go to the opera as it would be impossible to ever get him to go with me.

Madame Butterfly was playing that evening to be followed on successive days by *La Boheme* and *Tosca*. The latter two did not appeal to me so I decided now or never. The immediate problem then was to find the opera house and to obtain tickets. By means of directions from the Red Cross, a street map of Rome and some hot navigating on my part, I made it just in time to seat myself right behind a post in the mezzanine.

The only time I had ever seen *Butterfly* before was at Hollywood Bowl, so long ago, and so I had only a fair idea of the plot. The performance was smooth both in the pit and on the stage, the only fault that I could find was in MB. The part calls for at times rather coy and silly mannerisms. Unfortunately, our leading lady was rather on the hefty side, but after the first few minutes you became less conscious of her bulk and more aware of the quality of her voice. She was really wonderful, singing easily and well in all ranges.

In the second act her rendition of "One Fine Day" was so moving that she had to repeat the whole scene again. Ordinarily I hate to see the action interrupted by bows, encores, etc., but in this case, I had to hear it again. That encore cost me my supper but it was worth it and perhaps the best music I have heard in my life. Between acts, the theater is the same in Rome as in the States, and there is a mad rush to the lobby for a smoke, refreshments and the usual comments on the performance.

Returning to the hotel, Johnny was in the bar and we stayed there until it closed and even after, as we had ordered a half-dozen rounds just before closing time. This particular poison was a mixture of cognac and fruit juice in a really smooth blend—rare in these parts.

The next morning we managed to get in on the Red Cross tour and saw all the spots for which you know Rome is famous. It afforded us an opportunity to get a better look at modern and ancient Rome. The climax of the trip, of course, was St. Peter's.

The sheer size of the place is in itself amazing, but all the efforts of man are inside. If there is anything in the world to compare with it, I would like to see it. If you have been under the impression, as I was, that the walls inside are painted—this is the murals, not the columns, etc.— you will be surprised to learn that they are mosaic. I could not believe it when the guide told us, and would not until I moved up close enough to see the individual pieces which made up the complete picture. One particular shade of blue used in a cloak for Our Lord has been achieved by only three men in history. There are something like 28,000 different colors of mosaic and one place in the Vatican has pretty nearly all the colors.

It is impossible to describe St. Peter's. So much has been written about it for centuries that it is an effort to say even two bits worth of it. All I can say is that it is impossible to view even one little altar there without being conscious of something more than just a work of art.

I'm writing this in our new squadron club which was completed in my absence. Willy did the decorating and did a swell job. However, being at the club there are a number of the boys around making it rather difficult to concentrate.

The last day in Rome I made a special effort to be at the Vatican in time for an audience with the Pope. You have seen many pictures of the audience chamber and it is even more wonderful than pictured. On either side of the dais, up front the seats were reserved for Allied officers— American on the right, British and French on the left. The rest of the room was occupied by enlisted men with a space down the center for the coming and going of the Pope.

Shortly after twelve there was a stir at the rear of the chamber and automatically everybody rose to their feet and, as the Pope approached, knelt and received his blessing. He was carried in his chair by attendants preceded by some pretty husky guards sweating in their medieval uniforms. The Pope was dressed in white and appeared to be in good health and in high spirits. Descending from the chair, he went over to an American general and colonel who were with Archbishop Spellman and protested when they arose to their feet after being seated. He spoke a few words from the throne in French and English saying how glad he was to see us, and reminding us, above all, to live closer to God which was the only way of life.

After this he stepped down and everybody left their seats and crowded around to receive his blessing again, to shake his hand and he in turn had some comment to make to each individual soldier, sailor, nurse—everyone that could get close to him. He has a magnetic and inspiring personality and everybody instinctively felt that here was a great and holy man. I bought you some rosary beads which he touched. I could not get closer but it seemed even then to be too great a privilege for me.

Leaving finally with the crowd, I cannot describe my emotions. I had just seen and touched the Pope. Some of his goodness could not help penetrating my soul, and I felt ashamed of myself for every wrong I had ever done and knew in my weakness I would do again. If I could only keep that feeling of those few moments with me always…

Your loving son, Tommy

Tom didn't mention which Pope he saw. Google confirmed it was Pope Pius XII. My search also popped up a YouTube site, "Pope Pius Blesses 4,000 GIs in 1944." Tom's account exactly matches the 1:12 video, which surely made it easy for me to visualize him there.

TOM - THE SQUADRON SOIRÉE
Corsica, France, August 7, 1944

Dear Mom,

It's been a few days since I last wrote to you but not much has happened since then. Things are going along as usual except for the fact that our squadron club is now open and running in high gear. Its opening celebration was followed the next night by the usual soirée and both combined to leave your son slightly the worse for wear. However, yesterday was a quiet Sunday and I am now back in what for me passes as "good shape."

The other day I heard a rumor that Floyd, of my old preflight primary days, was on the island at an A-20 field up the road. So, with a day off on my hands I set out to see him. It was farther up there than I had figured and when I finally did get there, it was only to learn that he was in Rome for a few days' rest. By chance Smitty was piloting the courier ship from Rome Saturday and knew Floyd from the days at Mather Field. So Floyd came back with Smitty, went to the party with us and went to his field the next morning. Stan Gerry, also of the old gang, is in the 489th so we went down to see him and had a great time recalling the good old days.

Despite the fact that I only fly about one-third as often as I used to before I started leading, I am kept busy with practice missions and lectures so the time does pass very quickly. I cannot seem to get caught up on my letter-writing and the layoff I took when the typewriter went on the blink really put me behind the eight ball. Mail is still coming slowly though, about once a week the squadron has a fair-sized batch. The rest of the time it runs from a trickle to nothing at all. Yesterday I was pleased to get a letter from Bob and one from Falconer, the latter for the first time in a month or two.

I do have a request to make though I hesitate with the mail situation being what it is. The packages do make better time than they used to, they tell me. Anyway, if it is possible, I would like Pat to get me a book on figure drawing. There is an excellent one by Bridgeman and as a second choice, the work of Vanderpool on the same subject. Willy is, due to my nagging, taking more of an interest in his talent, and having somebody to work with, I like to do more drawing myself. The book is probably rather expensive but I think my allotment or next MO home will bear it. This month I am paying for my trip to Rome, but next month hope to send something over and above the usual amount. If my First comes through, it will mean a slight raise and I may increase the allotment so you will be sure to get it. Anyway, if Pat or you cannot locate these particular books, try to find a good substitute.

Tough that Jack could not get to see you but the way things seem to be going this may be over before I thought it would. I'll try to write Jack and Mark this week and will send them for you to forward. All for now— just to let you know things are OK.

Your loving son, Tommy

TOM - THE HAIR-RAISER
Corsica, France, August 7, 1944

Dear Jerry,

Being back to what used to be normal for the first time since the pre-Rome period, I have been ambitiously trying to get caught up on my letter-writing. I was back a couple days before I flew a mission and surprised everybody and myself by hitting the target. This was followed almost immediately by the housewarming of our new squadron officers' club and the night following the usual group dance was held—an auspicious occasion as it was the first time they have ever had any American whiskey to serve over the bar. Sooooo, except for the brief respite around that mission, the last week or so has been a series of drunks and morning-afters.

Now I am completely recovered, and it does not look like there will be any parties for a while, so I guess I can safely climb back on the wagon. Re-reading the above, it looks rather bad but it really is not quite that bad. Tension around here builds up and lets down, and if the circumstances are right when the tension is up, it gets very drunk out.

Missions are now quite different for me than they used to be. The success or failure of our efforts now rests upon my pilot and me, and though it is quite a responsibility, I no longer have to suffer for the mistakes of others, though that does not mean I am incapable of making plenty of my own. I guess it is something like driving on wet pavement or being a passenger and sweating out the other guy.

So far, we have been even more successful than I had hoped, but as failure is costly in more ways than one, I am keeping my nose to the old grindstone, and making an effort to keep my head from expanding. It is a kick to do better than some of the guys who were Pickle Barrel Boys back in my cadet class. There is a lesson to be learned every mission and I want to keep learning right up until rotation. (Rotation—Ha, Ha.)

I have really had a couple hair-raisers though as a rule have been pretty lucky. One fine day as we passed over the coast of Italy on our way to a hot target, I discovered that I had left my chute harness back at the field. Though I did have my chest pack I had nothing to attach it to if I had to use it. So I spent the trip trying to figure out various ways to use it anyway. Of course my worries proved groundless but I have never forgotten it since then.

For all you see in the papers and from propaganda the 12th Air Force puts out you would never think our 25s did anything over here. All you see is heavies and 26s. But you can keep the publicity—I'll keep my old 25. Boy, it is really OK and I would hate to be in anything else.

Well, of all things, I have got to go to an aircraft recognition class now so I'm going to the tent to get me a book and try not to waste the time down there. Hope you don't mind if I don't get to write you much but I know Mother forwards mine and I try to make them as interesting as I can. Gotta scram now. Say hello to those English-speaking frails for me. Take it easy.

Your loving bro, Tommy
P.S. FO'd the rekky class—took a shower instead.

TOM - FIELD TRIP TO THE 310TH
Corsica, France, August 13, 1944

Dear Mom,

Sunday evening and a quiet evening at home—if I can consider this club home, and quiet—when it is neither. Anyway, it is reasonably quiet. Quieter than in the daytime with that incessant background of airplane engines. It has been warmer than usual mostly because the usual breeze is still. Mass was said as usual over in the Red Cross club and I was able to go. Overseas there are no fasting regulations regarding Communion so it is very easy to go at any time.

As usual, there is practically no news. Your letter of July 20th, I believe, arrived about Thursday, but other than that there has been absolutely no mail. I did write to Jack at the APO you sent me and have caught up on some long overdue letters to all parts of the world. It is amazing to see all the addresses in my little black book—places in every theater of the war. (However, it is noticeably lacking in feminine entries.) But regardless of where Jack and Mark go, I am pretty sure I can recommend some good buddy of mine to look in on and possibly be of some assistance to them. I also mailed to you the rosary beads with the scarf which I got Pat in Rome. I was able to send them in a manila envelope, registered, and I think that was adequate protection. How long it will take to get to you is anybody's guess but be sure to let me know when it arrives.

I had an interesting afternoon the other day. I set out for the PX down at the 310th Group and while I was there I intended to visit Cancilla and some of my old gang who are stationed there. Accompanied by Morris and Barron, we set out in a beat-up command car. It quit on us entirely right in front of group headquarters. We told the driver to telephone back to the squadron for a tow and we would hitchhike.

In no time at all we were again in a command car, this time the guests of a lieutenant colonel and captain in the artillery. Of course, the talk in no time at all got round to anti-aircraft guns and we got some valuable advice on evasive action. The German guns are similar enough to ours that we may learn about them from experts on our own guns. The colonel soon suggested that we visit a battery and we said that would be nice sometime. Well, he had the afternoon pretty free and would enjoy showing us around personally.

In a while we were at one of his posts, and the captain in charge of the battery with his lieutenants were soon standing in a brace while we Air Force boys stood there with our hands in our pockets enjoying the whole show. The way they had enlisted men popping-to was reminiscent of the rough cadet days, and frankly we did not feel like we were really in the Army, to watch those guys. However, I don't think we were discourteous even though we do not go very much by the book. The crew actually picked up one of our planes in the sky for us, just like they would an enemy.

It was all the latest equipment and while the German version may not be as good as ours, it is still close enough to respect very much. It was quite a change to be on the other end of an ack-ack gun after looking down so many unfriendly barrels. To continue, the boys showed us the works and we were very much impressed and appreciative.

The colonel then took us to the PX (where they would not give us any rations) and we parted there. He was really a good Joe and does not think the Air Force is a bunch of brash kids raising hell with the old Army regulations. In return for his kindness, we promised him a trip to Rome any time he could get a day off. But lieutenant colonels don't have a free hand either. "I got a CO who was born swaddled in red tape and he wouldn't say - - - - if his mouth was full of it. I can't get a day off for love nor money!" So help me, that is what he said. So we punched his ticket for him and sent him on his way back to his "**!!**" CO.

We have had several new books added to our club's supply here so you can ease up on the book situation. However, I still would like the figure drawing book I asked for in my last letter. I would like for you to send me some food. Those brownies are swell, likewise the chocolate cookies. I am lucky to get one mission a week so my score now has crawled up to the total of 32. At this rate it looks like a long war so all the home-cooking will be appreciated.

I heard a nasty rumor that my promotion papers went through group and wing OK, but at the 12th Air Force they have frozen promotions for a while. That is not definite yet but if it is, the squadron, group and wing will just put the papers through again and again until they give up. Being in the lead now is certainly worth a promotion especially when in other outfits you are automatically put in after twenty missions or so. The damn thing ain't worth much in cash but it does make you feel like your work is appreciated.

Well, I had better not get griping or I'll get out of this unusually contented mood I'm in. Oh, yes, could you find out where Red Hopkins is. I heard he was in Italy and if I knew where, I could probably get to see him. Also, one of the veteran pilots of this outfit, Lt. Scott, went home on rotation the other day. He lives in Hollywood or someplace but has an aunt on Raymond Avenue whom he says he will be visiting and he hopes to drop by to see you too. He is a nice fellow and I think he'll keep his word. I guess he'll be there sometime about a week or two after you get this letter. If he can't get over he said he would call you anyway.

Last but not least, Smitty the other day became the father of an eight-pound boy and he's pretty proud. I was quite surprised to hear it as he lives right next door and did not act very expectant. He is a good fellow and keeps his worries pretty much to himself so I'm glad everything is all right. That is about it now.

Your loving son, Tommy

TOM - THE SUPERIOR OFFICERS
Corsica, France, August 14, 1944

Dear Mom,

This has been quite a day. It seems I spoke too soon about my promotion being held up, as today I am sporting silver bars in place of the gold ones.

The orders were dated the 9th so I've got five days in already. Whited got his today also and so now Willy is the only shavetail left in the tent.

Hopelessly outnumbered, he has spent the day mockingly standing in a brace, offering to fill the water can, sweep out the tent, and of course such other services as holding down a place in the chow line for us, shining our new bars every hour on the hour, and in general behaving quite properly before his superior officers. All in fun, of course, and we wish he had his. It just happened that I started leading and he hasn't, not that he cares one way or another. "Trigger" Phelps, the squadron bombing officer has been made a captain, passing on to me his old bars and one brand new pair never before worn.

That is not all. Just before supper, Henthorn (from LA by the way) came by with your package of cookies mailed June 16th. It took a little longer than the last but all mail has been slow. Carlos, Henthorn's Boy Friday, has just stopped by and sampled your cookies, venting his approval with a hearty "Bona!" He does all Henthorn's laundry, keeps his tent and area in good shape, shoes shined, etc., for his meals, a couple hundred lire per week (about $2).

There is another kid I'd like to have work here but never can quite make the decision. He is a good kid and taking him in would keep him out of mischief. Anyway, he takes care of about three tents. One pilot in particular he wakes up in the morning, rolls him out of bed, makes the bed up neat as a pin, and before the pilot is really awake, he plops him back down on top of the bed!

So now I have to hit the hay. I'll have some raise in pay and may be able to increase my allotment but if it is too much red tape, I'll just send it by money order.

Your loving son, Tommy

TOM - SAM'S BIG DRUNK
Corsica, France, August 17, 1944

Dear Mom,

Since the package which came Tuesday, and which I wrote you about, there has been no mail. At the same time I had a letter from Jackie—assisted by Little Pat—which I enjoyed very much and will answer tonight or tomorrow for sure.

So far, of all the foodstuffs you have sent, the Toll House cookies seem to stay the freshest regardless of how well you pack them all. The chocolate cookies are a bit too thin and are easiest to break. However, even when just crumbs are left, they are still swell and are eaten as quickly. The last box did not last long as I was treating the gang for my promotion. Now that the invasion is well underway, the mail service should improve.

We just received a new batch of books from special services among which I have just completed and enjoyed very much *Roughly Speaking*, by Louise Randall Pierson. If you have not already come across it, you should try to.

It is about the daughter of an old Massachusetts family whose troubles began when her father died and left them in relative poverty because "your father endorsed notes, that was the trouble." It is an autobiography, and with a few ups and downs, not unlike our own, though they operated on a larger scale.

Trigger Phelps, our squadron bombing officer, has been promoted to captain along with Sam Gibson our squadron navigator. Both have over sixty missions and don't fly any more combat.

Sam just got out of the hospital and how he got there in the first place is a story in itself.

About a month ago we had a big party over at group. I forget now the cause but no doubt it was worthy. Anyway, Sam, who does not drink very much but really winds up when he does, found himself getting wound up and there was not much he could do for himself. After the group club closed, the biggest celebrators returned to the squadron (I had had enough then and hit the sack) and took up where they left off, using the major's private stock for fuel.

As all things must come to an end, so did the party at about three a.m. It was a moonless night and the short walk to Sam's tent was made treacherous by deep, dark and obscured foxholes. Sam was doing strictly dead reckoning by now and in instrument weather. Well, you have already guessed it.

He fell in one of the aforementioned, but was in no condition to feel anything until he'd been in bed for about twenty-four hours in a vain effort to get back on an even keel.

After a couple days he was sent to the hospital, diagnosed as being in serious condition with torn ligaments, etc. So for about three or four weeks he lay up there, completed his six months in grade as first, got promoted to captain and due to his leg—which is about normal now— he'll probably not have to worry about a second tour of duty and is packing his things to go home. I have never seen such good results from a big drunk night as those.

I have been using our stool here in the tent for a typing table and it is not nearly as stable as the tables in the club. Consequently, you will find more than the usual number of errors for which I hope you will make allowances.

All for now. Keep me posted on Mark and Jack.

Your loving son, Tommy

The "invasion" mentioned is the Allied Invasion of Southern France, August 15.

TOM - LEAVING THE WAR AT THE DOOR
Corsica, France, August 21, 1944

Dear Mom,

Well, it is now D-day plus 6, and for more reasons than one this outfit is pretty happy. We hear by the BBC that all is going pretty well there, but what touches us most is the fact that mail is pouring through after being delayed so long. Just to help you keep things straight, I now have your letters of July 10, 15, 16, 22 (2), 26, 28 and 31. And for the month of August, the 8th and 11th—possibly a couple more which I do not have at hand or will receive tomorrow. The packages mentioned have not arrived but I expect them any moment. I have also had about a half-dozen from Pat which I never expect to get answered entirely unless she quits writing for the duration.

Your copy of Jack's letter about England is for my money, the best piece of writing I have ever received and far better than most of the reporters' efforts. It would have been nice having him over in Italy but I think he might be getting a better deal in the Eighth. At least he'll probably get a helluva lot more medals.

About the biggest news as far as I am concerned here is that Willy and I have new living quarters. We now occupy the tent which formerly belonged to Lee and Sellers. It is the best pitched in the area and has another tent about a foot over the top which keeps the place very cool during the day and for some reason dry at night. The front of the tent is at the back or the back is at the front—anyway, it goes in an opposite direction from all the other tents in the area. This lends a certain touch of privacy but just so they won't think we are being snobbish, Willy painted a neat sign—yellow letters on black—with "Cahill and Mravinec" on one side and "Mravinec and Cahill" on the other so there is no argument about top billing.

We both found it rather difficult living at our old place, "Maison la Bitch" we called it, not so much because of the occupants, but from reliving the war twenty-four hours a day, discussing it with everybody—

and I do mean everybody. Every officer from the major on down has sat out there and batted the breeze to say nothing of our enlisted men—the war, flak and the best way to bail out of a B-25.

If every day was as rough as the more outstanding events which are constantly being rehashed, then it would not be bad—but a fellow, in say fifty missions, spends a total of three or four hours over the target—the roughest time—plus coming home, now and then, slightly the worse for wear, but why they want to talk about it all day is more than I can see. I can honestly say that after thirty-five missions I am in as good shape for nerves as I was when I started, perhaps in some ways better. So Willy and I up and left.

Now, after a mission when only one of us is out, the homebody can ask, "How did it go?" and he can be answered with "Milk Run" or "Rough" and anything more than that will get him the job of sweeping the floor or filling the water can. The same applies to our visitors, hospitality or no hospitality. Our candy, smokes, literature—anything we have is theirs—but the war is left at the door.

While here we hope to improve on our drawing. This was made rather difficult in the old place by characters looking over your shoulder at some experiment you are doing—or perhaps what you hope is your best—and remarking, "You can't draw." I don't believe they mean any offense and most of the time are speaking only in fun rather than criticism. It seems that to those who have no interest in any form of interpretation, other than as prescribed for them by someone else, such efforts should be left to a few people whom the world recognizes as "artists." Having no illusions about my abilities—or lack of them—I am content to go along hoping to learn a little something every day, and if nothing else, feeling a certain satisfaction that I have something better to do than read comic books.

Comic books are quite a sore spot with me. Back in civilian days (what a memory!), I could see this plague which was creeping slowly but surely into our already not too intelligent literary diet. Surely in the service where I was going, where fellows were either on some rather uncertain crusade or at least avoiding a fate worse than the draft, and where these same individuals had to be "the cream of the crop," I expected to see the end of comic books. I did not expect anything as radical as a serious discussion of this mess we are all in, but normal interests of normal men. Alas, the comic book seems to be here to stay.

Out of the whole batch of magazines and books that special services sends us, the first choice is just about three-fourths for the comics. I can't see it. I can see a desire for "escape" as they say, and as Willy and I are seeking here, but not running that far away. I still read the regular newspaper funnies and enjoy the older ones, but it stops right there.

While on the subject of reading matter, I noticed in one of your letters you mentioned *U.S. Foreign Policy* by Walter Lippmann. I happen to have a copy of that here. The government has made pocket-sized copies of a great number of new books including that one, so unless you have already sent it, don't bother to, though I think Frank might like it. It is about the best book on that subject I have read, though I must admit I am not as well read on that subject as I might be. The two-party system we have now may be all right for some governmental problems, but I think the foreign policy is too big a problem to disagree so heartily upon, or to play politics with, as I think both gangs have done.

It is now Tuesday. I was interrupted last evening and it is again approaching bedtime. My train of thought, such as it was, has been pretty badly broken and I can't seem to get up much steam.

"White Christmas" is being sung now by Bing which makes us all wonder, and I suppose it will not be the last time we hear that song. It also reminds me that you mentioned something about presents. The things I want most cannot be bought at any price or sent in the mail. However, there are a couple things which might come in handy.

I would like a white silk scarf. I remember back at primary I was going to buy one when I soloed. Of course, by the time I got back from my solo ride, washout was staring me right in the face. A white silk scarf was the least of my worries as it looked like my flying days were at an abrupt end. Washing out removed just about whatever glamour I might have seen in flying, and as what I am doing now is no longer peaceful practice, the scarf will be used for what it was meant—warmth. Having a white one will be just a touch of brightness and will say "Boo" to this sea of olive drab in which we live.

Perhaps Bob might be able to get me some model airplanes. This may sound funny after practically living in one for so long and depending on them as much as I do my own heart, but I do like to make models. It keeps me busy and I have quite a bit of time. I prefer solid models but would like one or two flying ones. Ship models would also be welcome— modern or old sailing vessels.

Pat might be able to get hold of some modeling clay. I think Duncan-Vail has it. I don't know much about the stuff but I would like a fair-sized chunk, and the color does not particularly matter though I think the real stuff comes in a sort of terracotta. I remember at bombardier school I had some to work with, to get my fingers as sensitive as possible. My instructor never could figure out how my hands could be so clumsy, and many the rap on the knuckles I got for overcorrecting or reaching for the wrong knob. Anyway, now I'd just like it to putter around.

From the above it kinda looks like I may not be home for Christmas, doesn't it? When I first got here I was getting about twelve to fifteen missions a month, but since I have been leading I am lucky to get in half that many and later when Fall arrives, perhaps less. How many more I have to fly I don't know. Lead crews sometimes don't have to fly as many as wingmen. My pilot, Moyer, has a few more missions than I have, and when he is through I don't know as I'll want to fly with anybody else.

Whatever success we have had has been due to patience and teamwork with each other. We flew many hours of "dry runs" before we dropped a practice bomb, and plenty of bombs before we flew a mission in the lead. We cut our bomb run from a minute down to thirty seconds and even twenty if it is necessary. Flying ten or twenty seconds less, straight and level, may have already saved some of the fellows who fly behind us from getting hit. And of course, it has perhaps saved my own life. At times I think the war will be over before Christmas, at least for the Germans. They are being beaten and beaten badly. How they will behave when they are fighting in Germany proper remains to be seen.

The BBC has just announced that Toulon has been evacuated. Boy, that was a hot spot a couple days ago! So I don't know how many missions I will have to fly. If I can complete them before Christmas the next problem is rotation. I suppose those in a position to do so will go on rotation around Christmas and we underlings will have to wait. Anyway, my Christmas here will be better than last year at Columbia. Outside of a couple hours at Joe Callahan's it was about the most dismal I have ever experienced or hope to. Here at least I am doing something, and maybe some of the guys who have been away a lot longer than I have will be home because I am here.

Some of the fellows in the ground troops have been here almost three years. That is pretty rough on the combat troops. In the rear echelons you are away from home, that is true, but knowing you are safe and can expect to be, is compensation. Personally, I think I am through the roughest part right now. In fact, I have shaven off my mustache!

Well, that is about the biggest Christmas list I have made up since the dim days on Pleasant Street. However, I hope it won't be too much trouble and I hope I have explained my wants clearly enough. I'm going to the mess hall now to see if I can fix up a snack.

Your loving son, Tommy

P.S. Jocko's master got back from the States today with a new harness of green leather with silver trimmings. I don't think Jocko has ever seen one before, and when they put it on he crawled under the bed and refused to see anybody. It finally came time to eat and he showed up at the mess hall prepared I guess for quite a ribbing. After a while he caught on to the idea that he looked pretty sharp as no dog in all of Corsica had such a harness, so now he is acting pretty cocky and will no doubt be more spoiled than ever.

TOM - HAPPY BIRTHDAY 340TH
Corsica, France, August 26, 1944

Dear Mom,
As of yesterday, the 340th Bomb Group is two years old. To celebrate this fact we had a big celebration yesterday with the generals around, and all of us wearing clean clothes and thumbing through Army regulations, the *Officer's Guide* and other books on the subject of saluting, just in case we should be cornered by one of these star-studded specimens. The only contact I had with the general was at the dance at the officers' club where everybody but the general was dancing with the general's girl. Haaard Luck!

There being no halfway measure about this group, a book extolling the virtues and feats of our organization was published and issued to us yesterday. If you read it closely you'll see that come hell or high water this, as our motto states, is "The Best Damn Group There Is."...The Book says so!

Seriously though, we have got a good outfit. Col. Chapman, the CO, has brought some ideas out of the book which have worked and a few which he should have left in the book, but on the whole, our bombing accuracy has improved immensely. The dance last night was attended by the usual eight or ten females consisting of Red Cross, nurses and Corsican types. The bar was graced with the usual drinks and over it passed a dozen cases of American whiskey among other drinks, which had been "cossacked" for the occasion.

Alas and alack! I find that now I cannot drink anything with any particular enjoyment so I shot the bull with the old classmates, sucked on my pipe and took care of my ration of grapes, tomatoes and sandwiches and watched the other guys make jerks of themselves for a change.

Willy went over the falls in a barrel you might say. At about two-thirty a.m., half the camp busted into the tent to give Willy a P-call (which Jack so well described for you) for the simple reason that Willy never gets any.

They did everything but set the bunk on fire and still he lay with his arms crossed on his chest. This morning after breakfast I complimented him on the act he put on. "Act?" he says. "I don't remember a thing after about ten o'clock!" He was out colder than a mackerel.

The club was decorated with ferns and pictures of the group's bombing among which I was pleased to find a couple examples of what I had done with my own little hands. I'll send you the book when I can get to the post office.

Incidentally, our squadron CO is Maj. Hackney whose picture is toward the last page. How they ever caught him to take his picture I'll never know. He is never around except for a party, though I'll give him credit for flying on rough missions with us as well as the easy ones. He's quite a boy.

Had a letter from Jack written in Ireland. The way things are going in Paris and the rest of France I hope that we will be sending a courier ship up toward Paris and maybe even to London. I've got thirty-six missions now and may go to rest camp in another month or so if things are not too busy around here.

There are a bunch of the boys down in Cairo now, and if they can get down there, the trips up north should not be out of the question at a later date.

I've been doing a little experimenting with my drawing lately and have had fair results. I still work in spurts but I seem to be learning a little bit. Bob's song arrived after taking five weeks to get here, and as soon as I can get at the club's piano I'll try it out.

It has been pretty warm lately so we have been spending more time at the beach. The water is very clear here and we can kill time diving after rocks. I can swim better than I used to though I don't have much stamina. However, I'm learning to swim without wearing myself out so easily so I may strike a happy medium.

That seems to be about all there is today. Oh, yes, did I tell you that the mustache is no more? I got tired of taking the time for trimming it, and also decided that it had nothing to do with luck. Maybe I'll grow another before I go home but not for a while yet.

Received your letter with the clippings and enjoyed them all. Let me know when there is anything in the *Monitor* I might like to hear about. Mr. Tuttle sent the *Troubadour* the other day. Well, I'll write if anything new comes up.

Your loving son, Tommy

TOM - THE ALLOTMENT
Corsica, France, August 28, 1944

Dear Mom,

Willy is using the typewriter just now so I'll write you just a bit. Jerry sent me this stationery and it certainly is swell.

It has been hotter than blazes lately and I spend most of the time at the beach. The doughnut shop was closed this morning when we went by, so I hope to really catch up this afternoon. Those doughnuts are really a Godsend around here.

The candy ration is pretty small just now, and the doughnuts go a long way to relieve that between-meal hunger. In fact, if you don't have some doughnuts in the middle of the morning, it is just TC 'cause lunch is usually lousy.

What I mainly wanted to write about was allotments.

Willy's brother canceled the one he had and when Willy asked Capt. Meyers about getting one he not only got his allotment but it was retroactive to January 1st. This amounts to a pretty good sum, and if it would be to our advantage to have me get one and cancel the boys', I think we should do it.

As a first lieutenant I would get a dependency allotment of $96 per month which adds up to more than the rest of them combined could send. The way it would have to work would be for Jerry or whoever is carrying it to cancel the deal. That is cancel any money that the government contributes. Then I can start one retroactive to the date theirs stopped. So I would be sending the usual $100 of my own and the government would send $96. This only affects dependency allotments—money the government pays—not what they send home out of their own pay.

So if you find out what Jerry says and let me know when he cancels—if he does—and I'll start mine from that date. In that way the house will get more money and perhaps I can save some, and also the boys should be able to.

You might be able to get the details some place in Los Angeles. Anyway, try to get the thing settled and we'll get the deal underway. Going to the beach now.

Your loving son, Tommy

TOM - MEDITERRANEAN MORNING
Corsica, France, August 30, 1944

Dear Pat,

It's 09:30 here on the beach at Corsica. I am the only one on this particular stretch. The sea is as clear and smooth as glass, and except for a couple of fighters playing around upstairs, the only sound is the water lapping around my feet. Not only are my surroundings peaceful, but inside I feel serene and satisfied.

Physically, I have never felt better. I have done more swimming in the last couple weeks than I have in my life—and I am learning to swim better. Mentally, I have a quiet satisfaction in that my last mission (#37) was about the most successful I have ever had. It is not a feeling that I want to celebrate, as after winning a ballgame, because it is not sport—it is only fun when rehashed a month or so later, and the next time and the time after that, I must do as well and try to do better.

We have percentages on our records of hits and misses and bombs in the target area, and there is some measure for comparison between us bombardiers, but an unsuccessful mission may give Jerry an advantage for an hour or a week. The consequent lives involved can never be reckoned with, and any percentage on our part less than 100 might as well be zero. So I must keep all these things in mind, not rest on any temporary laurels and keep on without relaxing.

Bob's song arrived the other day. It took about a month getting here, and this afternoon I am going to see if I can get at the piano at the group club. I'm not much on reading music so I can't say anything about it now though the lyrics are clever.

I just had a brainstorm though about "Goodnight Little Laddie." I think it is a much better type of song to succeed than this latest. One thing which we have not considered, I believe, is that the last line might be either "Kiss your daddy" or "Kiss your mommy, goodnight," rather than "Kiss your teddy, goodnight." The second phrasing would also make it a good bet to send it to Kate Smith. Bing is now in England and the Crosbys might be hard to approach.

I would suggest Bob mail a copy of the song to himself, and send another copy of the song in a sealed envelope with a statement saying that the song has been protected by the composer, and that Kate or whoever he sends it to has his permission to use it. This protects her from having him say she stole it, and protects him from having it stolen, and I would also suggest doing it right away.

I'd like a copy of it here as I think the boys will enjoy it. If Bob gets no results, I'll send in a copy. The time is ripe and I don't think he should delay as already everybody is thinking of peacetime pursuits and songs, regardless of the fact that the war, as yet, is by no means won.

Well, it is getting rather uncomfortable writing on the beach. The B-25s are now up and around, and one just flew over so low that I had to fall flat on the ground. Honest, the only time I feel safe is *in* one of those things. A ride in a jeep or truck on these narrow winding roads the way the fellows around here drive gives me a worse case of jitters than any mission has. So, speak to Bob about the song and I'll try to write him in a couple days.

Guess I'll go in for a swim now. Haven't heard from Mrs. Miner in about a month now which is longer than usual. Say "Hello" to Mr. T. That's all.

Your loving brother, Tommy

TOM - THE GOOD OLD DAYS
Corsica, France, August 30, 1944

Dear Jerry,

Yours of the 22nd just arrived and I thought I would answer right away in case you did not get my last one to you. As you can see, the paper arrived, and though I usually use it for handwritten epics, this time I am out of the typing paper which I got from Mother. But I now find I can replace it from the orderly room supply. Thanks again.

This morning was a fairly average day. I went to the beach in the morning, picking up some doughnuts from the Red Cross on the way home, and spent this afternoon up with Capt. Trigger Phelps doing some practice bombing. The air was kinda bumpy so we didn't do so hot but it was something to do.

Trigger is quite a boy. He is the squadron bombing officer which is a soft job usually given to a bombardier who has completed his tour and happens to be around when there is a vacancy. He was flying back "in the good old days when it was *really* rough!" Everybody in the outfit is always telling everybody who has had less time in the outfit than they have about the days when it was really rough.

One day Smitty, who is from LA and whom I have mentioned in letters to Mom, came back with a whole aileron and part of the adjoining wing shot off. How it flew I'll never know. Anyway, he landed, and Trigger came driving up to the ship in a jeep like he always does after a mission. Smitty cut the engines, pulled back his window, and the first thing he yelled to Trigger was, "Say, kid, you should have been here in the days when it was *really* rough!"

Trigger bombed Cassino Abbey in the good old days.

I've got thirty-seven missions now. This month our squadron is running neck and neck with the 488th for top bombing accuracy. I can safely say that so far I have not hurt ours any this month though I did kinda screw up one last month. I'm pretty careful and try to let the bombsight do most of the work. That is what it was made for. I have no desires to be a "hot" bombardier with a bombsight just 'cause everybody else is using one. Incidentally, we have had heavies bomb some of the same targets we have bombed and we do better every time.

There has not been much doing around here socially. We had a big party a while ago with the general here and all the wheels to celebrate the group's second anniversary. They had American whiskey for the occasion—Schenley blended and some rye—but I could only drink one glass and the second one just would not go down, so I guess I'm on the wagon until I get back to the States and good old Coke Hi's. After drinking all this cognac, cherry brandy and vino for so long, I just have not got the taste anymore which is just as well.

I wrote to Mom the other day and told her that if nobody is collecting any money from the government, a la allotment, I can get 96 bucks a month. So if you have one, cancel it or something, and I think we will all come out ahead on the deal. I've been sending home 100 of my own each month plus about 50 more by money order and I don't think any of it is getting to the bank. I want Mom to spend it, of course, but I think this way we'll have more coming in for Mom, and we can all save some of our own money.

If about $200 per is going home in my name, you fellars should be able to save a good deal of your own. You probably know more about these things than I do, as I read in my *Officer's Guide* that commissioned O's could not draw dependency. Now that is all changed and anything I start will be retroactive to the date the canceled ones stopped. Willy just signed for one and will collect from January 1st—about 650 bucks. I wish I had known sooner.

Well, that is it. I hope your warrant officer deal comes through soon. I don't feel much different as a First though I may notice a slight change tomorrow—payday.

Your loving brother, Tom

P.S. Will try to look up Kay's brother but don't know when I'll get to Rome again.

P.P.S. Try to hear Sister Tharpe's recordings of "Rock Me," "That's all," "Rock Daniel." Solid.

MICHELLE - JACK: *SATAN'S LITTLE SISTER*, August 1944

Tom mentions in his August 26, 1944, letter to his mother that he received a letter from Jack, sent from Ireland as his crew was flying to their new base. Several of Jack's crewmembers were also Irish. What a time they must have had visiting the land of their common heritage. Jack, for sure, would have enjoyed seeing the sights, meeting the people (especially girls!) and sampling Irish beer.

After arriving at their airfield in England on August 1, Jack's crew exchanged the B-24 Liberator bomber they ferried from the States for another Liberator, *Satan's Little Sister*. They spent a few weeks acclimating to the area before flying their first mission August 25 to an aero engine plant in Germany.

Bungay, where Flixton Airfield was located, is in Suffolk County, a charming region of villages scattered across ancient landscapes. Like most bases, Flixton was self-contained with a post office, medical care, church services and tennis and basketball courts. The enlisted men's Aero Club had a library, game tables, snack bar and Red Cross girls who shared newspapers, magazines and conversation.

About fifteen miles northwest of Bungay is the somewhat larger town of Norwich. Historical references say that, early in the war, the British feared the Germans would invade England through this area, which never happened. When the Americans arrived, the townspeople were quite welcoming, especially the women who considered these men "a breath of fresh air." When soldiers left the base to go to "town," Norwich was where they went.

Tom's combat location, the French island of Corsica in the Mediterranean Sea, offered better weather and sunny beaches, compared to Jack's cooler English climate. But Tom doesn't mention any "dates" on Corsica, and I'm guessing Jack, in Norwich, had a much more interesting social life than his brother.

Fall 1944

TOM - ROOSEVELT VS. DEWEY
Corsica, France, September 1, 1944

Dear Mom,

Yours of the 21st came tonight though I had one from Pat of the 22nd the night before. I started to write last evening, but got so hopelessly involved in the subject of politics that I gave it up. In spite of all my raving on the subject, I don't believe I'm going to get to vote. I filled out an application blank then spilled grapefruit juice on it. For one reason or another, I never got another and now it is too late. I feel guilty about it, but I hope you will be sure to vote and I guess you know who for.

Personally, I think Dewey would make a pretty good man but not just now—and I can't see Bricker for beans. In fact, I'm pretty sore at both parties. I don't think the soldier vote will be influenced much by Roosevelt being Commander-in-Chief. I never think of him as that. As far as CO's go, about the highest I ever think of is our group CO. His influence is most important to me and his decisions affect me most. After that the wing commander, Gen. Knapp, comes in but not very much. I don't like his attitude about how many missions a guy should fly. Outside of that, I don't even know he exists. Cannon, Eaker and Arnold are just names I read in *Time*.

Walter Lippmann's *Foreign Policy* has had quite a bit to do with my thinking lately. It seems to me that before the American people say what they do or do not want for a foreign policy, they should find out what a foreign policy is—how the cards are stacked in the rest of the world regardless of the U.S. attitude.

I have not looked it up in the dictionary, but I think there is a difference between the word "policy" and the world "principle." Principles I would say are ideals (or sometimes they are really only "ideas") which we form or inherit such as to "keep free of foreign entanglements" or freedom for all nations, small or large. As Lippmann says, we have a couple different kinds of relations with Russia and England.

In Europe our relations with England are direct and we face the same problems as they, due to the Atlantic. In Europe our relations with Russia are only so much as they affect England and consequently ourselves. In Asia, it is the opposite. There our relations with Russia are direct due to the proximity to Alaska, our interests in China and our war with Japan. In Asia our relations with England are mostly in regard to how they affect Russia and us.

So I think that leaves us a rather obvious course to follow. I don't believe we are big enough to dictate to, even at our strongest, and if we can't agree on a policy at home, we won't stand a chance at a peace conference. This can be the war to end all wars—even for fifty or a hundred years, it would be better than the old set-up—but will it be?

So now it appears that, with all the heated discussions on reconversion and demobilization, we are taking our three years of active participation in the war with its priceless toll, the shaky position into which we have placed our economic life, the awakening of Americans to the greatness that is theirs in America, all this is being thrown in the gutter to be washed away by the drooling speeches of prejudiced politicians. That is a little more rhetorical than I had intended to get but I can't seem to say it any other way.

When we had our backs to the wall for a year or so after Pearl Harbor, we were looking at the skies and across the seas, but now that we are in the homestretch, it is the great "I" again and the almighty dollar. I wouldn't say that everybody feels that way. There are thousands of people, who like yourself have their sons away from home, others who have lost theirs, and others, who are unselfish and are doing their best to aid you, who had more to offer. Unfortunately, though they may be the majority, they serve silently with actions rather than talk, "unfortunately" because the minority who make the loudest noise are also in most cases the ones with the most material wealth and selfish interests.

Don't get the idea now that I think I am being imposed upon 'cause I am overseas. When my morale is normal or better, I still feel traces of what I was thinking when I enlisted. It is a privilege that I can get some enjoyment out of my work—that it is up to my capacities and not more or less—and that I am not alone but am working with millions of others who are probably having a lot tougher time.

What's left of my idealism tells me that we will come out all right, if only because of our sincerity. But I'm getting more realistic every day. I am inclined to despair that things will ever be right again, and to think that there is not much we can look forward to because the future, which we worked so hard to build, has been taken from our hands by a bunch of chiselers who may have been the ones that got us in this mess in the first place. Well, that's that. I can probably keep quiet for another month or so now.

Your loving son, Tommy
P.S. Could you tell me the dates of Little Pat's and Mary's birthdays? Thanks.

TOM - BROTHER BOB
Corsica, France, September 15, 1944

Dear Bob, Jackie and Little Patrick,
    You are collectively well ahead of me on the writing deal and individually I think I am only ahead of Patrick—or at least even with him. As usual I have been communicating indirectly to you through my letters to Mom, and at odd times I have also taken to getting in touch with old schoolmates and buddies from the would-be pilot days. However, I have not forgotten you all, by any means, and hope that for a while, at least, this letter will even things up just a little bit anyway.
    Life is just about as usual here now except that thoughts of home are more frequent than ever before—if that is at all possible—but now there is some possibility that our hopes may be realized. I have forty-three missions now and don't believe I have more than ten more to go. There was a time when forty-three looked so far away that there really was not much point in thinking about it, and even now those remaining missions hold as much question as any other number. It does seem that they have gone quickly—almost too well.
    Today has been spent reading, digging into Mom's last batch of cookies, with the late afternoon spent on the beach. The meals today were all poor. They seem to be getting worse every day and being noticeably lacking in fresh vegetables and meat. What is really making me mad is that, in spite of all this, I am as fat as ever and all the walking and swimming in the world does not seem to alter the situation.
    It seemed like I was never going to get over to the club to try out your song. Until the last week or so I have been flying practice missions, and as the club was not open in the morning I was rather stymied. However, the other day I did get over there and in my own laborious hunt and peck system managed to play it and liked it very much. The bartender happens

to be a trumpet player in one of the bands on the island and he liked it too. So I let him take it and he was going to see the leader about it and try to get an arrangement written.

I saw him yesterday and he said the guy liked it but did not enthuse, though he said he would try to write the arrangement. Just now his outfit is quite busy and may be for a while, just as we are, and incidentally, we are not having any dances scheduled. So music is more or less at a standstill here now, but I am keeping in touch with this guy and if anything further develops I'll let you know.

If you have a copy of the "Goodnight" song and care to send it along I think he will like it better. He said that one of the guys in the band had connections with a publishing house in New York, and if he is interested, some good might come of it. I wrote Patricia about this a couple weeks ago and she was supposed to talk to you about it. I got the idea when writing to her, and as I did not have a chance to write you then, I thought that would be the quickest way.

Little Pat's enclosures in Jackie's letters are really something. He shows signs of developing into quite a bull-slinger. Taking after his pappy and uncles, no doubt.

What is the latest on Frank and Nettie's doings? I have not heard anything about them in a long time. Say "Hello," will you. Well, that is about it. Trigger Phelps just dropped in for a session so I guess I'll wind this up now. Hope Bob's job is OK.

Meantime, take it easy and tell Pat to go easy on his flirting. I want to find a few girls left.

Your loving brother, Tom

Nettie was my mother's best friend from high school throughout her life, and Frank was her husband. I knew them both. Nettie and Tom were maid of honor and best man at my parents' wedding in 1940.

TOM - DEAR ELEANOR
Corsica, France, September 17, 1944

Dear Eleanor,

Just the other day I got to thinking about you and was going to write, but I decided that there would be a letter coming in a day or so. I thought perhaps, if I waited, I might be able to answer any question you ask. I don't mind telling you that, outside of Mom and Pat and one or two more at most, you are, luckily for me, one upon whom I can actually expect a letter at such and such a time, but what is more, have that letter arrive.

Thoughts of the holidays at Christmas time, while batting the breeze here with the boys, recalled that our acquaintance began and can be measured by those same days—the fourth one's coming up. The situation here now for most of the gang I came over with has reached a point where we can at least have firm grounds for hope that next Christmas will be in the States, and perhaps even at home—though of course we are not counting any chickens before they hatch.

I still have about eight or ten more missions to fly yet and any one of them may be worse than the forty-four I have already flown. Flying in the lead has slowed me down a bit—most of the fellows I came with have finished their tour—but I do have a bit of satisfaction which in their position I would not have been able to enjoy.

The business of leading continues, and I must admit that I have tried to quit it for the simple reason that I have been taking it too seriously. That sounds funny in such a serious business, though I have done as well as any of the others here on the average. When I have fouled up, the cause I can always trace directly to Yours Truly. However, I am gradually adapting myself to the downs as well as the ups, and I think all will turn out OK. I don't believe I'll have to fly as many missions as the wingmen, not because as you had mentioned it was more dangerous (all positions in the formation are the same as far as luck goes), but because the responsibility does have a tendency to wear on a fellow.

Don't get the impression that I am developing into a feeble shadow of myself and slightly flak-happy to boot. There have been changes in me— for the better I hope—principally in the evaluation of the world I am trying to live in. I do feel older and look hopefully for a couple grey hairs, which you must admit would look distinguished. But on the other hand I find myself seriously considering college after the war and other ideas like that, which seven years out of high school would usually put out of the question.

When I get home I'd like to talk to you about that sort of business. Just now it seems that I have absolutely no idea of what I want to do after the war. Singing in one respect does not seem like much of a way to accomplish anything in the world. After going through this business, anything I do in civilian life will have to be even more important, or all this effort now will simply be wasted. But again we are counting chickens too soon, so I won't bother you anymore now on that subject.

While in Rome I did have an audience with the Pope. Why I did not mention it in my letter I don't know, as it certainly was the most important part of that visit and certainly has made a lasting impression on me. No matter how I try when writing letters I cannot write the same letter to two people. I can write to everybody about, say, a trip to Rome, but after four or five letters on that subject—each with an attempt at distinctiveness, not telling the same thing in the same way—I run out of words and so switch to some other subject.

I have about twenty people I write to with some sort of regularity scattered about the globe, every place east from Hawaii around the world to Guadalcanal. Their chance of ever comparing notes is just about impossible. Besides the distance perhaps, no one knows more than two of the rest, but still I can't write the same way twice, and believe me, it does not make writing any easier.

I was in Rome three days before I found out that I could see the Pope just about any day around noon. Our plane was to go back to Corsica that afternoon so I skipped lunch and headed for the Vatican. I had been to St. Peter's a couple times before so did not pause there but went right up to the audience chamber. Being an American officer got me a seat at the front of the room on the right hand side about fifty feet from the dais. English and French officers were across from us on the Pope's left.

Shortly after twelve there was a stir at the rear of the hall and we knew that the Pope must be coming. I won't go into details about the chair he was carried in or any of the material splendors with which you are probably familiar anyway, but you could see a change come over the people assembled there when he came down the aisle.

Automatically everybody went down on at least one knee whether out of respect or manner I cannot say. There were all religions there, and men who call their president "Mister," not "Your Highness," but there it seemed as though all these men were simply children. The word "Pope" is I think "Il Papa" Anglicized from the Italian, and of course you know he is called the Holy Father.

He spoke in both English and French and in a few words reminded us that all this would be wasted unless after the war we remember the ideals which we have tried to preserve through this war. It was not a plea to Catholics alone but to all religions, all nations. After that he stepped down from the dais and everybody crowded around to shake his hand, have a word with him or just crowd closer, drawn by some magnetic force in the man himself.

I have tried a dozen times to describe just how I felt in those few minutes but it seems an impossible task. That such a frail little man could have stood up to Hitler the way he did, bear all the administrative duties as head of the Church, and hold to his ideals without compromise is remarkable. He gave the impression that he had the wisdom of the ages and more kindness and understanding than any other man in the world.

I suppose being a Catholic I had already made up my mind what to expect but it was not consciously, as I hoped to form my own impressions. Well, I formed them but I am afraid I can't express them.

When I left there I was unaware of the beauties of St. Peter's which I had marveled at for hours the day before. I had seen a man who knew our problems, our weakness and offered not criticism but understanding and encouragement. I felt that I had seen a saint. Not a man who shut himself away from the world and avoided all its temptations, but one who made his way in the world just doing his best, being very human, but still—well, I just don't know how to say it. It's something you'd have to see and feel yourself.

Well, I've had to move over to the club so I'd have some light, but what with the radio, the gang and all, it is pretty hard to concentrate. So until another time this will have to be all. Best regards to Grace and Johnny and keep your fingers crossed—may be home for Christmas!

Sincerely, Tom

P.S. Can't figure out why your letter took twenty-four days to get here. Had one from Mom the same date, though before this I have had letters in eight days.

The Cahills met Eleanor Hunt after they moved to Los Angeles. Like a few months back, with Tom's letter to Betty, Eleanor brought this letter to my grandmother, who captured another because of the kindness of a friend.

TOM - TOM AND WILLY'S MUSEUM
Corsica, France, September 18, 1944

Dear Mom,

Yours of August 24th arrived yesterday along with one from Eleanor. Why it took so long is more than I can understand as I have had much later ones arrive before it.

It is Monday morning and we have been until now straightening out the tent. The usual routine of airing the bedding and sweeping the floor was followed by a little decorating. We found an empty 90mm shell, and as it is just about the same as the German 88, it served our purpose. We washed it off and then painted on its side "To Willy and Tom, Love, Hermann." It now stands outside our tent and will be seen by everybody coming out of the mess hall.

Gradually our tent is looking like a museum of some kind. Willy is always painting leather jackets with pictures of B-25s, bombs representing the number of missions, names of the fellows' planes and all sorts of stuff. My jacket is and will be comparatively plain with a picture of "Dopey" with a "well—here-goes" look on his face, dropping a big bomb. When I finish all my missions, I'll print the number on the bomb and let it go at that.

Some guys just don't know where to stop on this jacket business, and I hate to imagine the results if somebody makes a portable neon sign. Actually, the jackets are not worn on the streets in the States anyway, but everybody seems to compete against everybody else to have the loudest jacket. My jacket and perhaps a few pictures of my missions will be about all the souvenirs I care to keep after this is over.

We also have a bulletin board in our tent with the accent on "bull." It has pictures of ourselves—to spite each other—and pictures of our brothers, girls, etc. Then we have a picture in color of two dogs, and Willy wrote a caption below, "I'm not a dog lover—I just don't want to get in a rut, (signed) Mravinec." It also has a parody on diarrhea in the cadence of Edgar Allan Poe's "The Raven." There is also the scoreboard of Willy's love life at Capri toting up to "Two smiles, four curious stares and one dirty look."

All the above material has been up for quite a while now, and we are currently dreaming up new material. A couple days ago the colonel was around, inspecting of all things, and told Capt. Shealy that we had the best tent in the outfit.

Right now we are paying considerable attention to the fact that winter is approaching, and we are going to try to put up some sort of a wall around our porch, and then we can rig a stove up without smoking ourselves out of bed. The hazards of combat will be increased considerably when we set up that 100-octane stove, but this is war, Mom.

We had quite a time in our mess hall last night. McMillan has finished his missions and is quite happy about the whole thing. Merkel got a nasty wound in the shoulder and is today seeing the medical board about going home, as it will be sometime before he will be able to fly. Well, the two of them got to jitterbugging and it was a riot.

Merkel could only use one arm, and to see him duck when Mac tried to grab hold of it was really funny. Then he (Merkel) would pull out the old insurance claim gag about how before the accident he could lift his arm "way up to here" but now could only lift it up half way. He'd lift his left arm straight up but his right would only go to his shoulder. Then they got Carroll to dance. Carroll is also a lead bombardier and they had just told him he only had a couple more missions to go so he was already celebrating. He gets the silliest grin on his face when he is crocked of anybody I know. With a Spike Jones recording being played he really went to town.

Carroll is from Kentucky and has led more missions than anybody outside of Staub. He is the one that recommended me for lead, and in spite of that we are very good friends. Lately, or really just the last time we fouled up a mission together, we went over to the club, and over beaucoup vino we gave the bird to the statisticians who only care about our bombing percentages in the target area and not whether it is a near miss or hit.

He is just a couple missions ahead of me, and there is a possibility that we might go home together. He wants me to spend three days at his home. Trigger wants us to spend three at his and at that rate it will probably take about three weeks to cross the country. Oh, that will be the day!

I have forty-four missions now and only eight or ten more to go. Looks good but keep praying because I haven't flown them yet.

. We had a lecture yesterday on the GI Bill of Rights. With the three years in the Army that I'll have in May, I'll be then entitled to three years of college at government expense. It sounds good but what I'll study I can't decide.

The guy said it was not just to give us something for our service, but also to improve the minds of the country as a whole. He's got something there.

The first year you have to make passing grades in order to go the next year and so on. After being out of high school almost eight years, college sounds funny but despite the fact that I feel thirtyish, I'm still only twenty-three and that is not too late. After putting so much into the last three years, it would be foolish for us to let our results deteriorate.

Well, I'd better not get into that. I'm going to send Jack a bond for his birthday. I'll mail it to the house sometime around the first of the month. I've got a music box for Pat which I'll try to mail to her in time for hers.

I don't know what the future holds about when I'll be home. I expect to be on Corsica here for a couple months maybe, but I would not send any more packages. You can concentrate on Jack and Mark for a while. That's all for now.

Your loving son, Tommy
P.S. Trying to work a trip to London to see Jack in a month or so.

TOM - THE SIDE JOB
Corsica, France, September 27, 1944

Dear Mom,

Inspiration has been lacking and, as writing a letter is more than just taking a pen in hand, the output has been practically nothing. This is perhaps due in part to the fact that there has been little or no mail for over a week now.

There is not very much doing here beyond the usual routine. However, I have now begun to help Willy paint the boys' leather jackets. I believe I have told you how they are covered with bombs per mission, B-25s in flight, nicknames, cartoons, insignia and anything else they want. Willy does the 25s and I take care of the insignia and printing. It is something to do. I also do signs for the tents. These are now getting quite fancy, as time on my hands increases and technique improves.

I am over at the club now and the boys are whooping it up so it is pretty difficult to write. So, unless I find something to add before I mail this in the morning, this is all. Just to let you know all is well, but as I said before, not a darn thing to write about it.

Your loving son, Tommy

P.S. The photo was taken at the group club. Who the characters are in the foreground I don't know, but that is Willy and I in the background right.

MICHELLE - JACK: GROCERY RUNS, September 1944

In September, Jack's crew flew nine missions: one supply drop over Holland to American ground troops, five bombing missions to Germany, and three "grocery runs." I didn't know what grocery runs were, but found the answer, paraphrased below from the book *The History of the 446th Bomb Group*, compiled by Harold E. Jansen.

In August and September, 1944, B-24 Liberator bombers were used for missions of mercy, hauling supplies to the airfields at Orleans, France. Empty ships flew from Flixton farther south where they were loaded by British Royal artillerymen. Cargo included penicillin, flour, yeast, beans, bacon, pork sausage, herring, milk powder, chocolate and maps of the evolving French landscape.

Sort of a "busman's holiday," the planes flew across the English Channel, giving the crews a view of Naval traffic and Normandy where, a few months earlier, Allied troops had first pierced Hitler's fortress. Reaching France, the pilots flew at treetop level over war-torn cities including St. Lo, Caen and Calais. Some of the planes skirted Paris to view the Eiffel Tower.

Not long before this, the Orleans airfields were in the hands of the Germans. From the air, results of Allied raids were still visible, pockmarked with craters and a maze of wreckage. Bombs lay abandoned where Germans began to wire them for detonation, but were thwarted when American forces arrived.

Destroyed trucks and tanks marked the landscape, and crashed fighter planes, both friendly and enemy, dotted the area. What were once large hangars were twisted girders, and American engineers put the runways back in order. Pitched tents were used by personnel running the field, and a shack served as a homemade control tower.

American planes were back, this time carrying food and medicine instead of high explosives. Frenchmen working in the fields stopped their plowing to wave at the approaching ships. After landing, French workers unloaded the supplies, and in a short while, American soldiers were on the road to Orleans to see the sights.

The French were very friendly. As the crews rode into town, people called "Vive L'Amerique" and gave the Victory sign. One of the crewmembers offered a pack of cigarettes to a Frenchman. It was intended as a gift, but the Frenchman would not have it so, and paid for it. He wanted the boy to have the French money as a souvenir and a bond of friendship. This rapport continued with more swapping, but no free giving. The American crews exchanged cigarettes, sugar and peaches out of their rations.

This was the first time men of the 446th landed on French soil. Previously they were greeted in the air by German flak and fighters. Now Americans were welcomed by the French as friends on solid ground.

I hope Jack was able to participate in these grocery runs. I know he would have loved seeing the sights, carrying food and medicine in a ship with no bombs and making new friends—friends whose freedom he joined the service to protect.

TOM - GROUNDED
Corsica, France, October 6, 1944

Dear Mom,

Just a few lines to let you know that I may not be writing for a while. I went to the flight surgeon about my cold, and am grounded for a week, so he is sending me to Capri for that time.

There is not much doing there now, but Adams is going with me and neither of us is so sick we can't have a good time.

Things like this make Christmas at home look farther and farther away but that is the way it goes. Perhaps for Christmas I can write and say I have finished my missions. Chances are still good though I'm not counting on a thing.

Will write when I can.

Your loving son, Tommy

TOM - THE ISLE OF CAPRI
Corsica, France, October 12, 1944

Dear Mom,

As this is the best day we have had so far, I'm taking the opportunity to spend it on the beach. Beach is really a compliment, as it is just a small cove with rocks where the sand ought to be. However, they call it the beach club so I'll let it go at that.

We have been having a swell time here and have two more nights before we go back to Corsica. Quisisana Hotel is our residence, and it is about the best hotel on the island and they have some good ones. It is just about all Air Force here but, as it should be, there is little or no talk about combat, though I think we would like to out-lie each other concerning heroic deeds.

I've been doing a little shopping but mostly bullion insignia for the boys at camp. There were some swell children's clothes, but Pat and Mary are still too small for what they have here. Shopping for the kids reminds us all of the approach of Christmas.

I brought my sketchbook and pencil with me today thinking I might do some sketching. However, I'm not much in the mood now and so probably will do nothing about it.

Adams and Gallatin are here with me and the three of us have quite a bit of fun and get along well together. They have movies (old ones every time) nightly and dancing afterwards. The odds are much better here for dancing than in Corsica, with only about twenty fellows for every gal instead of my accustomed 100 fellows to one. The fact that not all the fellows come to the dance makes the odds better.

Probably won't write until I get back to the outfit so don't worry if you don't hear from me for a while.

Your loving son, Tommy

TOM - CORSICAN CHRISTMAS
Corsica, France, October 24, 1944

Dear Mom,

Yours of October 9th and 11th plus Pat's of the 12th arrived tonight. Mail you can see is coming a little faster but not much.

It now looks as though it will be impossible to get home by Christmas. Certain changes in the rotation policy plus a couple unexpected obstacles make it quite certain now. I'll try to give you what reasons I can though I know you have never counted on anything positively.

For a while in September I thought that I would be sent home via the Medical Disposition Board. Lead crews usually have sufficient reasons for meeting the boards but they altered their rulings slightly, and I have also found that you have brought me up to be very sound and healthy, so after forty-eight missions, I am little the worse for wear. In fact, I think I feel much better. More important, my mental health is good, with nerves as they should be, backed by my now considerable experience.

The weather has been bad so that we don't fly as often as usual and now I fly less. I fly less because at present Johnny and I are the most experienced lead crew in the squadron. The four squadrons rotate leading the group, and whenever our squadron leads, Johnny and I will be the ones to do it. It is really not much different than just leading a box except that I'll get first crack at the target and won't have to bomb into anybody else's smoke. I'll get a good shot at it.

If I wanted to I could fly more often but as I said, due to my experience it would not be fair. I won't get any more out of it. A captaincy is not available so I'll just do it anyway. I am sure you would want it that way and there is still a good chance that I will be finished by Christmas.

By the time I am almost finished there will of course be somebody else to take my place, perhaps sooner if a couple of guys coming back from leave in the States get here. As long as I cannot get home for the holidays, I'll probably put in more time here without flying any combat missions as I'll have to wait for rotation anyway. So, will probably go to Cairo and Alexandria for a few days' rest and sightseeing.

Next month I think the weather should be better. Because I was at Capri for a week, I only have two missions so far this month. That is pretty slow after getting ten or twelve a month so don't worry as I won't be flying often or much more. There is still a chance the war might be over here by Christmas. Christmas is a very big day in Germany and Der Fuhrer has not been much of a Santa Claus.

We have a new "Pocket Book" out here called the *Official Guide of the AAF* with *AAF* in large letters on the cover. You should be able to get it for about two bits. In it you'll find out more about our 12th and Jack's 8th Air Force, B-25s, bombing and other stuff than I would ever tell you in a letter. This censorship! Anyway, you will find very encouraging information about our equipment, casualties, generals and stuff like that there.

That's about all now.

Your loving son, Tommy

P.S. If I can get hits on our next two missions, John and I will get a DFC.

TOM - THE AIR MEDAL

Corsica, France, October 27, 1944

Dear Mom,

I got the enclosed photos tonight from the squadron public relations sergeant. The photo with me in the foreground while Bylund is getting the medal is the funniest thing I've ever seen. Of course, I did not know the picture was being taken and now for the life of me I can't figure what I was thinking at the time.

I had been standing there for about twenty minutes waiting for Gen. Knapp to get to me and was tired of the whole business. You can see what the Air Medal looks like from the one Bylund has on. The fellows in the background are just a few of the entire group that were decorated that day, so don't think I did anything extraordinary.

In the second picture that is Gen. Knapp, wing CO, pinning the medal on. Behind him stands Col. Chapman, our group CO, and behind him is Lt. Col. Ruebel, group operations officer. Ruebel, by the way, is from Pasadena and is also the best guy in all the group headquarters gang. He shook hands with each of us with a kinda "Ain't-this-a-crock" attitude. He doesn't go for all this formality though he is a West Point man.

Incidentally, a month ago my pilot Johnny got grounded for a month for buzzing—that is, grounded for all but combat and training flights putting the kibosh on trips to Rome, Naples, etc. Anyway, when Col. Ruebel got to John he said, "Well, Moyer, your month is up now. If you get a DFC you can buzz the area twice." I guess he does not know that if we get hits on the next two missions John and I will get a DFC and then will be buzzing the place! That's all.

Your loving son, Tommy

TOM - BATTING THE BREEZE
Corsica, France, October 28, 1944

Dear Mom,

Tonight I'm alert officer which all boils down to the simple duty of putting the lights out in the club at midnight. So I'm sitting here writing, listening to the radio, batting the breeze.

Sitting across from me is Angelo Adams. I have just given him your address and phone number. His wife, Betty, will probably call you one of these days. From what Adams says she is rather lonesome there. We thought that through our mutual acquaintance, and the welcome I knew she'd get from you, that you would be all for it. It is not like Smitty's wife who lives in LA and has friends there. Angelo does not have her phone number there but I am pretty sure she'll call.

Adams is really a character and one of my best friends in the squadron. We were at Capri together, came in the outfit at the same time and so have a lot in common.

For the past two days Willy and I have been working on a project of the colonel's. He wants all the ship insignia and names painted on pieces of cloth 10"x10" to be sewed on to some kind of a curtain. So the first thing to do was get sketches to work from. Of course, you've read about how the boys like to decorate their ships. Our squadron is no different and the boys go at it with a vengeance. About four out of five have girls as the main attraction in various stages of dress and undress.

What these guys don't know about anatomy would fill the Congressional Library. However, they are all united on what parts of the anatomy they like best and the results are astounding. So we take their layouts, modify them enough so that we can work on them without having our artistic tastes offended and let it go at that. I do all the drawings, transfer them to cloth and Willy paints. I'm saving the sketches so you can see what they look like.

The ship just assigned to John and I is 6X, "The Alice L," with a blond in a blue bathing suit perched on a diving board. Anyway, we are just about finished now, and once more we'll have time on our hands. My drawings were much better than I thought I could do and Willy was surprised too, so I think that all my sketching and the Vanderpool book are paying off. Encouraging anyway.

Tonight I heard a German program. It was just a half hour of songs in the light classical vein—light opera—I only recognized a couple but it seemed that none of the songs were very cheerful. The girl singing had a beautiful voice and the way she sang "On Wings of Song" was the best I have ever heard. I couldn't help but wonder how much some German soldier enjoyed that program.

We are winning our war, and in spite of homesickness and other personal annoyances, we always have that feeling that we are winning. But the German is in another frame of mind completely. Even if he doesn't see his whole nation endangered, he no doubt has had plenty of setbacks in his unit. And that music! Does it comfort him, make him forget the war? Or does he turn the program off? I guess we'll never understand the Germans.

It's funny the ideas you get listening to a good program. I don't know of anything that I like better than to just relax and listen. I think it is when I really relax completely. It doesn't matter whether I'm in my bed or coming back from a mission. The music is priceless. Well, that's about all tonight.

Your loving son, Tommy

MICHELLE - JACK: MISSIONS TO GERMANY, October 1944

October was a busy month for Jack's crew. They flew ten bombing missions to targets in Germany, including marshalling yards, an airfield, a canal and an oil refinery.

In one of Tom's earlier letters, he mentions hoping to fly from Corsica to see Jack in England, though I found nothing that says he ever did. They did, though, continue to write each other and receive their mother's typed copies of each other's letters home, as well as letters written by their other brothers.

TOM - HELLO FROM ALEXANDRIA
Alexandria, Egypt, November 16, 1944

Dear Mom,

It is early afternoon now and I am writing this as you can see from the Red Cross. They have four places here, one of them for officers. This is a nice roomy house with vines growing all around, and as it is in the shade of a large modern apartment house, it is cool all day long though it actually has not been hot any place here. Alexandria is a swell city, far more modern, cleaner and generally better than Cairo ever will be.

Right now we are just waiting for our lunches to settle so that we can go down to Monaco's and indulge in their terrific pastries, ice cream and milkshakes.

Yesterday afternoon Jerry Rahatz and I had dates with a couple very nice girls here, and we went bicycling all around the city. There are a number of smooth, wide boulevards and thank heavens, hardly any hills. It has been a long time since I have ridden on a bike. The last time was about six months ago in a town in Morocco. There were eight or ten of us Americans—the only ones in town—and we went all through the local Kasbah and didn't miss a thing. There are hardly any Americans here, and as it is a British town, everybody—almost everybody—speaks English. The girls we were with yesterday speak five or six languages fluently.

We are also here for a little business. Capt. Shealy is buying liquor and beer for our club's Christmas and Thanksgiving parties. I think we are getting about twenty-five cases of whiskey and fifty of beer, plus a few candy bars and things from the PX. I'm getting some dark green material to have made into a battle jacket. Perhaps you've seen them. The British wear them. They are something like a mess jacket and much more comfortable than the blouse. I can have the jacket made in Naples. I also am having a pair of boots made in Cairo. They will be made just for me so perhaps I'll have one pair of boots that fit perfectly.

That's about all now. I'll write when I get back to the base and until then I'll be enjoying this almost civilian existence.

Your loving son, Tommy

TOM - EGYPT TRIP RECAP
Thanksgiving Day, Corsica, France, November 23, 1944

Dear Mom,

Well, here it is Thanksgiving again. Last year it was at Fred Harvey's in Kansas City and this year it is Corsica. We have a big dinner planned at 15:00, and of course the drinking started hours ago—in fact, last night. I've been pretty sober so far but wouldn't be a bit surprised if I start in after dinner. As a result of my trip to Cairo, I now have two quarts of Canadian Club and one of Three Feathers, so you can find some comfort in the fact that I'm drinking good stuff.

The vacation in Egypt was really something and by far the best rest I've had in a long time—not that I needed one but after forty-nine missions, it is nice to get far away from the war for a while. As I have given up all hope of being even on my way home by Christmas, I made the most of this trip.

Cairo was amazing. American civilian cars were all over the place, all bright and shiny though a bit dated. The streets at night were bright with lights and neon with plenty of movies and nightspots. Outside the city were the Pyramids and the Sphinx just as they have been for centuries. They are in the desert just outside the Nile Valley. I guess I have read as much about the Nile as anybody on the average and all about its richness and fertility, but I was in for a surprise.

The desert ends and the valley begins—as abruptly as that and as contrasting as black and white. There is no blending or gradual change but hot desert sand and cool green fields. It seems as though there is as much water surface as land though it is actually not the case. I took some pictures which I hope will come out alright. We were in Cairo a couple days not doing much but getting a pair of boots and trying to line up some liquor for our club.

From Cairo we went to Alexandria. There we stayed at a Red Cross place for boys on leave and received a royal welcome. Corsican Air Force men get a special treatment there as our location denies us some of the opportunities which the boys on the mainland have. The first thing we did was eat, and when they found out that we have marmalade here three times a day, seven days a week, they then and there took the marmalade from all the tables and replaced it with all kinds of different jams, and all the time we were there we never again saw orange marmalade. Seconds, thirds or fourth helpings just made the girl running the place feel better knowing that she had done a swell job.

Mom, I never felt so at home away from home as I did there in Alex. There was not a thing which they would not do for us. There were practically no Americans in the town and everyplace we went we were welcomed. All the time I was there I had a feeling which just filled up inside me of peace and contentment which I never expected to feel this side of the ocean. I can only describe it as that feeling when I am thinking of home and can almost feel myself there. I get it now just recalling that wonderful week.

And of course there were girls!

Ordinarily the pickings are pretty slim and there is always a language barrier. But at Alex they had a few American Red Cross girls and a few English-speaking girls to help out. Of course, everybody in the town speaks at least a little English. Anyway, the Red Cross had a number of girls for parties and dances and it was never difficult to get a date. Very nice girls and most of them extremely well educated with command of four or five languages and schooling in France, Italy, Switzerland and of course Egypt. The town had plenty of good nightspots, and believe it or not, I had a girl who had to be home by nine o'clock! Starting at six-thirty was essential.

Afternoons Jerry Rahatz and I with whatever feminine company we gathered would go out bicycling, but for the rest of the time we ganged up in teasing Magda. I would like to state here and now that Mag is without a doubt one of the nicest girls I have met in years, and one whom I could easily go for in a big way. Pretty, smart and as close to being an American girl as anybody over here will ever be. She worked at the desk at the place where we were staying and is engaged to an American Naval officer who is most fortunately for him stationed in Alex. She is rather doubtful about the deal, though, as he insists on talking politics when out on a date rather than dancing, etc. So we kidded the life out of her for the fact that he is a lawyer, and that she now realizes he is a "shyster" or perhaps an "ambulance chaser." He went to Princeton which does not even have a good football team. But last and not least, he is a Republican!

Oh, what a time we had. The funny part of it was that Jerry and I would both go out with her at the same time. The payoff came the night before we left. I came back from my nine o'clock date and found Mag at her desk knitting away, Jerry sitting there as usual and some unidentified woman sitting there, also knitting. As the girls often have friends there I did not pay much attention to her, and as there were no introductions I proceeded to make myself at home.

Well, I was pretty sharp telling her how much "we" would miss her and how outstanding she was and really spreading it on thick—she taking it all with a laugh. Finally it came time for her to go. The woman arose with her and at the door she paused to say good night and goodbye in case she did not see us in the morning. "Well, goodnight, Tom." She said, "And good luck in case I don't see you in the morning. Oh, by the way, have you met my mother? Mother, this is Tom." She'd been saving that all night and she and her mother really got a bang out of it. As for me, that is one girl that will always get the last word. Boy, that was funny. Ole Jerry was trying to tell me sooner but couldn't manage it from where he was sitting…and there I was.

A good part of my time was spent in Monaco's where they had super deluxe sundaes and pastries which were out of this world. I think I established a few records on the amount of chocolate cake I consumed.

Well, it is about time to go at that turkey. I'll write again in a couple days. Willy and Barney have finished their missions, and I am the only "fightin' man" left of the three. I refer to them now as the ground troops or rear echelon boys. I brought back a case of beer—which I don't drink—and every time we rearrange the furniture in the tent we have a housewarming!

I expect I'll be flying again soon and perhaps more often than before as the weather looks promising. This Thanksgiving I feel very thankful for a million things—things which I've always had before but I either did not realize it or appreciate them as I should. I never felt better in my life and I'm rarin' to go. Will keep you posted on things as they happen. That's all now.

Your loving son, Tommy

P.S. Send the drawing books along. I don't know how long I'll have to wait for rotation after I finish my missions.

After reading this letter, I looked in Tom's "little brown book" and Magda's address was in it. I wonder if he ever wrote to her? I know I'm biased, but Tom sure seems a lot more interesting than that politics-spewing shyster she was engaged to.

JERRY - AT DUGAN'S TAVERN
Ft. Lewis, Washington, November 24, 1944

Dear Mom,

Sorry to hear that you were laid up with a cold and hope you are feeling better now.

We had a pretty good Thanksgiving around here, but of course it wasn't the same as home. After dinner we had open house in "Dugan's Tavern" and carried on until midnight. It was almost like some of the parties we had at home in some ways. We even had two guys in that nobody knew. They just happened to hear the noise and dropped in.

Not much else to write about except to say that I got a letter from Jack and will enclose it. He has some good news too. Guess this is all for now. Will write again soon.

Your loving son, Jerry

P.S. Just heard that we are allowed two packs of cigs a day now instead of one. After I get paid I'll send more home.

TOM - UP IN MABEL'S ROOM
Corsica, France, November 30, 1944

Dear Mom,

It has been about a week now since I last wrote to you, but I did write Grandma on the 27th so you heard indirectly anyway. I just received yours of the 15th and was surprised to hear that Gram had a stroke. As from the wording, it must have been mentioned to me before, and evidently I have not received the letter as yet.

Today I went visiting up to the 319th to see some of my old classmates, particularly Hawrylak, the Mad Russian, as we call him, and it was a novelty to find somebody with less missions than I have (still 49 by the way). The fellows up there all trained in 26s so I had not seen many of them since graduation, one long year ago. It was like old times, and I guess I've changed a bit since then, as they all seemed a little different. Not much, though, but a little. The Russian got a jeep to ride us back—I went up with Bill Fischer, also of the old class—and he stopped in here long enough to sample my Canadian Club.

It seems that in the ten days I was in Egypt, the leaves all changed color and a number of them called it a year and fell off the trees. The drive up the road was nice with just enough clouds to give color to the sky and effect a brilliant sunset. The air is crisp and the fields are brown. Snow blankets the higher peaks and there is some sprinkled on the lower ones, and it is even money that we might get a little down here before the winter is out, but nobody knows. I guess we could look it up in an almanac or geography book, but once we did find out, that would be one less subject for speculation, and as such speculations are the favorite and only sport around here, we'll just wait and find out—and keep speculating.

Went to the movies last night and, cold as the evening was, we more than enjoyed *Up in Mabel's Room* from the old play of the same name. As a special added attraction, they had a newsreel showing of all things, the bombing of Cassino Abbey. What a crock! The heavies came over and hit the mountain but that was about all, even if the commentator did say "Right on the button!" A little thing called depth perception which we are supposed to possess showed that they hit to one side, though the smoke was in front of the Abbey. Then the mediums came over and really did hit it. Trigger Phelps, our bombing officer, dropped one load on it and they have pictures to prove it. If I couldn't hit a target that big, I'd turn in my wings. We have been getting a few short movies lately but never a cartoon, and for the life of me I can't figure out why.

For the first time in history, I guess, the 486th led the group in bombing accuracy this month. We've been in second place ever since we came out of the cellar in July and this month finally came out on top. This is probably due to the fact that I only bombed once this month. I knocked myself out of a DFC by getting a near miss instead of a hit, but as the bombs were in the target area it did not hurt the squadron average. I think that, weather permitting, I'll be flying as often as I used to from now on, as John and I have had enough rest camp for two tours. I'll still be here for a while though, and as long as I couldn't get home for Christmas, I might as well be getting time overseas.

Well I should get paid tomorrow and I'll enclose some dough with a note if I do. That is about all for now.

Your loving son, Tommy

MICHELLE - JACK: THREE-DAY PASSES, November 1944

In the middle of November, Flixton Airfield had a ten-day stand-down for runway repair. Jack's crew flew only two missions that month, both to Germany: one to a marshalling yard and another to an oil refinery.

Though their bombing times over targets were similar, a minute or less, Jack's flights to Germany were up to four times longer than Tom's flights to Italy and France. Based on accumulated flying hours, Jack had more frequent leaves than Tom. Jack got a three-day pass every five missions. London was a frequent destination for soldiers on leave. Perhaps Jack went there during this break in the action. He enclosed several postcards from London in his letters home, but he only wrote on one of them, saying he was disappointed at being unable to see the "King."

Winter 1944

TOM - A QUIET EVENING AT HOME
Corsica, France, December 3, 1944

Dear Mom,

On Sunday afternoons at home I used to listen to Andre Kostelanetz and the Family Hour after I got home from Church. Well, that is what I did today except that Mass is not until four p.m. The radio in the club sounded unusually clear today, and for the first time I heard Patrice Munsel sing. I had read about her in *Life* but until today had never heard her. She is wonderful to say the least. Not only does she handle opera, but she sings "I'll Be Seeing You" better than anybody I have ever heard. Most of those Met gals have trouble with that sort of stuff, but she goes to town on it. Jan Pearce on the Coke program also sounded good and better than the last time I heard him. Frank always used to plug his singing years ago and seems to have shown very good judgment.

I've been to Mass now and have settled down to a quiet evening at home. Mass was enlivened tonight with the news that orders came through sending Barney, Tip and Little home. Tip is from Ventura and Los Angeles, and I wouldn't be surprised if he dropped in on you sometime. I gave him your address, and as we have been good friends, I'm sure he'll make the effort. So to give you the dope on him, he is Capt. William L. Tipton. He was operations officer when I came in the squadron and I just found out the other day that he is only twenty-one years old and did not get out of high school 'til '40. That should make me an old man, but I had always figured him the older one due to his job and the way he handled it.

I think he has been overseas about a year and a half and flew over sixty missions. He is a swell pilot, and toward the end when he flew a few more missions, he always scheduled himself to fly off our wing, if he was not riding as command pilot in our ship. Anyway, if he gets around to seeing you he should give you a pretty good picture of what goes on here.

I don't believe I'm flying tomorrow so I should have a chance to send you a money order in this letter. I couldn't get one in the last, but I can say that I now have fifty-one missions. I don't know how many more I am expected to fly. Under the new setup the flight surgeon just tells you one day that you are through combat flying and that is the end. I think if I knew when I was flying my last mission, I'd be so anxious to get rid of those bombs that I might make a bad mistake.

Going to church tonight has done wonders for my morale. It did not need too much of a boost but a rise is always appreciated. I feel nice and comfortable inside, and even if Christmas is a long way from home, it certainly will not be a blue one. I've got more to be thankful for than I ever could have asked, and any complaining on my part would really be going too far.

Barney's going will make the place a little quieter. He is one of the knob twisters next door and spent half his time in here. He lives in Boston and has a boy whom he has not seen yet. He's been here about a year, was promoted from flight officer to first lieutenant and is beribboned with the Silver Star, DFC and cluster, Air Medal and about six clusters and a Purple Heart. He also left behind a bombing record which I don't think I can equal at my present rate so I am still in the small peanuts class.

Well, this is about all for tonight. I'm going to write a few more letters tonight as long as I'm staying in. Hope Gram is better now. Love to all.

Your loving son, Tommy

TOM - THE SKY WHERE I WORK
Corsica, France, December 3, 1944

Dear Mom,

Just a note on the enclosed money order. You won't have to carbon copy this for the boys. It is for $200 and, combined with the $100 allotment, I'd like you to do a couple things for me, and the rest as you will.

Jack wrote the other day saying something about Jerry being strapped for cash and probably wishing to invest in a ring. Jack said he'd put up $100 and I thought the least I could do was $150 to go with it. However, I did not know what Jerry would think of the idea, and advised Jack to write to you about it. So if you decide, the money is there.

That leaves $150. About the only specific requests I have are about $10 for Uncle John and five or so for the church Christmas collection. I'd like you to spend *at least half* of the rest on *yourself*. With the balance you might want to shop a bit for Christmas—perhaps sending something from the both of us to little Mary.

Money can't buy Christmas, or necessarily make it merry, but it will make mine, this one time, the happiest of all, if I know that you are getting a few necessary—and some silly—things for yourself. I already have the best family in the world, my health, a sense of enjoyment in such accepted things as the sky where I work, the beauty in the trees and fields, even though they are now bare and brown, and the beauty and strength of the mountains in my backyard here. They are all mine and can't be bought.

So don't worry about where the money goes. That's part of my Christmas.

Your loving son, Tommy

We found Tom and Jack's letters in a crumpled heap. While I put them in chronological order to read, the second to the last paragraph of this letter caught my eye. I was stunned by the depth of it. I now see that it foreshadowed the other letters, which collectively show the maturity and wisdom of my two young uncles. In addition to Tom's original copy of this letter, I found my grandmother's typed copy. Though he told her not to bother carbon-copying it for his brothers, she obviously saw the value of doing so.

TOM - THE CREATURE WAS STIRRING
Corsica, France, December 7, 1944

Dear Mom,

Another December 7 has rolled around. I can remember that first one as if it were yesterday. Around here it is just another day, and in the tent of Mravinec and Cahill that does not mean anything very exciting. It will be even less exciting if I don't start hitting the right keys here. About every so often I take a stab at writing without looking at the keys, and go for a while without messing it up, then Bang! I spell a word wrong and then I can't type whether I look at the keys or not.

Until a few days ago there were just two of us living in this tent. Now we have a third party in the form of a mouse who seems to possess the brains of Mickey and the strength of Superman. We keep our candy and foodstuff in a cabinet made of steel ammunition cans set inside a bomb fin case. At first, we were not troubled with our rodent rummager and all was well. The candy stayed fairly fresh, and as long as the supply held out we had no complaints. Then *he* came.

Well, all the candy I ever accumulated could easily be kept in a cigar box. Foo on you, Mouse! And my candy was safe. True, he could eat all the paper off the box and take some pretty good-sized chunks out of the wood. One time he even nibbled through the wood and got a taste of candy which was up against the edge of the box. *AhHA*! So I moved the candy to the center of the box, and he gnawed for "gnawding," if you'll allow such a pun.

While I'm laughing up my forest green sleeve, this rodent rascal is discovering that the box has a cover on it which lifts up at the edge. So help me, he lifted up the cover, got inside, ate through a fifty franc note (about a dollar) and into the Hershey bar which I had considered as safe as France behind the Maginot Line back in the late thirties. How he knows what time it is inside that box I don't know, but he is never there to be caught in the morning. When I came back from Cairo I had a whole carton of candy bars, and to protect them we put a wood thing over a couple shelves and once again felt ourselves secure—that ole mouse would have to go back on his old diet of our dirty socks and neckties.

But not this mouse! We are now at a point where we let him have the run of the place from eight p.m. to eight a.m., and then we take over for the rest of the day, but beyond that we refuse to compromise. We have boarded up our dwindling stock and either this mouse accepts these hours or we move out! Here we are out fighting for such goodies as Oh Henrys and Butterfingers, and this fifth columnist sneaks in and does us dirt. All I gotta say is that he'd better leave our Canadian Club alone, or he'll find himself living in an empty tent.

Your loving son, Tommy

P.S. Better send the books and have Bob send the airplanes. Little or no mail these days either.

P.P.S. Just found out that the fellow in the next tent lives about a half block from Lizbeth in Richmond. Knows the whole gang at 3111.

TOM - JOCKO GOES TO CHURCH
Corsica, France, December 9, 1944

Dear Mom,

This has been a red letter day in the squadron. A small red letter to be sure, but nevertheless it was no ordinary day. The reason is that I went down to the court and actually indulged in a game of basketball! I wasn't too fast on my feet; made no sensational plays; but there I was cavorting around, panting and perspiring. We officers were playing the GIs (beat them too!) and I got called some of the choicest names since I've been commissioned. So, once and for all, with this one exhibition, I have proved that I am not a walking dead man. I must be careful for the next three or four months not to overdo it though, as I ration myself on this commodity called Exercise.

Yesterday, being the feast of the Immaculate Conception, Willy and I traipsed over the hill to the chapel. With us came Jocko. We have not been too satisfied with all of Jocko's habits (fully realizing that none of us are perfect), and in his worst moments, he is sadly lacking in character. So a little church would do him good.

I had just returned from a practice mission so we were a little late arriving, but not too. We knelt toward the rear as that was the only place, and while we were kneeling things went well. I could keep a light grip on Jocko's harness but when I stood up, I had to let him stand for himself and trust that he would not embarrass us.

There is something of a dog in all of us, I guess, and like any of us, Jocko was distracted now and then from the service by a black female of his species. I've thrown a few winks across the aisle myself and realized what he was up against, so it was all right with me. But looking was not enough for Jocko. He had to *stare*.

For a tense moment we feared the worst, but Jocko somehow was reminded of where he was and left his eyeful to return to us. In a few minutes, he was sleeping. Well, I guess we've all slept a bit in church at one time or another. I'll bet even the bragging Pharisee dozed more than once. All went well until the bell rang. Old Jocko's ears stood straight up, and we thought he'd bark but he didn't. After that he behaved very well and, as Mass came to an end, like most of our brethren, he made every effort to be the first one out. Made it, too.

That is the most outrageous, out and out padding of a letter I have ever done. I have some consolation in the fact that all the events really happened, though I may have embellished them slightly. But there is no other news. Received yours of the 27th and 29th and am glad to hear that the books and packages are coming. Mail is fairly fast but there does not seem to be much of it.

One of my fellow bombardiers in the squadron I find is from dear old Richmond V-Ay, and is not only a neighbor but a friend of our cousins on Broad Street. His name is Al Bahen, and he says he might even remember when Pat was down there, as he knew Chigger, Jack Epps and all. I hear quite regularly from Lizbeth and she writes swell letters.

The missions still stand at fifty-one though things should speed up shortly. Would like to at least be finished by Christmas. It would be a swell present for both of us. Due to the delay in mail, I won't be able to inform you in time if I am, but take the bright outlook on it anyway. Hope Gram is feeling better. I didn't even know she was sick until you said she was better. That is about it, now.

Your loving son, Tommy

MICHELLE - JOCKO: THE PREQUEL AND THE SEQUEL

Tom's letter about Jocko accompanying him and Willy to church was his last mention of the canine flier. Unexpectedly, I was happy to learn more.

The Prequel: World War II veteran Sterling Ditchey, mentioned earlier in "Tom's Trip Over," emailed me a copy of the April 9, 1944, war diary for Squadron 486. Because Tom didn't arrive on Corsica until May, I had not read the April diaries. This diary excerpt reads: "Old Jocko, our squadron dog, is having a devil of a time with another pet of ours, little Penelope. He tries and tries, but the only result is a squeal and Penelope is off with Jocko right behind. For Jocko's sake we hope that he fulfills his mission someday, the little African orphan."

The little African orphan? I had assumed the squadron found Jocko on Corsica, but the April diary reference tells me that Jocko was found in Africa. In early April 1944, Squadron 486 was in Southern Italy, and later that month, relocated to Corsica. The crew took Jocko from Africa to Italy, then to Corsica, where he flew several missions, including those Tom wrote about.

The Sequel: Tom's stories about Jocko were such fun, I hoped to share them. I contacted Victor Hancock, a veteran Corsican pilot and editor of the 57th Bomb Wing Association newsletter, who was happy to print Tom's Jocko tales in the publication.

While emailing with Victor, he wrote: "In the 445th Squadron we had a little black terrier of some sort by the name of Butch. He was much loved, and he frequently flew missions. Some of the guys had rigged up a parachute for Butch, just in case. I had the distinct honor of having Butch ride on my lap during a bombing run. I was the co-pilot and I remember my instructions well: 'If we have to bail out, you make sure Butch is harnessed up, or don't you come back!'"

Victor provided me yet another answer I didn't know to look for. I had wondered: Why did Jocko's master bring him a harness when he returned from leave? There was no mention of a leash and Jocko was free-roaming. Now I realize it was a means to attach him to one of the crewmembers if they had to bail out.

When my story about Tom and Jocko appeared in the *Men of the 57th* newsletter, it prompted an email to me from 486th veteran tail-gunner and mission photographer Nick Loveless who knew Tom, though not well. Nick told me stories of two other Corsican dogs, "Monk" and "Moose." Nick also sent a picture of Jocko, in a jeep with an officer, whose identification I've not been able to determine, next to a Corsican resident. Nick took the photo in Cervione where many of the soldiers found families to do their laundry.

Ultimately, the sudden altitude changes on missions—dive-bombing—created discomfort in Jocko's ears, and he was grounded. I began to wonder what happened to him when the airfield closed at the end of the war. From Julie Martin, Membership Chairman of the 57th Bomb Wing Association, I learned that one of the boys (we don't know the name) adopted Jocko and brought him to the United States. Jocko flew here First Class with his crew on a B-25 bomber.

TOM - DEAR JERRY
Corsica, France, December 11, 1944

Dear Jerry,

Hope the enclosed reaches you in time to allow you to toss off a couple more glasses of good old Christmas cheer. Sorry it isn't more, but I sent most of what I had to Mom this month, and I guess she might be able to help you a little if necessary.

Yours of November 23rd was the last to arrive, and I wondered about what you said concerning being routed through your place as I hit the States, assuming if and when. From what I have gathered, I would be sent to the Presidio at Monterey, and from there to LA and home. I also thought that Santa Monica was a rest camp but not a redistribution center.

If I go home via the Medical Disposition Board—which I won't unless something makes me so nervous I can't fly any more combat—I would be entitled to rest leave at home plus three or four weeks at Santa Monica. I have also heard that I would go to Santa Monica for a few days even if I go home on rotation, so I'm thoroughly confused on the whole deal. What does your outfit do with me if I report there?

Actually, the Air Force does not give a hoot about bombardiers. We are the bastards of the outfit. For instance, each squadron calls for six pilots to be captains—the flight leaders—but calls for only one captain bombardier. He is the squadron bombing officer and is generally given the job when he has about finished his missions. Trigger has been SBO in this outfit ever since I came into it, though he has been relieved now to go home.

The new man is Freddie Sedach who just got back from a thirty-day leave in the States. He'll get his tracks any day now. So Woolcott, Barney, Davis and even myself have all led enough missions, bombed well enough, but can get no promotion as there is no TO for it. There is a group bombing officer and he is a major. He does not have to fly at all and got the job after being an SBO. Back in the States there is not much for bombardiers to do, just instruct cadets, or train to go back for a second tour.

Pilots can be instructors in all the cadet stages, OTU, or perhaps go into air transport. In B-29 outfits I hear that they have three captain bombardiers in each squadron. I also heard that the same would be applied to all bomber outfits, which would put me right in line for captaincy, but it is one of those nice, juicy rumors which spread like wildfire more on hope than any fact. Also a bombardier can never be a squadron CO or operations officer. There just are not any openings, that's all. So getting any kind of good job in the States will be a neat trick. B-29s sound pretty good.

I got pretty far off the track but it might be interesting to you. I'll close and try to get off a few more letters tonight.

Merry Christmas, Jerry. I hope you'll be able to get home for your own sake and to keep Mom's spirits up. Things are still OK here and with fifty-one trips behind me it looks pretty good ahead. Hope the new year is good to you. Perhaps your warrant officer promotion will go through. I sure hope so, as I know you deserve all that and more.

Your loving brother, Tommy

TOM - SANTA'S INVASION
Corsica, France, December 11, 1944

Dear Bob, Jackie and Little Patrick!

Unless I miss my guess Pat is having himself one helluva time with his Christmas tree right now. He is old enough now so that he probably is beginning to capish such things and is making plenty of trouble for Jacqueline May. (How about that JM?) Anyway, take the enclosed, and buy Little Pat a quart of good black market whiskey and write and tell me what happens. Wanna bring the kid up to be a man, don't you? Beer is a good chaser for youngsters. Coke is bad for the stomach.

Really though, here it is practically the night before Christmas, and you should have heard that mouse of ours stirring last night! It was bad enough when he chewed on my chocolate bars. I could scrape down that part and the rest was still good to eat. But no! He has to eat the candy, hang around until it is digested, and then he has the nerve to defecate and urinate on what is left!

Insult to injury! I would not be a bit surprised to find out that he is Herr Goebbels' vaunted "V-3".

Now, where were we? Oh, yes…As I was saying here it is practically H-Hour for Santa's invasion and I have not yet done even a little to fix up my Little Patrick. So do as you will with the enclosed—perhaps you might even have enough (what am I saying?) to have a snack some place. I'm sorry it isn't more but I sent Mom quite a sum and so am temporarily a bit short.

As a former employee of Douglas, you, Robert, may be interested to know that the other day I had a ride in an A-20. One of my old buddies in pilot training who *didn't* wash out buzzed the hell out of our area the other day. I knew it could be none other than Francis Floyd of San Francisco. He'd been over once before and so he knew where I was. He landed, had lunch here, then I goofed off a parade they were having for the general and we went bye-bye.

Warming up the engines he swung the tail parade-ward and managed in one fell swoop to "dust off" the whole 340th Bomb Group. I rode in the nose and could have reached down and grabbed off enough treetops to keep many a home fire burning.

We blew up the flaps on a few tents in the area, just missed a chimney on the mess hall, and then started buzzing through the mountain passes. If it wasn't wide enough between mountains to accommodate us, he'd dip one wing down or pull up over. All in all, it was an unforgettable ride.

After a few minutes of such horseplay I called him up on interphone and said, "Floyd, old boy, I am fully convinced that you can fly this airplane. I had my fill of buzzing back at Columbia where we were flying the cannon, and I've got fifty missions and am not quite as crazy as I used to be." "Roger," he says, "I know just how you feel. We'll make one more pass at those sheep down there and then we'll land." And we did. I was surprised that it did not make much noise. Our old twenty-fives make quite a racket.

Well, I've got a jillion letters to write in lieu of Christmas cards and so I'd better call this one finished. Merry Christmas, kids, and of course the happiest new year.

Hello to Frank and Nettie.

Your loving brother, Tommy

P.S. You mentioned model airplanes once and I hope you sent them. If not, will you? Thanks. My yo-yo is about worn out.

TOM - DISTINGUISHED FLYING CROSS
Corsica, France, December 12, 1944

Dear Mom,

About the only news around here is that our mouse is still doing his dirty work. However, by sheer diplomacy we enticed a cat to spend the night with us, and if that fails to stop him I'll give up.

My old buddy, Cancilla, was up this afternoon for a visit and we had quite a talk. He is in the 310th and, like myself, has not flown many missions. We went down to the 488th and found Bill Fischer, and went over to the 489th to see Alexander, but found out that that fortunate young man is on his way home. Alex and Cancilla were my roommates at Albuquerque for a while.

There was no mail for me tonight so I am not up on affairs Cahill. We had steak for supper which helped a great deal. The mess hall now looks pretty fancy. There are still a few minor inconveniences though. Don't be surprised if some time in the future, when I am at home, I sit down, take the cap off the salt shaker and pinch out my wants, dip the handle of my fork in the sugar bowl and then stir my coffee with it, wiping it dry on a piece of bread. Once in a while, we do have a spoon at a table and it is used by everybody.

In order to relieve the situation a little, our helper boys hover over us throughout the meal, ready to collect any weapon or utensil that you were foolish enough to lay down in plain sight. You can see that in no time at all the boys were called "Snatch" and answered to it much more quickly than "Garcon." For a while we had a couple Corsican kids and they were a kick. One boy would sit at the table, chin in hands and just watch you eat. As the plate was emptied, he'd take your fork and knife before you could lay them down. We have a couple new kids now, and I don't know where the other ones went.

This will probably be the last letter you will get before Christmas if it gets there in time for that. However, I'll be writing as often as usual. I have one little surprise in store for you. Staub told me the other night that we are going to fly a couple ships over to Rome the day before Christmas for the Catholics who would like to attend Midnight Mass at St. Peter's. The only thing that would prevent it is weather, but I think that will be OK. So, at least for a few minutes, you'll have a pretty definite idea of where I am and what I am doing.

So, it will be a very happy Christmas, even though I am so far away from home. There are still millions of fellows worse off than I am. I'll be thinking of you all and praying that we will all be together soon.

Your loving son, Tommy

P.S. Staub just said a DFC went through for me though the orders have not yet come back to the squadron.

TOM - HOT TARGETS AND MILK RUNS
Corsica, France, December 16, 1944

Dear Mom,

Yours of November 16th and 20th, Pat's of the 20th and the address book all arrived this evening. Contents noted, and I must say that the address book was elegant, and also send my thanks for same. We memorized the words to "Take Back Your Gold" already and believe me, the squadron will hear about it.

About the newspaper clippings: The one on the 340th had been posted on the bulletin board as printed in the *New York Herald Tribune* and it is nice to know that the word gets around.

The one on bombardiers was very good and remarkably true except perhaps for the glamour part. However, he expressed our ideas very well. Going back to a target is the worst of all because the boys know just what to expect. The lead bombardiers seldom go back the second time as the lead crews are rotated each mission, so actually the guy who misses does not get the chance to even things up but does "sweat out" the fellows who must go back to finish the job he started. That is the worst part of the whole deal. I've only missed on one "hot" target but am sorry to say it was the hottest one of all. Why it is I don't know, but I've done my worst bombing on milk runs. I don't get cocky, but having no flak to worry about, I get to thinking about how I will bomb and so do not do things mechanically or instinctively.

The guy also mentioned an outfit which hit 62 consecutive missions— that was the 340th, thank you, and I'm glad to say that I was not in a slump at the time. I think I have just come out of one though and expect to be doing some good work again. Incidentally my pilot was promoted to captain a couple days ago. He's also assistant operations officer but he got the captaincy primarily for being a flight leader. Don't expect one for me though. They provide for six pilot captaincies per squadron but only one for a bombardier and that is the squadron bombing officer. C'est la guerre!

It seems that every time I write to you we are rearranging our quarters. We have just completed the biggest and I think final work on the place, and we now have much more room and comfort. If I can I'll try to enclose a couple sketches of the place. Willy expects to go home shortly after Christmas and I guess Jerry Rahatz will move in.

I just heard last night that my radio is being fixed. Floyd gave me a small Stewart-Warner which needed repairs which he could not have made on it. Communications said they had no parts for it so I just left it there, but now they tell me it will soon be ready. There are a number of good programs on the air and so help me, in the evenings I find the best music coming from the Third Reich. Can't understand the words (except when it is English propaganda) but generally can recognize the music.

As I can't tell when I'll be finished or on my way home, you could send along some of those packages. For the Postmaster I am writing that you please send two or three of the packages which you had intended to send for Christmas but which I told you to keep. They should reach here in about six weeks or possibly sooner.

That is about it for now. I sent Gram a Christmas card which should reach her in time. I'll try to draw those pictures now and then hit the sack. I'll probably have to get up in the morning for a few practice bombs. That reporter was right when he wrote about how much we trained over here.

Your loving son, Tommy

TOM - THE GANG'S ALL HERE
Corsica, France, December 19, 1944

Dear Mom,

For some of the boys in the squadron it is still "the morning after," even at the present hour of 21:00. It seems that Willy and I played host to the gang last night for a farewell party in honor of McMillan who went home this morning. It started quite simply with a meeting of Mac, Willy, Woolcott and myself to eat the fruitcake which Pat Salley sent me. As we all knew Pat back at Columbia, it was fitting that we all ate the cake.

Well, seeing as Mac was going to leave us, a drink was in order, and before you could say "down the hatch," we had a good old-fashioned party a la Cahill with about twenty guys in the tent, about half of them uninvited but welcome.

Before it was over, the major and about everybody else had taken part in some measure. A couple enterprising young boys went over to the Red Cross doughnut factory and brought back a whole carton of sinkers and so we had food to spare. The tent in its last improvement has had a good housewarming, and after a morning cleaning it up, it is now ready to settle down to normal existence.

Willy went to Naples today for some shopping and he is still over there. He was in rather tough shape but not too bad. Your son is feeling fine and has suffered absolutely no after effects—which is quite marvelous I think. We are also without a drop of stuff in the place, which does not make me sad at all. We'd been saving the other stuff for months, and we were glad it went for a good cause. We had Canadian Club, White Horse, Three Feathers and some Johnny Walker Scotch. Where it all came from I don't know, but Willy and I provided about half of it. So Mac after flying his tour has gone home. He is a grand little guy, and hardly looks big enough to reach the rudder pedals, but he's a swell pilot.

The general was supposed to hand out some medals yesterday but the weather kinda snarled things up. I was up for my fifth cluster to my Air Medal. John is up for a DFC. Col. Ruebel told him that when he got one he'd let him buzz the area without getting himself grounded as he did the last time. We're waiting for the colonel to get back from Cairo and then we'll take him up on the offer.

Col. Ruebel is, I think, from Pasadena. He flew with us the other day when we led the group and he is really swell. He's a West Point man but not a bit stiff. He thinks a lot of John and says that our squadron is the best in the group. I think John can go home a major if he wants to. I was really lucky to get him for my pilot. Incidentally I have fifty-two now and got out of that "near miss" rut with a hit on the last mission. Perhaps now I can start a streak again. I hope so. You have enough worries without wondering if you're going to hit the darn bridge.

Before I forget it, I have a request to make. Until now I have been getting my onionskin paper from the orderly room or operations, but they are not too well supplied now so could you send me some? Just the paper will do as I use the stamped envelopes most of the time. If I use the lightweight envelopes I have to buy stamps, and they get sticky and I have a devil of a time before I'm finished. So if you could send along two or three packs of typing paper I'd sure appreciate it.

Well, Mom, there is no more news at present. Received your December 5th letter yesterday which is better than the time lately. I also got an announcement from Jim and Eli about their baby and it was postmarked October 9th so you see anything can happen. I wrote them the 22nd of October, but I don't know as they have received it or not.

That's it now. Good night!

Your loving son, Tommy

P.S. You should have heard Davis and I sing "Take Back Your Gold" last night.

TOM - THE DEPOT STOVE
Corsica, France, December 22, 1944

Dear Mom,

Looking through the little brown book in which I record my letter-writing, I find that I last wrote to you on the 19th. There has been no mail since then so I can answer no questions.

Subject matter being scarce, I'll try to give you some idea of how our stove operates. That does not sound very interesting but the fact that it is a gasoline stove puts a new light on the subject. Gasoline we all know is very dangerous stuff unless handled just so. Six months ago the only interest I had in gasoline was in knowing how much we had left in the tank and if it was enough to get us home. Now it is something which I must handle daily—several times a day even.

About the only use I have ever found in all my bombardier training and in combat for the rules and formulae of physics which we were forced to study back in preflight has been incorporated in our stove. Namely the law of gravity and the fact that if you heat a liquid it will turn to a gas. I am not bragging about being bright, but I can safely say that I knew that before I went to preflight. Anybody knows it. So what good did the physics do? But that is getting off the subject.

First, I want the gasoline to flow from the tank outside down to the stove. So by raising the lowest level of the gas above the burner, a constant flow is assured. You capish? Good. By sealing the end of my burner tube and punching a few holes in it, the gas first squirts out into a pan placed underneath. When I have a puddle of it, just shut the flow off, toss in a match, and after the first big flame, turn the gas on again, so that the gas in the tube starts to burn before the gas in the pan is all gone. In a second, the tube gets hot enough so that the gas vaporizes in the tube and behold! We have a burner quite similar to the one on your stove—except that your gas is not a liquid in the first place.

The only worry seems to be that a vapor lock will form in the lines and the flame will almost go out for a second, then all of a sudden the stuff is flowing again, and about the same time you hear the blast, you are ready for the hospital. Willy, being very ingenious, fixed ours some way so that this cannot occur. We have absolutely no trouble whatever. In fact ours burns so evenly that there is hardly any smoke or soot. Some of these stoves really blacken the area.

The fuel itself is 100-octane. When not flying airplanes around it is burning in stoves, cleaning woolen clothes (just dunk them in a can and rub out the spots) or performing a dozen other tasks. We are quite economical. A five-gallon can lasts from fifteen to twenty hours of steady burning. As it is used mostly in the evening and on rainy days, it is not too much trouble keeping a supply. Just go down to the field, flag a gas truck and fill 'em up. Some of the guys burn 80-octane which is used for motor vehicles, but we think it is sootier and besides you can't clean clothes with it.

To burn wood, you have to have a great deal of time to pick up a load, store it some place where it will keep dry, and carry ashes, so we use gas. Simply twist the valve and you can have just a small, cheery glow or a blaze that will roast you in no time at all.

Tonight for a while, we (Willy and I) were designing a poster for a dinner-dance which the enlisted men are having. Posters are going to be displayed in Bastia and a couple other towns inviting girls to show up at such and such a time on a certain date at the place where the poster is located, and a nice big GI truck will take them to and from the scene of festivities. The 489th had one a few days ago and it was quite a success. Had about thirty-five girls there I understand which is about thirty more than I have ever seen at one of our dances at the officers' club. Anyway, we made a layout in English, they're going to send it back in French, and we will then make the poster.

They have to get the approval of the mayor or somebody in authority so that the gals will know what goes on. The parents here are either very strict or else don't give a damn what the daughters do. They must have it all figured out though, or they would not be making such plans. They are going to use our officers' club for the dinner, and the dance will be at the EM's Red Cross.

Speaking of the club, it now looks very fancy. A ceiling—or the illusion of one as you will—has been furnished through the medium of burlap stretched flat under the crosspieces. Bamboo—corn stocks technically—are nailed in just the right places to hold the burlap taut and break the dullness. The bar has a solid wall behind it of bamboo and shelves have been put in the windows.

I supplied a couple "dead Indians," which are now embalmed with tea and look good anyway...recalling memories of when they were alive and kicking. The gals which Willy painted have endured the winter so far. Failing to find anybody capable of painting goose pimples on the gals— just to show we realize how they are taking the cold—we made grass skirts and bras out of tinsel and put them on. The newcomers persist in exploring under the tinsel to make sure all is in order and I guess they (the gals) must feel the draft. Still better than nothing, we figure. C'est la guerre! I offered the name "Corsicabana" for the place but I think it will forever be just "the club."

Say "Hello" to Gram and I hope she's feeling better. As for the nurse, what I send home should cover it and more. I personally would rather have the nurse there all the time than to have you doing so much extra work. I'd like to have you write that you've just finished another landscape with your pastels, or that you even got yourself some oils, rather than report on another day of bedpan carrying. This war will last long enough so that I can still save plenty of money—not that I wouldn't like to have it end tonight. I'd rather we didn't go any further in the hole on your health. Bank accounts can always be replaced. I don't care what it costs but I wish you'd take it easy.

Well, I can hear Christmas carols from the club radio. Funny but I haven't heard many this year. I hope someday I'll have studied and practiced enough so that I can sing a Christmas carol that will sound halfway decent. I wish we were stationed near Rome or Florence, then I could probably take some lessons. If wishes were horses beggars would ride.

That's all for tonight, Mom. You might dish up a batch of brownies or Toll House one of these days. Rations aren't so hot now as they used to be and they'd hit the spot. Love to all.

Your loving son, Tommy

TOM - MISSING IN ACTION
Corsica, France, December 23, 1944

Dear Mom,

Pat's letter about Jack just arrived. I can't find words to express what I feel at this moment. I'm sure our mutual faith in Quinn will be justified.

Confidence in your pilot is of the utmost importance and that confidence is gained only by proving that he was capable of handling his ships. Pilots can fool themselves about their ability but they can't fool their crewmen. So that is one hope to hang onto.

I've tried to find out all I could about operations of November 21st. From what I could discover there was nothing unusual and so you can try to figure on the high percentage of crewmen saved, though the ship may be lost.

Jack, being the radioman, would be constantly in touch with the whole crew and would notice any interruption in communications. He would also be located close to the pilot—and the escape hatch—so there would be no delay in finding out what went wrong, and he would be in a convenient position to bail out when the time came.

These things are all in his favor and Germans do treat Air Force prisoners well. Nothing fancy, you know, but still adequate. He will probably be listed as "Missing" until there is a report that he's a POW. Any other information is usually forthcoming fairly soon. He might even evade capture in which case there will be no word until he is captured or returns through our lines.

I wish I could offer you more comfort but for now I can only warn you that there may be long months of waiting with no word. During that time we can all pray that the news will be good. I wish I were more worthy to ask God for such a favor, but I will do the best I can.

While Grandma has the nurse, I do wish you would go to San Francisco for a few days. Monette and Tom would love to have you, and I'll send the money the first of the month.

I hope perhaps by the time you receive this you will have heard some word. If you don't get a fairly regular report write to the Adjutant General's Office, Washington, DC. They can tell you more than his squadron or chaplain are allowed to write.

Must go to bed now. Tomorrow is Sunday and Mass and Communion will have a special purpose. Goodnight, Mom.

Your loving son, Tommy

TOM - ROOMMATES
Corsica, France, December 29, 1944

Dear Mom,

It has been about six days since I last wrote to you, and I am sorry if it caused any undue worry, but I did not feel much like it, after writing the letter about Jack. Added to that, I have also been quite "busy" and I now have fifty-five missions, and if the weather holds I should add quickly to them. I keep having my good and bad days with my Norden, but am still managing to keep up with the average but no more than that.

Due to the weather, I was unable to get to Rome for Midnight Mass. It was a great disappointment of course, but under the circumstances of Christmas this year, it did not matter so much. We had Midnight Mass here in the group and it was every bit as nice as any in previous years. The chaplain said that this year being overseas we perhaps came as close to the true meaning of Christmas as we ever will in our lives. There was a quality about it, which is hard to feel under the pressure in the States of last minute shopping, nightclubs and Christmas cards with Christmas spelled with an "X".

On my part it was also a sober Christmas. There was plenty of liquor to be had but I didn't have the thirst. Today some son of a - - - - - said that John and I picked which missions we flew on, missing the rough ones. John works in operations you know, but the schedule is always made up before the target is known. We take our share as they come, and because of the way we plan our bomb run we can get in and out of some hot spots without a scratch, while some other joker is blundering through and paying for his ignorance. The major is really going to do things to the loudmouth if he ever catches him.

There are not many of the old gang left around here. Most of them have gone back to the States—Willy goes in a couple of days by the way—and the new boys just believe what they see in the movies about the Air Corps. They come into the squadron fresh from the States and think they are pretty sharp. They'll find out before very long, I'm thinking.

Anyway, Christmas was sober, and the next day the weather lifted and we were flying again.

As I mentioned above Willy is going home in a couple days. He has waited for his orders for about six weeks or more and was getting restless. He's one of the best buddies I've had in the Army and I'll miss having him around. I think Jerry Rahatz will move in the tent after Willy. Rahatz is pronounced Rawtz by him and by everybody else Rats, Ray-hats or whatever else they can make out of it, but it all boils down to "Mouse." We used to chant "Ignutz Ruhutz is Nutz." Despite that, he is a very hot bombardier. He knows it too, and so I have quite a time keeping his ears down. Down in Alex we were going to bed one night and Chief Glade was talking about his date. Jerry made some crack and Chief said, "Oh, you're just jealous, Rahatz, 'cause you didn't have a date." And the Mouse came back with, "Jealous, hell! The horse that pulled our jerry-buggy home let me kiss her goodnight!" I'll have to change the sign outside from Mravinec and Cahill to perhaps Tom and Jerry even if the Mouse is a teetotaler.

That's about all the news now, Mom. Oh, yes; I've been flying with Adams lately and we make a great pair. He flies with me when we lead the group which is fairly often now.

How's Gram? I'll try to write her again soon. What do you think about going to San Francisco? Even if just for three or four days, I think it would do you good. Out of the next money I send, you can get a bond for Mark's birthday. That's all now.

Your loving son, Tommy

TOM - NEW YEAR'S EVE
Corsica, France, January 1, 1945

Dear Mom,

Yours of December 15th and 18th just arrived and I hope it is some indication as to the 1945 mail calls, as I had cards also from Bill Bohlman's mother, Grace Stark and Peggy Broderson. Was glad to hear that things on the Cahill front are about the same as usual. This letter probably will not be very long, as I am going to dinner in a few minutes, and to church from there.

Last night, New Year's Eve, a bunch of us knob twisters (Davis, Rahatz, Mravinec and Yours Truly) went up to the hospital to see the movie, which incidentally was nothing to write home about—and so I won't. While there we also visited Charlie Vail. Charlie is a navigator who has flown with me several times and is in bed with a broken leg.

Like almost all the casualties on this island, the accident was not incurred in combat. Charlie was pretty much in his cups one night and had good cause, as he was told he did not have to fly any more missions. Well, he got rather surly in the mess hall where a poker game was in progress, and in the ensuing fracas Charlie got a broken leg.

Like Grandma, Charlie has an aversion toward that monstrosity called a bedpan. Being subject to regular and frequent laxatives up there, whether he needs them or not, Charlie's hate is further aggravated. Until the other day, the Red Cross girl just breezed through his ward which contained mostly jeep victims and catered to the wounded men down the way. Well, you can easily guess what happened. The day she does take an interest in Charlie he is riding high. Now Red Cross girls didn't go to school just to eat their lunches and Charlie's predicament was immediately apparent.

She thought it very funny and even Charlie could see the humor in the situation for a while, but after a few minutes, the fun wore off for Charlie. She finally left him but Charlie says that she no longer just passes him by everyday as before, but stops to have a word no matter how pressed for time she might be.

Christmas Eve our bedridden friend talked three different nurses into bringing him a little liquid cheer. All three complied and kept the secret from each other, but Charlie had enough to almost fall out of bed and then the girls caught on.

After the show we stopped over to the group club for a while and said "Hello" to all the guys from the other squadrons. I only had enough to launch one of my old classmates, Dearborn, homeward bound. Davis had to fly this morning and so it was a pretty quiet evening for all of us.

I guess I told you last time that I now have fifty-five missions. I don't know how many I'll be required to go but it will be around sixty. I'm still flying lead and John and I are pretty experienced, so we know what is going on. With Adams flying as navigator with us, we work well together.

I'm not going to mail this until tomorrow probably, at which time I'll enclose a money order. You can do just about as you like with it except buy Mark a fifty-dollar bond for his birthday. Each month I would like you to take Pat out to dinner and a show at least one night. With a nurse there now there is absolutely no excuse. Absolutely. You could also include Betty, Mrs. Miner or anyone else you care to. In my present location I'm hardly able to keep up my social duties and you could very well.

If Bob is going into the service as your letter mentioned, it would be good to take the 81st Street Cahills out before he goes. That's all now. Tonight I'll try to write the Slavens.

Your loving son, Tommy
P.S. Money order will be in the next letter.

TOM - JUST ANOTHER DAY AT THE OFFICE
Corsica, January 2, 1945

Dear Mom,

The enclosed is what I told you I'd send in my last letter. You can do just about what you will with it except for the couple ideas I mentioned before.

Today was windy again and we spent most of the time working on the tent. It seems there is always something needing to be attended to and always fairly important. We rearranged things again. I know I said the last time would be the last, but I decided to have Davis move in with Jerry and I when Willy goes, and the changes were necessary to accommodate three bunks.

We still have as much room as before. Davis was over in his old tent with some new guys who came in and he was not too contented. So it was decided a threesome would be ideal and there you are. He has loads of packages and is never at a loss for food. He is a comedian to boot and that in itself is enough.

One night Davis went down to operations with Willy to check the schedule for the next day. The office was empty but the schedule was up. There was his name in black and white. Down on his knees he went before Willy, pleading, "Take me off that schedule, please! I know tomorrow is My Day! They're going to get me, I know. If I don't fly tomorrow they'll have missed their chance and then I'll be safe for the duration. Please! Please!" By this time tears were streaming down his face, sweat beaded his brow and Willy entered into the spirit of things too. "No," he said, "who do you think you are asking favors of me? I can't help it if we both love the same girl! I made out that schedule and you're staying on it!" More pleading by Davis.

In walked the major and Capt. Shealy. Well, old Davis tried to explain it was all a gag (Willy offering no help) and the more he tried to explain, the worse it seemed to appear. To this day, the major raises an eyebrow every time he sees Davis. No matter what Davis does, he is always misunderstood. Anyway, there is never a dull moment around here, and you should hear what we do to "Take Back Your Gold."

Went to the movies this afternoon at the club and saw *San Diego I Love You*. Pretty good, too. In one scene, the hero and heroine, with four of her kid brothers, were visiting the zoo. The kids ran from say six to twelve years old. Tiring of watching the bears, one of the older kids said, "I want to see a stork." With a very disgusted manner, the youngest kid pipes up with, "Boy! Are you dumb!"

That is about all, Mom. Sorry there is no more news but I think I covered everything last night.

Your loving son, Tommy

P.S. Tell Bob if he can, when he goes into the service, bring along a small radio. Almost any place he goes he will be able to use it.

TOM - FRIENDSHIPS
Corsica, France, January 9, 1945

Dear Mom,

A couple days ago I started a letter to you, but never did get it finished. In it I wrote that I perhaps would not be writing as much as before, though I would try to write as often. This is due mostly to the fact that our recently acquired radio is usually going in the evening, and I can't seem to get back to writing by hand.

The weather finally cleared and Willy has gone on his way back to Pittsburg. With him went Trigger Phelps who was our squadron bombing officer. Both were very good friends and I shall miss them. It seems that in the Army your best friends are the ones who get transferred or somehow separated from you. Willy left me a number of his cartoons, which I intend to keep and bring home with me.

George Henthorn also went with them. He is an LA boy and will perhaps call you. He and Adams had been living together in his shack, and when he left we bought their radio, as Adams thought it was too much money for him to have tied up in it himself. My Boy John is in Cannes for four or five days, and so I have very little to do around here with no practice missions or anything. I might have gone with him but, alas, Cannes is for "Staff Officers Only."

Yesterday was quite a bona day for mail. I received a package from Dick Frodl's mother and sister and from Theda a book (*St. Paul The Apostle* by Sholem Asch) and a wooly scarf. In the letter department was yours of December 14th and one from Mrs. Miner. As a special bonus, Wells Morris, who has gone home, got a package of nuts and candy, which we appropriated according to his wishes. We also got a few very old copies of the *Times*.

I have been reading quite a bit lately. J.P. Marquand got a going over when I came across both *The Late George Apley* and *H.M. Pulham, Esq.* Then we somehow got hold of *The Razor's Edge*, by Somerset Maugham, and enjoyed it very much. I should now be able to start on *The Apostle*.

It sounds good to hear that Tom and Monette are at last moving back to LA. It will be a swell deal all around and I am looking forward to seeing them both. I seem to be so close to finishing my missions that I can imagine myself at home quite easily, even though it may be a while before I actually get there. One thing in my favor is that when I do finish, there will be little or no delay in putting through my rotation papers, as I am now one of the oldest combat men in the squadron.

Mom, I'm going to call this bit a letter. I can't seem to get going on it with the radio so I'll close now with the promise of more later. This will let you know that I am well anyway.

Your loving son, Tommy

TOM - THE LIBRARY
Corsica, France, January 10, 1945

Dear Pat,

I've long since given up trying to answer each of your letters. It simply can't be done and I hope you will understand that you are very much in my thoughts whenever I write home.

There has been a great reading boom going on here for the last few days, as the weather has been so-so, and my companions are sack artists supreme.

I read *H. M. Pulham, Esq.* and passed it on to Davis. If you have read it you will perhaps recall that Pulham is not too sharp on the take and manages to turn down his true love, marry an old friend of the family and in general miss out on a lot of good things in life.

Comrade Davis takes the book right to heart, and the silence is often broken with his anguished cries directed at the fictional Pulham. "Pulham, you jerk! You dope! Wake up! Don't marry that gal. She's hooking you!" And later on when his wife rather obviously (to the reader) steps out on him, he tries to make excuses for her and never suspects the truth. "Ohhhh, my God! Pulham! I give up, Pulham. I give up. If you can't help yourself, I sure as hell can't." And long after lights are out, we go over Pulham and his follies.

Rahatz is currently reading *The Razor's Edge* by Somerset Maugham. Really a marvelous book and Jerry definitely does not beat about the bush about anything. His remarks are mostly about the women in the story, or in certain chapters the lack of them. He is a riot, but I'm afraid I can't go into details here.

Jerry is the married man of the trio, looks the youngest, is the smallest—and the hottest bombardier in the squadron.

We form quite a trio. I furnished the tent with typewriter and a few books. They provided a bumper crop of Christmas packages. We have so much food on hand now that I don't know when we'll eat it all.

Today I flew in a new capacity. This morning and afternoon I was up with a new bombing crew checking on their procedure and offering a few suggestions of my own. The bombardier used to be an instructor in the

States and knows more about the bombsight than I do, but I have the edge in experience in combat bombing. The improvement this afternoon over the morning's work was marked. I'm glad I was able to help. It was beautiful up there today but cold—13 below, thank you.

Don't know what it is but lately I can't seem to write a thing. So this will have to be all. Best to Mr. T. and take it easy.

Your loving brother, Tommy

JERRY - HOPING AND PRAYING
Ft. Lewis, Washington, January 14, 1945

Dear Mom,

Got your letter today and of course I was sorry to hear about Bob. It could be worse though, and he might be better off to have his hernia repaired right away if he can. I know just how he feels though because as you remember I had to hit them three times. Tell him if possible to keep out of the Army Limited Service. He would soon get fed up with the whole thing.

This afternoon I finally unpacked my bags and got my stuff thrown about in some semblance of order. I threw out a lot of stuff, but I know if I ship out, I'll have to throw still more.

Last nite there were two big parties at the sergeants club. One was Dugan's going away party (furlough) and the other was the married members of the survey team with their wives. I stayed with Dugan's outfit for about an hour and a half, and most of the time was spent in refusing drinks of Four Roses.

They finally put away four fifths with absolutely no help from me. I left too early to go through the same thing at the other affair and came back to the room to read *Lost in the Horse Latitudes* by H. Allen Smith.

Jack's letter was certainly swell and it brought a lump in my throat too. I think that the whole family is just beginning to know each other now that we are so widely separated.

Just keep hoping and praying, and I know Jack will turn up none the worse for wear.

It looks as though Tom should be getting through before very long and I sure wish that I could get to see him. It's hard to tell where I'll be by then though. I have my papers for OCS and will submit them this week sometime.

Well guess this is all for now.

I'll keep you posted on anything new that turns up.

Your loving son, Gerald

P.S. Will send home some stuff that I want to get rid of soon and will try to include some cigs. Found another letter of Jack's and also that one of Frank's.

FRANK - CHRISTMAS WITH MARY ELIZABETH
Lebanon, Pennsylvania, January 15, 1945

Dear Ma,

I should have written sooner, but I have been working about 20 hours a day, what with school, regular work and all that goes under "addition to your other duties." In this case it's a question of writing a training program for the troops we have here.

Sis wrote a while ago and I guess none of us had too fancy a Christmas. Somehow, neither Peg nor I could get enthusiastic about anything in the Lebanon stores, as a result of which we felt very little satisfaction from our shopping.

Mary had a nice Christmas, I guess, which is only normal, and we did get a kick out of her. I wish you could see her. Friendly, effervescent, and hot-tempered. Gets that from the Cushings, I think.

I don't suppose you've heard anything from Jack yet. Don't worry though, his chances of coming through are still good. If he is in occupied territory and under the aegis of the Underground, why naturally you won't be hearing from him for a long time.

Anyhow, keep your chin up.

It's snowing here, and quite cold. Mary and Peg don't get out much anymore. Frankly, I don't think they would object a bit to leaving here for home. I wouldn't object much to that myself.

This is not much of a letter, but it seems to be the best thing of this type that I can do at this time. Peg sends her love and Mary would.

Love, Frank

TOM - DOUBLE SOLITAIRE
Corsica, France, January 16, 1945

Dear Mom,

Already a week has gone by since I last wrote to you. Where it went I have no idea but I certainly haven't been doing much.

The enclosed pictures were taken before Christmas and the scene is our squadron officers' mess. I am only in one of them, and am right behind that pipe and under that mess of hair. The wall decorations were all done by Willy, and as you may note, tinsel skirts have been added to a couple of the girls. That was simpler than trying to paint goose pimples, we found.

Comrade Adams appears in all three pictures. He is playing cards in two of them (Hearts I think was the game) and in the third picture he is leaning against the wall near the bar in the make-believe downing a snort. I say "make-believe" because I am sure those bottles were empty at the time—otherwise there would have been a larger group in the pictures.

In the bar picture also is Garnett Carroll being served by Fisher who is behind the bar. Over the fireplace is our squadron insignia. The fellow that I am playing cards with (Double Solitaire) is Jim Clarke of Upper Darby, Pennsylvania. That is Davis nearest him at the next table though hardly clear enough to identify him. The slot machine in the background was purchased out of the mess fund for an ungodly sum, and then it was discovered that nowhere in this theater were there coins to fit it. And there it sits.

Freddie Sedach, our squadron bombing officer, is going away for a couple weeks so during that time I'm going to take over his job. It will help pass the time, and it is interesting at times. It is mostly paperwork such as keeping a record of bombing training and making a schedule for same, writing alibis for bombardiers who missed the target by very much, and sending them to group—be embarrassing to have the job of writing one for myself!—and generally keeping an eye on the bombing business. It makes me realize that I am now the "oldest" bombardier in the squadron—except for Freddie of course. In fact, in May I'll have three years in the Army and will get a 5% raise in pay.

Today a few of us who have had colds or any sort of ear trouble went up to the hospital for a lookover. The flight surgeon who examined us was a specialist in that sort of thing. He had a long probe which he ran in each nostril, and it had a light which showed him if the passage back there was clear or blocked. I don't know the medical terms but anyway nine out of ten of us were found to have that passage closed and were recommended for a radium treatment which we all took.

It will be repeated next month and also the following one. What it does is to burn away the clogging tissues which only collect germs. These germs help along anything resembling a cold, and hinder breathing. It also makes it difficult to "clear" your ears when coming down from high altitudes. So, though the trouble I had was slight and only occurred once,

I should have no trouble now. There is less chance of getting a severe cold too. He said the same treatment in civilian life would cost a couple hundred bucks.

Well, I'll close now so this will get off in the morning. Oh, yes. Have you been stuffing any dates lately? Or just the plain dates would be swell if you could send some. I like them better than candy and they would be easy to keep. Don't go to any bother as I know you are very busy, but the candy ration has fallen off to about nothing and my new tent-mates' packages are just about gone.

Say hello to Gram and let me know Tom and Monette's new address when they settle down.

Your loving son, Tommy

TOM - MAIL CALL
Corsica, France, January 23, 1945

Dear Mom,

How the weeks go by! I checked in my little brown book, and it has been seven days since I last wrote to you. It seems as though I have spent most of the time carting bombardiers down to the trainer and flying with some of the new bombardiers. It is now raining outside and it is not very cheery weather.

We have been listening to the radio and the news from the Russian front is very encouraging. But we have been victorious before and been stopped later on, so there is not much sense in being overoptimistic. Sometimes I have the idea it will never end.

Mail Call paid off last night with Pat's letter of the 24th and a couple or three packages from you and Pat including the brownies and dates (all gone this morning), the box of cookies (just started on them) and one half of a Monopoly board. Pat's model airplane also arrived the other day with one from Bob. Many thanks for all and they help me hold up my end of the food supply here. I've been eating Jerry's and Davis' ever since they moved in. We did get a good ration this week which also helped.

Davis is overdue from Cairo but nothing is wrong. They simply decided to stay longer, and there is not much anybody here can do about it until they come back. Evidently they're having a good time and are perhaps staying longer to buy something special in the way of food. We chip in to the mess fund so that each month we can have fresh vegetables and fruit, which we would not otherwise have. Last month they did not have much luck down there, and so we have been having nothing but dehydrated stuff and hamburger. Each time the hamburger tastes a bit worse. But I really shouldn't complain as all things considered I'm pretty lucky.

For the last few days now I have been reading *The Apostle* by Sholem Asch which Theda sent to me for Christmas. It is a wonderful book and if you get a chance, be sure to read it. There are a good eight hundred pages but each of them is worth reading. I would like to read the *Nazarene* which is also by Asch, but I'd rather not ask you to send it just now with me so close to being finished.

One of the favorite indoor sports here in the evening is listening to the German news broadcasts, directed at the Americans and British. Their broadcasts say: The whole war is being waged for the Jews; the Russian advance into Germany is a crime which the Allies should prevent because Germany is fighting to protect the whole of Europe from the barbarian in the Kremlin, and they really pour it on thick.

They do get in some good digs when they talk about our handling of affairs in Greece and Italy where I guess things are not quite what they should be. Poland is brought into the news every night. I do think that in the long run the Poles will be left high and dry, and that the United States should have more to say about affairs in Europe. It seems to me that we are the first to say that an aggressor is wrong, but for diplomatic reasons, do nothing. If we don't like something, I believe that we should do something about it. It is no more isolationism to crawl into a shell, than it is to preach and not back up what we say. Our responsibility will not end on V-Day.

Well, I'll close before I go really off. It makes me mad to have an opinion and be unable to express it properly. Will write again soon, and in the meantime will hope to have more news.

Your loving son, Tommy

TOM - MAJOR HACKNEY
Corsica, France, January 27, 1945

Dear Mom,

The last twenty-four hours have had more life packed into them than the last couple weeks. First, Davis returned from Cairo and that called for a celebration last night. They were having a dance at the club and the Mouse was playing the drums so we had to be there. There was no whiskey so we had to be satisfied with cognac, Yours Truly falling off the wagon, which he has been riding for the last couple months. Jerry was really hot on the drums and took one break which lasted about five minutes, with everybody including the colonel just standing by and cheering. What an ovation!

After the dance (four girls in all) we came back to our own squadron club and sat around playing Sister Tharpe records until the wee small hours. Determined to get up for breakfast and get off to a good start, we set the alarm and turned in—more remarkably we got up too, feeling unusually good and peppy. After breakfast we went down to operations to see what was cooking. Nothing doing there so back we started.

Passing the basketball court we noticed it was not being used so we got a ball and started shooting. Davis is a very good player (our squadron officers' team has not been beaten this year) and he said I had a good eye but my shots under the basket were all wrong. One thing led to another, and soon I was getting a complete lecture on the fine art of basketball.

The time passed quickly, and before we knew it a couple of hours had gone by, and I had done more exercise than I have in the last six months. However, I do think I have learned a few things today and with more practice may get to play a mediocre game! Davis is very patient and really knows his basketball. Perhaps I can take off some of this excess weight I have. I hate to say it, but it is true that I am getting fat off the war.

Never a dull moment. Jerry and I were down to the bomb trainer a couple afternoons ago and when we came back we were greeted with the news that our tent had burned down. Jerry didn't believe it, but I'm a pessimist on some points and expected the worst. It just happened that a hole was burned around the chimney and could be repaired that afternoon. We took off the back part of the tent and, as the inside was thus exposed, Maj. Hackney came by and looked in.

My new book of figure drawing was in plain sight, and the cover you will recall is eye-catching, to say the least. Well, Maj. Hack has just the eye to be caught easily and with a yelp he was inside the tent. "Cahill, you've been holding out on me!" While giving the book the once-over Junior came down to tell him that the colonel wanted him on the phone and he had difficulty tearing himself away. "Don't let that get away," he warned and off he went. In about five minutes he was back. "Now where did I leave off"? "About page eighty, Maj. Hack." "Thanks, Cahill." And he was undisturbed as he finished the once-over.

He wants me to do a few sketches for him, but I don't feel quite up to it. Major flew with us the other day on a mission. What a character.

He also saw my scarf and said he had one just like it but not quite as clean now. He's not in his best humor just now, though, as one of the other squadron CO's got his silver leaf the other day and his has been long overdue.

He was in the first Tokyo group but didn't get on the mission as he was only a spare, but he had to make the carrier trip and all.

The mouse trap arrived and already has a kill to its credit! Thanks a lot. The cookies are all gone and in fact have been for a couple days. The store-boughts keep pretty well and I wouldn't mind some more if you could send them. It will be easier for you than to make them, as I know how busy you are.

The drawing book is wonderful, and I agree with Betty and Andy that it is better than Bridgman. There has been quite a burst of enthusiasm along art lines lately and I find myself in the position of teacher and supply store for other would-be artists. The biggest trouble around here is that when a fellow is in the mood to draw, there is always some joker who has to look over his shoulder and say, "What in the hell is that supposed to be?"

Whether he is your best friend or your bitterest enemy, it never fails to make a fellow boil. Politely but firmly you tell the guy that you are not an artist and make no claims. You did not ask him to look at your work, and therefore no criticism on his part is asked or desired. If you really thought you could draw you would mount your pictures in the mess hall for all to see and criticize to their heart's content.

Despite telling him this, it does tend to dull your outlook and you begin to lose out in your battle for improvement. I have done my best to encourage anybody who has an interest in drawing and place my books at their disposal but try not to make suggestions on their work, unless the fault is glaring and my criticism would be approved by the authors whom I have read. I have a surplus of drawing pencils which I bought over by the Vatican, and have passed a few of those around as a hard pencil is not much help to a beginner. There are a couple fellows here who can teach me plenty, and I make no bones about asking for help.

My back is about broken from that game this morning and so this will be all. Everything is under control here, and I'll try to write as soon as anything comes up. A good break in the weather should finish my tour. Thanks again for everything—meaning you too, Pat—and take it easy.

Your loving son, Tommy

P.S. Two packages arrived tonight, yours and Jackie's mailed November 29th. Everything intact and you batted 100% on the selections. Mrs. Slaven's cookies in perfect shape. The pencils are swell and give me the variety I needed. Had only one type before. From the modeling tools I assume that the clay is on the way. Correct? Song sheets solid. Incidentally, did you know that "Take Back Your Gold" is unofficially the drinking song of the 486th? Hope that covers everything and God love you all!

TOM - TOM'S LAST LETTER
Corsica, France, January 31, 1945

Dear Mom,

Payday again. The enclosed is not as much as I usually send, but with the allotment I hope it will be sufficient. I am keeping about a hundred for myself in case I should go up to Cannes this month. I'd rather not borrow as most of the boys have enough financial troubles of their own. However, if you need any just let me know as I may not use this money after all and can if necessary get more.

On my home front things are going as usual. The modeling clay arrived but I have not as yet had the chance to use it. When I had plenty of time on my hands I had nothing to do on my own hook. Now with the models, clay and the new drawing book, I have an extra job to keep me busy when I'm not flying. As I told you the bombing officer is away for a while going to a school, and since he has gone I have been taking care of his job.

Capt. Dozier the other night told me that I'd probably have to keep at it even when he got back. There is some possibility that I might work into the job for myself with the attached promotion, but it is as yet but a possibility and I am not assuming anything. It would not entail flying any more missions than I would have to ordinarily, but would mean a delay in getting home. Being overseas in itself is not bad at all, and if I were through with my missions, it might even be enjoyable.

Speaking of missions I now have sixty. How many more I'll have to go is not known to me now. I feel like I could go on indefinitely, so you know that I am in pretty good shape. John will have seventy-five when I have sixty-five and I don't think he'll fly anymore. He could quit now but wants to finish me out. I'd rather not fly with anybody else anyway. Col. Ruebel says that John is one of the best men in the group and I am very lucky to fly with him.

Weather is picking up now so I might even be finished this month. So all in all things look good and by the time this letter reaches you I should be even closer to the end of my tour than I am now. It seems that every time things look good something comes up to spoil it, but the way things are now I am pretty happy about the whole deal.

We heard Adolph speak last night. At least I presume it was he. It did not sound much like the old tyrant at Munich. Preceding the speech was a long march played by a typical German band. Somehow German marches seem different than ours. The downbeat is very decided and sounds brutal rather than inspiring. He never once raised his voice and though I could not understand what he was saying except for a few unmistakable words, he sounded very much as he should, taking a licking in the East and being threatened in the West. After his speech they played a slow, solemn piece like a funeral march. It sounded like the Third German Reich was buried then and there.

The days are now much warmer and not unlike California at this time of year. The evenings still get cold and there is usually ice in the foxholes but it soon thaws when the sun comes up. Woolcott says that they are swimming at Cannes now. Perhaps I'll go there soon but I'd rather not until I finish my missions.

Well, we have a couple new bombardiers now and I have to give them the setup here so I'd better go now. Hope Gram is better.

Much love to all.

Your loving son, Tommy

Epilogue

BAD NEWS

Through Tom and Jack's letters, the uncles I never knew became fully alive. It was both exciting and frightening for me to accompany them vicariously through World War II. Spending three years before I was born "with" my parents and their mother, sister and brothers, who were my family as I grew up, was a surprising and delightful bonus.

It was my goal in writing this book to share Tom and Jack's vibrant young lives—let their voices finally be heard. The time has come, however, to finish their story.

On November 21, 1944, Jack's plane, *Satan's Little Sister,* departed Flixton Airfield in Bungay, Suffolk County, England, on the crew's 19th mission. The ship did not return to base as expected and was classified Missing in Action.

After dropping its bombs over the target, an oil refinery in Hamburg, Germany, the ship encountered heavy flak on its way back to England. Over Holland, just five miles from safety in Belgium, *Satan's Little Sister* could no longer fly after losing its hydraulics, fuel, automatic pilot and two of its four engines.

Losing altitude, seven crewmembers bailed out on the pilot's order. The pilot and co-pilot remained on the ship to ensure all crewmembers escaped safely, then they bailed out. The pilot counted eight parachutes in the air in addition to his own.

An unexpected change in wind direction blew the crewmembers who bailed out first into the icy waters of the Ijsselmeer, a freshwater lake off the North Sea. They all drowned. Jack was 21 years old and is buried at Netherlands American Cemetery Margraten.

The pilots who bailed out later at a lower altitude landed near coastal villages. Both were rescued by the Dutch in separate locations and protected until hostilities ended in May 1945.

This was a static crew, normally ten men, who had flown together exclusively for seven months and were very close. Only the navigator was not on this mission. Because Jack's ship was flying deputy lead, second plane in the formation, no navigator was needed.

On February 5, 1945, Tom's plane departed Alesan Airfield, Corsica, France. He was flying as navigator, rather than his usual bombardier position, and with a different pilot and crew.

On this mission to the Brenner Pass in Italy, Tom's plane and two others attacked threatening gun positions at Rovereto so the main ships, a formation of twelve, could accurately bomb German supply lines four miles north at Calliano. The mission was recorded as 100% accurate.

After dropping its bombs, Tom's ship took a flak hit and crashed at the base of the Alps in northern Italy. Tom was 23 years old and is buried with his crew at Fort Scott National Cemetery in Kansas.

A few days prior to his death, Tom received the Distinguished Flying Cross for outstanding achievement in action against the enemy.

I wondered over the years, before I knew of my uncles' letters, why Jack was buried in Europe and why Tom was not buried in California. At the very least, why were they not buried somewhere side by side? But I never asked anyone.

Through the Freedom of Information Act (FOIA), I acquired government files about my uncles' deaths. There were many letters between my grandmother and U.S. government authorities discussing burial options for the boys. In one, my grandmother wrote that, after Jack died, other boys who came home from overseas told her, if they were to die on foreign soil, they would want to be buried where they fell.

Until I found my family's letters and documents, I didn't know that the remains of Tom and his crewmates could not be individually identified and were therefore buried together. The government suggested the Kansas location, which was central for the crewmates' families who lived around the country.

Subsequent to Jack's death, my grandmother became friends and corresponded with several very kind Dutch people related to his crew's loss. In another of her letters in Tom's FOIA file, she told the government of her concurrence with the suggested Kansas location for the crew's burial.

She also said, "Had identification been possible I would have asked to have Tommy laid beside his brother at Margraten, where Dutch friends would visit his grave as though he were one of their own."

BETTER NEWS

Knowing Tom and Jack, when I never thought I would, is one of the high points of my life. My awareness of my father's family was fragmented. I had only bits and pieces and never thought about what was left to know.

I find it astounding that I knew my grandmother for twenty years, and my parents, aunt and other uncles longer, but had no idea of the preciousness of these brothers, the enormity of their loss and its long-term impact on my family. They weren't discussed with my generation that I remember, which I now know is common among those who experienced loss in World War II. Though the questions my generation asked our parents were always answered, we never thought to seek more substantial information.

After eavesdropping on my family for the letters' duration, the puzzle pieces came together and liberated me. I now understand that the deaths of Tom and Jack triggered a lingering, stifled sadness that trickled from their generation to mine and resulted in a tangle of emotional family issues. There is a quiet Tom-and-Jack-shaped empty space in our lives.

It was a privilege to compile my uncles' story. Though emotional, it also felt spiritual and cozy, being with my grandmother again. Forever linked to each other their last few years, Tom and Jack lived separately yet parallel and are now colorfully alive for their descendants. In addition to glimpsing the joy of the boys' existence, I learned how much my family cherished them, and that they knew how loved they were.

My brother Patrick and our cousin Liz, both mentioned in the letters, were too young to remember knowing Tom and Jack when the boys left home in 1943. The year 1945 used to be just the year I was born, as was my cousin Katy, Frank's second daughter. Now I see that year as the time everything changed for our family.

Over time, I've realized the futility of struggling with life as it evolves. There are some things I can control but a lot I cannot. As much as I have improved my ability to discern the difference, grappling with the loss of Tom and Jack is rough. Even knowing that we were not alone—hundreds of thousands of people suffered losses during World War II—I still wonder, "Why our family, why both boys?" Sometimes when the question is "Why?" there is no answer.

Tom and Jack touched places in my heart I did not know were there, and now I cherish these boys I never knew. As my past merged with my present, I became whole, grew closer to God and found a peacefulness I never knew I could have.

Appendices

HIGH FLIGHT

By John Gillespie Magee, Jr.
1922-1941

Oh! I have slipped the surly bonds of Earth
And danced the skies on laughter-silvered wings;
Sunward I've climbed, and joined the tumbling mirth
Of sun-split clouds—and done a hundred things
You have not dreamed of—wheeled and soared and swung
High in the sunlit silence. Hov'ring there,
I've chased the shouting wind along, and flung
My eager craft through footless halls of air...

Up, up the long, delirious burning blue
I've topped the wind-swept heights with easy grace
Where never lark, or ever eagle flew—
And, while with silent lifting mind I've trod
The high untrespassed sanctity of space,
Put out my hand, and touched the face of God.

TOM'S MISSIONS

From the island of Corsica, France, Tom flew sixty-two bombing missions with Squadron 486 in twin-engine B-25 Mitchell bombers. He couldn't write specifics about his missions in his letters, but the squadron kept detailed crew lists and war diaries, both *Secret* at that time.

Decades later, these documents were *Declassified.* They are now in public domain, available through the website of the Mediterranean Theater of Operations' 57th Bomb Wing Association. Aligning crew lists with daily war diaries for the dates of Tom's missions, I gained a better picture of what Tom's life was like beyond the letters he sent home. The diaries were respectfully and colorfully compiled by Lt. Glenn L. Pierre, who certainly had the literary style—and heart—for this assignment.

June 3, 1944, Lagaro, Italy (Railroad Bridge, 18 planes)

Our family will be without the friendly personalities of Lts. Sellers, Coons, Tupper and Sgts. Koebcke, Carey, McDonough because they have, during their mission, been shot down. We hope to see them soon after their escape.

June 6, 1944, Orvieto, Italy (Road Bridge, 12 planes)

Invasion of Normandy, France, D-Day! Yes, a time for celebration; for prayer; for work and for thought. Invasion pool paid off $49 to T/Sgt. Economos, $10.50 to Cpl. Sanford and $10.50 to S/Sgt. Addison. Ears were glued to the speakers and talk indicated how many ways the war could be won.

June 22, 1944, Grisigliano, Italy (Railroad Bridge, 12 planes)

Mission today was rather rugged. The boys were still talking about it four hours later.

June 30, 1944, Pietrasanta, Italy (Railroad Bridge, 12 planes)

Another mission started the day; unfortunately results were not good. Mr. Dixon from the Associated Press has been with us for a few days now and has made friends with a number of the personnel. Mr. Dixon of Virginia says, "Pass the bottle."

July 2, 1944, Ostiglia, Italy (Fuel Dump, 6 planes)

Mission today was a popular success. The men have been bombing bridges so long that a change to an oil dump that blew up gave them a thrill.

July 3, 1944, Ferrara, Italy (Fuel Dump, 12 planes)

Big event today was a rough mission—another oil dump. Lt. Pike's hydraulic brakes failed on his return and his ship barreled off the end of the runway.

After losing landing gear on the rough ground, his ship slid to a stop in the gully 100 yards from the end of the strip, then crumpled in two about 12 feet from the tail. Fortunately the ship did not burn and the crew experienced only a shakeup, except for Sgts. Diehl and McHale who were bruised.

Lt. Martinson who was cut by flying Plexiglas came back on one engine with Capt. Shealy as bombardier. They said that they buzzed a weather station of Jerry's so close on a mountaintop that they could read Jerry's weather map in the shack. Flak also hit Sgt. Housken, with Sgt. Slocum and Sgt. Schmitz in the hospital with moderate injuries.

Lt. Mell's ship is said to have cut the "sagebrush" like a lawnmower on the mountaintop on his way home. After precariously missing the mountain they discovered they were about 30 miles from Leghorn with so little altitude that Jerry's tracers and small arms fire was directed at them. One of the gunners fired back and said the ground fire ceased. Lt. Fisher was cut by flak and is in the hospital; nothing serious, we hope.

The outstanding feature is the display of "guts" by this "soft and decadent" democratic progeny. Jokes and humor dominate. Youth finds it difficult to believe that mortal injury can be so close, and as a result it does not take danger seriously or cowardly, but it looks into danger's eyes and thumbs its nose.

To maintain the war-like atmosphere, the local flickers are flicking away with *Destination Tokyo*. Pictures were taken today for civilian passports in the event they may be needed if combat crews are shot down behind enemy lines.

July 14, 1944, Corbola, Italy (Road and Railroad Bridges, 12 planes)

It seems the bomb-loaders Joe Kolcz, Abe Heller, Vin Douglas, Glenn Blair and "Buf" Falo almost had some excitement. When wheeling up a 1,000 lb. bomb, it jumped the dolly and sheared its fuse. Despite it being fully armed, Blair defused it amid the dust caused by scampering personnel. Cool work Blair, take a bow.

July 15, 1944, Ferrara, Italy (Road Bridge, 12 planes)

Again today Ferrara was hit twice. The morning flight came back with one serious casualty, Sgt. Keller the radio-gunner was hit in the chest and jaw. Several ships made belly landings and were perforated with flak. Patterns traveled in the target area but most bombs straddled the bridge.

The afternoon mission had its tense moments but if any fear was present there was no outward manifestation. Over a period of time injury is relatively light and consequently much joviality and fun exists everywhere. If the missions were to become very hazardous there would be no flinching, only perhaps a more serious demeanor about the squadron. Results of the afternoon mission, good.

July 17, 1944, Alessandria, Italy (Railroad Bridge, 6 planes)

Mission today, but light, as each squadron put up only six ships. Target was a milk run and was bombed to dust. All squadrons received 100% except one.

The nature of the mission was reflected in the attitude of the combat crews because their spirits were high and joviality was dominant at the finish of the mission.

July 26, 1944, Ostiglia, Italy (Railroad Bridge, 12 planes)

Successful mission today collapsed the Ostiglia RR bridge which was getting to be an obsession with the crews. The line, armament, etc., certainly have been keeping up their end of the work. Theirs is routine labor but they get it done and that's what counts. Our compliments for their steadfastness.

August 11, 1944, Raphael, Southern France (Gun Positions, 15 planes)

Mission today was quite a challenge to the skill of the combat crews: gun positions on the coast of Southern France. Returned crews reported excellent results, we shall see!

Weather was forbidding till late afternoon at which time the group's 48-ship mission left.

August 15, 1944, Allied Invasion of Southern France
Avignon, France, and Issambres, France (Beach, Bridge and Gun Positions, 33 planes)

The group sent 72 ships into the air and over the South France coast by 0730 this morning. Very few boxes dropped their bombs because of the damned weather which blanketed the coast. This was very disappointing, however, because little or no flak was observed, everyone returned safely and we are grateful for that at least.

In the afternoon, bridges at Avignon were selected as targets. This indicated the B-25s could be taken off ground support work and put back on semi-strategic work. A French major general and his aide-de-camp accompanied the invasion during the afternoon after being initiated about the group by Col. Chapman. The mission was rough; three ships did not return and most were holed. Two went down over the target and one over the sea. Lt. Hoschar's ship, struck in the right wing, flew apart and set the ship into a flat spin. No one was seen chuting out but chutes may have been overlooked because of the excited state of the crews due to the intense and accurate flak. Some are inclined to believe several men may have gotten out safely and the writer is one who believes.

On the return trip, pilots J.D. Smith and Morrison spotted a 488th ship going down, and when the crew landed in the water, they each dropped spare dinghies and radioed the fix for air-sea rescue. The squadron was not happy and groups of men could be seen about the area in discussion, quiet and soberly talking about the mission. The squadron's turn for stand-down tomorrow will serve to help them forget about the mission.

Quite a few boys drained their sorrow with some beer and whiskey, in fact, singing could be heard during the small hours. The manpower shortage in the armament section left Bob Sturgis with no one on his flight but Jim Sheldon, so he is once more a regular armorer, while "Buf" Falo, John Dietzen and "Tex" Dyson, who hardly knew what armament was six weeks ago, have learned the hard way and now take care of their own ships.

August 21, 1944, Parma, Italy
(Railroad Bridge, 12 planes including 3 each with Sq. 487 and Sq. 488)

Morning mission to Italy for a change, results good. The bridge is down. Early evening found the air liaison officer a guest for supper and as a lecturer on the war fronts.

Although a goodly number of personnel follow the various fronts avidly, it is quite surprising that a considerable number pay little heed of day-to-day development. Especially is this so among combat officer personnel. As this is from the writer's observations, he cannot yet submit a reason why.

August 23, 1944, Avignon, France (Gun Positions, 12 planes)

Squadron stand-down today was unexpectedly canceled when a mission was called for Avignon, a dreaded target! After great apprehension, the combat crews discovered all flak at Avignon was silent! It may have been removed, no one seems to know. However to spoil a free ride the ships came home over Marseilles accidentally and there was a small amount of flak observed. The target was so unexpected that the combat gunners were required to assist in loading bombs—they went to work cheerfully and Capt. Bridges said without their help the mission would not have been on time.

November 5, 1944 Padua, Italy (East and South Bridges, 12 planes)

Again a mission—fine results. Lt Brandle's ship, *Schapps YoYo*, with tail designation 6M, did not return, and it was last seen entering a cloud bank en route to the target. We expect word that he landed at another field.

November 6, 1944 [follow-up]

Lt. Brandle and his crew have not returned—we are hoping fervently!

November 8, 1944 Casarsa, Italy (Railroad Bridge, 18 planes)

Mission again—again 100% and again coffee and doughnuts at the return of the mission. No word on 6M and it is feared that Lt. Brandle's ship is definitely "missing."

November 10, 1944 [follow-up]

Lt. Brandle's ship is now considered lost, and to the memory of the crew, we say "Happy Valhalla." *[Author's note, 2015: Valhalla, in Norse mythology, is a majestic hall of honor where souls of heroes, fallen bravely in battle, go when they die. In spite of multiple searches, Lt. Richard Brandle, pilot, his crew of five, and their ship have never been found. Schapps YoYo disappeared forever without a trace.]*

December 2, 1944 Rovereto and Calliano, Italy (Railroad Bridges, 15 planes)

Mission again, this time to Rovereto and Calliano bridges. The Calliano target was a hot one. Lt. Cooley barreled off the end of the runway because his hydraulics were out. Lt. Calloway arrived home with 58 holes and Lt. Cantino luckily escaped an 88mm explosion when the shell passed through his wing. As it was, no one was injured for which we are all very thankful.

December 26, Rovereto and Calliano, Italy (Railroad Bridges, 18 planes)

A mission today near the Brenner Pass. The chaff and phosphorus bombs helped reduce the accuracy and amount of flak. The mission was declared successful—they get more successful every day.

Crews were given doughnuts and coffee after interrogation, and then hurriedly returned to the squadron for a dinner of fresh pork with applesauce.

<u>January 20, 1945, Trento, Italy (Marshalling Yards and Gun Positions, 15 planes)</u>

In spite of freezing mist and drizzle early this morning, the day resolved itself into a fairly sunny one, and we had a mission to the Trento Marshalling Yards. Very hot target. Twelve ships with bombs and three with chaff and phosphorous. Three ships holed but no casualties. One of the other squadrons, the 487th, lost one ship in flames over the target.

<u>January 22, 1945 Dogna, Italy (Railroad Bridge, 12 planes)</u>

Today was extremely cold and the boys on today's mission report that it was 22 below, Fahrenheit. This, combined with the extreme length of the mission, made for some runny noses and frozen fingers. They went to the Dogna RR Bridge way up by the Austrian Border, and just a few miles west of Yugoslavia.

It was a refrigerated milk run and we got another 100% and one box got probable hits. The Russian advance (and I use that word although it inadequately describes the stupendous drive) is the big news around here. Keeping up with their front lines on our map is really wearing out the grease pencils.

<u>February 2, 1945 Chiusaforte, Italy (West Railroad Bridge, 12 planes)</u>

Mission today to Chiusaforte, just south of Dogna up near Austria. Results 100% for the box that dropped, no flak and all went well.

<u>February 5, 1945 Calliano, Italy (Railroad Bridge, 12 planes) Rovereto, Italy (Gun Positions, 3 planes)</u> *[Tom's last mission]*

Today a bursting star. A star with seven points; points of valor and duty and courage. Today seven men went down in a flak killed ship and tonight seven empty bunks bring lumps to men's throats. Lt. Ross and his crew, on an operational mission over the Brenner Pass, attacked gun positions so that the main flights could bomb accurately and they did— the mission was recorded as 100% accurate. We hope the report of one chute seen means at least one chute. And so it is again proven; where the Yanks are duty placed, they rise to the task like men.

JACK'S MISSIONS

In 1944, Jack's crew flew nineteen combat missions over Europe and three grocery runs to France. This information was taken from the 446th Bomb Group website. Lt. John Quinn, Jack's pilot, sometimes added comments specific to their ship, *Satan's Little Sister*, a four-engine B-24 Liberator bomber.

August 25, Rostock, Germany
Thirty-six planes hit the Heinkel aero engine plant, amid accurate flak. *Ronnie* ended its streak of seventy-nine straight successful missions by aborting. *Happy Go Lucky* crashed into the North Sea, killing all ten aboard. It is assumed it suffered engine failure. Another plane also crashed, killing four, with seven taken prisoner.

September 2, 6, and 9, Beaulieu, France, Grocery Runs
These were non-combat missions, grocery runs, requiring only two enlisted men and one officer. Food and medicine were ferried to Orleans, France, for the people recently liberated from German occupation. Empty bombers left Flixton Airfield for Southern England to be filled with provisions.

They then flew to the airfields in Orleans which lay in ruins after recent bombardment by these same bombers to clear German militants. The crews were met with open arms by the French citizens, who helped unload the planes.

September 10, Heilbronn, Germany
Rail yards were attacked, with fair results. *Rough Buddy* was hit by flak and went down, killing nine crewmen with one taken prisoner.

September 12, Kiel, Germany
Thirty-six planes bombed a jet engine plant with good results. Lt. Quinn's comment: "Flak through navigator's window and left waist gun."

September 18, Supply Drop, Groesbeek, Nijmegen, Holland
Gasoline, food, and ammunition were dropped to American ground troops, which had just parachuted into the area. The group commander, Col. Jacob Brogger, was injured by an explosive bullet and was sent home. Lt. Quinn's comment: "Rifle fire through command deck."

September 21, Koblenz, Germany

The crews were unable to see the signal given by the lead plane and, as a result, missed the target by about a mile. One plane, *T.S.*, was hit by flak and crash-landed at Bredfield Aifield, killing all ten on board. It was the crew's first mission.

September 22, Kassel, Germany

Twenty-two planes bombed the marshalling yards through heavy clouds, with unobserved results. Flak was intense, but inaccurate.

September 28, Kassel, Germany

In the second day of a two-day mission to Kassel, twenty-seven planes bombed the locomotive works. The group saw seven enemy jet fighters. Lt. Quinn's comment: "Five flak holes."

October 2, Hamm, Germany

The marshalling yards were hit with good results. The yard was left in flames and freight cars were destroyed. Accurate flak caused damage to fifteen of the 446th's planes, but all returned. Lt. Quinn's comment: "Flak and No. 3 engine failure. Bombs fell along railroad tracks on right side going in. Saw P-51s apparently attacking enemy aircraft after crossing the Ijsselmeer in Holland."

October 3, Lachen/Speyerdorf Airfield, Germany

Twenty-five planes attacked the airfield with good results reported. Lt. Quinn's comment: "Squadron ahead dropped their bomb load in southeast corner."

October 5, Lippstadt Airfield, Germany

Several errors caused the 446th to drop short of the target. One plane crash-landed on its return to base with no injuries reported.

October 6, Hamburg, Germany

Thirty-one planes attacked an oil refinery with poor results. A pilot was killed by flak; the co-pilot was able to return the heavily damaged plane to base. Lt. Quinn's comment: "Hole in No. 3 engine, which then failed."

October 9, Koblenz, Germany

Thirty-five planes attacked target with unobserved results. Contrails from jet fighters were seen in the area.

October 12, Osnabruk, Germany
Twenty-nine planes hit the marshalling yards with unobserved results.

October 15, Cologne, Germany
A return visit for group saw fair results on the marshalling yards. *Lady Luck* received severe flak damage and returned on two engines. Upon landing, it crashed, killing three crewmen. Lt. Quinn's comment: "Flak in nose turret. U.S. lost thirty-four planes."

October 17, Cologne, Germany
The marshalling yards were again hit, with unobserved results.

October 19, Mainz, Germany
Marshalling yards on the north side of the Rhine were hit with poor results. *Slightly Dangerous* was hit by flak and crashed, killing three, with the remaining seven taken prisoner.

October 26, Minden, Germany
In spite of a solid undercast, a canal was hit with very good results. Several miles of the canal dried up as a result.

November 5, Karlsruhe, Germany
Thirty-one planes bombed the marshalling yards through cloud cover with unobserved results.

November 21, Hamburg, Germany *[Jack's last mission]*
The group's first mission after a ten-day stand-down for runway repair was not a good one. An oil refinery was hit and intense flak brought down *Satan's Little Sister*. Seven crewmen were killed and two more evaded capture.

HOW I FOUND MY UNCLES

After I found my uncles' letters, I became determined to learn more about them. I was surprised how easy that became once I made the proper contacts.

I found enough information in Tom's letters to determine he was in Corsica, France, Squadron 486. Googling led me to the Mediterranean Theater's 57th Bomb Wing Association, to which Tom's squadron belongs, and which is open to surviving service members and descendants. I since have learned that many groups like this exist, created by veterans hungry to keep World War II history alive.

I emailed the membership contact, Julie Martin, and said we had just found family letters, Tom was stationed on Corsica and that I'd like to join the group. Because I thought it was sweet, I tossed in that his squadron had a dog named Jocko. I received a rapid reply from Julie and her friend Doug Culver with the particulars of joining, including additional website information with references to Tom.

Julie said that her father, B-25 pilot Jim "Red" Martin, was also in Squadron 486. He and Tom had about a month in common there, but we don't know if they knew each other. Julie's father survived the war, and what really sent a chill up my spine was her comment, "My dad used to talk about Jocko." Now I had not only met my uncle through his letters, but I connected with "someone" in his life 70 years ago: a dog. Julie sent me a website photo of Tom with squadron friends, and Jocko, standing at attention in the front row. This one connection had me hooked. I'm proud to say I'm a card-carrying member of the Mediterranean Theater's 57th Bomb Wing Association, on Tom's behalf.

In this flurry of emails with Julie and Doug about Tom, I mentioned that I would next seek similar information for Tom's brother Jack, but I didn't have the squadron number lead I had for Tom. I didn't even know where Jack was stationed when he was in Europe.

In about two minutes, Doug wrote back with Jack's information. He was stationed in England during the war with the 446th Bomb Group. Doug provided me with the website for the survivors and descendants association for the European Theater, which I joined on Jack's behalf.

I learned a lot about Tom's combat activities from his letters, but I was missing similar information for Jack, and the Army information online for him is more limited. I had hoped that we would find the letters Jack wrote from England, but had to conclude they were lost in the fire. I am thrilled, though, that we have Jack's letters from training which introduced him to me.

Once I knew Tom's and Jack's bomb group associations, I became obsessed with internet searching to know more. I was amazed how much information is available, including government documents originally *Secret* that are now *Declassified*.

Though I will never hear Jack's words from England, other than one postcard from London, I did find a stirring Dutch connection for him that I never could have anticipated.

JACK'S DUTCH CONNECTION

I was a goofy college kid when I traveled with a high school friend outside the United States the first time. It was 1966, and we were encouraged to travel to *Europe on Five Dollars a Day*, as the popular book title coaxed. We left New York and landed in Amsterdam eight hours later.

I felt like I entered a storybook...welcoming people, centuries-old buildings, lush landscapes and, of course, windmills. It was the perfect place to launch our five-week tour. I lived high-on-the-hog and spent *eight* dollars a day.

The beauty of Holland charmed me, and I took new pride declaring my one-eighth Dutch heritage. I didn't realize then that, nearly fifty years later, my Dutch connection would be rekindled and my life forever interwoven with this country and its people.

I remember as a child hearing that my uncle, John "Jack" Cahill, my father's younger brother, an Army flier killed during World War II, was buried in Europe...Belgium, Holland or somewhere. In my mind, Jack was lumped with other Cahill ancestors my generation would never know, including his brother Tom, also an Army flier killed during the war. My family never forgot Tom and Jack; we all had their photos in our homes. Growing up, though, my generation learned little about them.

Through the 446th Bomb Group Association, I learned that Jack was stationed at Flixton Airfield in Bungay, Suffolk County, on the east coast of England. He was with the Eighth Air Force, belonged to Squadron 706 and flew bombing missions as radio operator, primarily between England and Germany. Because Jack's letters from England were lost in my grandmother's fire, information about him from other sources was crucial. I contacted veteran Bill Davenport, historian of the 446th Bomb Group, who said he would snail-mail to me related material.

A few days later, I received a copy of a book chapter that tells of an American plane shot down over Holland. It was my Uncle Jack's ship, *Satan's Little Sister.*

Bill suggested I contact the Dutch author of this chapter, Jaap van der Woude, and gave me his email address in the Netherlands. Jaap was born a few years after the war ended in the town of Eemnes, Holland, next to the Ijsselmeer, a freshwater lake off the North Sea. This is where Jack's plane came to rest in 1944, and that proximity sparked Jaap's interest in the area's wartime history.

Jaap speaks fluent English and we were happy to meet online. He and I nearly met in 1982 when he began his research. He had written to wartime addresses for the families of crewmembers on Jack's plane, but received a response from only one family. His letter to my family in Los Angeles was returned—we had moved from there in 1950. Jaap and I both found it astonishing that, thirty years after he wrote to us, he finally got a "reply" to his letter when I popped up in his email.

Through Jaap's research, he became committed to the memory of the deceased fliers and, when he traveled to the United States, he met the surviving pilot, Lt. John Quinn. The chapter Jaap wrote about Jack's crash filled in pieces of family history that had been missing all my life. Of Jack's crew of nine, seven perished and two survived under Dutch protection until hostilities ended in 1945.

The Eemnes Freedom Memorial, dedicated to Jack's crew and the crew of a British plane that also crashed nearby, was erected in Jaap's hometown. Each year's class of eighth-grade students maintains the memorial as part of their World War II curriculum. A summary of the history of *Satan's Little Sister* and the establishment of the memorial to its crew appears in the article that follows, written in 1987 by British Flixton Airfield historian, John Archer, for the *Beccles and Bungay Journal.*

Jaap, whose name in English is Jack, and I exchanged a multitude of emails with photos and documents, including photos I sent him of Jack and our family. Jaap also sent photos taken in 1993 when he, his wife and friends visited the Memorial to the 446th Bomb Group in England and walked the grounds of the former Flixton Airfield. He said his friend noticed he was staring at the start of the runway for several minutes. "He asked me what I was thinking. I still don't know, but it was an overwhelming feeling. This is the area where crews including your Uncle Jack's left their footprints and took off for the next uncertain mission into enemy territory."

On November 21, 2012, the 68th anniversary of the loss of the crew of *Satan's Little Sister,* Jaap sent me the following email: "Hi Michelle, Today we light a candle for your uncle and his crew. We will never forget their sacrifice. A grateful Jack, Maria and children."

Uncle Jack is one of 8,301 American soldiers killed in World War II and buried in Netherlands American Cemetery Margraten. Also memorialized there, on the Tablets of the Missing, are names of 1,722 soldiers, whose remains are unaccounted for.

One way Dutch individuals and families have shown their respect and gratitude is by adopting graves of those buried in Margraten, as well as names listed on the Tablets of the Missing. After learning this, I emailed the foundation that oversees the adoption initiative to ask for information on Jack's Dutch adopters. They gave me the name and mailing address, but had no email, so I prepared to write a letter.

The foundation emailed me again promptly. They had phoned the adoptive family, Koosje Crolla van der Velden, her husband Math and their daughter Anita. The foundation gave the family my email address, and Koosje gave her email address to them to forward to me. Almost to the minute, Koosje and I emailed each other for the first time. She knows little English and I speak no Dutch. But thanks to internet translation resources and Koosje's English-speaking family members, we communicate.

To this point, Uncle Jack was "John" to his adopters, and they only had one photo, the same soldier photo that my brother, cousins and I had all our lives. I learned they adopted Jack's grave in 1996. He is one of three American soldiers whose graves they adopted. A second soldier is buried at Margraten and the third is buried at Henri-Chapelle American Cemetery in Belgium.

In 2009 Koosje obtained Jack's forty-page Deceased Personnel File through the United States government's Freedom of Information Act (FOIA). She emailed those documents to me, and I shared with her photos of Jack as a child and young adult, as well as photos of our family. Koosje and I had the same experience for years, knowing very little about our shared soldier, but in an instant, we both learned much more.

Each of us is grateful to the other. I helped her get to know Jack, and I am comforted knowing that her family watches over his grave. They refer to him as "our liberator." Though he lies nearly 6,000 miles from his California home, Jack has a family in the Netherlands that visits his place of rest and brings him flowers and gratitude. Though Koosje, Jaap and I connected through Jack originally, both asked me to tell them about Tom, and their gratitude now extends to him also.

Because Koosje speaks little English, I obtained FOIA files for her other two American adoptees. I am in regular contact with her and her family, but not always related to Jack. We are now friends beyond our connection through him. Koosje is a photographer and sends beautiful photos of her travels around Europe, and we share a love of animals.

As I communicated with Jaap and Koosje, I realized they might enjoy knowing each other. Both had shared information with me that I thought the other would like to have, but it was theirs to share, not mine.

Jaap had tried before to get the names of Jack's adopters but the foundation would only share it with Jack's family. I was the missing link and emailed Jaap and Koosje to see if they were interested in meeting online. They connected quickly upon receiving each other's email address.

Jaap volunteers at the National Liberation Museum in Groesbeek, and Koosje and her husband traveled from their home in Valkenburg to meet him and see the museum. Koosje sent me pictures of their meeting, and they remain in contact.

In addition to Koosje visiting Uncle Jack's grave, Jaap has a friend, also named Jack, who often visits the grave of another soldier at Margraten. For several years, he has visited Uncle Jack's grave on Jaap's behalf. In 2012, Jaap's friend Jack sent him a touching photo of himself saluting Uncle Jack's grave, and Jaap forwarded that photo to me.

I never could have foreseen the fascinating path I traveled to get to know my uncles. I haven't met either Jaap or Koosje in person, but we are all connected. They live in the same country a couple hours apart, but it took a zigzag to Uncle Jack and me in California to introduce them to each other.

It's comforting for me to know that, though Jack is laid to rest far away from family, he certainly is not alone. The Dutch continue to honor his memory.

SATAN'S LITTLE SISTER REMEMBERED
By John Archer for *Beccles and Bungay Journal,* Friday, August 21, 1987
Reprinted with permission of John Archer

A Liberator named Satan's Little Sister *flew many missions from Flixton Airfield during the Second World War, before finally crashing in Holland. Recently a memorial was erected to it at its last landing place, and Flixton Airfield's historian, John Archer, is recently back from visiting it. In this article he recalls the Liberator's last mission from its Suffolk base.*

Satan's Little Sister had been around for several months, I had seen her going out on missions in the early mornings and often returning during the early afternoons.

Through May to November 1944 this B-24 Liberator of the 446th Bombardment Group had flown across Germany and the occupied countries of Europe, always returning with the group. On November 21, 1944, the Liberator took off and assembled with the rest of the group for a raid on Hamburg.

But that day was the last time she would take off from Flixton Airfield.

While the aircraft was over the target area, anti-aircraft gunfire was intense. Two engines, both on the port side, were hit, the fuel lines were ruptured. The crew were in deep trouble. The aircraft began to lose altitude, and the controls became difficult to operate. Members of the crew calculated how much fuel was left and, if at all possible, a short route back to Flixton.

Whatever they tried, an emergency landing at sea was a big risk and dropping into the icy North Sea was not very inviting.

A course was plotted for a possible emergency landing behind Allied lines across the Zuider Zee. Over the Zuider Zee the lone B-24 slowly glided down towards the icy waters of the Ijsselmeer, close to the mouth of the River Eem. The crew bailed out, but unfortunately the SW wind drifted seven of the parachutes back in the direction of the Ijsselmeer. They all drowned.

The pilot and co-pilot being last out of the plane, landed near the coastline and were hidden by the Dutch resistance until the end of hostilities.

Shortly after the crash, Northern Europe experienced one of the severest winters of the century. The Ijsselmeer froze over and stayed frozen until the end of January 1945. When the thaw began in February, the bodies of the drowned airmen were recovered.

Jack van der Woude, a young boy at the time, remembers the large formations flying over Holland. That particular day will never be forgotten. Jack lives in a village called Eemnes, quite near to the last resting place of *Satan's Little Sister.* I have been in touch with Jack over the years concerning this particular crash.

In May, a memorial was erected and dedicated to the crew of *Satan's Little Sister.* Names of an RAF Lancaster bomber crew, lost February 20, 1944, are also listed. The local school children have adopted the memorial, they are very much involved in keeping the surroundings neat and trimmed.

A few weeks ago I was most fortunate to meet my Dutch aviation friend Jack, and aviation historian Harold Jansen of The Hague. It was a great experience to see, after 43 years, the place where *Satan's Little Sister*'s tragic end came, after leaving Flixton on that cold November morning.

A FEW WORDS FROM BROTHER BOB

There are no letters from my dad Bob in this book, so I have included a few below so readers can hear his voice. He called my mother "Jack" not Jackie as I used to differentiate her from my Uncle Jack in our family's letters.

My mother and I took the train to Vancouver to visit her parents in March 1949. I was three and remember that train ride, my first. My brother was seven years old. On March 20, 1949, my dad wrote:

Dear Jack,

It's a shame to start a letter with an apology, but it looks like one is in order—never again will I call you the world's champion bed and blanket hog. The title will remain in the family, but you'll have to be content with second place. Your boy, to add insult to injury, invasion and exposure, asked for a glass of milk about 3 a.m. No doubt to replenish and bolster his energy to protect the conquered territory for which he had battled so vigorously.

Hope you enjoyed your trip despite the fact that I forgot to give you the pocketful of change I had accumulated.

In a sense, I'm enjoying your trip as much as you are. You may not know it, but for some time, I've wanted you to have a rest, but it was just one of those things. Inability to provide same has been one of the little things stuck in the corner of my mind. I feel quite relieved knowing that you're getting a vacation, despite the fact that I had very little to do with it. Therefore, make the most of it and have fun.

Don't worry about Pat, he has been a very good boy so far. Write and tell us all about your trip.

Love, Bob

In May 1952, my dad went to Wichita, Kansas, for a yearlong engineering assignment. The rest of us followed several weeks later when the school year ended. He wrote this letter to my brother Patrick and me (my nickname is Mikey), May 17, 1952, then ages ten and six.

Dear Kids,

I received your wonderful letters yesterday. I was certainly pleased with Mikey's wonderful coloring and writing and Pat's wonderful penmanship.

I'm living in a big two-story house made of bricks. When I go to work, I go down the street a few blocks and through the park which has a zoo. Generally, the big black bears are still sleeping when I go by. Then I go over the bridge across the river. A lot of people fish from the bridge for catfish and bass. I had catfish for dinner last night. After crossing the bridge, I have breakfast downtown and then go to work. We are building a training plane for Beech Aircraft. I will send a picture in my next letter to Mommy.

This is a pretty good little town. It is not as large as Los Angeles, but big enough. We have all kinds of weather here. Since I have been here, we've had nice days, rainy days, hot days, cold days, thunder and lightning.

I hope you are both getting along well in school. I hope you, Pat, are getting along well in baseball, and Mikey, I hope you're still doing that fine cooking. Try to help Mommy because she has a lot more to do. I'll write again soon.

Lots of love, Daddy
P.S. Love to Mommy, too.

Another letter, to me, from Wichita a few weeks later, June 2:

Dear Mikey,

You are sure getting to be a fine letter-writer. I certainly enjoy your letters. Just want to tell you that you're still my favorite girlfriend.

Seeing your letters reminds me of when I was about your age going to school and I had to sit with a girl for talking in class. When I told my Daddy, he laughed and told me not to worry because, in a few years, all these things would seem very funny.

Thanks for the nickel. I'll save it toward my next batch of presents.

Love, Daddy

This letter had an unexpected treat. My Grandfather Patrick, who I never met, came to life. Seeing him laughing "animated" the still pictures we have of him. I could also morph this into an image of him "live" with Nana.

Author "Mikey" with Daddy in Los Angeles, 1946.

FRIENDS

Finding Tom and Jack's letters launched me on a quest to know about people in their lives during the war. Seven decades had passed, but I hoped the emergence of the internet would help with my search. After all the years that I knew nothing about my uncles, it was amazing to see their names appear in books and on websites and government documents.

The one hundred sixty-five pages of letters we have from Jack mention buddies occasionally, though no one consistently until he linked up with his crew. Connections to the 446th Bomb Group Association, books, and websites yielded a wealth of information about Jack's bomb group and Flixton Airfield in England, but nothing of his personal connections or activities there. Through research, to fill in for his missing letters, I included in this book monthly updates about some of his likely experiences.

In the early 1980s, Dutch writer Jaap ("Jack") van der Woude, was researching Jack's ship's loss for a chapter for a book in progress. He hoped to connect with *Satan's Little Sister's* pilot, John Quinn. Lt. Quinn and the co-pilot, both initially listed Missing in Action, were protected by the Dutch and repatriated at war's end.

Lt. Quinn always refused to grant requests for interviews about the ship's crash for fear the writer would not treat the deceased crew with the respect they deserved. After receiving Jaap's request and confirmation from a mutual friend that Jaap would be most respectful of the crew, Lt. Quinn agreed to meet with him. On a subsequent trip to America, Jaap and his wife Maria had a wonderful visit with the Quinns in New York, and Jaap interviewed Lt. Quinn. Jaap's account of the loss of *Satan's Little Sister* appears in the book *The History of the 446th Bomb Group*, compiled by Harold E. Jansen.

Lt. Quinn's wife Marion subsequently wrote a fourteen-page narrative for their children, which details their father's wartime experience and the lost crew. Until that time, as is true with many families of World War II veterans, following generations knew little about veterans' military careers. In Mrs. Quinn's narrative, four decades after the war, she wrote, "I knew all these crewmen very well, having traveled with them from base to base—Tennessee, Texas, Colorado, Nevada and Kansas—while Dad was in training to fly heavy bombers. The loss of the seven crewmembers haunts both of us."

During the war, when soldiers were Missing in Action, the Army connected crewmembers' families by sharing their mailing addresses. Mrs. Quinn corresponded with relatives of *Satan's Little Sister's* missing airmen.

She said in her narrative that my grandmother sent Christmas cards to her family yearly after the war until Nana died in 1965.

Jaap gave me a 1980s address he had for John Quinn's son Pat, and we corresponded. The commonality I have with Pat is unusual but comforting. He generously said I could excerpt for this book any information I chose from his mother's narrative.

We have more than twice as many pages of letters from Tom as we do from Jack. Tom's letters mention many buddies consistently, in particular while he was on Corsica. I hoped to make a connection with at least one person who knew him.

For a while, it seemed like Jocko the dog was going to be my only connection. I love dogs, but wanted more, a *human* who flew with Tom. I searched the internet and military websites for names mentioned in Tom's letters.

The internet eventually connected me with families of three of Tom's best friends from his squadron: the daughter of Angelo Adams, a navigator; the wife and son of John Moyer, the highly skilled B-25 pilot Tom flew with on forty-seven missions; and two nieces of Willy Mravinec, fellow bombardier and tent-mate for several months. Tom mentioned Angelo, John and Willy often in his letters.

My first connection, Angelo's daughter, Joni Adams Sesma, had been searching for our family before I knew to look for hers. In 2012, I entered Tom and Jack's information on www.fold3.com, a military database. The historian for the 57th Bomb Wing, Barbi Ennis Connelly, daughter of Tech. Sgt. Edward C. Ennis, knew of Joni's query on this site and connected us upon seeing my entries.

In Tom's letter dated October 28, 1944, he mentions to his mother that he gave her name, address and phone number to Angelo to send to his wife, Betty. Betty lived in Los Angeles also, but knew very few people. Joni has her father's letters to her mother during the war. In one, also dated October 28, Angelo gives his wife the information and says, "That's the mother of one of my buddies over here and I thought you might like to get in touch with her. If she and his sister are as nice as he is, you should like them very much."

Joni found mentions in her mother's letters to Angelo that she, my grandmother and Aunt Patricia met several times, but at some point, after Tom's loss, they lost touch. Joni learned from her father's letters that her father was devastated by Tom's loss, and her mother told her that this bothered him all his life. Also, Angelo knew Jack was listed MIA, but heard nothing further after Tom's ship went down, and he always wondered if Jack survived the war. Joni found those answers on the internet shortly before she and I met online.

Joni and I regret that our families lost touch and agree that remaining connected could have helped everyone in the grieving process. She and I were happy to meet in 2015 when she traveled to Southern California for a family vacation. We reconnected our families, seventy years later.

As I continued to search, some things were difficult to hear, but I came to understand that knowing the truth was better than the *nothing* that I knew all my life. From John Moyer's son, Randy, I learned that the mission on which Tom was killed, his 62nd, was his last scheduled one before rotating home. That was painful. However, John's wife Eleanor, who met John after the war, told me, "John used to talk about Tom a lot." Once again, Tom was remembered. That was uplifting.

Willy was called Bill by his family, and I met two of his nieces online. From them I learned Willy did pursue his natural artistic talent that Tom encouraged and wrote about several times. In an email, Willy's niece Suzanne (Mravinec) O'Toole wrote: "Bill was an excellent artist and many of the pictures he did are hanging in our family homes, I have four of them. His works that we have are mostly in oil and watercolor." I remain in contact online with Sue, as well as Willy's great-niece Kristin Mravinec, who connected me to Sue. Together we reconnected Tom and Willy to each other, and I feel more connected to Tom through them.

Eleanor suggested I write to Gordon Davis, a bombardier-navigator who she said flew with John and Tom. She maintained contact with him after John died and heard from him shortly before I wrote her. She gave me his address in Northern California. I kept thinking, Gordon? Gordon? The name didn't ring a bell at all from Tom's letters. Then it hit me: Gordon *Davis*. He was Tom's good friend referred to as *Davis* in several letters. Gordon also became Tom's tent-mate after moving in with him and Jerry Rahatz when Willy rotated home.

I wrote to Gordon and enclosed one of Tom's letters, "Just Another Day at the Office," January 2, 1945, where Davis was a comedic performer and Willy was the straight man. I received a wonderful letter back from Gordon confirming he was the Davis who shared quarters with Tom and Jerry. He said it was a special time for him, learning through Tom about closeness of family that he didn't have in his own family as he grew up. He said Tom was a great guy, a good influence on him and well respected in their squadron.

Gordon touchingly concluded his letter saying that he and Jerry didn't invite anyone else to share their tent after Tom went down. They felt no one could quite take his place.

ONE MORE FRIEND

Just before finalizing this manuscript, I had a happy surprise.

The connections I made with a few of Uncle Tom's Corsica squadron friends and relatives were through email and letters. I never sought the opportunity to converse with any. Truth be told, I was afraid...it was easier to stay at arm's length. Reading Tom and Jack's letters drained me emotionally at first, though I ultimately received tremendous joy in return. But how much further would it undo me to actually talk with someone who knew them? Luckily, connecting with Curly happened fairly quickly before I chickened out.

In an online site related to the 57th Bomb Wing, to which Tom's squadron belonged, I mentioned "Morrison" in a quote from one of Tom's entertaining letters. One of the people who saw that comment was John Spoonamore, brother of Tech. Sgt. Robert Spoonamore, also stationed on Corsica, killed in action on a bombing mission in November 1944.

John posted that he had been in contact with Manley J. Morrison, nicknamed Curly, over the last several years, and that he lived on the East Coast. Before I remembered to be afraid, I found myself asking John if he thought Curly would connect with me, actually still thinking via email or letter. He checked with Curly, who said he remembered Tom well and would be happy to talk with me. But John recommended calling him because he wasn't sure how often Curly checked his email. Call? Gulp.

On the afternoon of June 6, 2014—how fitting, the 70th Anniversary of D-Day—I called Curly. We talked for over an hour, then another hour a couple of weeks later. Both times we laughed a lot. Recalling 1944, tent-life on Corsica, Curly said, "Tom was brilliant, he could do anything."

Curly was a pilot and told me that his plane and Tom's, with their crews, stayed together for five weeks on the Trip Over from the United States to Corsica. On Corsica, Curly was one of Tom's three tent-mates for several months. The other two were pilot Vern Whited and bombardier/navigator Willy Mravinec, both mentioned often in Tom's letters.

After reading Tom and Jack's letters, one question kept nagging at me: Were the boys as happy in real life as they seemed in their letters? Or did they write entertaining letters only to keep up their mother's spirits? Curly said Tom was always happy, always had a smile on his face, was friendly to everyone and well liked. His letters were not a cover-up for fear or dissatisfaction, but he could be serious when he had to be. Though it was war, they had a great time on Corsica, loved being there and flying. Yes, there was danger, but they didn't personalize it. Its presence didn't mar their adventure of "seeing the world," as Tom and Jack had looked forward to.

Though I don't have a Curly-equivalent among Jack's friends, I transferred this same sentiment to him: Jack was happy and loved flying too, I told myself.

To my surprise, Curly had a question for me. After he finished his missions on Corsica, he didn't want to go back to the States because, "They probably would have made me an instructor." He opted to stay in the war and transferred to mainland France to work as a pilot for a general. While in France, Curley heard that Tom died; he was shocked and saddened. But he never heard what happened. I told him what I had learned—what is included in this book. Seventy years later, he has his answer.

When Curly and I met, this book was still a few months from being published, so I sent him a mini-book. It contained the opening chapter, several letters in which "Morrison" was mentioned comically and a few others letters I thought would interest him. He was surprised to learn how well Tom documented the squadron's antics.

SUNDAY JOYRIDE IN CORSICA

World War II Memoir by USAAC Crew Chief Frank B. Dean
57th Bomb Wing, 310th Bomb Group, Squadron 380
Permission to Publish via Dominique Taddei

The essay *Sunday Joyride in Corsica* by Frank B. Dean was forwarded to me by French author Dominique Taddei, who, by his contributions to American war history, merits introduction and recognition.

During World War II, Dominique lived in the Corsica, France, village of Migliacciaru, the location the American Army chose for its 57th Bomb Wing Mediterranean Theater headquarters. Though only six years old, Dominique remembers when the planes and soldiers, including my Uncle Tom, were on the island.

As an adult, Dominique served in the French Navy, worked twenty-six years as a purser for Air France, then became a farmer before retiring in 1998. Dominique subsequently researched the men, missions and planes of the 57th Bomb Wing. He compiled his findings in a book, *U.S.S. Corsica*, the title of which aligns the island to an aircraft carrier on land.

Combat veterans once stationed on Corsica are grateful for Dominique's contributions to the preservation of their history during the war, as are we veterans' descendants who seek to learn about family members who were there. Many of these people have been in contact with Dominique over the years, and some have traveled to Corsica to meet him and visit the island. Dominique generously shared documents and photos with me, as I sought to learn more about the island where Tom wrote so many letters to my grandmother. Lastly, Dominique helped to establish a monument to the American airmen who were stationed there.

The first of Dominique's research contacts was Crew Chief Frank B. Dean, an aircraft mechanic who was stationed with the 310th Bomb Group at Ghisonaccia Gare, an airfield south of Tom's field, Alesan. Whether flying combat missions or for fun, the safety of our highly trained, conscientious airmen was dependent on ground crew personnel like Frank who maintained the ships.

Frank was also a poet and writer. After returning home to Warner Robins, Georgia, he wrote *Sunday Joyride in Corsica* from notes he made after an unforgettable wartime experience. This piece was originally published in the *Men of the 57th* newsletter mailed to the membership of the 57th Bomb Wing Association.

Perhaps less heralded than fliers, ground crews were equally essential, and I include this eloquent essay to give them a grateful salute.

Sunday Joyride in Corsica: April 1944 came to Ghisonaccia Gare, Corsica, and nothing had changed as far as we aircraft mechanics were concerned. We were still responsible for the maintenance, repair and guarding of our assigned bombers in the midst of combat operations.

Even when most of the B-25s of our 310th Bomb Group were out on combat missions, the rest of the remaining aircraft were not always idle. There were other flight requirements for training, test hops, freight runs, and sometimes just because some of the pilots felt like flying.

Some of these latter flights offered us mechanics, who normally remained on the ground, a chance to see the country from the air. One such opportunity came when Major Clyde Grow arrived with a co-pilot to fly *Tissyprissle* for a while. I chose to go along. I crawled through the aluminum tunnel to the Plexiglas enclosed bombardier's compartment where the view was virtually unobstructed.

Preflight inspection complete, we idle down the dirt taxi strip to the end of the runway. Maj. Grow talks to the tower, makes the required power checks and pushes the throttles forward. The brakes are released and the plane hurtles down the steel-matted runway at ever-increasing speed. The two engines turn three-bladed propellers, set at full pitch.

The nose rises and the main wheels tiptoe prior to liftoff. The plane flashes over the end of the runway, nose high and climbing steeply. The solid clunk of the landing gear locks and the slamming of the nacelle doors lets me know that the gears are "up and locked."

We level off about two hundred feet above the ground and make a gentle downward turn. The nose of the aircraft points east, down the asphalt highway. The tips of the telephone poles seem close enough to touch as they file past at almost two hundred miles an hour. The slate roofs of the houses of Ghisonaccia Ville flash into view then vanish behind us. The silent shadow of our aircraft follows us across the green of the salt marshes.

The water of the Mediterranean Sea stretches before us like a sheet of blue glass. We streak above it, the slipstream of the propellers rippling the calm water as we pass. From my vantage point I gaze through the clear Plexiglas panes. The sunlight dances on the blue surface of the water as we bank slowly to the left. The lower wingtip hangs just above the blue of the water as we turn. The line of foam where the shoreline is married to the sea rushes to meet us and is lost behind.

We laze over the level ground, just above the top of the thick brush. Their branches nod at our passing. There is a freedom and a wonder. We are not hindered by obstacles. Rocks and trees do not impede our flight. The rush of the wind and the muted sound of the engines are the only distraction.

We glide over the hills and sneak into the valleys. We are never more than a hundred feet away. We flash from the valleys into the sunlight and duck back into the shadows. We seem suspended in space as the sides of low mountains rush past our wingtips. The freedom of flight is intoxicating.

We climb into the mountains, through the passes, and past villages clinging to mountain slopes. Towns like Vezzani, Venaco, and Ghisoni quickly display their gray slate roofs then quickly snatch them away.

We skim over the tops of tall pine trees, shaking their topmost boughs. We ride on wingtips down mountainsides and soar upwards toward the top of the peaks where only eagles dare to fly. We ride the winds with carefree abandon. We climb the slopes and slide down the mountainsides. The smooth, easy, lazy turns and gentle rise and fall of the plane as it follows the exact contour of the land show the hand of a master craftsman at his best.

Maj. Grow pushes me into vistas of scenic pictures unwinding. The ever-changing, ever-moving kaleidoscopic views rush to meet me and unveil their beauty for a brief glimpse as we hurry past: Blue skies; swaying trees of oak, beech, chestnut and pines; towering majestic mountains; nodding fields of wildflowers; glints of silver streams leaping rocks or plunging off stone ledges; small stone houses hiding beneath leafy boughs and peering at us through glinting window eyes; ribbon-like roads clutching tenaciously to steep, rocky mountainsides; open-mouthed children standing startled in village streets; rolling green hills; and sunlight and shadows that shift and change and blend, and separate and blend again, in a symphony of colors and delicate hues.

We descend the mountain, cross the low hills and move toward the sea over dense thickets of arbutus, heather, juniper, lavender, myrtle and rosemary. I watch as nature paints a panoramic view with brush strokes of sky azure, sand white, Mediterranean blue and marsh green, as we head out to sea.

The tip of the wing is again suspended over the blue waters as we turn the nose toward our base. We slide across the shoreline, the salt marshes, and the low, dense undergrowth. To our left, in the distance, the bulk of Mount Incudine, with Furmigula, Punta della Cappella and Pointe Tintennaja, rises more than two thousand meters above the level of the plain.

We climb gently and the long steel-matted runways, the dirt taxi strips and the olive drab colored bombers standing in their circular dispersal areas come into view. The plane shudders as wing flaps and landing gear are lowered, and the slowing of the plane as the throttles are retarded shakes me back into the present.

The main tires feel for the runway, touch and roll. The nose tire touches seconds later. The aircraft lurches and dips as the brakes are applied. It continues to nod its head until the speed reaches an acceptable level. We wheel off the runway onto the taxi strip and head for the dispersal area. Harry Drake waves us into place. The engine dies in a final burst of power and the propellers coast to a halt.

The honeymoon is over and it is now time to pay the piper. There will be refueling, replenishing the oil tanks, checking, cleaning, inspecting and all the other chores that follow a flight. However, this time I am content. Whatever the cost, it was worth it.

In 2002, Dominique traveled from France to Warner Robins, Georgia, to see the U.S. Air Force Museum of Aviation and to meet Frank Dean, who volunteered there for twenty years. They remained in contact until Frank died in 2006. In one of Frank's letters, he urged Dominique's continuing conservation of 57th Bomb Wing history: "Dominique! Don't let our history die with us!"

THE GRAND PIANO'S SECRET

I'll never forget the splendor of the Steinway, regal in the room where other furnishings played only minor roles. Aunt Patricia's piano is a cherished memory.

Patricia began studying piano around 1920 in the Cahill family's hometown of Concord, New Hampshire. The only daughter of Patrick and Mary, she filled the large brick home with music, juxtaposed with the cacophony of eight brothers. My father Bob was the middle child.

After the stock market crash of 1929, business reverses and the death of my grandfather interrupted the music of the once financially comfortable family. On her own with the children, school aged through young adults, my grandmother saw greater opportunity for her brood in California where she and my grandfather spent their honeymoon, and where her mother and sister relocated in the 1920s.

In 1937, the family moved to Los Angeles. They were welcomed by Gram into her home, downtown on Van Buren. The house, built in 1916, was a stately two-story place, 5,000 square feet, with eight bedrooms, three balconies and concrete pillars framing a large front porch.

Still struggling financially, Los Angeles was the perfect place for the family to restart their lives after several difficult years. They acclimated happily to the beaches, warm weather and abundant live entertainment.

The entire family was musical, all loved to sing and some were professional musicians. My father met my mother Jackie when he played bass fiddle in a band for her high school dance. He also sang with the band and wrote music and lyrics.

Patricia's music was center stage often when their home was the venue for jam sessions with friends, as well as for bands that rehearsed there. Good times would roll late into the night, sometimes quieting only when police arrived after neighbors complained, thought by some in the family to be the sign of a truly successful party.

Classical music was Patricia's passion. She longed for a new piano, a Steinway baby grand, and got her wish in the early 1940s. Over the next few years, as brothers moved out of the Van Buren home, my aunt and her Steinway remained with her mother. In 1945, my parents and rascally toddler brother filled the empty rooms, and I was born a few months later.

When Gram died in 1948, Nana and Patricia inherited the home. In 1950 they sold it and bought another, a few miles south near the Pacific Ocean, in the Newport Beach village of Corona del Mar. This house had the perfect spot for the piano, knotty pine walls and cathedral ceilings with great acoustics. Nana told us grandchildren that, in addition to good piano placement, she liked the home's distance to the beach. It was close enough for us to walk there, but far enough that all the sand fell off us before we got back home.

My family and my father's brothers and their families all lived near Nana. Multitudinous Cahills went there often as my generation increased, topping out at thirteen. Over the years, the Steinway was the core of every celebration, regardless of the celebratory cause. At every gathering, as Nana, her children and in-law daughters yakked, we youngsters would nag "When is Patricia going to play the piano?" until we finally got our way.

Jam sessions were the best part of every get-together. We sang for hours—children's songs, pop favorites and show tunes. I loved it when Patricia and my dad belted out "Shine on Harvest Moon." My childhood request was always "How Much is that Doggie in the Window?"

Our parties must have been tamer than the earlier ones in Los Angeles...the police never came.

Nana's house became my personal vacation home every summer when I brought a friend to stay a week or two. We went to the beach every day. Evenings, after Patricia returned from work, she played the piano for her own enjoyment. As I watched her hands fly along the keyboard, I was awed by Chopin, Beethoven and the boys. Staying at that house was like living in a concert hall.

My aunt was quite social and loved the beach locale. In addition to her real estate job, she often played piano in posh seaside restaurants. I remember, as a young adult, going with her to a gig at El Pescador, a fancy place on Lido Isle. As she played the piano, obviously in her element, she crooned with her audience.

In 1964, a fire devastated Nana and Patricia's home. Thankfully, they were uninjured physically, but the emotional toll was huge. The fire destroyed most everything in the home, including the Steinway that was the heartbeat of our family.

Well into adulthood, my cousins and I explored keepsakes that survived the fire and had been in storage for decades. We never could have dreamed the family history they would reveal. Among the still smoky-smelling treasures were mounds of photos dating back to the late 1800s. Some were scorched and water-spotted from the fire.

We also found over 500 pages of letters to our grandmother from our World War II Army flier uncles, Tom and Jack, "the boys." My cousins, my brother and I never knew them. Both were killed on bombing missions in Europe a few weeks apart near the end of the war.

When I was a child, I always looked at the boys' silent portraits on Nana's gallery wall. They would remind me that our uncles weren't with us, and I'd feel a vague sadness. I don't know how Tom and Jack's archive survived the fire when so much else was lost. As I read their touching, hilarious letters, and eavesdropped on their lives, I finally "met" my uncles. When I look at those once quiet pictures now, I see the boys laughing, through the stories they wrote home to their mother.

With the letters, we also found old news clippings about the fire where Nana said Patricia's Steinway was a gift from Tom and Jack. They bought it for her with money they sent home during the war. I don't remember ever knowing that the boys gave her the piano, but knowing this now makes its memory even more precious. The music Patricia played was Tom and Jack's gift to all of us, including my generation they never met.

Aunt Patricia at her baby grand, Corona del Mar in the 1950s. A bonus in this photo: The feet under the piano belonged to my grandmother, "Dear Mom." I think she ducked down to let her daughter have the limelight in the picture.

References

Related to Tom Cahill, Mediterranean Theater, Alesan Airfield, Corsica, France

WEBSITES

57th Bomb Wing Association:
http://57thbombwing.com/

57th Bomb Wing Association,
340th Bomb Group, Squadron 486 War Diaries:
http://57thbombwing.com/340th_History/
486thSquadronHistory.php

A Son Remembers Hymie's War, by Dan Setzer:
http://home.comcast.net/~dhsetzer/

Pope Pius XII Blesses 4,000 U.S. GI's 1944 (YouTube):
http://www.youtube.com/watch?v=VKfzmzmicZc

BOOKS

The True Story of Catch 22, by Patricia Chapman Meder
Truth Flies with Fiction, by Dale J. Satterthwaite
U.S.S. Corsica: L'Ile Porte Avions (U.S.S. Corsica: The Island Carrier), by Dominique Taddei, in French only

Related to Jack Cahill, European Theater, Flixton Airfield, Bungay, England

WEBSITES

446th Bomb Group:
http://www.446bg.com/

Eemnes Freedom Memorial, Netherlands:
http://www.446bg.com/memorials/eemnes.htm

Fields of Honor Database Margraten:
www.fieldsofhonor-database.com

National Liberation Museum, Netherlands:
http://www.bevrijdingsmuseum.nl/
basis.aspx?Tid=746#.VCsms010xMw

National Museum of the Mighty Eighth Air Force:
http://mightyeighth.org/

Netherlands American Cemetery Margraten:
http://www.fieldsofhonor-database.com/

Norfolk and Suffolk Aviation Museum:
http://www.aviationmuseum.net/

BOOKS

B-24 Combat Missions, by Martin W. Bowman
B-24 Pilot: Remembering My War, by Lt. Col. Paul Armentrout
Bombs Away Buckaroos, by Rick Albright
The Flixton Story, by Bob Cossey
The History of the 446th Bomb Group, compiled by Harold E. Jansen
The Margraten Boys, by Peter Schrijvers
The Mighty Eighth, by Gerald Astor
One Last Look, by Philip Kaplan and Rex Alan Smith

OTHER MILITARY REFERENCES

Fold3.com Military Database, by Ancestry.com:
http://www.fold3.com/

National World War II Memorial, Washington, D.C.:
http://www.wwiimemorial.com/

The Official Guide to the Army Air Forces by U.S. Army Air Force,
published in 1944 by Simon and Schuster

U.S. Air Force Museum of Aviation, Georgia:
http://www.museumofaviation.org/

Made in the USA
San Bernardino, CA
04 June 2015